W9-CBJ-622

COLLECTED WORKS OF ERASMUS

VOLUME 82

COLLECTED WORKS OF
ERASMUS

CONTROVERSIES

DECLARATIONES
AD CENSURAS LUTETIAE
VULGATAS SUB NOMINE
FACULTATIS THEOLOGIAE PARISIENSIS

edited, translated, and annotated by
Clarence H. Miller

Introduction by Clarence H. Miller and James K. Farge

University of Toronto Press

Toronto / Buffalo / London

The research and publication costs of the
Collected Works of Erasmus are supported by
University of Toronto Press.

© University of Toronto Press 2012
Toronto / Buffalo / London
Printed in Canada

ISBN 978-1-4426-4115-0

Printed on acid-free paper

Library and Archives Canada Cataloguing in Publication

Erasmus, Desiderius, d. 1536
[Works]
Collected works of Erasmus.

Each vol. has special t.p. ; general title from half title page.
Includes bibliographical references and indexes.
Partial contents: Controversies : declarationes ad censuras Lutetiae
vulgatas sub nomine facultatis theologiae Parisiensis / edited,
translated, and annotated by Clarence H. Miller.
ISBN 0-8020-2831-4 (set). – ISBN 978-1-4426-4115-0 (v. 82)

1. Erasmus, Desiderius, d. 1536 – Collected works. I. Title.

PA8500.1974   199'.492   C74006326-X rev

University of Toronto Press acknowledges the financial assistance to its
publishing program of the Canada Council and the Ontario Arts Council.

 Canada Council Conseil des Arts
for the Arts du Canada   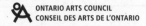 ONTARIO ARTS COUNCIL
CONSEIL DES ARTS DE L'ONTARIO

University of Toronto Press acknowledges the financial support
for its publishing activities of the Government of Canada through
the Book Publishing Industry Development Program (BPIDP).

Collected Works of Erasmus

The aim of the Collected Works of Erasmus
is to make available an accurate, readable English text
of Erasmus' correspondence and his
other principal writings. The edition is planned
and directed by an Editorial Board, an Executive Committee,
and an Advisory Committee.

Contents

Introduction

This volume presents Erasmus' final arguments in a decade-long controversy with the theologians of the University of Paris – especially with their
elected syndic, or director, Noël Béda. At the heart of the controversy were
two principal issues: the textual integrity of the Latin Vulgate Bible and
the validity and utility of the traditional method of the schools for the
study, interpretation, and teaching of Christian doctrine. In essence it was
a question of which approach was of more value to the church. Should
theologians adopt the humanistic approach advocated by Erasmus, which
employed philological textual criticism of the Bible and showed a preference for the works of the early church Fathers over those of the medieval
theologians? Or should they retain the scholastic method, which deployed
a systematic, dialectical investigation of God's revelation to man and man's
relationship to God and to the church, and also a strong moral obligation to profess, defend, and pass on to future generations a tradition of
dogma, moral teaching, and popular devotions as essential expressions of
the Catholic faith?

The challenge of humanism to the domination of scholasticism had already been active for more than a century. With the publication of Erasmus' *New Testament* (1516), which juxtaposed his own lightly revised Latin
text with the traditional Vulgate text and the Greek text – along with a myr-
iad of innovative annotations on them – Erasmus had become humanism's
supreme advocate. It was therefore inevitable that he would find himself in

* * * * *

Works cited frequently are referred to in abbreviated form. A list of these
abbreviations and full bibliographical information will be found on 328–30
below, and a list of short-title forms for Erasmus' works on 331–5. References
to Erasmus' correspondence are to the English translation of the letters in cwe
where these have already been published, or to the Latin edition of Allen. In
this volume references to the Bible are to the Vulgate version.

controversy with defenders of scholasticism not only in Paris but in many parts of Europe.

Nevertheless the appearance in July 1531 of *Determinatio facultatis theologiae*, a short book containing the Paris theologians' formal censures of 175 propositions drawn from various works of Erasmus, took him by surprise.[1] Two years had passed since the latest exchange of polemic between him and Béda. Although Erasmus tells us that he considered simply ignoring the new attack, that was never really in question. Never before had he failed to answer his critics, whether Catholic or Reformed, and he had already written several books or tracts against Béda.[2] This new attack, launched under the imprimatur of the most prestigious theological faculty in Europe, could not be ignored.

Erasmus' initial response to the Paris theologians appeared early in 1532 under the title *Declarationes ad censuras Lutetiae vulgatas sub nomine facultatis theologiae Parisiensis.*[3] Several months later, after making extensive

* * * * *

1 *Determinatio facultatis theologiae in schola Parisiensi super quam plurimis assertionibus D. Erasmi Roterodami* 'A Determination of the Theology Faculty in the University of Paris concerning Many Assertions by Desiderius Erasmus' (Paris: Josse Bade, July 1531); Renouard *Imprimeurs* II 266 no 672. It also contained the 1521 Paris condemnation of Luther and a 1523 censure of propositions concerning the veneration of saints, the canon of the mass, and the practice of accepting stipends for sacramental ministry. The *Determinatio* follows closely, but not exactly, the manuscript text recorded in the *Liber secundus registri determinationum* (fols 65v–109) that was kept by the faculty's beadle. Argentré *Collectio judiciorum de novis erroribus* II-1 53–77 published this manuscript version, not the 1531 printed version, which employs a different system of numbering the propositions. The faculty published a second, more elaborate edition (undated but probably later in 1532), which contains minor changes in the order of certain of its sections; see Renouard *Imprimeurs* II 297 no 774.
  Ninety-seven of the 175 offending propositions appeared under 32 headings; 8 more were added in a separate section; and 70 others were drawn from Erasmus' *Colloquies*. It should be noted that no more than a dozen of those 176 matters employed the word 'heresy,' although a number of others were labelled Arian or Lutheran or Wyclifite. In many cases the faculty resorted to more nebulous charges such as giving scandal, posing danger to the faithful, or offending pious Christians.
2 See xx–xxvii below. In all Erasmus wrote about thirty-five books or tracts in reply to his Catholic critics and another seven in criticism of Protestant reformers.
3 'Clarifications concerning the Censures Published at Paris in the Name of the Theology Faculty There' (Basel: Hieronymus Froben and Nicolaus Episcopius 1532). This first edition, in octavo format of 386 + 6 pages, bears no month-date, but it must have appeared either in January or early February, because Erasmus wrote to Bishop Piotr Tomicki on 4 February 1532 that he was sending

revisions, some of which took into account criticisms and suggestions made by a young Dominican theologian named Ambrosius Pelargus, Erasmus published a revised and augmented edition of that reply.[4] It is this second, authorized edition of Erasmus' *Declarationes* that is translated and annotated in the present volume.

The Latin text from which this translation was made was established by a complete collation of the first edition (using a microfilm of the copy held at the Bibliotheek der Gemeente, Rotterdam) with the copy of the second edition conserved at the Centre for Reformation and Renaissance Studies, Victoria University, Toronto, and a microfilm of that same version held by the Bayerische Staatsbibliothek, Munich.

ERASMUS, PARIS, AND THE PARIS FACULTY OF THEOLOGY

This new and final chapter in the polemic between Erasmus and the Paris theologians that was taking place in 1531–2 can be properly understood only if situated in the longer perspective of Erasmus' involvements with Paris, its faculty of theology, and Noël Béda.[5] In 1495, when Erasmus was about twenty-five years old, he had received permission and financial support

* * * * *

him a copy of it (Allen IX Ep 2600). The Antwerp printer Robert de Keysere issued an unauthorized reprint of it in April 1532 (Wouter Nijhoff and M.E. Kronenberg *Nederlandsche bibliographie van 1500 tot 1540* 3 vols, 2 supplements [The Hague 1923–71] no 813).

4 (Basel: Hieronymus Froben and Nicolaus Episcopius, September 1532), issued in quarto format of 397 pages. Like Erasmus, Pelargus (1493/5–July 1561) had taken refuge in Freiburg-im-Breisgau from the Zwinglian reformation in Basel. He received his doctorate in theology at the University of Freiburg in 1533. Although trained in scholastic theology he was also well versed in the Greek and Latin Fathers and was sympathetic to Erasmus' theological program. On his role in *Declarationes* see xxx–xxxii below.

5 The most comprehensive study of Béda remains the three-volume thesis by Bense. Farge 'Noël Béda' 143–64 draws on that monumental work. For a short sketch see CEBR I 116–18. For studies of the polemic between Erasmus and Béda see Rummel *Catholic Critics* II 29–59; Mark Crane 'Competing Visions of Religious Reform: Erasmus and Noël Béda' *Erasmus of Rotterdam Society Yearbook* 25 (2005) 39–57; and Charles Nauert '"A Remarkably Supercilious and Touchy Lot": Erasmus on the Scholastic Theologians' *Erasmus of Rotterdam Society Yearbook* 22 (2002) 41–2, 45–53. A new article by Edwin Rabbie, 'Long and Useless: The Polemic between Erasmus and Béda' *Erasmus of Rotterdam Society Yearbook* 30 (2010) 7–21, appeared too late, unfortunately, to be taken into account in CWE 82.

from his bishop to take leave of absence from the monastic life at Steyn that he found to be intellectually stifling. He went to Paris, where he resided, off and on, for about forty-eight months during the next six years. Probably following arrangements made by his bishop, he spent the first year in the Collège de Montaigu, where the ascetic regime of room, board, and discipline imposed by the principal of the college, Jan Standonck, suited him not at all. Twenty-five years later he would denounce it bitterly in the colloquy 'A Fish Diet.'[6] At Montaigu Erasmus would certainly have encountered his future *bête noire*, Noël Béda, whose whole career as a student in arts and theology and later as the principal at Montaigu for ten years was closely tied to that college.

Although Erasmus told his bishop and his friends that he was going to Paris to take a degree in theology, he neither followed a course of study nor fulfilled a period of residency that would have led to any degree at all, whether in arts or theology, at the University of Paris.[7] To free himself from dependence on his bishop and the life at Montaigu that he could not endure, Erasmus began to tutor students. He became friendly enough with some of them that they invited him to England and provided him with hospitality there, where he came under the life-changing influence of John Colet, Thomas More, and other English humanists. There, too, he met faithful patrons like Archbishop William Warham and Bishops John Longland, Cuthbert Tunstall, and John Fisher.

For some years before he began to publish, Erasmus had already come to the conclusion that the scholastic thought and method that dominated the curriculum of most European universities had outlived their usefulness to both education and the church. Many of his early published works constituted a thoroughgoing critique of scholasticism.[8] It is therefore worthy of note that, although this open warfare on scholastic theology drew early and extensive fire from traditionalist theologians in the Low Countries, Spain, and England, the Paris faculty of theology remained silent about works like the *Praise of Folly* and – for a full seven years – Erasmus' version of the New

*   *   *   *   *

6 CWE 40 675–762. This colloquy must also be seen as part of Erasmus' controversies with Béda, who remained the *éminence grise* of Montaigu even after he resigned as its principal in 1514.

7 See James K. Farge 'Erasmus, the University of Paris, and the Profession of Theology' *Erasmus of Rotterdam Society Yearbook 19* (1999) 18–46.

8 Notably his *Antibarbari* (begun c 1487 but published only in 1520); *Enchiridion* (1506); *Praise of Folly* (1511); the *Colloquies* (begun c 1498, first published in 1518); the Greek and Latin versions of the New Testament, treatises on theological method in *Ratio verae theologiae*, *Paraclesis*, and even parts of *Parabolae* (all published first in 1516)

Testament.[9] The Paris theologians cannot therefore be accused of rushing to judgment about Erasmus' works. Still, once that judgment began, it would continue for nearly ten years, culminating in the exchange of censure (1531) and response (1532) that concerns us here.

The first documented evidence of a Paris censure of Erasmus came on 22 August 1523, when the faculty concluded that new versions of the Bible, whether they were Latin translations from the Hebrew and Greek or vernacular translations – 'for example, those of Erasmus and Jacques Lefèvre' – posed real dangers to the faith of Christians and must therefore not be allowed to circulate.[10] The faculty was blocked from implementing this decision, however, because just at that time King Francis I was planning to invite Erasmus to take up residence once again in France, and he let it be known that the theologians should cease their opposition to him. The doctors prudently backed away; however, seeing that Noël Béda wanted to carry on the opposition, they authorized him to send the king, under his own initiative and in his own name, the list of errors that he had already drawn up.[11] Béda apparently did nothing with his notes at that time, but he saved them and from time-to-time added to them for future use.

That opportunity was not long in coming. In January 1524 the Swiss-born Paris printer Konrad Resch, who had already published Erasmus' *Para-phrases* on the Gospels of Matthew and John, requested a *privilège*, or copy-right, from the Parlement of Paris (the supreme court in France) to print Erasmus' *Paraphrase on Luke*. François Deloynes, the president of one of the four courts in the Parlement and one of its few members who favoured the humanist approach to learning, followed the court's standard procedure when considering a copyright for books concerning religion. As required by a law passed on 21 March 1521, Deloynes sent the text to the faculty of theology to determine whether it contained anything harmful to Christian doctrine or the church. The faculty appointed three masters to examine it, and then met at least eight times to discuss their findings.[12] Although

* * * * *

9 See Rummel *Catholic Critics* passim. The sole exception was the Paris graduate Jean Briselot, an auxiliary bishop of Cambrai and confessor of Charles v, whose criticism in 1517 was made independently of the faculty.

10 Clerval *Procès-verbaux* 380. In 1525 the Parlement of Paris adopted this same policy; see Paris AN x¹ᴬ 1528 723v–724r (28 August 1525).

11 'sed posset honorandus magister noster Natalis Beda syndicus facultatis suo privato jure, si vellet, (quia ad hoc se ultro exhibuit)': Clerval *Procès-verbaux* 401–2.

12 On 15, 18, 22 January, 6, 12, 16 February, 5 March, 1 April 1524: Farge *Procès-verbaux* 4B, 5A, 6B, 8A, 9A, 9B, 10A, 11A, 16A, 18C. The three delegated masters were Guillaume Le Sauvaige of the Collège d'Harcourt, Pieter Fabri, a

no final judgment on the *Paraphrase on Luke* is recorded in its minutes, we know that the faculty sent the Parlement a list of the errors it perceived in the book, along with its recommendation that the copyright not be granted. As a result the *Paraphrase on Luke* was never printed in Paris. Deloynes took it upon himself, however, to alert Erasmus to the faculty's opposition by sending him the list of propositions that the theologians had censured.[13]

Erasmus came to the faculty's attention again in May 1525 when the theologians were asked to examine French translations of some of his books by the evangelical humanist Louis de Berquin.[14] They found the translations to contain 'many things that are impious or absurd or pernicious to good morals, or heretical.' This was, however, not a direct attack on Erasmus but a judgment against Berquin who, to Erasmus' great dismay, had mixed into his translations texts drawn from works of condemned reformers like Guillaume Farel and even Martin Luther himself. On 20 May and 1 June 1525 the doctors formally condemned Berquin's translations of Erasmus – without, however, mentioning Erasmus as the author.[15]

* * * * *

Dominican friar from Nijmegen, and Jean Gillain, the grand master of the Collège de Navarre.

13 Béda would certainly have contributed to that list. He wrote that on a Saturday (he does not specify the date) in January 1523 (that is, 1524 new style) at four o'clock in the afternoon he began to read Erasmus' *Paraphrase on Luke* and to make notes on the errors he found in it. Erasmus later published Béda's notes (as *Annotationes Bedae theologi in Paraphrasim Erasmi Rot. in Lucam*, which carries the running head: 'Notata per N. Bedam in Paraphrasim in Lucam'), along with his refutation of them, in the omnibus volume of anti-Béda materials entitled *Supputationes errorum in censuris Natalis Bedae* (Basel: Froben 1527) part II 63v–73v.

14 The books in question were *Encomium matrimonii* (Basel: Froben 1518); *Brevis admonitio de modo orandi* (not Erasmus' *Modus orandi Deum*, but rather a collection of excerpts from his *Paraphrases* on Matthew and Luke, with an introduction by Guillaume Farel, which Berquin translated as *Briefve admonition de la maniere de prier*); *Symbolum* (that is, the colloquy *Inquisitio de fide* 'An examination concerning the faith,' which Berquin translated as *Le symbole des apostres de Jesuchrist*, and into which he inserted excerpts from Luther's writings); and *Querela pacis* (translated as *Declamation de la paix*). See Farge *Procès-verbaux* 96–7 nos 94A, 95A and nn44–6; cf Margaret Mann (Phillips) 'Louis de Berquin, traducteur d'Erasme' *Revue du seizième siècle* 18 (1931) 309–23. On Berquin see James K. Farge 'Les procès de Louis de Berquin: épisodes dans la lutte du Parlement de Paris contre l'absolutisme royal' *Histoire et Archives* 18 (2005) 49–77.

15 Although the decision stipulated that the books 'translated in this way' should not be allowed to be printed in Paris, they had already been published there

The disastrous defeat of the French army at Pavia in late February 1525 and the resulting captivity of King Francis I in Spain for more than a year gave the faculty and its allies in the Parlement of Paris a much freer hand in taking action against evangelicals and humanists in France. The reform measures in the diocese of Meaux that were inspired by Lefèvre d'Étaples and implemented by Bishop Guillaume Briçonnet were strictly curtailed; a number of evangelicals were imprisoned and at least two were executed for heresy. Fearing the worst, Lefèvre fled to Strasbourg.

Erasmus himself, having received Béda's list of errors and aware of the heightened climate of fear and repression in Paris, began an exchange of letters with Béda – a correspondence that would amount to eleven letters in all.[16] The exchange reveals much about Béda's deep-seated antipathy toward the humanists' approach to learning and the reform of religion and about Erasmus' defence of that approach. Erasmus was anxious to prevent a formal censure of his works; thus, in the initial letter (Ep 1571, dated 28 April 1525) he invited Béda to point out any errors he perceived in Erasmus' books, and he promised to give due consideration to them in the projected fourth edition of his *Annotations on the New Testament*. A good deal of the letter, however, is devoted to an indignant rejection of attacks on him that had been made by Pierre Cousturier and 'Taxander.'[17] In reply (Ep 1579, 21 May 1525) Béda singled out for criticism not so much individual errors but the whole Erasmian project of producing new Latin or Greek versions of

* * * * *

anonymously and clandestinely by Simon Du Bois (Moreau *Inventaire* III 249–51 nos 813, 816, 819). There is no evidence to support Moreau's statement (250 no 818) that the faculty condemned Erasmus' own Latin version of *Querela pacis* (Paris: Simon de Colines 1525).

16 Epp 1571, 1579, 1581, 1596, 1609, 1610, 1620, 1642, 1679, 1685, and 1906; see CWE vols 11, 12, 13 / Allen vols VI and VII. Allen VI 65–7, a lengthy introduction to Ep 1571, provides Béda's own account of the circumstances under which his dealings with Erasmus arose.

17 Cousturier (Latin *Sutor*), a Carthusian graduate of the Paris faculty of theology in 1510, had criticized Erasmus' credentials as a theologian and his biblical scholarship in *De tralatione Bibliae et novarum reprobatione interpretationum* (Paris: Pierre Vidoue for Jean Petit 1525). Of all his critics Erasmus held Cousturier most in contempt. On him see James K. Farge *Biographical Register of Paris Doctors of Theology, 1500–1536* Subsidia Mediaevalia 10 (Toronto 1980) 119–21 no 123.

'Taxander' was the pseudonym under which several Dominicans in Louvain published *Apologia in eum librum quam ab anno Erasmus Roterodamus de confessione edidit* (Antwerp: Simon Cocus 1525). Its principal author was Vincentius Theodoricus.

the Bible and Erasmus' advocacy of vernacular translations of it. He argued that Erasmus' scorn for scholastic doctors and his partiality for the church Father Origen, who had been condemned by an ecumenical council, would bring nothing but harm to the church, put at risk the souls of Christians, and perhaps even bring danger on himself. He recommended that Erasmus read Augustine and Jean Gerson. Scholasticism, Béda says, has given great service to the church. It could not have come into common use in Catholic theology without the working of God's Holy Spirit.[18]

Erasmus' reply (Ep 1581, 15 June 1525) is a particularly important apologia for his approach to exegesis and theology.[19] He insisted that he had always kept away from dogmatic theology, since that could 'only result in peril alike to myself and many others.' Moreover, he expressed regret for having introduced emendations to the Vulgate Bible, pleading that it was only the pressure of learned friends which pushed him into doing so. But he also insisted that, rather than seeking to replace scholastic method, he and other humanists sought only to complement it:

It has always been my aim to inspire a renewed interest in the liberal arts and to bring about a marriage between them and those subjects with which you and your colleagues are concerned. Part of my purpose was to give literary studies a Christian voice, for up to that time, as you are aware, humanists in Italy concentrated on pagan themes. But I also hoped, by adding an interest in languages and fine literature, to bring something valuable and illuminating to the existing curriculum of the schools. Both sides, I believe, have been at fault in this controversy: the devotees of literature bitterly attack those whose interests are different from their own, while those on the other side refuse

* * * * *

18 CWE 11 Ep 1579:118–19
19 When Béda later published his *Apologia adversus clandestinos Lutheranos* (Paris: Josse Bade 1 February 1529) he appended to it eight of the eleven letters exchanged with Erasmus – the only source we have for several of them. Ep 1581, however, was one of the three he did not include. In CWE 11 Ep 1609:9–10 he had already disingenuously termed it 'a waste of effort,' calling it prolix and useless, on the grounds that Erasmus' later, more irenic Ep 1596 showed that he had recovered from the attack of pride and anger which had inspired Ep 1581. One may indeed wonder if Béda simply preferred to avoid giving publicity to Erasmus' arguments for a new and fresh approach to theology. Erasmus, however, did not fail to include Ep 1581 in his *Opus epistolarum* (Basel 1529), and in his *Responsio ad notulas Bedaicas*, written in the same year, he said that Béda's suppression of such an important letter was characteristic of him and showed him to be a 'crack-brained theologian' (LB IX 718D).

to accept the humanities into partnership, although they could have profited greatly from them; instead they dismiss them unceremoniously and reject what they do not understand.[20]

Erasmus argued, moreover, that Christian doctrine is not fixed in what he calls the static forms of current scholastic theology but must be continually rethought in the light of changing circumstances. If the Holy Spirit had indeed inspired scholastic theologians in recent centuries with insights that escaped the church Fathers, what is to prevent the same Spirit in these present, perilous times from revealing truths that no one had noticed before?[21] In the same letter Erasmus pointed to reputable theologians – even Paris graduates like Ludwig Baer – who approved of his works. Finally, he insisted that he had always submitted his work to the judgment of the church, but he denied that the judgment of the scholastic theologians of Paris – no matter how pre-eminent their faculty was among the universities of Europe – should be considered as the single, immutable, or unassailable criterion of orthodoxy. It was an argument that would underlie his 1532 *Declarationes* in reply to the official censure by the Paris theological faculty in 1531.

For lack of a courier to Paris Ep 1581 was carried only as far as Strasbourg, from where it was returned to Erasmus in Basel. He then composed the shorter and milder Ep 1596 (dated 24 August 1525) to accompany his second attempt to send Ep 1581. In it Erasmus again noted how important he considered his revival of interest in the ancient Fathers, and this time he was more forthcoming about the advantage of employing the oldest versions of Scripture to emend the Vulgate Bible. Pleading the critical needs of the time, he stressed again the necessity of providing for the Christian people translations of Sacred Scripture into vernacular languages.[22] Erasmus also mentioned that he hoped his courier could bring back to him Béda's annotations.[23]

Béda replied (Ep 1609, 12 September 1525) to the two letters in a friendly but condescending tone. He termed Erasmus' lengthy Ep 1581 'a

* * * * *

20 CWE 11 Ep 1581:121–33. Erasmus' harsh and satirical rejection of scholasticism, however, was a matter of long public record. This apologia could therefore only be interpreted by Béda as disingenuous.
21 CWE 11 Ep 1581:614–26
22 CWE 11 Ep 1596:41–7
23 CWE 11 Ep 1596:7 mistakenly treats Béda's 'annotationes' as a printed book, but the book did not appear until eight months later, in May 1526. Erasmus is looking here for the most up-to-date draft of Béda's manuscript notes.

waste of effort.' He wrote that Baer's approval of Erasmus' *De esu carnium* (1522) merely showed how Baer had gone astray in approving a book which had given aid and comfort to Luther and his followers, who, as a result, could now boast that Erasmus agreed with them.[24] Béda felt confident that he could entrust Gervasius Wain, a German-born Paris theologian who had Erasmus' confidence, with warning Baer about his error. Béda could boast that, in contrast to Erasmus, the important and prolific Paris theologian Josse Clichtove, who had once been an avid supporter of the humanist methodology of Lefèvre d'Etaples, was now regularly asking Béda to vet his books. Finally, in response to Erasmus' request (in Ep 1581:895–907), Béda included with Ep 1609 an updated manuscript of his annotations on the errors he perceived in Erasmus' books.

Erasmus' Ep 1610 (undated but tentatively placed in September 1525) had only one purpose: to deny in detail false rumours charging that, during his visit to Besançon in the spring of 1524, he had made an irreverent remark during invocations to the Blessed Virgin before dinner.[25] His next letter (Ep 1620, dated 2 October 1525) is a moderate plea aimed at forestalling an official censure by the whole faculty of theology. He does charge that Béda's manuscript annotations are often concerned with issues that are matters of opinion, not doctrine – issues such as the authorship of the Epistle to the Hebrews, fasting, and celibacy of the clergy. He adds that the important issues, such as the real presence in the Eucharist – increasingly denied by Sacramentarians like Andreas Karlstadt, Huldrych Zwingli, and Johannes Oecolampadius – would be better refuted by persuasive argument than by resorting to propositions, as the scholastics do.[26] Béda's response (Ep 1642, 21 October 1525) shows increasing impatience with Erasmus' refusal to retract his 'errors.' No one, he says, seems acceptable to Erasmus who does not agree with him. In reply to Erasmus' remark that Béda is too often concerned with non-essential points, he asserts that accusations like that are just what allow 'countless people to do enormous damage to the church, and that rascal Luther shelters behind the same doctrine.'[27] As for the Sacramentarians, he wishes that Erasmus would write against them. He defends the role of the faculty of theology in censoring doctrinal errors: anyone must be held suspect, he says, who shows himself hostile to theolo-

* * * * *

24 'I assert it as an unalterable article of truth that [Baer] and anyone who is of the same opinion have gone pitifully astray' CWE 11 Ep 1609:20–7.

25 CWE 11 Ep 1610:60 n20

26 CWE 11 Ep 1620:94–103

27 CWE 11 Ep 1642:14–24

gians who are duty-bound by their profession to examine new teachings and who, by condemning those they find to be in error, warn the faithful of their danger. He forewarns Erasmus that he has now cast his notes and censures of Erasmus in the form of a book which he would append to another book he had already prepared against Lefèvre d'Etaples. Béda concedes that the language used by Pierre Cousturier in *De tralatione* to describe Erasmus and Lefèvre was 'excessively arrogant and sarcastic,' and says that he had reproved Cousturier for it. Still, he insists that the doctrinal points that Cousturier was making are valid, and that it was those points, not Cousturier's style, that the faculty of theology had approved.[28] Finally, in a postscript he implies that he is far from certain that Erasmus did not make the irreverent remark in Besançon about prayer to the Virgin Mary.

Erasmus was growing weary of the exchange. In Ep 1679 (13 March 1526) he accuses Béda of confusing his personal opinions with orthodox theology. He once again defends the humanists' approach to the Bible: they seek to restore it to its pristine form, not to destroy its true integrity. The real innovators, Erasmus says bitterly, are the sophistic scholastics who have substituted Aristotle, Averroes, and Duns Scotus for the Bible. Erasmus takes credit for advising the city fathers of Basel to suppress Oecolampadius' second book on the Eucharist.[29]

After a hiatus in the correspondence of twenty months, during which the first exchange of published polemical books between Erasmus and Béda took place,[30] Erasmus wrote his final letter to Béda (Ep 1906, 16 November 1527); in it he exhorted him to reconsider his censures – or, as Erasmus calls them, his calumnies.[31] No reply to it from Béda is extant. The same courier who carried it also brought letters from Erasmus to the faculty of theology (Ep 1902) and the Parlement of Paris (Ep 1905). Erasmus obviously sensed that the condemnation he had tried to avoid was imminent. He asked the

* * * * *

28 cwe 11 Ep 1642:33–63
29 cwe 12 Ep 1679:9–17, 63–8, 102–15. At the end of the letter Erasmus admits that, in Besançon, he had found the litany to the Blessed Virgin Mary to be overlong, and that he had indeed spoken words that some may have thought irreverent; but he contends that the reports about those words did not take into account the context of the incident as a whole.
30 See xxi–xxvi below.
31 Like Ep 1581, this letter also went astray, forcing Erasmus to send it again; but we cannot be certain that Béda received it. As with Ep 1581, Béda did not include Ep 1906 with those he published in *Apologia adversus clandestinos Lutheranos*.

faculty to act without passion, but he affirmed that if they did condemn him the truth would nevertheless prevail. He asked the Parlement to recognize the danger of Béda's leadership in the faculty.

This epistolary exchange was obviously unsuccessful. There was never a real meeting of minds. Erasmus' arguments were partly rhetorical (his enemies are inconsequential, and his many supporters are notable and learned) and partly substantial (theological argument cannot be immutably frozen but must be adapted to changing times, always subject to the judgment of the church). Béda's letters, on the other hand, show an unyielding sense of the legitimate role of theologians whose professional training has been duly certified by the Holy See to teach doctrine, to defend traditional church practices, and especially to uphold the validity and exclusive use of the Latin Vulgate Bible. Béda was convinced that Erasmus and other humanists, by employing their literary skills to dismiss many of the church's traditions and to emend or translate the text of the Bible used for a thousand years, would endanger the salvation of Christian souls.

While these letters were being exchanged, Béda was exercising his office as syndic of the faculty of theology to marshal it for a formal examination and condemnation of Erasmus' works. The faculty met numerous times in committee and general session before voting unanimously on 16 May 1526 to censure Erasmus' *Colloquies*, deeming them to be particularly unsuitable for young people on the grounds that they satirize church traditions and practices such as fasting and abstinence, the veneration of the Virgin Mary and the saints, and the consecrated life of monks in religious orders.[32] Then, on 16 December 1527, the doctors pronounced a general condemnation of propositions drawn from several of Erasmus' books.[33] This 1527 censure along with the 1526 censure of the *Colloquies* would essentially comprise the faculty's 1531 *Determinatio*.

Six months later Béda successfully convinced the whole university to ratify the faculty's censure of the *Colloquies*.[34] The university's rector

* * * * *

32 Farge *Procès-verbaux* 136–7 no 152A. The decision was copied into the faculty's *Liber secundus* 63v–64; cf Argentré *Collectio judiciorum* II-1 47. The faculty's censures of the *Colloquies* were listed and sent to the Parlement of Paris (*Liber secundus* 99–109).

33 This critically important censure was not recorded in the faculty's *Procès-verbaux*, but it was inscribed in the faculty's *Liber secundus* 65v–99; cf Argentré *Collectio judiciorum* II-1 53–77.

34 The faculties of law and medicine supported Béda's request with no hesitation, but the four 'Nations' comprising the faculty of arts were divided. The Nations of France and Germany supported the censure without reservation, while the

mandated that the censure be posted on every bulletin board in the university precincts. It is important to keep in mind that, since none of these censures were published until 1531, Erasmus probably did not have them when he composed his books and tracts against Béda, although some of their features may have reached him unofficially through contacts in Paris. The faculty of theology, on the other hand, certainly did have access to Erasmus' arguments against Béda's *Annotationes* when it censured him in December 1527 – thus judging those arguments to be either unconvincing or in error.

Indeed, as those official proceedings in the faculty were taking place, Béda and Erasmus were already replacing their epistolary exchange with a series of mutually recriminating books and tracts.[35] As early as 1525 Erasmus had begun to compose a work that he entitled *Divinationes ad notata Bedae*[36] (LB IX 454–96). It was his first response to Béda's notes on the *Paraphrase on Luke* that François Deloynes[37] had sent Erasmus, and to additional notes on other paraphrases sent directly by Béda himself. Hoping to forestall a censure of his works by the faculty itself, Erasmus included a manuscript

* * * * *

Nations of Picardy and Normandy wanted to allow Erasmus time to retract the offending parts (something Erasmus would never have done). On 23 June 1528, therefore, the university's rector ruled that the majority favoured the formal condemnation of the *Colloquies*. See Archives de l'Université de Paris (Sorbonne) Register 15 151r; cf C.-E. Du Boulay *Historia universitatis parisiensis* (Paris 1665–73) VI 210, 235; and Argentré *Collectio judiciorum* II-1 52. Because this was an act of the whole university, it was not recorded in the faculty's *Procès-verbaux*. It was, however, entered in the *Liber secundus*, where it is dated vaguely 'circa finem julii,' the same dating copied later into the 1531 *Declarationes*.

35 Apart from his manuscript notes, Béda published two books critical of Erasmus; Erasmus wrote six books or tracts against Béda. The most accessible guide through these works is Rummel *Catholic Critics* II 33–46; the most detailed is Bense 671–725. Because some editions bore no precise day, month, or even year of publication, we cannot be certain about the order of composition and publication of Erasmus' books and tracts. We will frequently refer the reader to LB, the 1703 Leiden edition, which used the 1540 Basel *Opera omnia* as its basis, because it is the most accessible edition. It must be said that both Erasmus and Béda repeated themselves endlessly, and that many of the arguments put forth by both sides in 1531 and 1532 had already been proposed and answered in the earlier books and tracts, seeming almost to fall on deaf ears.

36 The title *Divinationes*, which translates as 'Guesses,' implies that, since Béda had merely listed Erasmus' alleged errors without supplying any arguments against them, Erasmus could only 'guess' what those arguments might be.

37 See xiii–xiv above.

of *Divinationes* with Ep 1664 (6 February 1526),[38] adding: 'I have replied briefly to a few of the points raised, though I have had to guess what it was he objected to [*divinare coactus quid illam offendent*].'[39] He also enclosed with Ep 1664 another document, signed on 7 April 1525 by Béda and the late Doctor Guillaume Duchesne, which Béda had written to dissuade Carthusian monks from reading Erasmus' works. Erasmus complained that it contained barefaced lies and calumnies and that its legal form made it look like an official condemnation by the faculty itself.[40]

Only a few months later, anticipating the publication of Béda's *Annotationes* and working again from notes received from Béda and reports sent by friends in Paris, Erasmus composed his *Elenchus in censuras Bedae* (LB IX 495–514).[41] On 14 June 1526 he enclosed it with a letter to the Parlement of Paris in which he complains that Béda failed to take into account the objections he made in *Divinationes*, which he had sent to the faculty together

* * * * *

38 In the Introduction to Ep 1664 Allen states that Erasmus included with that letter to the Parlement his treatise *Prologus in supputationem calumniarum Bedae*. He drew that conclusion solely from the fact that Erasmus published *Prologus* with Ep 1664. That publication, however, did not appear until August 1526 – six months after Erasmus wrote Ep 1664 (6 February 1526). The text of Ep 1664 itself shows, instead, that Erasmus sent the faculty not his *Prologus* but his *Divinationes. Prologus*, written some months later, was Erasmus' first, hasty response to Béda's *Annotationes* (published 28 May 1526). Erasmus followed it up later with his more considered *Supputatio errorum in censuris Bedae*. On these two later treatises see xxiv–xxvi and nn49 and 51 below.

39 CWE 12 Ep 1664:25–7 / Allen VI Ep 1664:24. *Divinationes* responds to 45 alleged errors that Béda drew from the *Paraphrases* on Matthew and Luke, 55 others from the *Paraphrases* on the Epistles, and the rest from some of Erasmus' other works. Matters treated at length concern the sin against the Holy Ghost (LB IX 454A–455E), the translation of Scripture into vernacular languages (LB IX 456C–457C), the renewal of baptismal vows (LB IX 459A–F), the prohibition of oaths (LB IX 461E– 462E), the punishment of heretics (LB IX 464A–C), fasting and the choice of foods (LB IX 474B–E), and the celibacy of the clergy (LB IX 484D–485E).

40 In March 1527 Erasmus published this short document, which he entitled *Calumniae Bedae*, in the omnibus volume *Supputationes* (part II 13v). It is followed by Ep 1664 to the faculty of theology (14–15v), and then by *Divinationes* (15v–72v).

41 Erasmus does not use 'elenchus' in the strictly Socratic sense (a series of questions designed to demonstrate from the opponent's own answers that his original argument cannot be true); he uses it in the general sense of 'refutation.' Like *Divinationes, Elenchus* is relegated to part II of the omnibus *Supputationes* (75–98).

with his own explanations and defences.[42] He did not publish them at that time,[43] he avers, but now he wishes that he had, because in the meantime Béda has shown his censures to the faculty of theology and to others. The Parlement's only response to this new letter from Erasmus was to send it and *Elenchus* to the faculty and to ask its advice about how the Parlement should respond to Erasmus.[44]

In *Elenchus* Erasmus does not reveal the propositions to which Béda objected but simply gives the ordinal numbers of Béda's notes.[45] His responses in *Elenchus* tend to be brief. Only a few of them would find their way into *Declarationes*. In his peroration (LB IX 513E–514E) Erasmus expresses the hope that the reputation of the faculty will not be damaged by the 'absurdities' of Béda. He felt bound to reply to them to prevent some unknowing persons, reading only Béda, from thinking Erasmus belonged to the Lutheran faction, since Béda constantly links his name with every sort of heretic. Moreover, using his 'brave and splendid lies,' Béda has distorted the meaning of Erasmus' *Paraphrases on the New Testament* by interpreting them as if they applied to the present time and circumstances instead of reading them in the context of the apostolic times in which the Scriptures were written.

Béda's *Annotationes*, about which he had forewarned Erasmus, finally appeared on 28 May 1526.[46] In contrast to the first set of notes that he had

* * * * *

42 Ep 1721. The Parlement register records reception of the letter and of 'a little treatise he has written in opposition to Noël Béda and [Pierre] Cousturier.' Contrary to his usual practice, the Parlement secretary did not copy the text of the letter itself into the register (AN x^{1A} 1529 307r–308r).

43 *Divinationes* appeared in print only in March 1527. We consulted the copy in the Centre for Reformation and Renaissance Studies, Victoria University, Toronto.

44 AN x^{1A} 1529 309r

45 This is the opposite situation to *Divinationes*, where Erasmus complained that Béda's notes were simply rebuttals without any indication of where the propositions that he objected to could be found. In *Elenchus* Erasmus turns Béda's method of detailed and lengthy numeration against him. But this cumulative rhetoric, whether employed by Béda or Erasmus, is neither very coherent nor generally analytic.

46 *Annotationum ... in Jacobum Fabrum Stapulensem libri duo: et in Desiderium Erasmum Roterodamum liber unus* (Paris: Josse Bade 28 May 1526; repr Cologne: Petrus Quentell 31 August 1526). The first 80 per cent of Béda's text concerns the errors he found in the works of Lefèvre d'Etaples, while only the remaining 20 per cent deals with the errors he perceived in Erasmus' *Paraphrases on the New Testament*. CWE Ep 1609:110–12 n16 misinterprets Béda, who does not

sent to Erasmus, he published here both the offending propositions and his censures of them.[47] In the Preface Béda places Erasmus and Lefèvre among the 'theologizing humanists' who, being educated only in the humanities and languages, write erroneously about the orthodox faith and disrupt the morals of the faithful. In this way, he says, they attempt to usurp the title of theologian for themselves; instead, like the heretics of old, they disagree among themselves and fall into the same old heresies about faith and morals, free will, church councils, penance, veneration of the saints, and the nature of the church.

Erasmus could not fail to comprehend the danger to himself when such a book was unleashed in the public forum. On 16 June 1526 he wrote to King Francis I (Ep 1722) to ask him to suppress the book. He charged that Béda was blocking the progress of learning in France, that he was making the University of Paris a laughing-stock in Europe, and that he was even plotting against the authority of the king on the pretext that the king was failing to suppress heresy. Francis ordered the Parlement to confiscate all copies of the book, but the printer reported that he had already sold or sent 600 of the 650 printed copies for distribution throughout the Continent and in England.[48] The Cologne printer Petrus Quentell immediately reprinted it (August 1526) and circulated it widely.

After receiving and reading Béda's *Annotationes* Erasmus began to prepare a lengthy and detailed refutation of it: *Supputatio errorum in censuris Bedae* (LB IX 516–702). In order to get something out more quickly, however, he first published *Prologus in supputationem calumniarum Natalis Bedae.*[49] It opens

* * * * *

say that he had not read through the entire *Paraphrases*; rather, he remarks that he consulted only those parts of Erasmus' *Annotations on the New Testament* that had a direct bearing on his censures of the *Paraphrases*.

47 Béda's book deals with the *Paraphrases* on all four Gospels, on almost every Pauline Epistle, and on the seven canonical, or apostolic, Epistles. In many cases his 'censures' fall far short of a refutation or even an explanation, and are sometimes limited to short opinions such as 'this is Lutheran.' See Erika Rummel 'Why Noël Béda Did Not Like Erasmus' Paraphrases' in *Holy Scripture Speaks: The Production and Reception of Erasmus' Paraphrases on the New Testament* ed Hilmar Pabel and Mark Vessey (Toronto 2002) 265–78.

48 Paris, AN x[1A] 367v–369v (17 August 1526); cf Farge *Procès-verbaux* 142–3, nos 161B 161C; and Farge *Orthodoxy and Reform* 260–1.

49 (Basel: Froben August 1526). It was reprinted in the omnibus *Supputationes* volume (March 1527) with a variation in the title: *Prologus supputationis errorum in censuris Bedae*. He used this same tactic earlier that year, when he hurriedly issued *Hyperaspistes 1* (February 1526) against Luther, following it up later with the longer and more detailed *Hyperaspistes 2* (summer/fall 1527).

with a Protestation in which Erasmus declares that he wishes to be heard as if
in solemn testimony at a theological disputation, speaking for himself alone,
and dealing only with the censures of Béda, with whom he is prepared to be
reconciled if only Béda would adopt a more Christian frame of mind (LB IX
441–442B). Claiming lack of time to deal as fully as he would like with Béda's
book, he says he must here be content only to give examples of three kinds
of errors in it: inaccuracies (some of them merely shameless, others consciously malicious), slanders, and blasphemies. He provides two examples
of shameless inaccuracies: those concerning the authorship of the Epistle to
the Hebrews and Erasmus' notion that baptismal vows should be repeated
in early adulthood. He characterizes as shamelessly and maliciously inaccu-
rate Béda's accusation about Erasmus' remarks on Christ's knowledge of the
last day. As an example of slander he notes Béda's charge that Erasmus is an
Arian – slanderous, he says, because he had already refuted that charge in
Divinationes.[50] Béda slandered him again, he says, by charging that Erasmus
was siding with Lutherans and schismatics merely because he pointed out
that some learned men have taught that *Ecclesiastical Hierarchies* was not written by St Paul's Athenian convert Dionysius the Areopagite (Acts 17:34). As
for Béda's blasphemies, they are said to be more hysterical than conscious
ones, as when he again called Erasmus Lutheran or heretical for holding
doctrines taught by St Paul and widely believed in the church. Finally, *Prologus* lists thirteen methods by which Béda consciously and maliciously distorts Erasmus' works: he misidentifies the person speaking in a paraphrase;
he misidentifies the time and circumstances of some of the paraphrases; he
deliberately misreports Erasmus' words; he chooses the unfavourable sense
of an ambiguous expression; he adds words; he omits words; he miscon-
strues statements that are made clear in another place; he confronts one passage with another that is seemingly contradictory to it; he rejects legitimate
figurative interpretations; he attributes obvious printers' errors to Erasmus;
he engages in trivial quarrels about diction; he confuses the reader with
specious quibbles; and he indulges in bad faith by characterizing as heretical passages in Erasmus' works that are found in Scripture or the Fathers.

In this lengthy Preface to *Supputatio*[51] Erasmus responded in prickly,
indignant, and outraged detail to the opening remarks in Béda's *Annota-*

* * * * *

50 Erasmus had sent *Divinationes* (in manuscript) to the faculty in February 1526
   with Ep 1664. See xxi–xxii and n38 above.
51 The Preface alone comprises 52 pages in the 1527 octavo edition and 27 fo-
   lio columns in LB IX 515A–542B. The entire *Supputatio* occupies the first 470
   pages in the omnibus edition: *Supputationes errorum in censuris Natalis Bedae*

tiones. In the *Supputatio* itself he enumerated (or 'counted up') and replied to 198 censures of Béda, in which he delineates 181 inaccuracies, 310 calumnies, and 47 blasphemies by using the marginal notations v (*vanum*), c (*calumnia*), and b (*blasphemia*).[52] The points listed in *Supputatio* are found in Béda's criticism of the *Paraphrases* as well as *Enchiridion militis christiani*.

The Paris theologians obviously found Erasmus' arguments to be unconvincing, for many of the charges that Erasmus refuted here reappear in their December 1527 censure (and thus in the 1531 *Determinatio*), even though *Supputatio* was probably available to the faculty and its committees.[53] The final censures, however, omitted many of the propositions that Béda had listed in his *Annotationes*.

Instead of publishing still another book in response to *Supputatio*, Béda orchestrated the three formal condemnations of Erasmus in the faculty and the whole University of Paris that were discussed above.[54] The faculty judged it imprudent to publish these censures in the political climate of those first years after Francis 1's release from Spanish captivity. But the publication of faculty censures against humanists and reformers had been on Béda's mind for some time. At least three times – 1 April 1525, 7 March 1526, and 10 December 1526 – he had proposed that the faculty publish a

* * * * *

(Basel: Johannes Froben, March 1527). In a second, repaginated part *Supputationes* contains all of Erasmus' anti-Béda books and tracts up to that time: *Prologus supputationis errorum in censuris Bedae* (2–13r); *Divinationes ad notata Beda* (15–63v), with Béda's early notes on Erasmus' *Paraphrase on Luke* (January 1524) (64–72v); *Elenchus in censuras Bedae* (73–97v); and two tracts against the Paris-trained theologians Pierre Cousturier and Josse Clichtove. See Ferdinand van der Haeghen *Bibliotheca Erasmiana: Répertoire des oeuvres d'Erasme* (Ghent 1893; repr Nieuwkoop 1961, 1972) 178; Jacqueline Glomski and Erika Rummel *Annotated Catalogue of Early Editions of Erasmus at the Centre for Reformation and Renaissance Studies, Toronto* (Toronto 1994) no 465; Erika Rummel and Dale Schrag *The Erasmus Collection in the Herzog August Bibliothek* (Wiesbaden 2004) 151–2 no 1252; *Index Aureliensis: Catalogus librorum sedecimi saeculo impressorum* (Baden-Baden 1980–   ) xv 169.

52 *Enumeratio* is a feature of classical rhetoric but only on a much smaller scale: the listing of arguments in the *partitio* or in the *peroratio* of an oration. See Heinrich Lausberg *Handbook of Literary Rhetoric: A Foundation for Literary Study* trans Matthew T. Bliss, Annemiek Jansen, et al, ed David E. Orton and R. Dean Anderson (Leiden 1998) 299–302 nos 669–74. Reformation polemics employed it frequently to refute a text sequentially, piece by piece, as Erasmus did, for instance, in *Hyperaspistes* 1 and 2; but the censures by Béda and the faculty of theology do not employ it.

53 Farge *Orthodoxy and Reform* 194–5

54 See xx–xxi above.

book containing all the censures that it had passed since 1523 against persons accused of Lutheranism, as well as certain works of Lefèvre d'Etaples, and on the third of those occasions Erasmus himself was included.[55] By 1531 Béda and the faculty obviously thought the time was finally ripe to publish, and they issued their *Determinatio* against Erasmus. They included with it the university's 1521 condemnation of Luther and a 1523 censure of propositions preached in the diocese of Meaux.

Noël Béda was also involved in other controversies. In 1529 he composed his *Apologia adversus clandestinos Lutheranos*,[56] the chief purpose of which was to respond to an anonymous little book accusing him of heresy.[57] But this *Apologia* also provided him with the opportunity to include Erasmus and Lefèvre d'Etaples in his category of 'clandestine Lutherans,' charging once again that they had made possible the success of Lutheranism and other heretical movements in France. Erasmus replied with *Notatiunculae quaedam extemporales ad naenias Bedaicas* (LB IX 701–36),[58] in which he calls Béda 'the most stupid of bipeds' and a 'hot-headed monster who is also impotent, stupid, doting, and out of his mind.' He urged King Francis I to have Béda deported to the most remote region of his kingdom.[59]

* * * * *

55 Farge *Procès-verbaux* 92 no 87c, 130 no 144b, 160 no 182b
56 'Apology against Clandestine Lutherans.' See n19 above.
57 *Duodecim articuli infidelitatis magistri Natalis Bedae ... ex libro suarum annotationum ... reprobantur & confutantur* 'Twelve Articles of Infidelity of Master Noël Béda ... Drawn from the Book of His Annotations ... Confounded and Reproved' (np nd [Paris: Josse Bade 1527]). Béda believed the book was composed by Louis de Berquin; but Berquin denied under oath that he was the author, and his fervent evangelical conscience would not have tolerated a false oath. The author was more likely Béda's long-time colleague and adversary Jacques Merlin, whose lawyer had spoken in the Parlement of 'a large number of erroneous propositions, suspect in the faith, drawn and excerpted from the books of Béda' (Paris, AN x^{1A} 8344 17).
58 'Some Little Notes against the Trifling Ditties of Béda' (Basel: Froben, March 1529)
59 This is exactly what the king finally did. Francis had personal reasons for ridding himself of Béda who, like his mentor Jan Standonck, did not hesitate to oppose royal initiatives openly when he deemed them dangerous. In 1530 Béda had fought unsuccessfully against Francis' efforts to get the Paris faculty to declare Henry VIII's marriage with Catherine of Aragon null and void. In 1533 he opposed the public sermons of Gérard Roussel, who was the favourite court preacher of the king's sister Margaret of Navarre. Finally, in 1534, Béda brought suit in the Parlement to keep the king's appointed professors of Greek and Latin – *lecteurs royaux*, the nascent Collège royal (later the Collège de France) – from commenting on biblical texts in their lectures; see

There were no further polemical exchanges between Erasmus and
Béda during the next two years. It seemed that everything that could be
said had been said – until the publication of the faculty's *Determinatio* in
1531 and Erasmus' *Declarationes* in 1532. In response to the latter, Béda's last
direct action against Erasmus occurred in April 1532, when he showed *Declarationes* to the faculty. Its first response was to direct the faculty beadle to
caution all booksellers not to sell Erasmus' book and to forbid the printers
in Paris to reprint it.[60] A committee appointed to examine it found it to contain so many issues which they considered erroneous or heretical that the
faculty instructed the committee to narrow the list down to the most important ones. On 2 May Béda concluded that, even though all those propositions had already been condemned by the faculty, a book so pernicious to
the Catholic faith should be suppressed. The faculty decided to consult the
Parlement, the papal judges-delegate in France, and the ecclesiastical court
of the bishop of Paris. But no one on the faculty, not even Béda, rose to
the challenge to respond once again to Erasmus in print. This was, perhaps,
because of the publication of the second, revised and augmented edition
of Erasmus' *Declarationes*, which would have entailed still another process
of examination and censure. One may plausibly speculate, however, that
the faculty responded to Erasmus' second edition by issuing its own second, more elaborate edition of *Determinatio*.[61] It can be regarded as the final
response of Béda and the Parisian faculty of theology to Erasmus and his
humanist approach to Scripture and theology.

ERASMUS' REVISED AND AUGMENTED EDITION OF *DECLARATIONES*

Many of the changes Erasmus made in the second edition of *Declarationes*
are of the minor sort that he often made to new editions of his works in

* * * * *

James K. Farge *Le parti conservateur au XVIe siècle: Université et Parlement de Paris
à l'époque de la Renaissance et de la Réforme* (Paris 1992) 41–6, 117–31. To punish Béda for 'a thousand reasons,' as he put it, Francis first subjected him to a
public humiliation outside the cathedral of Paris and then committed him to
a state prison housed in the abbey of Mont-Saint-Michel, where he was kept
in degrading circumstances until his death in January 1537. See Farge 'Noël
Béda' n100.
60 Farge *Procès-verbaux* 263–4 nos 339B, 341A
61 See n1 above. Bibliographers have noted briefly some changes in the faculty's
second edition: some headings and numeration were changed, and some passages were shifted; but a scientific collation of the two editions has not been
done.

order to clarify, intensify, or qualify statements and arguments.[62] For example, in revising a section of censured propositions that the theologians had added (almost as an afterthought, alleging the printer's deadline), Erasmus made only two very brief additions and one longer one of about 50 words (at the end of the sixth additional charge). Here he was attempting to clarify how some of the church Fathers regarded the non-apostolic opinions of early theologians. To his long appendix on the censures drawn from the *Colloquies* Erasmus now added 18 very brief phrases and longer additions to the following four sections: 150 words on the fourth charge about sacramental confession; 125 words on charge 52A about calling the Father 'the Source' and the Son 'the Lord' (terminology, he explains, that was drawn mostly from Hilary of Poitiers); 90 words on charge 55 about 'Credo sanctam ecclesiam' instead of the traditional 'Credo in sanctam ecclesiam';[63] and 250 words on charge 56 about whether the church consists only of good persons. His clarifications about propositions from the *Colloquies* usually resort to the argument of dramatic context, in which he argues that the opinions found objectionable by the faculty were not his own opinions but were merely those held by one of the speakers in the colloquy, while still another character refutes what the faculty found to be objectionable.[64]

Some of the changes, however, are quite substantial, making the second edition almost 50 per cent longer than the first. These additions must, at least in some instances, reveal the issues that Erasmus thought to be most important. Topic 9, dealing with 'The Old Law,' underwent the most extensive revision, adding 2650 words to its treatment in the first edition. Three other topics – 4 'Oaths,' 3 'Fasting and the choice of food,' and 7 'Faith' – were all augmented by more than 1500 words. He added between 600 and 900 words to the following six topics: 8 'Certain wishes regarding the faith,' 19 'Vocal prayer,' 2 'The death of Christ,' 5 'Reparation for injuries,' 10 'The authors of the books of the New Testament,' and 23 'The punishment of heretics.' Six topics were augmented by between 200 and 500 words: 32 'Scholastic theology,' 11 'The Apostles' Creed,' 12 'The translation of Holy Scripture into a vernacular language,' 1 'The baptizing of infants,' 26 'The church,' and 27 'The Blessed Virgin Mary.' Additions of 100 to 180 words

* * * * *

62 The second edition also tidied up the headings and numeration of the first edition and shifted two passages to more appropriate locations.
63 He cited the Fathers and Jean Gerson on this point.
64 Franz Bierlaire *Les Colloques d'Érasme: réforme des études, réforme des moeurs et réforme de l'Église au XVIe siècle* Bibliothèque de la Faculté de Philosophie et Lettres de l'Université de Liège 222 (Paris 1978) 216–66

were made to four topics: 22 'The temporal punishment of children because of the sins of their parents,' 30 'The apostle Paul,' 15 'Some propositions in which the writer did not fulfil the duty of a paraphraser,' and 20 'The celibacy of priests.' The remaining 13 topics were either augmented by less than a hundred words or, in the case of topics 6 'Matrimony' and 21 'Original sin,' by no changes at all.[65]

This list shows that, on the whole, the longest additions appear in the earliest sections of the work. It is not surprising that a busy, prolific author like Erasmus would have been less and less inclined to revise his work as he progressed further into it. It is also worth noting that some topics central to the religious conflicts of the time, such as original sin, merit for good works, and ceremonies (topics 16, 17, 21), were expanded very little or not at all. That could be because Erasmus had treated them so often and so thoroughly in his previous works or simply because he considered them to have been adequately treated in the first edition.

Many of the significant changes can be attributed to Erasmus' consultations with the young Dominican friar Ambrosius Pelargus.[66] Even though not a full-fledged doctor of theology until 1533, Pelargus was a seasoned polemicist; he had entered the fray against Zwingli in 1527 and published two books against Oecolampadius' view of the Eucharist. After taking refuge in Freiburg Pelargus also wrote tracts against the Anabaptists, iconoclasts, and other Protestants.[67]

In the exchange of seven letters between Erasmus and Pelargus in June 1529 Pelargus shows himself to be self-effacing and respectful, while at the same time sufficiently learned to win a place among Erasmus' correspondents and visitors.[68] Despite Pelargus' tendency to point out errors and other weaknesses in Erasmus' works, their friendship developed to the extent that in the summer of 1532 Erasmus, who was preparing the sec-

* * * * *

65 The word-counts are close approximations based on the Latin texts, not the English translation of them.
66 See xi n4 above. *Pelargus* is the Latinized form of *Pelargos*, the Greek equivalent of his German name, *Storch* 'stork.' See CEBR III 63–4.
67 In 1533 Pelargus was moved by his order to Trier, where he served as both preacher and professor in the university, and there he translated John Chrysostom's *Divine Liturgy* from Greek into Latin. He took part in the Colloquy of Worms (1541) and perhaps in that of Regensburg (1546). He represented the archbishop of Trier at the Council of Trent, where he engaged in sessions on justification, the sacraments, and the residency of bishops. He preached to the assembled council Fathers in 1552.
68 Epp 2169, 2170, 2181, 2182, 2184, 2185, 2186

ond edition of his *Declarationes* and knew that Pelargus had read the first edition, asked him for his help:

> I am required to revise my *Clarifications*, since the printers are demanding it. Hence I beg you to send me your notes, so that I can see if they are of any help. For I certainly do not want to have any admixture of Lutheranism in what I write. If you are willing to do it, there is no need for you to take the trouble to make a fair copy. I have assistants who can read anything. But if you wish to make a fair copy, I will not fail to be thankful for it. But I would not want you to take the trouble to do so until, after sampling the matter, we have talked about it.[69]

Pelargus thus submitted suggestions for the revision of *Declarationes* by means of a manuscript notebook. For the most part his suggestions are lengthy, thoughtful, expert, and fair-minded. Only occasionally do they digress somewhat into irrelevance and even ostentation.[70] He did not hesitate to point out places where Erasmus' arguments were tenuous. He found not at all convincing Erasmus' argument that criticisms in the *Paraphrases* were aimed exclusively at the entourage of the scriptural writers, not at groups or institutions of Erasmus' time (such as monks and mendicant friars).[71] When dealing with the section about the *Colloquies* Pelargus made only six comments. In one he insisted that, although opinions in the *Colloquies* are voiced by the dramatic characters – not directly by Erasmus – and although their views are often counteracted by other characters, it was nevertheless quite apparent that Erasmus composed his remarks with contemporary groups and institutions in mind.[72] Pelargus even went so far as to wish that the *Colloquies* had never been published, because he feared that they might be harmful to the morals of young people. Although he did not condemn the *Colloquies* in the same terms as

* * * * *

69 Ep 2666. The correspondence on the *Declarationes* continues with Epp 2667–9, all in July 1532. The letters reveal that Pelargus could be bluntly critical when he thought Erasmus was wrong, whether on points of grammar, exegesis, or doctrine.
70 Summaries of Pelargus' suggestions are presented below in the appropriate places in the annotations on the text.
71 See 188 n683 below. In fact the whole aim of paraphrases as such was to make Scripture more immediately accessible and applicable to a contemporary audience.
72 See 310 n1110 below.

the Paris theologians, Pelargus certainly shared their apprehensions about them.[73]

Erasmus did not reply to such objections in his second edition, but he did take some of Pelargus' criticisms and his suggestions that Erasmus provide additional evidence for his arguments quite seriously, as certain long sections in the second edition make clear.[74]

Not long after the publication of the second edition Pelargus discovered by chance that, in a letter to Thomas More in 1529, Erasmus had blamed Pelargus (without naming him) for stirring up the troubles in Basel that had made it impossible for Erasmus to continue living there.[75] After that, although they continued to correspond, the relations between Pelargus and Erasmus were never as trusting or as close as they had previously been.[76]

THE SIGNIFICANCE OF ERASMUS' *DECLARATIONES*

Reading the *Declarationes* is hardly an exhilarating or even very satisfying experience. In comparing it to other polemical works that Erasmus had produced during the 1520s and early 1530s, whether against his Catholic critics or Protestants, one recognizes that the two parts of *Hyperaspistes*,[77] Erasmus' long and detailed defence of his *De libero arbitrio* against Luther's attack in *De servo arbitrio*, remain perhaps the most theologically substantial and valuable of Erasmus' polemical works. Other works, such as *Ratio verae theologiae* and *Enchiridion militis christiani*, give a more general and clearer view of Erasmus' *philosophia Christi* than *Declarationes*, while the text and copious annotations of Erasmus' edition of the New Testament exemplify and spell out the details of his programme in an extended and multifarious but still ad hoc fashion. However, *Declarationes* has its own strengths. One of its important contributions is that it consolidates and orders most of the polemic exchanged between Erasmus and Noël Béda during the previous decade.

* * * * *

73 See 269 n945, 310 n1110 below.
74 See the following notes in the text below: nn57, 104, 118, 152, 172, 206, 233, 330, 348, 365, 377, 399, 694, 749, 767, 790, 826, 1093–4, 1098.
75 Ep 2211, dated 5 September 1529, thus not long after their initial friendly exchanges
76 For additional insights into the issues that Pelargus raised and the way that Erasmus reacted to them see Rummel *Catholic Critics* II 55–8 and CEBR III 63–4. It was only in 1539, three years after Erasmus' death, that Pelargus published his notebook, *Iudicium Pelargi de Declarationibus Erasmi*, along with their correspondence, in *Bellaria*.
77 *A Warrior Shielding a Discussion of Free Will* CWE 76 91–321 and CWE 77.

Moreover, although *Declarationes* presents the censured propositions of the Paris faculty of theology bare of their context, it organizes them according to the thirty-two topics initially delineated by the theologians in *Determinatio*. Erasmus' replies in *Declarationes* can therefore be set against them in a detailed and direct manner. Those topics cover most of Erasmus' religious programme in a fairly systematic manner: doctrine, exegesis, pastoral practices, the religious orders, and other ecclesiastical concerns. Some of them are treated in depth, others only lightly, using a patristic and philological approach. Further, because Erasmus is addressing not a particular opponent, such as Noël Béda, Pierre Cousturier, or Alberto Pio, but rather the faculty of theology of the University of Paris (which he must at least feign to respect), the tedious arguments *ad hominem* and whining complaints about unjust treatment that mark some other polemical works of Erasmus are for the most part avoided in *Declarationes*. It must be admitted that his defence of the *Colloquies* in *Declarationes*, though remotely based on the literary integrity and intention of its pieces, tends to be rather weak and tenuous. Yet the only major dimensions of Erasmus' work not included or implied in *Declarationes* are his educational works, directly devotional works, and literary concerns. It would otherwise be hard to find a single work of Erasmus in which the two contrasting (and tragically conflicting) methods of theology – the scholastic/systematic approach of the faculty and the rhetorical/philological approach of Erasmus – are set out in such a detailed and clear fashion. Unfortunately, the confrontation did not lead to any real mutual understanding or reconciliation.

Erasmus tried to depict Béda as the monolithic head of a small clique of theologians who did not truly represent the opinion of the full, more sensible majority of the faculty. A close reading of the *procès-verbaux* of faculty meetings, however, does not justify that view. Béda had twice attempted to withdraw from his position as faculty syndic, and both times the faculty persuaded him to continue in it. Moreover, the faculty comprised several dozen theologians and could therefore draw on a wide range of colleges and religious orders when appointing deputies to examine the works of Erasmus and others. There were also members of the faculty who opposed Béda on a variety of issues – even on his opposition to Erasmus. A few eventually espoused the Reformation, and several others had sympathy for some of its ideas, although they were never a significant enough number to make a difference to the faculty's conservative, traditionalist inclinations. Indeed, Béda was able to mobilize not only the faculty of theology but also the other three faculties of the university, the great majority of judges and councillors in the Parlement of Paris, and many influential laymen who shared his view that humanist approaches to religious affairs posed danger to church doctrine and traditions. This does not mean that they were right and Erasmus was wrong. Many of Béda's positions would be clearly untenable today. At the same time many of Erasmus' positions were less than conclusive or entirely convincing. The exchanges between Erasmus and Béda were multifarious, verbose, complex, intricate, and often tedious. Still, the arguments for both sides that we shall find in Erasmus' *Declarationes* provide us with a strong and memorable sense of the issues and the rhetoric that prevailed in the momentous clash of humanist and scholastic approaches to Christian doctrine and proposals for reform of the church.

CHM and JKF

ACKNOWLEDGMENTS
We are indebted to Father James Farge, Pontifical Institute of Mediaeval Studies, for his contribution to the Introduction. Drawing on his editorial work on Erasmus' correspondence and his intensive research in the archives of the University of Paris, Farge describes in detail the complex and bitter relations between Erasmus and Noël Béda, which culminated in 1531 with the publication of the Paris faculty of theology's official censure of Erasmus. Farge presents a balanced view of the controversy, and at the same time clarifies the tangled publication history of Erasmus' works against Béda.

We also wish to thank Joan Bulger for her thoughtful and meticulous copyediting of the manuscript, Lynn Browne and Philippa Matheson for their expertise in typesetting the volume, and Ruth Pincoe for providing the excellent index.

THE STRUCTURE OF *DECLARATIONES*

The faculty's preface / 3–4

The faculty's list of topics / 5

Erasmus' preface / 6

* * * * *

* Propositions on which Pelargus commented are indicated by an asterisk.

Propositions added

The faculty's determination concerning the *Colloquies* / 269–71

CLARIFICATIONS CONCERNING THE CENSURES PUBLISHED AT PARIS IN THE NAME OF THE THEOLOGY FACULTY THERE

Declarationes
ad censuras Lutetiae vulgatus
sub nomine facultatis theologiae Parisiensis

CLARIFICATIONS
CONCERNING THE CENSURES[1]
PUBLISHED AT PARIS
IN THE NAME OF
THE THEOLOGY FACULTY THERE

The Preface of the Faculty

THE DEAN AND THE THEOLOGY FACULTY OF THE UNIVERSITY
OF PARIS TO ALL THE FAITHFUL IN CHRIST, GREETINGS
Since, toward the end of June in the year 1526, we were asked by many
eminent persons what should be thought about some propositions excerpted from Desiderius Erasmus' *Paraphrases on the New Testament*,
and likewise about some others excerpted from his little book defending the said propositions, which is called *Elenchus*, and also about some
others found in other books by him, and since we wished to render
an account of the faith which is in us,[2] after looking into the matter
at length and at the proper time and discussing it among ourselves,
at last we not only thought that a reply should be given concerning
the said propositions but we also took care to provide our reasons
and some brief scriptural evidence, according to the narrow scope of

* * * * *

In *Declarationes* Erasmus reprints the *Determinatio* of the Faculty of Theology,
answering the censures point by point. The first two editions of *Declarationes*,
published in the spring and fall of 1532, present the faculty's prefaces and
censures in a smaller type size than Erasmus' responses and clarifications. In
this translation the prefaces and censures of the faculty are indented at the
left margin to distinguish them from Erasmus' responses, which are set full
measure.
1 'Censure' (Latin *censura*) is a technical term referring to doctrinal or theological condemnations of various kinds and degrees, issued by popes, councils,
bishops, and the theological faculties of universities. The censures of theological faculties have considerable standing and importance but lack the official
authority of censures issued by popes, councils, bishops, and some other figures or bodies. See DTC II 2101–2 sv 'censures doctrinales.'
2 Cf 1 Pet 3:15.

our enterprise, where it seemed to be needed, as a precaution, so that those who would read our responses might recognize that the force of truth is so great that, however much it is sometimes assailed by stupid men in their shameless temerity, it can still never be shattered. For if the gates of hell cannot prevail against it,[3] certainly no power on earth will do so. Accordingly prudent men, even among the pagans, are not accustomed to defend with stubborn vehemence what they have asserted, perhaps capriciously or inconsiderately, after the truth itself has been rationally defended and clearly recognized. But in the conclusion of this present work the reason for this undertaking of ours will be more fully explained.

* * * * *

3 Matt 16:18

**An Index of the Topics Which Were Discussed
and Determined by the Aforesaid Assembly of Doctors**

DESIDERIUS ERASMUS' PREFACE
TO HIS CLARIFICATIONS

I certainly hoped there would finally be an end to such quarrels, if for no other reason because the determination of my attackers had petered out, and if that did not happen, I was myself determined to buy some peace from unpeaceful critics by my stubborn silence. For I replied to Alberto Pio because of his famous reputation, which it seemed to me would weigh me down more than his argument itself. But as soon as the censures attributed to the Paris Faculty of Theology were published, quite unexpectedly, my mind was totally divided, thinking that it was not safe to remain silent lest I seem either to hold the majesty of such a famous college in contempt or to acknowledge that their accusations are true, and also not safe to reply lest I should be thought arrogant because I did not fear to defy the pronouncements of that most sacred faculty. Of the two evils, since I could not avoid both, I preferred to incur the one which seemed lighter. For I would consider it lighter to be considered arrogant than to be thought the promulgator of evil teachings. But at least my response is far removed from the blameworthy stubbornness of some people who not only defend and vindicate themselves from charges made against them but also go from bad to worse and redouble their error, and while they avoid seeming to be mere men, they become heretics.

But my response will be so modulated that I will both give the authority of theologians the honour it deserves and also, wherever I have erred through human carelessness, negligence, or ignorance, acknowledge and correct my error; on the other hand, when the obscurity or ambiguity of my language gave rise to a misunderstanding, I will clarify in good faith what I meant. But whenever it happens that something is simply pointless, or wrongly understood, or slanderously distorted, I will candidly reject it, throwing it up not to the body of the sacred faculty but to the delegates or other persons to whom this task was assigned, who foisted off on the most sacred faculty my points either truncated, or corrupted, or taken from some other person and wrongly assigned to me, or falsely interpreted. For since the faculty is bound to perform very onerous tasks, it is not surprising that its members do not have the leisure to examine my lucubrations in an intense and detailed fashion, but make their pronouncements only about what is brought to them; and if that is falsely set forth, they condemn not what is mine but what is brought to them.

For certainly it is my deepest desire that the dignity, together with the authority, of that college should be upheld intact to the utmost degree, since I am not unaware that it is of the greatest importance to the integrity of the Christian religion that everyone should have the loftiest opinion of the fellowship of the Sorbonne and accept as nothing less than oracular whatever it decrees by a unanimous vote or issues by some similar consensus. And in writings both serious and light I have always striven not to injure any nation or group, precisely because I know that everywhere the good are mixed with the bad and the bad with the good. Whenever I have said something rather harsh, it has been spoken against the morals of particular persons, not against the groups themselves. Furthermore, just as whoever taxes the vices of mankind does not hinder the Christian enterprise but promotes it, so too whoever tears apart approved groups disturbs and tears apart the fabric of the church. Among such groups I know of hardly any other which is owed more honour than the theologians, who have taken over for themselves what used to be the prerogative of the bishops. Then too among theological colleges the whole world agrees that the school of Paris holds the highest rank, and everyone rightly calls it the very citadel of the Christian religion – so it is far from being right to derogate from its dignity in any way. Accordingly, in this defence I will take less care about how I defend my own innocence, namely in such matters where I am undeservedly accused, than I will about being careful that my defence does not injure or diminish the authority of the fellowship of the Sorbonne in any way.

To be sure I do not know any of the deans or the delegates or the amanuenses, but nevertheless it is clear on the face of it that there are some there who are inflamed with an unbridled hatred of me; and perhaps there are some who are carried away by zeal for the church, but it is a zeal that is more vehement than rational. And perhaps there is no lack of those who vote out of fear. Some go along out of personal attachment; others either look the other way or withdraw, considering it preferable to yield rather than to struggle with unquiet spirits and persons born for strife, thinking they would soon hear themselves called Lutherans if they said anything fair. Nevertheless, I would have wished that these censures had been published under any other aegis than that of this faculty, not only for my own sake, since I will be overwhelmed beyond measure by the splendid reputation of the Sorbonne even if there were no error on my part, but also because it is important for the faculty itself that nothing should issue from it that can rightly be reproached. And though I can easily believe that these matters were vigorously discussed at a sitting of the theologians, I find it unlikely that they were decided by the clear votes of everyone and published by their legitimate consensus. Certain points seem to be mixed in, especially in the topics, conclusions, and prefaces, which manifest more hatred than judgment. And I hardly know whether some theologian or amanuensis has gone so far as to take upon himself the right to add something of his own even in the middle of the censures, privately indulging his own burning anger. Such things the faculty either does not know or pretends not to know. Not everything that is vigorously discussed among theologians should be immediately published. Many things are aired among them for the sake of exercise. If it had pleased the faculty to issue these judgments, why are they now published at last after four years?[4] Moreover, when the censures against Luther were published, the day of the determination, and right afterwards the day on which it was decided to issue the decisions, and also a list of the rector of the university, the royal counsellors, and other trustworthy persons, were carefully added to the judgments; but here there is no mention of the authority for publication.[5]

But even if it is granted that these are the judgments of the entire college, and that they are not pronouncements based upon fragments brought to it but upon a continuous reading of my writings, and that they were published by a legitimate and unanimous consensus, at least I still have as much right among the theologians as a convicted criminal had before the Macedonian king, Philip, namely the right to appeal from the faculty dozing to the faculty awake.[6] For just as Paul confesses that he can do nothing

* * * * *

4 The judgments of the Paris theologians against Erasmus, published together with their judgments against Luther in *Determinatio facultatis theologiae in schola Parisiensi super quam plurimis assertionibus D. Erasmi Roterodami* (Paris: Josse Bade nd [July 1531]; 2nd ed Paris nd [c 1532]), had been discussed and agreed upon in 1527.

5 On sig d7 of the condemnation of Luther (see n1) the Paris theologians note that they had reached their decisions against Luther on 14 November 1523 and published them on 2 December of the same year in the presence of the rector of the university, the royal counsellors, and many other trustworthy persons. But in the preface to their condemnation of Erasmus there is no mention of dates or of specific authorities.

6 Plutarch *Moralia* 178F–179A; Valerius Maximus 6.2.ext 1; Erasmus *Apophthegmata* book 4 Philippus Macedo 24 LB IV 195A

which would harm the church,[7] even though he was such a great apostle, so too theologians have no authority against the manifest truth; they too are merely men, and even though neither emotion nor carelessness nor ignorance causes them to err, they can be deceived by the trickery of wicked persons. What if the assignment of examining is not made by an unimpaired judgment but sometimes by the ambition of some persons? And then it can happen that the matter is managed by persons not sufficiently learned in the Latin language, so that they condemn what they do not understand; or it can be done by persons not trained to read ancient writers, so that, if they do not see conclusions, aphorisms, and corollaries, they seem to be in another world; or by persons corrupted by hatred, so that they condemn even what is said with piety; or by people so lazy that they read only what is marked, though the mind of the writer is clear from what precedes and what follows.

I think, however, that I see the source of the offence some take at my books. First, since I measure the minds of others by my own, I utter what I think freely and straightforwardly, not expecting to be ambushed by some slander. And then they take offence because I abstain from scholastic phraseology and try now and then to say what I think in somewhat better Latin. Some people, however, are displeased by what they do not understand and they carp at what they understand wrongly. Furthermore, they are offended because almost everywhere I delight in following each of the most ancient Doctors of the church rather than the opinions of the scholastics, some of which are of doubtful validity, some also controversial among themselves, some obviously falling short of the forcefulness of the gospel. Consequently, since I usually follow the ancient Fathers, to examine my reflections according to the opinions of recent theologians is just as if you should analyse a song in the Lydian mode according to the canons of the Phrygian mode. But if anyone were to use the same standards to examine the books of Basil, Chrysostom, Ambrose, Jerome, Augustine, he will find thousands of propositions which require more unfavourable censure than most of mine. Certainly it is very unjust to excuse everything in their writings, even serious errors, and to bring false charges against even what is piously said in mine. For sometimes it happens that what is read with approval in Augustine or Cyprian is given a black mark in my writings. Among lawyers someone who follows a good authority is cleared of the crime of malicious prosecution.[8] But as for me, neither Augustine nor

* * * * *

7 2 Cor 13:8, 10; cf 2 Cor 10:8.
8 Erasmus seems to refer to *Codex Iustiniani* IX titulum 46 *De calumniatoribus* 'Malicious Prosecutors' section 3; see *Corpus iuris civilis* ed P. Krueger, T. Mommsen, et al 3 vols (Berlin: Weidmann 1915–28) II 648.

Jerome, the most approved of all authorities, offer me any support, but in reproving me even Haymo and Richard of St Victor[9] have weight. Indeed it is held against me that I follow the custom of the early theologians and even of Holy Scripture itself by not refraining from figures of speech, whereas those who waste their time with scholastic aphorisms do not acknowledge figures.

But the most frequent occasion of maligning me unjustly is taking something said by another person which applies to the early years of the church and setting it down as if I were saying it now against the present condition of the church. Furthermore, those who will not accept the excuse of quoting what other persons say in subject matter which consists of such quotations, what are they doing but confessing that they do not wish to function as just judges? To excuse ancient writers the evidence of one place is sufficient, and to prove that they held what is correct one little sentence is sufficient, even though it seems from many places that they held something different. But when it comes to me, even though I have expressed the approved opinion in hundreds of places, one passage is thrown up to me and twisted into a false accusation, and all those many passages in which I said what is right are of no avail.

Finally, in dialogues where one person says something which the other refutes, who does not understand how very far it is from even the appearance of justice to accuse me of holding the wrong view and to ignore the other opinion? But that is how I am treated time and again in the censures which evaluate my *Colloquies*. This will be abundantly clear in the relevant passages. Less serious, to be sure, but still sometimes damaging to me is the fact that the criticism has one point of view and my discourse has another. In every matter they contemplate what is, or should be, best; my discourse looks at how far the morals of mankind have degenerated. And though sometimes we are making the same point, they by exhorting and I by reproaching, nevertheless we seem to disagree. Here I get some help from literature which is pagan, to be sure, but nevertheless sufficiently relevant to what I am talking about: when the tragedian Philoxenus was asked why in his plots he introduced bad women whereas Sophocles introduced good ones, he said: 'he introduces them as they should be; I, as they are.'[10] Some-

* * * * *

9 Haymo of Feversham (d 1244), general of the Franciscans, theologian and liturgist, author of a commentary on the *Sentences* of Lombard. Richard of St Victor, d 1173, renowned especially for his works on mystical theology; see n543 below.

10 Erasmus tells the same story in *Apophthegmata* book 6 Chirosophus 17 LB IV 313D. For this apophthegm Heribert Philips *Erasmus von Rotterdam Apophtheg-*

one who presents a pattern of honourable behaviour, exhorting people to be virtuous, and someone who sets forth and pillories vices (especially those that disguise themselves under the appearance of virtue) are both working toward the same goal.

Long ago, in my responses[11] to Noël Béda, I treated almost all of the propositions in the first part of this examination.[12] It is clear that the delegates read this response, since they cite some passages from my *Reckonings* and my *Listing*. But even though in those works I responded on many points in such a way, I think, as to satisfy unbiased theologians, they overlook all of that and only bring up what damages me. I will cite one example. At one place in the *Paraphrase on Matthew*, chapter 16, Béda took exception to the phrase I had written, 'Christ the son of God by a singular love,' accusing me not of a minor offence but of the execrable impiety of the Arians,[13] as if I meant that Christ is the son of God not by nature but by adoption.[14] But I showed this was a typographical error, introduced by a careless printer in the later edition, which changed *more* 'manner' to *amore* 'love.' The first edition, which was published in 1522 in small type, clearly proves this. There I found written 'Son of God in a singular way,' that is, son of God in such a way that there is none other but him. The second edition was produced without my knowledge, and even if I had been very much at hand, I would not have been able to correct all negligent errors. I expressed a thoroughly Catholic opinion and still I am called an Arian. If the delegates had reported in good faith to the faculty that I had carefully

* * * * *

mata: Spruchweisheiten herausgegeben, eingeleitet, übersetzt und mit Anmerkungen versehen (Würzburg 2001) refers to Aristotle's *Poetics* 1448a, where Aristotle discusses narrative and dramatic characters better and worse than normal people and mentions the dithyrambist Philoxenus of Cythera (443/436–380/378), but Aristotle does not make the reply given by Erasmus, which I have not been able to find.

11 These occupy columns 442–720 in LB IX and include *Elenchus* 'Listing,' LB IX 495–514 and *Supputationes* 'Reckonings,' LB IX 515–702. Naturally they cover much of the same ground as in this reply to the Paris censures.

12 Erasmus means the part before the eight propositions which allegedly arrived late at the printshop (257–68 below) and the additional criticisms of the *Colloquies* (269–326 below).

13 Arius was a leading proponent of the fourth-century heresy which denied the coequal and coeternal divinity of Christ. At the First Council of Nicaea (325) it was rejected in favour of orthodox trinitarian doctrine, but its mutations led to disputes (often violent) for more than a century.

14 Erasmus had explained the misprint in *Divinationes ad notata Bedae* LB IX 464D–F, pointing out that Béda should have recognized it from the context and was quite aware that Erasmus held no Arian beliefs.

and unmistakably indicated this, they would by no means have added that censure,[15] and I have no doubt that they would have done the same in many other places.

Moreover, some unfair persons were also offended because, in imitation of the ancient Fathers, I adapt my language to the matter at hand, bearing down forcefully on the one side that offers the graver danger to the morals of mankind, as, for example, when I frighten people away from the fury of warfare, perjury, trusting in our own powers and works, trusting in ceremonies, the superstitious veneration of the saints, judging things in a topsy-turvy way. Whoever treats such matters in an uninterrupted flow of speech is sometimes so carried away by his fervour that he seems to condemn totally what he is frightening people away from – according to the old proverb, 'to demand more than justice in order to get justice.'[16] We see to what lengths Jerome's love of virginity sometimes carries him.[17] You would say that he gives marriage less than its due. On the other hand, someone who is praising matrimony mightily can hardly avoid sometimes seeming to disparage virginity. The same person sometimes urges contempt of the world with such vehemence that if you stress the words alone he could seem to deprive all Christians of salvation except monks. In another place he frightens clerics away from the love of riches to such an extent that he seems to deprive them of the right to any private property. Somewhere else he overthrows the tyranny of some bishops to such a degree that he demotes them and puts them on the level of priests. Not to be longwinded in giving particular examples, many such places are found both in Holy Scripture and in the writings of men famous for their holiness, especially the ancient Fathers. This is the reason why in the writings of the apostles and Doctors some points seem to be diametrically[18] opposed to one another. Indeed what would it be like if an orator were vehemently exhorting a belligerent audience not to fight a war and urging concord upon them, and someone should interrupt him thus: 'Hey you, why are you condemning war, which it is sometimes right and necessary to wage?' What should be said to such a heckler? Isn't it this? 'Friend, what you say is true, but now we are dealing with something else. I am curing a disease of this audience and your medicine is of no help in doing this. Keep it for another time.' It is one thing to examine a truth with exactitude in a scholastic debate; quite

* * * * *

15 But the censure was in fact added; see proposition LXXXIX below.
16 *Adagia* II iii 26
17 Jerome defends virginity most forcefully in *Two Books against Jovinian*.
18 *Adagia* I x 45

another to sweep along human emotions toward improved morals by the force of language. Urging us to be kind, the Lord cries out, 'give to everyone who asks you for something,'[19] commanding us to make even our enemies beholden to us. When he does this, would it be fitting to chirp up with the scholastic dogma that no one is obliged to give his own property to his neighbour except in cases of extreme need, but even then he has the right to ask for it back when the recipient is in better circumstances?[20]

But I do not say these things as if to deny that there are any mistakes in my writings. I am not more fortunate than Jerome, Ambrose, and Augustine – who were not so fortunate. But I would not be at all afraid to swear by all that is holy and even in the presence of Christ that my outlook and intentions were never perverted. Nevertheless I praise the pious vigilance of the theologians, for whom it is not enough to pull up the tares of wicked dogmas[21] but who must also take pains to prevent any offence from being given to the weak. For that is what they indicate both in many of the censures and in the preface, where they say 'as a precaution.' But in my opinion they would have taken precautions for the sake of the weak more properly if they had delegated to certain persons the task of excerpting from my reflections whatever is there that conflicts with the doctrines concerning which the church is in such turmoil[22] (and they are innumerable) or if they had tempered their language thus: 'if Erasmus meant this, he is wrong.' As it is, from words inappropriately excerpted, they sometimes make pronouncements even about my outlook, and that without any just cause, as I will demonstrate in the proper places. Why do they not see what I stand for as a reason not to make accusations since the enemies we have in common see them as a reason to attack me? But since up to now I have constantly adhered to the Catholic church, since I have stirred up against me the minds and the pens of those whom they consider to be the enemies of the church, if I seem unworthy of the favour of being granted a friendly interpretation of what I expressed in a somewhat unguarded way, I could at least have seemed not unworthy of the fairness of not having

* * * * *

19 Luke 6:30
20 Scholastic theologians regularly discussed the circumstances requiring that alms be given to someone in need; see, for example, Thomas Aquinas *Summa theologiae* IIa–IIae q 32 aa 5–6. I have not found any scholastic saying that the giver may ask the recipient to return the donation when he is able to do so.
21 Matt 13:27–8
22 That is, if they had excerpted orthodox passages which refute heretics such as Luther and Zwingli

what I neither said nor meant pelted with such hateful names and of not being dealt with by means of ill-chosen fragments which have been twisted so as to have a wicked meaning. Finally, if someone who strives to forestall the dangers faced by the simple and the weak has a pious intention, I think I would be performing a pious deed if I forestall the danger faced by those who might fall into error or be confirmed in it if they are persuaded that I hold what certain persons of great reputation interpret me to mean, because they think I am somebody (though I am not). What would you think of a physician if, while he was striving to heal the sores of some people, he inflicted wounds on others who were healthy? It is an incautious sort of precaution to look out for somebody or other who is weak, or rather captious or unfair, in such a way as to inflict grave injury on an innocent person.

Furthermore, I am full of praise for the theologians for not begrudging us an accounting of the faith that is in them, though it was not without reason that the apostle added 'with modesty and fear,'[23] so that the rebuke would savour of Christian gentleness and the judgment would be circumspect, taking into account human weakness, lest perhaps the one who brands an error should himself be deceived. It would have been a more clear-cut example of Christian gentleness if it had stuck to teaching and not also mixed in some insults – such a thing was not done even against Luther. Nor do I see at whom the following words are hurled: 'so that those who would read our responses might recognize that the force of truth is so great that, however much it is sometimes assailed by stupid men in their shameless temerity, it can still never be shattered, etc.' If this is being spoken against someone other than me, it is being spoken in the wrong place; if against me, it is spoken insultingly; if it is spoken as a general admonition, anyone who wants can snatch it up; as for me, I profess that such feelings have always been quite foreign to me, and I rejoice that they still are, and with the help of Christ I am confident they always will be. Finally I grant that even among the pagans it was shameful to oppose truth that is known and evident, but among them it was likewise never honourable to assail someone with slanders.

Having made these prefatory remarks, I proceed to the matter itself. But first I want to advise the reader that if anything in the preface or in the following clarifications seems to be said less than reverently, let him understand that it does not apply to the faculty, which made its pronounce-

* * * * *

23 1 Pet 3:15–16

ments only on what was brought to it. And so if there is anything bad, let it fall on the 'bringers,'[24] as if on Pyrrha,[25] as they say. But whatever I ordinarily say in legitimate protest, I want that to be taken as clearly intended here.

The End of the Preface

* * * * *

24 Latin *delatores*. This word refers to those who brought the excerpts to the theologians, but in Tacitus and Suetonius it is used frequently to refer to underhanded accusers in the intrigues of the court.
25 *Adagia* III ii 1. Pyrrha was a town very unpopular with its neighbours. If something bad was threatening, they said 'let it fall on Pyrrha.'

THE CENSURES OF THE PARIS FACULTY
OF THEOLOGY ABOUT THE PROPOSITIONS
OF ERASMUS

Topic 1. The baptizing of infants

1 *Erasmus' proposition in the epistle prefixed to his* Paraphrase
on Matthew
It seems to me it would be of no small use if baptized children,
when they reach the age of puberty, would be enjoined to attend
sermons which would clearly explain what is contained in the professions made at baptism. Then they would be carefully examined in
private by men of good character to see whether they retain and remember well enough what the priest has explained. If they are found
to remember it well enough, they would be asked if they approve of
what their sponsors promised for them at baptism. After they have
heard the profession, if they approve of what was done by their rep-
resentatives, everything should be attempted to see to it that no one
backslides from his original belief. But if this cannot be achieved, perhaps it will be expedient not to force the backslider but to leave him
to his own thoughts until he comes to his senses, and in the meantime
not to sentence him to any punishment except to forbid him the Eucharist and the other sacraments. But he would not be excluded from
divine service or sermons.[26]

CENSURE
This advice, in so far as it urges us to seek out those baptized as infants
when they are grown up and to ask them whether they assent to what
their godparents promised in their names at baptism, and, if they do
not approve, finds it perhaps expedient to leave them to their own

* * * * *

26 Erasmus defended this proposition in *Prologus supputationis* LB IX 445B–F, in
Divinationes ad notata Bedae LB IX 459, and at even greater length in *Supputatio*
LB IX 557D–563B.

thoughts until they come to their senses, and in the meantime not to punish them except by not administering the sacraments of the church to them, is ungodly and tends toward the destruction of the faithful, opening up a path to the abolition of the Christian religion.

The Grounds. For if those baptized as infants, when they are asked as adults whether they assent to what their godparents promised in their name, say they do not, they will persevere in their perversity and will soon fall away from Christianity, both they themselves and many others by their example. Furthermore, to call into doubt whether those baptized as infants, when they reach the age of discretion, can be forced to hold to the Christian faith is on the face of it clearly ungodly. Since we hold by faith that baptized infants are faithful children of God and heirs of heaven, so too we must hold by faith that those same children, when they have grown up, are in the bosom of the church and therefore are subject to the same laws as bind other orthodox Christians, just as infants belonging to other communities, when they reach the years of puberty, are bound by the laws of their governments, although they did not agree to them formally by their own act. Hence it is no less just to force the baptized infants of Christians to keep the faith of Christ than to force the circumcised infants of Jews to keep the law of Moses; but concerning them it is wrong to have any doubt. For the Apostle declares that those circumcised under the Law are bound to keep the entire Law;[27] and in the Old Law the Lord decreed that whoever fell away from the Law once he had accepted it should be punished with death.[28] Likewise some popes have declared that those baptized as children who, when they have become capable of wrongdoing, convert to the Jewish worship should be proceeded against as heretics.[29]

ERASMUS OF ROTTERDAM'S CLARIFICATION CONCERNING
THE FIRST CENSURE[30]

1 I have never doubted that baptized infants belong to the body of the church, nor have I ever doubted that the church has the right to punish

* * * * *

27 Gal 5:3
28 Deut 13:5, 9
29 As Erasmus himself later points out the theologians here refer to the decretals of Boniface VIII 5 tit 2 cap 13 *Corpus iuris canonici* II 1075.
30 Pelargus sigs B7–8 finds Erasmus' suggestion dangerous and destructive of the church, especially because it would open the door to Anabaptist arguments.

those who backslide from the faith of their baptism, so that those words of the censure, 'concerning them it is wrong to have any doubt,' do not apply to me at all: I doubted only whether it would be expedient. For many things are permissible but not expedient. Furthermore, as for the point to which the censure is limited, it cannot properly be called 'advice'; rather it is 'a general inquiry.' For someone who advises has already reached a judgment. But someone who proposes something as a doubt seeks rather than gives advice; and he does not judge but leaves judgment to others. But to stop quarrelling about words, how can something proposed with godly intentions be called ungodly? For there is no reason why each of the sides, being led by an equally godly spirit, may not agree in general but differ concerning means. Considering the extraordinary propensity to adopt every newfangled opinion, especially in these times, they have thought it necessary to put down headlong precipitousness by displaying a cudgel. As for me, considering how many thousands there are, even among Christians, who either know nothing at all about the teachings of the faith or who do not believe them at all – which I have learned in part from conversations with many persons and discovered in part from what I have been told by those who are employed in hearing private confessions – I sought a remedy for such a great evil. And I hoped that if the catechesis of adults were restored by the authority of the bishops and if, after the philosophy of the gospel was learned, it were newly professed, the church would have more true and genuine Christians. But it seems that the outcome would be better if people were led rather than forced. For the faith delights more in being persuasive rather than compulsory.

* * * * *

He thinks Erasmus' contention that he is asking for, not giving, advice merely specious since Erasmus is such an expert theologian that he needs no advice about the law in such matters. Pelargus thinks that the force of the law might be mitigated after the first attempt to reconvert but that successive failures should bring on threats and punishment. He agrees with Erasmus concerning the theologians' argument that membership in the church or commonwealth brings with it being bound by laws not accepted by infants, and also their argument that Paul considers those who are circumcised to be bound by all of the Mosaic law; Pelargus thinks these arguments elegant and true but not applicable to Erasmus, since Erasmus recognizes the force of such laws but considers they should sometimes be mitigated. Pelargus considers that, though Erasmus' suggestion is impious, his motive is pious and charitable; he praises Erasmus for withdrawing the erroneous proposition.
In what he added to the second edition Erasmus reiterated that neither the ancient Fathers nor Boniface thought heretics should be punished with death,

Moreover, I hoped that, with Christ assisting the vigilance of the cate-
chists, there would be no backsliders or certainly very few; concerning them
I proposed we should give some thought to whether it would be expedient
not to turn them over immediately to an external judge but rather to challenge them with admonitions, exhortations, shame, and gentler remedies in
accord with Christian charity, until they make a sincere profession. In the
meantime they would not be free from the severity of the princes' laws if
they either vomited out blasphemies against Christ or solicited others to
defect or attacked our religion brashly.

Finally, I did not argue to abolish the law but to moderate the application of the law. For who does not know how leniently heretics were
once treated and how long it took to come to capital punishment, though
the right to punish was the same. I grant that the church has no less power
over its members than the synagogue had over its members; but increased
charity weakened the severity of the Old Law in many respects, the church
being more concerned with what was expedient for her children than with
her own rights, just as St Paul certainly recognizes the power which he received from the Lord, but frequently does not use it when he is pursuing
what is useful for his disciples, who are still nursing at the breast.[31] The
punishment of adultery was mitigated by the gospel.[32] Also, Paul is sometimes angry at the false apostles, but he never even names them, much less
does he hand them over to Satan,[33] not because he lacked the authority but
because charity and the progress of the gospel called for something else.

But, they say, such lenience will invite the wicked to be bold. I saw
this danger also, and for that reason I added 'perhaps.' On the other hand
it appeared that fear of punishment was causing the church to be full of
pseudo-Christians. They did not want this condition of the polity to be
changed lest things should get worse; I hoped to introduce a certain number
of more sincere persons, with no more loss to the church, as it certainly
seemed to me at the time, than it now suffers. For those who do not believe
have already slid back in the eyes of God. Perhaps they would infect others
less and would come to their senses more quickly if they were sequestered,
as the profligate, contumacious, and those doing penance were formerly
sequestered for a time; for fear of the law frequently produces hypocrites

* * * * *

and he interpreted the Pauline text (Gal 5:3) in context to show that it is not
an applicable argument.
31 1 Cor 3:2, 6:3
32 John 8:3–11
33 2 Cor 11:13–15; 1 Tim 1:20

and binds the tongue more truly than it corrects the mind. But charity accommodates the law, as much as is allowable, to what is useful. Even today many wonder whether it would have been wiser to allow the Jews to stay in Spain where they were than to have them mingled among us as they now are, changed more in name than in belief.

They rightly cite the rescript from book 5 of the Decretals of Boniface VIII (title 2 concerning 'heretics,' chapter 13) against Christians. But with what kindness and gentleness did the ancient Fathers of the church treat heretics who were seduced by persuasion or erred through ignorance? They even called upon emperors to refrain from capital punishment, lest there be no one left for them to heal. In fact, even Boniface, though he is not a much praised pope, does not urge the extreme penalty in such cases but suggests ecclesiastical censure, which is paternal, not royal, and hence does not always exercise its rights but is more inclined to heal than to punish, partly because in this way it imitates its Lord and partly because it hopes to gain more from such a procedure.[34]

Now the law in Deuteronomy 13[:6–11] which threatens backsliders from Judaism is aimed more at those who urge impiety than at those who have been seduced, and everywhere it adds going over to other gods. But let us have nothing to do with lenity so great that if perhaps some baptized infant should (God forbid) refuse in adulthood to keep to the profession made at baptism, he would be permitted to worship idols or demons, which is not even allowed to Jews, though they are foreign to the power of the church. Furthermore, I grant that infants entered into the jurisdiction of the synagogue through circumcision, but only in so far as I also believe that those born of Jewish parents were subject to the same jurisdiction. For circumcision was discontinued on many occasions, as during the Babylonian captivity. Nor could the uncircumcised, I think, go over to pagan worship with impunity. Indeed there is some doubt that a child born of pagan parents but secretly circumcised by Jews would be bound by the Mosaic Law. Moreover, Paul does not seem to say what he thinks to the Galatians but rather he discourages the Galatians from circumcision out of a hatred for the other Jewish observances, which were repellent to the gentiles. Otherwise who could be said to be bound by Paul to do something useless? Much less something destructive? If, after the light of the gospel had risen, the cutting off of a little bit of skin did not bind to the Jewish form of worship those born of Jewish parents and circumcised according to the Law, how

* * * * *

34 The Latin 'quod hinc sperat plus lucri' would certainly include the notion of fines and monetary gains but would not be cynically limited to them.

could it bind the Galatians, professed worshippers of Christ? How could
something be said to be required if its omission is praised by the godly?
But, as I said, Paul is frightening them, as if he were saying: if you listen to
the false apostles in this matter, you will be casting yourselves into miserable servitude. For they will demand that you keep the entire Law, bound,
as it were, by the earnest money of circumcision.

But these things are almost beside the point, and I say them for myself, not because the theologians cited a passage with little relevance. It is
clear, I think, that my thoughts were very far from impiety when I wrote
these things, and for that reason my mind shuddered in deep abhorrence
when I read those words in the censure: 'this advice is ungodly, tending
toward the destruction of the faithful, opening up a path to the abolition
of the Christian religion.' In fact, how can it tend to destruction when the
church first spread most felicitously and grew very strong at a time when
no one killed backsliders? At that time, when backsliders were rewarded,
the church had many thousands of men and women who refused no punishment, no form of death, for the sake of Christ. Nowadays you can hardly
find anyone who scorns money. And so let us divide the praise between
us, if you please: the theologians were prudently afraid, I was generously
hopeful; and in them zeal for the faith was more watchful; in me charity,
according to Paul, hoped for all things.[35] And nevertheless, all these words,
since they seem to give offence, will be deleted. Indeed the whole decora-
tive insert has been long since rejected. For it is not a preface to Matthew,
as it is said to be here, but a piece of patchwork thrust in impromptu to fill
up some pages which were left blank through the negligence of the person
who cast off the copy.

Topic 2. The death of Christ

11 *Luke 23[:27–8]. Erasmus' first proposition*
Jesus did not want his death to be mournful but glorious, nor did
he want it to be deplored but rather adored, since it was willingly
accepted for the salvation of the whole world.[36]

CENSURE
Though Christ's death is precious and glorious, since it destroyed
death and the founder of death, it does not immediately follow that it is

* * * * *

35 1 Cor 13:4–6
36 Erasmus defended this proposition in *Supputatio* LB IX 617C–619D.

not mournful and to be bewailed by the faithful, for whose salvation it was willingly undertaken. For since Christ lamented through the royal prophet, saying 'I looked for someone who would grieve together with me, and I did not find anyone,'[37] and since it was foretold by Zechariah that 'they will mourn for him as one normally mourns for the death of a first-born son,'[38] and also since a sword of sorrow pierced the heart of the holy Mother at the passion of her Son, according to the prophecy of Simeon,[39] it is clear that Christ did not in the least forbid us to weep over his passion and death, but that he wanted us to grieve not only for them but also for the sins which he expiated with his death, since they are the cause of such great sorrow, for (as Isaiah writes) 'he was crushed for our sins and by his bruises we were healed.'[40] Therefore, since this proposition is opposed to the opinion of Catholic Doctors, and to the liturgy of the universal church, according to which we abstain from meat on every Friday, and also to a correct understanding of Holy Scripture, it is rash, ungodly, and heretical.

ERASMUS' SECOND CLARIFICATION[41]

11 Certainly I did not suspect that such a scorpion lurked beneath this rock.[42] In my paraphrase explaining the words of Christ I followed orthodox and approved authors who are very far removed from any heretical opinion. First, I will report the words of Theophylactus: 'Certainly women are the sort of persons easily given to tears and lamentation, and so, as if some-

* * * * *

37 Ps 68:21
38 Zech 12:10
39 Luke 2:35
40 Isa 53:5
41 Quoting Peter Lombard's obvious distinction between sorrow for Christ's suffering and joy because of the redemption, Pelargus sigs B8v–C2v complains that here and in the following clarification Erasmus speaks not in the person of Christ but in his own name and thus seems to condemn mourning for Christ's suffering in an unqualified way. He also blames Erasmus for using 'in the usual way' (*vulgari more*) somewhat ambiguously: does he refer to ordinary, acceptable human emotion or to the unfitting lamentation of the women who thought that Christ was helpless in his suffering? He also argues in the scholastic manner that from the fact that Christ and Paul do not require that Christ's death be mourned, it does not follow that it was not mournful. Here as elsewhere he overlooks Erasmus' pastoral intent: to correct superficial and misdirected grief. But in general he thinks that Erasmus' clarification makes the necessary corrections and qualifications.
42 *Adagia* I i 34

thing awful had happened to the Lord, they weep and show signs of great compassion, lamenting an injustice. But he does not approve but rather rebukes them. For he was suffering voluntarily. It is not fitting to lament for someone who suffers willingly and for the salvation of all, but rather it is fitting to extol, praise, and celebrate him. For through the cross both death was destroyed and hell led captive. For lamenting about those who suffer willingly provides them no consolation and therefore the Lord reproaches those who mourn for him, etc.'[43] Something quite similar was written by Bede, called the Venerable, a writer praised by the theologians themselves: 'Do not grieve for me as I go to my death, since my swift resurrection can dissolve death, and since my death will destroy all death and the very founder of death.'[44] This is what Bede says. But Ambrose, though he passes over this speech of the Lord to the women, nevertheless, at the mention of the cross, immediately bursts out into triumphal, not mournful, language: 'but now let the victor lift up his trophy.' And then, 'now, since we have already seen the trophy, let the triumphant victor get up onto his chariot, etc.'[45] And the Lord himself, committing the memory of his passion to us, does not say 'you will grieve for the death of the Lord' but 'you will announce the death of the Lord,'[46] that is 'you will preach and celebrate it.'

Indeed, even the church calls the commemoration of the Lord's death not lamentation but the Eucharist, that is, thanksgiving. 'Eucharist' is a word expressing joy, not sorrow. Thus how could it be fitting for the church to celebrate the deaths of other martyrs with such enthusiastic ceremonies, though they were not without sin, and to celebrate the death of the Lord with general mourning? Furthermore, Psalm 68[:21], 'I looked for someone who would grieve together with me, etc,' does not urge us to grieve but prophesies how the Lord in his passion had to be deprived of all human consolation. And at that time the Lord certainly needed consolation according to his human nature, and his disciples rightly grieved with him as he grieved, though at that time it was still a human emotion. Then, too, what is strange about all creatures being disturbed when the Lord of all things died? Even today holy people mourn no less if he suffers something like that. But now it is both more helpful and more appropriate to rejoice with him as he rejoices, and it is more useful to weep for what caused

* * * * *

43 Theophylactus *Enarratio in Evangelium Lucae* 23.28–31 PG 123 1100C
44 Bede *In Lucae Evangelium expositio* 6.23 PL 92 614B
45 Ambrose *Expositio Evangelii secundum Lucam* 10.107, 10.109 PL 15 (1845) 1830B, 1831A
46 1 Cor 11:26

him to suffer so bitterly. As for these words of Zechariah, 'they mourned with grief as if for an only son,'[47] Jerome interprets them as applying to the wicked at the last judgment. 'Then,' he says, 'they will grieve that they crucified him when they see him reigning in splendour.'[48] But to make this place apply most closely to the grief of the disciples and the holy women at the death of the Lord, it is a prophecy of something done, not an exhortation to do something.

And further, on Good Friday itself, when the death and burial of the Lord are principally celebrated, the church still does not repress its glory in the death of the Lord, singing the hymn 'Faithful cross, of all trees the single noble one,'[49] which is anything but mournful, just as throughout Holy Week the triumphal hymn 'The banner of the king comes forth' is sung.[50] Likewise on Fridays, when the commemoration of the Lord's death is enacted, the church sings 'But we should glory in the cross of our Lord'[51] and does not show any sign of grief. The reason the minds of the disciples

* * * * *

47 Zech 12:10
48 *Commentaria in Zechariam* 3.12 vs 10 PL 25 (1845) col 1515A
49 This was the eighth stanza of the hymn *Pange lingua gloriosi lauream certaminis* by Venantius Fortunatus (d c 600), which was sung on Good Friday as a sort of refrain to some other verses of the hymn during the veneration of the cross. See *Missale Romanum* no 17, I 172–3.
50 This famous hymn, also written by Venantius Fortunatus, was composed as a processional for the presentation of a relic of the true cross to Queen Radegund at Poitiers; it was then sung on Good Friday as a processional when the Eucharist was brought from the repository to the high altar. See Connelly 79–82; and Matthew Britt *The Hymns of the Breviary and Missal* (New York 1922) 123–6.
51 *Commemoratio* here seems to be a technical term since weekday masses could be assigned to a principal feast or saint but could also 'commemorate' another feast or saint, and particular weekdays could have particular commemorations assigned to them. Saturday often commemorated the Blessed Virgin, Monday the angels, and Friday the Holy Cross (and hence the passion). And the Friday mass of the Holy Cross contained the prayer Erasmus mentioned, which continues 'in whom is our salvation, life, and resurrection and through the cross we are saved and freed.' See, for example, *Missale ad usum Ecclesiae Westmonasteriensis* ed John Wickham Legg, Henry Bradshaw Society 1, 5, 12 (rpt Woodbridge, Suffolk and Rochester NY 1999) 1114–18. But missals in Erasmus' time were not consistent in such matters. *Missale Romanum* no 17, I 433, for example, has a *Missa in honore sancte crucis* with the prayer Erasmus mentions, but it does not seem to be merely a commemoration, and it is not specifically associated with Friday.

were so disturbed by the death of the Lord was partly weakness, partly failure to believe. They did not yet fully understand the mystery of the redemption, and they despaired of the resurrection, or at least had doubts about it. It was not expedient that they should remain in that frame of mind, nor is it fitting that we should, since we know that Christ dies no more but reigns immortal with the Father. And so how can we now consider that death mournful which is the wellspring of all consolation, all joy, all our glory?

But his mother, they say, felt a sword of sorrow. I will omit a differing interpretation of this passage, for Augustine interprets it to mean a sword of disbelief.[52] His mother felt an emotion of nature but she struggled against it in the spirit. But all that sorrow, I think, was wiped away by the joy of the resurrection. For that is what the Lord promised his disciples: 'But I will see you again, and your hearts will rejoice, and your joy no one shall take from you.'[53] Nevertheless, the emotion of those who grieved for Christ at that time out of an ordinary fellow feeling because of his horrible suffering should not be condemned, nor does Christ reproach the tears of the women unreservedly, but rather he tells them what they should weep for instead; and using them as a springboard he admonishes their posterity that, when they commemorate the death of the Lord, they should weep not for his death but for the sins committed by them and theirs, since that is what put a completely innocent man on the cross. A person who grieves mourns either for the lot of the one who has died or for his own lot or both; but Christ had thirsted for that hour and for us his death was a wellspring of life. Ordinarily those who mourn for a dead person are tormented by a desire for the person they loved when he was with them. Who could approve of such grief among Christians? For Christ is with us till the end of the world,[54] and do we still mourn for him as if he were absent? We mourn well if we mourn for our sins, which caused Christ to undergo death; we mourn more justly when we fall repeatedly into sin and crucify Christ, in so far as we can, time after time. And it is not clear that Christ was reproaching holy and pious women but rather it is more probable that they were ordinary women, for they are called a crowd, which sheds tears not out of judgment but because of feminine softness. With such tears, I think, Christ does not want his death to be mourned.

* * * * *

52 *Quaestiones veteris et novi testamenti* 73 PL 35 2267–8
53 John 16:22
54 Matt 28:20

III *His second proposition in* Elenchus, *note 7*[55]
If Christ wanted his death to be mourned in the usual way, why did
he reproach the women of Jerusalem as he was carrying his cross?[56]

CENSURE

Christ did not want the daughters of Jerusalem to weep for him as
if he were weak or incapable of defending himself from injuries inflicted on him, in the same way as the women needed to be wept for
because of the imminent destruction of the city of Jerusalem. But he
did not for that reason prohibit what nature prompts, reason urges,
and sacred eloquence approves: namely that Christians as members
of Christ should be conformed to their head and should suffer and
grieve with him when he suffers and grieves, as the liturgy of the
church generally observes. By this question this writer intimates the
contrary, misunderstanding the scriptural text he cites, and is clearly
in error.

ERASMUS' THIRD CLARIFICATION[57]

III If the Lord did not in the least forbid that his death be wept for, what
is the meaning of the words 'Do not weep over me'? They say he did not
want to be wept for in this way. I both say and mean the same thing: he
did not wish to be wept for in the ordinary way. And so there is a certain
kind of mourning which he does not wish to be directed toward him. If
they grant that, my proposition is not false. Again, if (as they concede) the
death of Christ is glorious and triumphal, then it is in some sense pious
to deny that his death should be mourned by us. But even though it were
conclusively proved that the death of the Lord should be mourned by us
in some sense, it was not appropriate for me in a paraphrase to say the
opposite of the passage I was explaining. Christ says 'do not weep.' Am I
to say on my own: certainly all Christians should mourn for the death of
Christ? Finally, though human emotion called forth tears during Christ's

* * * * *

55 *Elenchus in censuras Bedae* LB IX 499E. In *Elenchus* this is n70, not n7.
56 Luke 23:28
57 Pelargus sig c2v–c3 comments only briefly on the first few sentences of this
clarification, noting that since Erasmus speaks in his own person he should
have specified what kind of grief was not appropriate to Christ's death.
In the second edition Erasmus added a long section describing a holy sort of
grief which is appropriate to Christ's death and various sorts of secular or
superficial grief which are not appropriate.

passion, since human emotion is sometimes prompted by hearing or seeing the death of a person, even a wicked criminal, what shall we think if, after death has been conquered and fifteen hundred years have passed, someone still mourns the death of the Lord with human emotion? 'The members,' they say, 'should be conformed to their head.'[58] I grant it: that is, they should imitate the cross of Christ by mortifying the emotions which fight against the spirit, not by bewailing Christ as if he were miserable. For this is what Paul calls 'to suffer together with Christ,'[59] to be afflicted for the sake of justice according to his example, so that we may reign with him.

In addition, it hardly seems appropriate to the loftiness of Christian doctrine to require ordinary emotions of us. Paul enjoins husbands to love their wives, but he adds something worthy of an apostle, 'as Christ loved the church.'[60] He enjoins slaves to be obedient to their masters, but he adds 'as if to the Lord.'[61] I am surprised that they think they should call to mind that on Fridays the church abstains from eating meat in memory of the Lord's passion. For that, as I see it, is not to grieve at the death of the Lord but to imitate it. They should rather have called to mind that in the last days of Lent the church in some of her ceremonies represents the distress of the disciples, the uproar and madness of the Jews, the splitting of the temple veil, and the burial. But these are not properly speaking grief but a sort of representation of what was done at that time. So too on Easter Sunday the church represents the joy of the resurrection by white vestments and other ceremonies, not because it has put away grief for Christ but rather because the garments of penance are changed to symbolize renewed innocence. Finally, if we are required to mourn for the death of Christ, why, by the same token, are we not ordered to mourn for the sufferings, dangers, and death of Paul? For if this reason based on the fellow feeling of the members has any validity, all the martyrs are our fellow members, some of whom suffered so horribly according to their legends that the mind sometimes shudders when it merely calls them to mind. And yet how joyfully, how enthusiastically, the church celebrates their deaths! It does not speak of their deaths but of their birthdays, their victories, their palms, their triumphs. And in these circumstances, where is that fellow feeling of the members? It consists in this: when the struggle is over, it is followed by a joyful victory.

* * * * *

58 Rom 12:5; Eph 5:23; Col 1:18
59 Cf Heb 4:15.
60 Eph 5:25
61 Eph 6:5

It is natural to shed tears at the death of a friend. But worthy of praise are they who overcame this emotion of nature by the strength of the spirit. Neither nature nor reason dictates that someone who has died a beautiful death should be a perpetual object of mourning, as women once mourned the death of Adonis. Who could approve of someone who still wears mourning garments and grieves for the death of a remote ancestor who bravely died in battle for his fatherland two hundred years ago? Who would not laugh if the Romans should now weep for Quintus Curtius or the Decii,[62] who sacrificed themselves to save their fatherland? Or if we should recall with sorrow the death of our first parents, Adam and Eve? To weep when others suffer belongs to the human condition, but what is one to think of still remembering grief in the midst of a triumph? The apostles lamented when the Lord was captured and died because they were still following him out of fleshly emotions. When the triumph of the resurrection flashed forth, when they had accepted the heavenly spirit and said with Paul 'though I knew Christ according to the flesh, but now I no longer know him so,'[63] all their grief was changed into joy, which the Lord himself wished to be complete;[64] nor do we ever read that they wept for the death of the Lord or spoke of it in mournful language but rather that they proclaimed it as triumphant with the greatest alacrity.

But if the theologians mean that some holy men, by calling to mind the passion of the Lord, recreate (as it were) for themselves what the Lord suffered and are moved by it as if it were presently happening, that has nothing to do with my paraphrase, which deals with ordinary grief. As for me, I cannot condemn such emotion felt by holy men who in this way also rejoice to be conformed to the Lord. But, as I see it, this very feeling is not so much grief as the imitation of the Lord's death, and that emotion has more joy than sorrow, and the tears that are shed spring from charity, not grief. When I wrote those words, I was referring to the temporal weeping of ordinary people. Sometimes at theatrical performances, when the death of Christ is presented even by trifling persons,[65] some spectators, especially

* * * * *

62 These three sacrificed themselves for the sake of Rome; see Livy 7.6.1–6, 8.6.8–13, 8.9.1–12.
63 2 Cor 5:16
64 John 16:20–4
65 Erasmus has in mind the crucifixion episode from the mystery plays, a long cycle of plays presented both in England and on the continent by the guilds. The performances were elaborate and vivid; see Rosemary Woolf *The English Mystery Plays* (Berkeley and Los Angeles 1972) 257–63. Erasmus refers to the actors as 'trifling persons' (*homines ... leves*) in contrast to the clerics who

light-minded women, burst forth in sobs and tears. Pictures, though unreal, have the same effect, as, for example, those which present Christ fallen down nine times. Similar results are produced by orators who render the torture of Christ even more pitiable by making up enormities, and also by pictures or statues portraying a most miserable spectacle, based not on the gospel narrative but on the imagination of the artist. Thus some paint the mother of Jesus falling in a lifeless swoon at the foot of the cross, but over the objections of Chrysostom.[66] They also paint her pierced with seven swords. Uneducated people sigh and weep at the sight of such images. But these same people would weep if they saw a performance of Euripides' *Hecuba*. So too Augustine before his rebirth could not read the fourth book of the *Aeneid* without tears even though he knew that the whole story of the love and death of Dido was made up by the poet.[67] To such Christians, I think, Christ says today 'do not weep for me but weep for yourselves.' They groan at an image of the Redeemer and they do not groan at their own sins by which they crucify the Lord (in so far as they can) once more.

And so if someone should ask whether I condemn natural emotion, I would immediately respond 'not at all.' For it is a sign of a humane and sympathetic personality. But what does this have to do with the energy and majesty of the evangelical philosophy which I was paraphrasing at that point? Much less do I condemn the emotion of holy persons who, by contemplating the death of the Lord, are moved to a sort of sympathetic sorrow, as long as they do not get stuck there. But in fact, as I said, I think that even the tears of such men spring more from charity and joy than from grief and sorrow. Grief is a dismal and hateful word, more fit for Jews than for Christians, who are the children of the resurrection. As a type Moses was buried with mourning;[68] Christ is not assiduously mourned. And so what is the objection to me? That I approve of the Stoics' 'apathy'? Far be it from me to do so. That I condemn natural emotion? Nothing like that is expressed in the paraphrase. But I should have added that I do not condemn natural 'sympathy.' The gospel did not add it, nor did Theophylactus in his interpretation. I was so intent on the glory of the Lord's death that that quasi-grief which is now thrown up to me did not even enter my mind, since none of the ancient Doctors mentions it.

* * * * *

venerate the cross and recite the *improperia* in a somewhat analogous ceremony on Good Friday.
66 *Homiliae in Iohannem* 85.2 on John 19:25 PG 59 462
67 *Confessions* 1.13.20–1 CCSL 27 11–12
68 Deut 34:6–9

And then, considering how many uneducated people there are who bewail Christ as if he were somehow pitiable and do so with tears that are temporal, fruitless, and displeasing to Christ, I preferred to bend in the opposite direction. Even so, what they want me to say is not entirely absent. For the paraphrase says as follows: 'Jesus, who did not want his death to be mournful but glorious, and who did not want it to be deplored but rather adored, since it was willingly accepted for the salvation of the whole world, repressed their lamentation as inappropriate, though it arose from a pious emotion.' If someone calls an emotion pious does he seem to condemn it? But I wonder with what intent the reporters left out these words? Now if someone examines the matter closely, he will perceive that the theologians teach the same thing that I do. For if, when they say 'the Lord did not in the least forbid us to grieve,' they mean the statement to be universal – *minime* 'in the least,' that is, meaning 'in no way,' the censure contradicts itself, since it grants that Christ did not wish to be mourned as if he were forced to suffer like other people. But when my paraphrase says 'since it was willingly accepted for the salvation of the whole world,' does it not clearly express the manner in which our Lord did not want his death to be mournful, in agreement with the interpretation of the theologians? For it does not say he does not want it to be mournful in any way at all, but rather he did not wish it generally. If they counter that a general statement is sometimes taken to be universal, then in turn what they say, 'he did not want it to be mourned in the least,' will be a universal statement and they will encounter the difficulty I pointed out before. Then Christ's language will be universal, making no exceptions when he says 'do not weep.' But even if I had made a quite universal statement, the paraphrase would have had to accommodate its language to the passage which was being interpreted, especially when it expresses the manner of mourning.

Finally, when they say that the women were reproached because they wept for Christ as if he necessarily had to suffer, they are partly right, but that was not the only respect the Lord was taking into account. Nevertheless, the paraphrase does also express this. But in fact, if they were rightly reproached for their grief at that time, those who mourn with similar emotion today are also justly reproached. Accordingly, since nature is content with brief mourning, since reason does not dictate that splendid triumphs should be spoiled by mourning, since I followed orthodox and approved authors in my paraphrase, since my words, taken in the context of the passage, do not conflict with any passage in Scripture or any liturgical ceremony of the church, there is no reason why I should be said to misunderstand the passage I am explaining or to propound a heretical opinion.

Topic 3. Fasting and the choice of food

IV *Erasmus' first proposition in the epistle prefaced to the paraphrase*
on the First Epistle to the Corinthians
It seems to me to represent a purer Christianity and be more in keeping with the teaching of the gospel and the apostles not to prescribe a
certain kind of food but to admonish everyone to eat according to his
physical constitution so as to promote good health as much as possible, not luxuriously but temperately, with thanksgiving and in pursuit
of a good conscience.[69]

CENSURE
This proposition, signifying that it is more in keeping with the teaching of the gospel and the apostles to free Christians from all distinctions of food so that everyone can eat as he sees fit whatever he thinks
will contribute to his health, as long as he does so temperately and
thankfully, is based on an erroneous understanding of Scripture, undermines ecclesiastical discipline, and is opposed to the teaching of the
gospel and the apostles, which commands obedience to superior authorities. It shows contempt for the Catholic church, which religiously
and prudently prescribes such a choice of food for the faithful, and
it agrees with the heresy of Aeris,[70] Jovinian,[71] the Waldensians,[72] and

* * * * *

69 Erasmus defended this proposition briefly in *Supputatio* LB IX 678B–679C.
70 Aeris of Pontus (fl 350) was a priest at Sebaste who propounded several heresies: no special character distinguishes bishops or priests from laymen; fasts
and abstinence should not be required by law; it is useless to pray for the dead.
Protestants found him significant as a precursor of some of their doctrines.
71 Jovinian was an opponent of asceticism condemned as a heretic (390). Our
knowledge of his positions derives principally from *Contra Jovinianum*, a fierce
tract launched at him by St Jerome. Jovinian apparently asserted that virginity
is not superior to marriage, that abstinence is no better than eating with the
right disposition, that a person baptized with the Spirit as well as water cannot
sin, that all sins are equal, and that in the afterlife there is only one level of
punishment and one level of reward. In *Contra Vigilantium* PL 23 (1845) 340A
Jerome remarks concerning the death of Jovinian: 'amidst pheasants and pork
he rather belched forth than breathed out his life' ('inter phasides aves et
carnes suillas non tam emisit spiritum quam eructavit').
72 The Waldensians were a sect founded in the twelfth century by a wealthy
merchant of Lyon named Waldo (Waldes). In reaction against the wealth
of the church and the dissolute lives of some clergymen, the Waldensians
placed great emphasis on poverty and preaching. They denied purgatory,

Luther. Finally it displays the intolerable arrogance of the person asserting it, who shamelessly prefers his own unique opinion to the
judgment of the whole church.

ERASMUS' FOURTH CLARIFICATION

IV No place will be found in my writings where I criticize the church's
custom of abstaining from meat, but some places will be found where I
oppose those who heedlessly and unnecessarily eat forbidden food. Here,
too, I make no assertion, but I only say what seems right to me, not at all
to the prejudice of the rules or custom of the church; for I do not want
any innovation without the authority of our overlords, and for that reason I
do not infringe the commandment 'obey those placed over you,'[73] no more
than if I were seated in a council concerned with changing some accepted
practices in the church and should say that this seems expedient to me,
leaving to the church the authority to decide.

I call Christianity purer in so far as it is more removed from the
appearance of Judaism, which was so shunned by the ancient, orthodox
Fathers that in religious practices they preferred to borrow many features
from the gentiles, lest they should seem to Judaize. And Chrysostom very
earnestly admonishes Christians not to fast on the days on which the Jews
engaged in fasting.[74] There is hardly any other practice which has crept into
the church which comes closer to the appearance of Judaism than the choice
of foods; it is the source both of little fruit for promoting true piety and
of many stumbling blocks. And I think that Christianity was purer in the
time of the apostles and martyrs than it is now, when men's charity has
grown so cold. In those times, when there was no rule about differences in
food, more people willingly abstained from meat, and even from fish, than

* * * * *

indulgences, and prayers for the dead; they refused to take oaths and condemned capital punishment and war. Some of their more radical members in
northern Italy insisted that the validity of the sacraments depends on the wor-
thiness of the minister and rejected the entire organization of the church in
so far as it was not based on Scripture. Their members were divided into two
groups: the 'perfect' (*perfecti*) and the 'friends' or 'believers' (*amici* or *credentes*).
They spread throughout most of Europe and were frequently condemned. A
crusade against them was called by Innocent VIII at the end of the fifteenth
century. Some of their groups survived, especially in the Savoy, but many of
them were assimilated into various forms of Protestantism in the sixteenth
and seventeenth centuries.

73 Heb 13:17
74 *Adversus Iudaeos* 1.1–4 PG 48 843–50

people do now when they are bound by law. We praise the philosopher who, when he was asked what profit he gained from philosophy, said 'to perform willingly what the laws require.'[75] And St Paul said that the law does not bind a righteous man because where the spirit of the Lord is, there also is liberty.[76]

Accordingly, if someone were asked which church he preferred, the one where the people were once led by the fervour of the spirit and did not need external rules about food and drink, or the one which is now so lazy that it can hardly be compelled by so many rules to practise some sort of temperance and cannot be prevented by so many barriers from breaking out into wantonness and drunkenness, would he not immediately confess a preference for the former? And Erasmus is stoned because he hopes for the same thing the church hopes for, and even the theologians themselves, if I am not mistaken. A multitude of prescriptions does not bespeak the purity of Christianity but the decline of piety. For just as a multitude of physicians shows that many are ill, so too the multitude of laws bespeaks the wickedness of mankind. Now when the Lord says 'what enters into the mouth does not defile a person,'[77] he surely advises more against the choice of foods than for it. So too Peter in Acts freed the gentiles from such observances.[78] Likewise Paul is always crying out against those who judge their brother because of food and drink and try to introduce into Christianity superstition about food.[79]

I know that the church does not prohibit foods as inherently unclean but rather as excessively nourishing. But there are many people today who are not much different from the Jews in that, even when they are sick and both physicians[80] urge them to eat meat, they shrink from doing so, and (what is even worse) when their brother is in difficulty and the physician encourages them to give him meat, do not dare to do so and judge that he is eating rightly and justly according to the will of the church. I do not criticize the custom of the church which sees charity growing cold and many persons degenerating into luxury and fleshly delights and hence has reined in human frailty and proneness to evil with such prescriptions as if

* * * * *

75 Diogenes Laertius 5.20; *Apophthegmata* book 7 Aristoteles Stagirites 22 LB IV 339A
76 2 Cor 3:17
77 Matt 15:11
78 Acts 10:11–17, 11:2–11
79 Rom 14:2–20
80 That is, the doctor and the priest

with a bit, going beyond rather than against the teaching of the apostles. Nor is obedience to superior powers at all impaired where no innovation is introduced except by their authority. No injury is inflicted on the church if what she has prudently and religiously instituted is equally prudently and religious changed, for reasons which have recently emerged, into something that is more expedient for the times.

But I did not wish to do away absolutely with differences among edibles but only in so far as to promote perpetual temperance in all kinds of food, instead of requiring abstinence from certain foods, so that the loss of external observance would be a gain of true piety. For these are my words: 'not luxuriously but temperately, with thanksgiving and the pursuit of a good conscience.' Therefore, since I make no assertion but express my opinion, since in many passages in my writings I rebuff those who heedlessly violate either the prescriptions or the customs of the church in these matters, since I do not want any innovation without the authority of the church, how, I beg you, do I display contempt for the church? I do not know any Arians,[81] Jovinians, or Waldensians. Perhaps they taught that there is no difference between eating and not eating, between fasting and dining. As for me, I am not talking about voluntary fasting but about a prescription. The theologians also act as though, if the obligation of the commandment were removed, no one would live temperately, though the church flourished most in fasting and abstinence at a time when it was not threatened with any human prescription.

Unless I am mistaken, Luther teaches that the bishops have no right to make any laws and that those they have made should be stoutly broken because they are unholy; and so it is clear on the face of it how different my proposition is from his teaching. I have always approved of those who subdue and master their flesh by eating sparing amounts of food; and in the books I have published I have excoriated those who use the pretext of the gospel to indulge their throats and privy members. And so I differ a great deal from the Aerians, Jovinians, and Waldensians, since in published books I have also condemned those who unnecessarily violate the public customs and decrees of the church even in the slightest matters. How brazen, then, is it to say that my words agree with the teachings of Luther! Furthermore they blithely accuse me of intolerable arrogance because I prefer my unique opinion to the judgment of the whole church, though I do not proclaim

* * * * *

81 'Aerians' refers not to the followers of the trinitarian heretic but to the followers of Aeris of Pontus, with whom the theologians had associated him. See n70 above.

anything and I think that there are thousands of holy men who have the same opinion as I do.

However, in this regulation the church does not profess that it is following a purer Christianity or coming closer to the teachings of the gospel or the apostles, but rather it has provided a remedy for the declining morality of mankind according to the times. It would be another matter if it were clear that these rules were established in such a way that the church neither could nor would ever wish to revise them, since many decisions of the apostles have been revoked. Has there never been anyone before me who complained about the multitude of regulations? Never anyone who had any doubts about whether it would be expedient to revise some ecclesiastical regulations? Certainly Jean Gerson,[82] a writer of no little renown and reputation among the theologians, does it sometimes. If someone proposes such a thing to the leaders of the church, is he suffering from intolerable arrogance? And how were so many serious innovations introduced into the liturgy and regulations of the church, if no one proposed them? Is there really no difference between those who say 'if you starve your body in the pursuit of holiness, you are not at all more holy than someone who gives himself over to pleasure' and someone who wonders whether it is expedient in our times to change the obligation about choosing food into an exhortation, with the idea that the loss in ceremony will add to spiritual holiness? Or between those who proclaim that such regulations are thoroughly wicked and spring from the spirit of Satan and someone who wants no innovation to be introduced except what is useful to the church, and that it be done by the authority of those who preside over the church?

v *His second proposition on the same point, which implies many propositions.*
   In the paraphrase of the eighth chapter of 1 Corinthians
   I approve of what you say: 'Food does not recommend us to God.'[83]
   For since God created the universe for mankind to use and demands
   nothing from us except holy living, what difference does it make to
   him whether we eat fish, or four-footed beasts, or winged flesh? For

* * * * *

82 Jean Charlier de Gerson (1363–1429), a renowned scholastic theologian and chancellor of the university of Paris, was exiled from Paris after 1418 because of political and ecclesiastical strife. He was critical of excessive subtlety in theological speculation and was admired by humanists like Thomas More and Erasmus. See Louis B. Pascoe *Jean Gerson: Principles of Church Reform* (Leiden 1973) 58–68, 99–109, 128–35.
83 1 Cor 8:8

none of these either adds to or detracts from holiness. Choosing among them may make someone superstitious but it will by no means make him holy. Christ taught no distinction among them. Accordingly it is foolhardy for some little human nobody to burden anyone with regulations of this sort. Let everyone eat whatever he wants according to the constitution of his body, as long as he does so soberly, sparingly, and (above all) giving thanks to God.[84]

CENSURE

However much the Apostle asserts, as in those words 'food does not recommend us to God,' that food and drink or the consumption of them are, of their own nature, neither morally good nor morally bad and do not render anyone holy or unholy, nevertheless abstinence from them is praiseworthy and meritorious when it is undertaken to promote virtue according to the precept of the church or when it is voluntarily undertaken according to the status of the person because of a vow or out of devotion; and it contributes to holiness, preparing for it and providing it with great assistance. Otherwise Scripture would not have recommended abstinence and sobriety so often, nor would the church, addressing God, sing as follows: 'You who by bodily fasting repress vice, lift up the mind, bestow virtue and rewards.'[85] Therefore that dogma, so indistinctly propounded and asserted on the basis of Scripture badly understood detracts from holiness and sides with the error of the aforesaid heretics Aeris and Jovinian, condemned a thousand years ago, and afterwards once again rejected in the Waldensians,[86] Wyclif,[87] and Luther. The writer does not so much explain the

* * * * *

84 Erasmus defended these propositions in *Divinationes ad notata Bedae* LB IX 474B–E, in *Elenchus in censuras Bedae* LB IX 507D–E, and in *Supputatio* LB IX 680F–681C.

85 This is the beginning of the preface in the mass from Ash Wednesday until Palm Sunday; *Missale Romanum* no 17, I 202.

86 See n72 above.

87 John Wyclif (1324–84) was a doctor of theology and professor at the University of Oxford. A partisan of the anti-clerical party of John of Gaunt, Wyclif attacked not only transubstantiation but also the wealth of the clergy and religious orders, holding that no respect is due to the commands or the property of the wicked. He laid great stress on preaching and on the Bible as the chief and almost the only source of orthodoxy. He was responsible (directly or indirectly) for the Wyclifite translation of the New Testament into English. He was officially condemned at the Council of Constance in 1415. His heresies concerned not so much matters of ascetical practice as questions of church property and the sacramental system.

text of the Apostle as twist it to give it a heretical meaning, particularly if we take into account the preceding proposition (namely, 'it seems to me to be representative of a purer Christianity, etc'), which reveals the mind of the writer with sufficient clarity, particularly when we have ascertained that the choice of foods was introduced by the apostles themselves, who taught abstinence from blood and what was strangled.[88] It was by their decree, according to Ignatius, Jerome, and Maximinus,[89] that Lent was established. And though Christ does not teach any discrimination of foods as such, we cannot rightly conclude from that that it is foolhardy for the church to establish laws in these matters to be of use to the faithful. Nay rather, it is very foolhardy to strive so arrogantly to tear to shreds what the church has established.

ERASMUS' FIFTH EXPLANATION
v The words which are recited in the paraphrase in the person of St Paul and which were spoken devoutly and piously at that time to express the Apostle's mindset against those who were striving to mix into Christianity a Jewish superstition about food or who thought that meat sacrificed to idols would defile a Christian eating it in good conscience, these words they report just as if they were spoken by me in my own person against the regulations of the church. In many places Paul struggles against the choice of edibles.[90] That was certainly what the times required, when the integrity of the gospel was threatened by pseudo-apostles trying to introduce Judaism. When that danger was eliminated, the church then introduced different regulations against a tidal wave of luxury. And so, if we distinguish persons and times, that place in the paraphrase is not at all opposed to customs which arose long afterwards; and I think that I have rendered Paul's meaning faithfully according to the explanations of the ancient Fathers and have not corrupted it by giving it a heretical meaning (as the censure claims, more

* * * * *

88 Acts 15:20
89 Ignatius of Antioch has nothing to say about Lent, much less about its apostolic institution. Jerome does claim (erroneously) that Lent was instituted by the apostles (*Epistle to Marcella* 3 PL 22 475). St Maximinus (d 352), bishop of Trier, has left behind no writings in which he could express an opinion about the institution of Lent. St Maximus of Turin (380–465), however, claims that Lent was not established by men but by Christ himself (and hence handed down by the apostles, though he does not draw that conclusion); see his *Homilies* 38–9 PL 57 307–11.
90 For example, Rom 14:17

insultingly than truthfully). In Paul's time it was right to say that it was foolhardy for some little human nobody to try to burden the people of Christ with such constitutions. For this passage is directed at the pseudo-apostles who, on their own private authority, were imposing some Jewish rules, proclaiming 'do not taste, do not touch, do not handle.' However you distort it, this passage cannot apply to the church, which is not a little human nobody but rather the mystical body of Christ or those who are the vicars of this presiding Christ. It is spoken in the person of Paul against some pseudo-apostle, not against the church.

But I am surprised that at this point they think Christian fasting should be praised, since the present passage and also the previous one speak only of the choice of foods, especially since fasting is recommended by me in many places, even in my little pamphlet *The Choice of Food*, for example, and in my pamphlet *How to Pray to God*,[91] and since I certainly never taught what Aeris, Jovinian,[92] Wyclif, and Luther do. Nor do I see why they mention here that James in the council imposed on the gentiles that they should abstain from blood and what had been strangled. For this decree did not spring from the opinion of the apostles but was a temporary concession to the invincible importunity of the Jews. Otherwise the apostles preferred to leave the gentiles completely free, as Peter decided in that council without exception.[93]

Then again Lent is not relevant here, since (as I said) the subject is not fasting but discriminating about foods, unless perhaps they think that abstinence from meat and dairy products is always connected with fasting. But even today it is disputed whether the choice of foods is a matter of custom or of law. For it is one thing to introduce, another to prescribe. First came exhortation and usage; regulation was meant to stem the dwindling holiness of Christians. But these ideas are beside the point, since (as I said) the paraphrase deals with the time of the apostles, not with the regulations of the later church when it was already growing old. And so the inference they draw, taking it as if I were accusing the church of foolhardiness because she has prescribed fasting and abstinence from foods and as if I were arrogantly striving to tear to shreds what the church has established, is beside the point and utterly undeserved; it is an attack more truly inspired by hatred than by learning, since in many places I urge people to observe the constitutions of the church.

* * * * *

91 *De esu carnium* LB IX; *Modus orandi Deum* LB V / CWE 70
92 See n71 above.
93 Acts 15:11

Nor does Paul condemn those who in the pursuit of holiness abstain from gourmet food and wine; for it is probable that at that time there were many Christians who abstained completely from wine and meat throughout their lives, content with vegetables and beans; but the Apostle condemned Jewish regulation of such matters, for that time to be sure, when Jewish observances posed a danger to the liberty of the gospel, just as Chrysostom in his age condemned those who fasted on the same days as the Jews did according to what was prescribed by the Law[94] – a practice which has completely disappeared today. It was set forth in ancient canons that those who voluntarily wished to abstain from eating meat were not permitted to do so until they had tasted meat before some witnesses, lest they should seem to be abstaining because of the superstition of the Manichees rather than out of a love of holiness.[95]

Some explain this text in Paul, 'food does not recommend us to God,' as if it were spoken by someone raising an objection,[96] and the paraphrase certainly follows these exegetes, but whoever is taken as the speaker of the text, Paul does not reject it, since he emphatically expresses the same opinion in many other places; here he adds only that whoever has wisdom

* * * * *

94 *Adversus Iudaeos* 2 PG 48 857–8
95 St Martin (c 520–80), archbishop of Braga, records three canons requiring that those who wished to abstain from meat should first taste meat or vegetables cooked in meat; if they refused to do so they were to be excommunicated as following the heresy of the Manichees or Priscillianists. The first two canons were laid down by the First Council of Braga (562); the third by an unspecified eastern council. See *Martini Episcopi Bracarensis Opera Omnia* ed Claude W. Barlow (New Haven 1950) 108, 113, 138. These canons circulated in manuscript in the Middle Ages and were well known in Erasmus' time. Martin of Braga would have interested Erasmus because he knew Greek well and had produced an adaptation of Seneca.
96 It is possible to read 1 Cor 8–9 in the sense 'in God's eyes food is of no importance one way or the other; hence we should not scandalize weaker Christians by eating food sacrificed to idols even though we know we could do so without offence to God.' Chrysostom takes it so in *Homiliae in epistolam primam ad Corinthios* 20.4 PG 61 166, as does Theophylactus in *Expositio in epistolam primam ad Corinthios* 8:8 PG 124 661A–B. But 1 Cor 8:8 may also be taken as a rejoinder to the scruples of weaker Christians about food sacrificed to idols, as, for example, pseudo-Ambrose does in *Commentaria in epistolas beati Pauli, in epistolam ad Corinthios primam* 8:8–9 PL 17 [1845] 227C–D; Rabanus Maurus repeats pseudo-Ambrose's interpretation verbatim in *Enarrationes in epistolas beati Pauli* 10 and *Expositio in epistolam ad Corinthios primam* 8 PL 112 77A. The answer to the rejoinder is 'Yes, but pay attention to the requirements of your weaker Christian brothers.'

avoids being a stumbling block for the weak. And so where is this person who so arrogantly strives to tear to pieces what the church has established? If it is Erasmus, then Paul, whom he is explaining, does the same. But if the Apostle makes no judgment against the constitutions of the church which are yet to come, then I too make no judgment against them when I explain the Apostle's meaning. But if no account is taken of the persons and the times, frequently the less attentive are given a handle to make false charges.[97] Since in that place I am paraphrasing and speaking in the person of Paul,[98] it was not proper for me to stray very far from his words. He says, 'neither if we eat will we abound, nor if we do not eat will we be lacking.'

The paraphrase interprets this according to the opinion of the ancient Fathers: 'for such things do not at all either contribute to holiness or detract from it. Choice in these matters can make someone superstitious; it cannot by any means make a person holy.' Chrysostom and Thomas interpret it to mean that from eating and abstinence there is no increase or decrease in virtue. Ambrose writes as follows: 'because we do not please God precisely by eating all things nor offend if we scorn some kinds of food.' Thomas dares to add on his own, 'because food is good for the stomach, not the mind,' and he finds a parallel to this place in a text from chapter 14[:17] of the Epistle to the Romans, 'the kingdom of God is not food and drink,' and also in a text from the last chapter of the Epistle to the Hebrews [13:9], 'it is good to ground the heart in grace, not food.'[99] In chapter 10[:25, 27] of 1 Corinthians the Apostle says, without any qualification, 'eat whatever comes to the meat market,' and 'if one of the unfaithful invites you, eat whatever is placed before you, asking no questions.' To such a degree did he wish those initiated in Christ to be unconcerned about discriminating one food from another.

In Luke 10[:7] the Lord holds forth to them, 'remain in the same house, eating and drinking what they have there.' The paraphrase explains this text as follows: 'But if you should happen to go into towns, eat what is placed before you, with no choice and no fastidiousness.' Why was this passage

* * * * *

97 *Adagia* I iv 4
98 See Jane E. Phillips 'Sub Evangelistae persona: The Speaking Voice in Erasmus' Paraphrase on Luke' in Hilmar Pabel and Mark Vessey eds *Holy Scripture Speaks: The Production and Reception of Erasmus' Paraphrases on the New Testament* (Toronto, Buffalo, and London 2002) 127–50.
99 For Chrysostom and Ambrose (pseudo-Ambrose) see n96 above. Erasmus reports accurately what Thomas Aquinas says in *Expositio in omnes s. Pauli epistolas, in epistolam primam ad Corinthios* 8 lectio 1.

not thrown up to me as contrary to the regulations of the church? They will say, I think, it is because at the time Christ was speaking the regulations of the church had not yet been issued and he was also engaged in freeing them from legal prescriptions. I accept the answer, but there was no more reason to attack the passage in which I present Paul speaking at a time when there were still no prescriptions about kinds of food, his intent being rather to recall Christians to the liberty of the gospel and to keep them from backsliding into Judaism. But if they do not want the consideration of time and person to do me any good, then it should do no good in the passage from the gospel just cited and in innumerable other places.

They will say it is necessary to counteract these new teachings. But when I wrote these things in 1519, I did not so much as dream of these new teachings. And even if I had been very much aware of them, it was not proper for me to do in a paraphrase what I would have been permitted to do in a commentary. But neither Thomas nor Theophylactus nor Chrysostom counteracts them in their commentaries where it would have been permissible, and I am accused even though I was not allowed to do so in a paraphrase.

Someone will say that the weak will be offended because they do not know about the decorum of persons or the category of time. What can I do for such persons if they ignore the title and learn nothing from so many prefatory admonitions? In his commentary Thomas says 'food is good for the stomach, not the mind,' and his comment is accepted as congruent with the meaning of Paul, and in my paraphrase I am said to corrupt the words of Paul, giving them a heretical meaning.

VI *His third proposition. From his book* The Prohibition of Eating Meat
What stumbling block arises from those things the use of which is not forbidden in the gospel? Indeed in his writings the Apostle condemns those who forbid the use of them: 'prohibiting,' he says, 'food which God created to be eaten.'[100]

CENSURE
This proposition, which alleges that the church established a precept concerning fasting and the choice of food on certain days contrary to the teaching of the Apostle, is asserted at the prompting of the devil

* * * * *

100 1 Tim 4:3. In *Divinationes ad notata Bedae* LB IX 484D–489A Erasmus has a long defence of the legitimacy and appropriateness of what he wrote in *De esu carnium* about fasting, feast days, and the celibacy of the clergy. He defends this particular proposition at LB IX 487E–F.

and is heretical; and it is an affront to the Catholic church and strives to introduce an insane liberty in agreement with the aforesaid heretics. It is not in agreement with the intention of the Apostle who in the cited text condemns only those who assert that creatures are by nature evil, but not those who abstain from certain foods at fixed times according to what the church has established, either to make satisfaction or to gain virtue.

ERASMUS' SIXTH CLARIFICATION[101]

VI Here again they mix in fasting, whereas the passage is concerned only with the choice of foods. Neither Christ nor the apostles nor the holy Doctors ever condemn fasting undertaken in pursuit of holiness, and it is often praised by me. For the time being I will not examine their point that the pseudo-apostles condemned by Paul forbade certain foods as if they were in themselves unclean and contaminating; but nevertheless, to keep Christians as far as possible from this danger, the apostles left them completely free in the choice of foods. Nor does my language insinuate that the rules of the church concerning food are opposed to the teaching of the Apostle; far be it from me to be so ungodly. I merely compare one scandal with another. Nowadays it is a huge scandal if someone eats eggs or solid cheese during Lent, but if someone gets drunk or goes whoring, no one is offended, though that is forbidden by the writings of the Apostle and the other is forbidden by the rules, or rather the customs, of men. Formerly some concession had to be made to the stumbling block encountered by the gentiles, who could not bring themselves to believe that a Christian could eat sacrificial offerings with a good conscience; likewise to that encountered by the Jews, who could not bear that the gentiles should eat ordinary food because of the deep-seated belief handed down by their ancestors. But now there is no place for a stumbling block if someone sees his brother eating food forbidden only by human beings, since it could be that he does so with a good conscience for some hidden reason. But in doubtful matters one should tend toward a kind interpretation.

* * * * *

101 Pelargus sigs c3–c3v notes that Erasmus has already admitted in his fourth and fifth clarifications that what Paul says about the choice of foods does not conflict with the regulations of the church. But he claims that Erasmus here takes Paul's statement universally as forbidding dietary prescriptions to all Christians. In clarifications IV, V, and VI Erasmus makes it quite clear that he had no such intention.
In the second edition Erasmus added only a few brief sentences.

Moreover, the clause 'indeed the writings of the Apostle condemn those who forbid the use of them' is added to the turning point of the sentence, as if I had said 'so far from true is it that the gospel forbids the use of foods that the writing of the Apostle actually condemns those who prohibit it.' Now it is hardly likely that the Jews were so stupid as to think that food is evil by nature, as the Manichaeans did; rather many of them strove to mingle Judaism with Christianity and hence they thought that this part of the Law also had to be observed by Christians. Against them Paul defends the liberty granted to the disciples by the Lord. And so when they say that the Apostle is speaking only about the Manichaeans, that is hardly likely. Certainly he did not mean our regulations, which had not yet arisen. What we call 'unclean,' the Greeks call 'ordinary,' that is, 'secular.' So too the priests abstained from eating the bread of laypeople not because it was by nature unclean but because it was forbidden.[102] That whole people, which belonged to God in a special way, held as sacred what the Law granted, and as secular what it forbade.

Nor is there immediately a conflict between the church and the Apostle if he rightly taught what was fit for his times, whereas the church has made different rules according to different times. And so the prompting of the devil and the attempt to introduce an insane liberty in agreement with heretics, that was far from my intention, and nowhere (I think) do my writings express anything like that. I am merely checking the foolhardiness of some who shrink from their neighbour because of what he eats as if he had slaughtered his parent with a sword. But I confess that I said this with too little circumspection, especially in this age; and because of the weak I will also correct that passage the first chance I get.

VII *His fourth proposition. Mark 2*
The fasting prescribed by the Law is sad and therefore displeasing to God, who loves a cheerful giver.[103]

CENSURE
This proposition, which falsely asserts that fasting is sad and that whatever is done according to a precept is always done in a servile state of mind, whereas it is often performed with free charity, is erroneous

* * * * *

102 Lev 24:4–9. Priests were to eat only holy bread (*panes propositionis*). David and his men were forced to eat holy bread because no ordinary bread was available; see 1 Sam 21:3–6, Matt 12:3–4.
103 2 Cor 9:7

and is asserted by distorting Holy Scripture, which shows that obedience offered to the precepts of superiors is extremely pleasing to God. It is also opposed to the order of natural law, which appoints that inferiors be directed by the laws of their superiors. But if it should happen that someone should observe such fasts in order to avoid the punishment which would be incurred if he broke the rule, that does not always mean that his fasting is displeasing to God and that therefore it has lost any relationship to merit.

ERASMUS' SEVENTH CLARIFICATION[104]

VII At this point they also ineptly twist the words of the paraphrase, which are spoken in the person of Christ, applying them to my person and to these times. The comparison in that passage is between the fasting of the Pharisees, condemned by God in Isaiah and despised by Christ in the gospel, and the spontaneous fasting which the apostles were about to undertake without any precept after they had drawn in the spirit of heaven. For in that passage the Lord excuses his disciples for not fasting as the disciples of John and those of the Pharisees did, since he himself had not imposed any fasting on them. This comparison has nothing to do with the regulations of the church, which came much later. And in that passage the Lord is talking mostly about the laws and rules of the Pharisees. I did not by any means either conceive in my mind or express in words the notion that whoever fasts according to the prescriptions of the Law always fasts out of a servile fear, for there can be no doubt that there were also many among the Jews who observed the prescriptions of the Law with alacrity of spirit. But I was talking generally about the ordinary fasting of the Jews, which was

* * * * *

104 Pelargus sigs c4–c5v spends considerable effort refuting what Erasmus does not say, namely that fasting is sad because it is prescribed by the law. He says no one is likely to believe Erasmus when he claims that he is not criticizing the regulations of the church since he does so in other writings, such as his letter to Jean Gachi (cwe 13 Ep 1891). On Gachi see CEBR II 68. He claims that Christ did not despise the fasting of John's disciples since he said his own disciples would do the same in the future. He also argues that the text against fasting from Isaiah 38 is irrelevant because the fasting condemned there was not pharisaical and probably not prescribed, but was practised by evil men.

In the second edition Erasmus added long sections arguing (from context and patristic evidence) that the pharisaical fasts in Isaiah 38 were performed out of fear, not joy; that his phrase 'displeasing to God' can be taken to mean 'less pleasing to God'; and that the theologians' view of the force of law and Erasmus' can be reconciled.

performed without charity. But that 'always' was inserted by some persons or other on their own, to provide an occasion for a false accusation, since it is not to be found in what I wrote.

As for the merit earned by someone who would murder his fellow human being unless the law deterred him, I will leave it to others to consider that question. But certainly this is what the Lord said: 'If a man sees a woman and lusts after her, he has already committed fornication with her in his heart.'[105] So too someone who fasts without charity and would not fast unless he feared the punishment of the law seems already to have violated the fast and is displeasing to God on two counts, both because he hates the law and because he is a hypocrite, pretending to fast when in fact he does not. Origen calls such fasts Jewish, not because all Jews fasted in this way but because most did.[106] Moreover, if someone fasts out of fear and would not fast unless he was compelled by the law to do so, his fasting is certainly sad and displeasing to God in so far as it lacks eagerness of spirit, which is what chiefly delights God. And so I do not urge anyone to be disobedient to his superiors, but rather I show what is more pleasing to God. If someone urges that what is prescribed should be observed with alacrity rather than out of fear of punishment, is he urging that higher powers not be obeyed? Nor are the weak free from regulations just because God prefers those who fast eagerly and willingly over those who fast because they are coerced by the law rather than moved by their own impulse.

Furthermore, I see that the theologians mean nothing different from what I mean; the quarrel is merely about words. Law has a double force: it directs and it compels. It directs sons by lighting their path; it draws and forces slaves by compelling them. But when my paraphrase compares the spontaneous fasting of the disciples with the fasting of the Jews, it calls the precepts of the Law compulsion. But when the theologians say that fasting which is performed because of a precept is often undertaken with free charity, they are referring to the directive force of law. Otherwise how can there be free charity where a depraved will is repressed by fear? Then too, when they add that obedience offered to the precepts of superiors is extremely pleasing to God, no one denies that this is true, especially if we are speaking of divine precepts. But those who fast with a depraved will and no charity or merely out of fear of punishment and do not tend toward the goal for which the fast was established do not supply the obedience

* * * * *

105 Matt 5:28
106 *Homilies on Jeremiah* 12.13.38 *Sources chrétiennes* 441 vols (Lyon 1942–) 238
      46–8

owed to the precepts, omitting in fact the very purpose which was in the mind of the lawgiver.

Then, too, when they say 'but if it should happen that someone should observe such fasts in order to avoid the punishment which would be incurred if he broke the rule, that does not always mean that his fasting is displeasing to God and that therefore it has lost any relationship to merit,' they admit that it is sometimes displeasing to God; otherwise the adverb 'always' would be superfluous. And so, if I am not mistaken, they mean that fasting is not entirely displeasing when fear adds a stimulus to languishing charity, but that it is displeasing when there is hatred of the law, or a depraved will, or hypocrisy. But if weakness driven on by fear does not lose all relationship to merit, it certainly loses the best part of merit. On these points, I think, we are in agreement.

Now if I had written 'and for that reason less pleasing to God,' there would be no difficulty. And yet my paraphrase makes it clear that that is what I meant: 'The fasting prescribed by the Law is sad and therefore displeasing,' that is, displeasing to God in so far as it is performed not out of free charity but out of Jewish fear. Furthermore, if I used 'displeasing' to mean 'less pleasing,' it would be a figure of speech not uncommon in Scripture. That is clear from the testimony cited by the Lord from Hosea[107] in Matthew 9[:13],[108] 'I want mercy, and not sacrifice,' meaning 'I want mercy more than sacrifice.' That is clear from the clause proclaimed right afterwards by the prophet: 'the knowledge of God more than a holocaust.' 'And not,' which he had said in the first part of the sentence he changed here to 'more than.'

Furthermore, it is quite clear from the words of the Gospel that Christ is speaking there about the compulsory and sad fasting of the Jews. Matthew says: 'The sons of the bridegroom cannot mourn while the bridegroom is with them.'[109] See, he calls the fasting of the Jews mourning. Luke says as follows: 'Can you make the sons of the bridegroom fast while the bridegroom is with them?'[110] Here he uses 'make' to mean 'force,' signifying that the fasting of the Jews was forced. In this passage Jerome freely condemns the fasting of John's disciples not only because they used it as an occasion of pride but also because they looked askance at Christ's disciples

* * * * *

107 Hos 6:6
108 See also Matt 12:7.
109 Matt 9:15
110 Luke 5:34

and scoffed at Christ himself.[111] And Chrysostom pronounces their fasting useless both because they were pleased with themselves and because they looked down on others, taking pride in their external fasting while their inner lives were saturated with sin.[112] The paraphrase compares such fasting of the Jews with the fasting of Christ's disciples after they had drawn in the spirit of heaven. They persevered in fasting and prayer, out of a free alacrity of spirit, not to comply with compulsory precepts.

The paraphrase could not even speak about the regulations of the church, since it speaks in the person of Christ, in whose times there were no precepts of the church about fasting. Still, if someone today should say generally that the fasting of Christians is sad and displeasing to God in so far as they fast not out of charity but only because of an obligation and pay no attention to the purpose for which fasting was ordained, he would not be straying very far, I think, from the teaching of the gospel.

Topic 4. Oaths[113]

VIII *Erasmus' first proposition. Matthew 5[:12]*
To keep men safer from perjury, the law of the Gospel completely condemns all swearing, so that now it is not right to take an oath.
His second proposition. Matthew 5[:35]
Christ totally forbids us to swear oaths.[114]

CENSURE
It is manifest that Christ and the apostles swore oaths, which they would not have done if all oaths were illicit according to the law of the gospel. The process of the law often requires an oath, as the Apostle says 'that the end of all controversy is an oath.'[115] Hence each of these propositions is an affront to the law of the gospel and its promulgator Christ, is foreign to a sound understanding of Scripture,

* * * * *

111 *Commentariorum in Evangelium Matthaei ad Eusebium libri quatuor* 1.9.14 and 2.11.1–2 PL 26 (1845) 46D–57A and 69C–D
112 *In Matthaeum homiliae* 30–1.3 PG 57 366
113 In *Supputatio* LB IX 575A–576C Erasmus briefly defended all the propositions in this section. He also did so very briefly in *Responsio ad notulas Bedaicas* LB IX 713A.
114 Erasmus briefly defended this proposition in *Divinationes ad notata Bedae* LB IX 462A–B
115 Heb 6:16

and is taken over from the condemned teaching of the Catharists,[116] the Waldensians,[117] and those who boast that they belong to the order of the apostles.

ERASMUS' EIGHTH CLARIFICATION[118]

VIII Farewell to the Catharists, together with the Achatharists[119] and the Waldensians, and the Apostolics,[120] with whom I have nothing in common. It is obvious that Christ prohibits all oaths in the Gospel expressly and in clear language, and the apostle James chimes in with Christ.[121] But since this passage is handled variously by the Doctors of the church, it was not suitable that a paraphraser should stray very far from the words of the Gospel and trace out the ramifications of human opinions. I touch on only two opinions,

* * * * *

116 A dualistic, hyperascetic heresy that grew up in France in the eleventh century and spread (in various forms) throughout Belgium, northern Italy, Germany, and the Balkan countries for more than three centuries. Catharism was frequently condemned and many of its adherents were burned at the stake. It finally died out in the fifteenth century. The Albigensians (see n479 below) can be thought of as a subdivision of the Catharists.

117 See n72 above.

118 Pelargus sigs 5v–6v misguidedly thinks that Erasmus should have paraphrased as follows: 'you should in no way desire to swear, in so far as you can avoid it' ('Ne omnino affectaveritis iuramentum, quod quidem in vobis est'). He asserts that Augustine and Hilary agree with his interpretation and flatly rejects the interpretations of Theophylactus and Chrysostom. Hairsplitting in the usual way, he finds contradictions in Erasmus' clarification. He notes rather slyly that when Erasmus wrote to Alberto Pio he offered to take an oath in order to be believed.
In the second edition Erasmus added two long sections, one pointing out that he (like the Fathers) makes some allowances in some of his other works, and another pointing out the interpretation of Thomas Aquinas that even asseverations are forbidden and highlighting the misuse of oaths among the Christians of his own time.

119 Erasmus jests by adding a negating prefix to the Greek name Cathari (pure), thus producing 'impure.'

120 The Apostolics of the twelfth century sprang up in France and Germany. They forbade marriage and the eating of meat. They also rejected infant baptism, veneration of the saints, prayers for the dead, purgatory, and the use of oaths. They were condemned by St Bernard Sermones 66 PL 183 1093D–1102B. In the thirteenth and early fourteenth centuries there was also a sect of Apostolics founded by Segarelli and later led by Dulcin; they were frequently condemned and finally repressed in the fifteenth century by a crusade organized by Clement V.

121 James 5:12

one of them Augustine's, though he is not the only one to hold it: oaths are totally forbidden that we may better avoid the danger of perjury.[122] The other is that of most scholastics, who hold that this passage in the Gospel is a counsel, not a precept, and that it applies only to the perfect.[123] For the Lord is there setting forth an image of a perfect Christian, which, if realized, would make oaths superfluous but instead in all interchanges 'yes, yes' or 'no, no' would be sufficient, since they would be between persons one of whom would not distrust the other or plan to trick him but rather each would speak in straightforward language and fulfil what he had said no less faithfully and scrupulously than if he had sworn an oath. There is also no lack of those who explain the difficulty by saying that an oath taken to advance the gospel is allowable but not in secular and extraneous affairs.[124] And in this way they excuse Paul when he swears.[125] But surely there is no getting around the fact that it is somehow or other wrong to do what the Gospel so expressly and in so many words forbids, as does the apostle James. Otherwise this statement of Christ would be completely superfluous if it were to forbid only perjury or rash oaths.

But if it is objected that oaths are ordinary human practices, then if any command differing from human customs is delivered, it is more equitable for us to correct our lives in accord with the rule of the gospel rather than to twist that rule to match our customs. For in that passage the Lord is not concerned with oaths in court, since he is shaping a people who could have no lawsuits. Jerome explains the passage even more strictly than I: he thinks the Jews were permitted to swear by God for no other reason than to keep them from swearing by demons. His words are as follows: 'And the Law makes this concession to those who are, as it were, not grown up: just as

* * * * *

122 Augustine *Sermones classis primae de Scripturis* 180.1–2 PL 38 972–3; *De sermone Domini in monte libri duo* 1.17.51 PL 34 1255

123 The notion was widespread because it was mentioned in the *Glossa ordinaria* on Matt 5:37 PL 114 96c. See, for example, Alexander of Hales *Summa theologica* III-II inq 4 tr 2 q 3 tit 1 cap 1. But the scholastics usually mentioned it only as marginal or subsidiary. They stressed the exceptions from Augustine, Jerome, and others mentioned by Erasmus

124 It is not uncommon for exegetes to point out that oaths to advance the gospel, as Paul uses them, are allowable, but I have not found commentators who claim that only such oaths are permitted. Mitigation and various modifications of the seemingly absolute prohibition of oaths in Matt 5:34–7 and James 5:12 began earlier in the West than in the eastern church; see Ulrich Luz *Das Evangelium nach Matthäus: 1. Teilband Mt 1–7* (Zurich 1985) 286–9.

125 See 2 Cor 1:23; Gal 1:20; Rom 1:9.

they sacrificed victims to God to keep from sacrificing them to idols, so too they were permitted to swear by God, not because that was the right thing to do, but because it was better to swear by God than by demons. But the truth of the gospel does not accept oaths, since all the speech of a person of faith is equivalent to an oath.'[126] That is what he says. And Theophylactus is no more lenient when he says: 'to swear and add anything more than "no," comes from the devil.' If you say that the Law of Moses was evil because it commands oaths, know that it was not evil to swear at that time; but after Christ it was evil, just as circumcision was, and generally whatever is Jewish was evil.'[127] So says Theophylactus. Hilary also does not disagree with them; for when he had said that it was permitted to the crude Jewish people to swear by God, he adds concerning Christians: 'But the faith eliminates the practice of swearing, establishing all our affairs in truth, removing the desire to deceive, and prescribing simplicity in speaking and listening, etc.' In this passage Hilary uses *sacramentum* 'swearing' to mean what we call *jusjurandum* 'oath,' and that is good Latin usage. And a little later he says: 'Therefore those who live in the simplicity of faith have no need of oaths, etc.'[128] Chrysostom sings the same tune about this passage, teaching that oaths were conceded to the weakness of the Jews, but that Christians ought not to swear even when an oath is demanded or urgently needed; rather among Christians all oaths are evil, so much so that it is a sin deserving hell; and he threatens clerics who had no fear of holding out the book of the gospel to those who are to take an oath.[129] In his commentary on Psalm 118 Ambrose does not permit anyone to swear if there is any danger of perjury; but because every human being is deceitful, he concedes oaths only to God and to those who by divine inspiration are certain they can carry out what they swear to do.[130] These are the opinions which approved Doctors of the church have dared to put in writing.

But I did not entirely follow them in the paraphrase; I merely say that among perfect Christians oaths are superfluous. Nevertheless I do not mean that a perfect person immediately sins if he swears for some serious reason or is constrained by some grave necessity; but wherever there is an

* * * * *

126 Jerome *Commentariorum in Evangelium Matthaei ad Eusebium libri quatuor* 1.5.34–7 PL 26 40A–B
127 Theophylactus *Enarratio in Evangelium Matthaei* 5.37 PG 123 200B
128 Hilary *In Evangelium Matthaei commentarius* 4.23 PL 9 940A–B
129 Chrysostom *In Matthaeum homiliae* 17.5–6 PG 57 261; *Ad populum Antiochenum homiliae* 15.5 PG 49 160
130 Ambrose *In psalmum David* CXVIII *expositio* 14.14 PL 15 (1845) 1396B–C

oath, there is some evil, even if no more than that of weakness. The words of the paraphrase are as follows: 'What need is there, then, of any oaths among persons who out of simplicity do not distrust anyone and who out of sincerity do not desire to deceive anyone, even if they could get away with it unpunished?' And a little further on: 'If anything is added, it must be added out of some vicious motive. For either the person swearing does not entirely mean the thing he is swearing to or else the person who demands the oath is distrustful. But neither motive is fitting for you, whom I wish to be perfect in every way, etc.' This is as far as the paraphrase goes. And so it concedes oaths to the imperfect, but neither praises nor prescribes them. Why then should my proposition be an affront to the law of the gospel and its author Christ, since I explain the very same thing which he expressly teaches and which orthodox Doctors expressly explained in their interpretations, at the same time, nevertheless, indicating a reason that oaths ought to be permitted? And how can it be just to say that I have drawn in error from the Cathars, Apostolics, and Waldensians, since what is condemned as error is clearly expressed in so many and such great luminaries of the church? If I meant that oaths could neither be demanded nor taken without sin, I could have seemed to have drawn upon approved Doctors of the church. Augustine says nothing like this about the Cathars and the Apostolics. What kind of animal the Waldensians are I neither know nor care to know.

They will say that the approved Doctors of the church make it clear in other places that they do not completely condemn all oaths. Granted that this is true, I do the same. For in my annotations on the fifth chapter of Matthew I not only indicate that this discourse of Christ applies to the perfect, and that oaths are conceded to the weak, but I also display a new way of clearing up the difficulty. I will quote my words: 'In this way, then, many knotty problems could be solved if we understood that Christ did not absolutely forbid these things but that he forbade that they should be done in the way that people ordinarily do them. Thus he forbade anger, etc.'[131] This, I think, is not the language of someone who absolutely forbids all oaths.

But if they say that they are making pronouncements only about my proposition, I have reported much harsher judgments from very approved Doctors of the church, though they were at liberty in their commentaries to try in various ways to resolve the difficulty, while unlike them I was not free in my paraphrase, since there I speak in the person of Christ and the

* * * * *

131 *Annotations on the New Testament* LB VI 29F

evangelist. Would it have been right to suppress what the Lord so clearly expressed? Those who write commentaries recite the words of the Lord. What crime was there if a paraphraser faithfully rendered their meaning? If someone should say that a paraphraser ought to indicate how the language of the Lord is to be understood, I did not omit that, though the delegates did. My opinion agrees with that of the theologians; the dispute is only about individual words, since where the evangelist says *omnino* 'altogether,' the paraphraser says *in totum* 'totally.' But if they press us about the words, which one seems closer to the appearance of heresy, someone who says 'totally abstaining from oaths' in conformity with the gospel and the apostle, or someone who says 'in very many cases an oath is quite useful and praiseworthy,' which we never read in the written Gospels? The Lord expressly says one thing; men say another, do another.

Now in order to find some way to make it seem right both to say and to do this, it was not appropriate for the paraphrase to recount how useful oaths are; for that would not be explaining the language of the Lord but rather diminishing the energy of the evangelical philosophy. Should I have said in the person of Christ: 'I say to you, do not swear at all but let your language be "yes, yes, no, no"; anything beyond that comes from an evil source. But though I speak thus, there are still many ways in which oaths are useful and even necessary, in controversies, in judgments, in the treaties of princes, in undertaking positions as magistrates, in initiating persons into holy orders and liberal studies, and thousands of other occasions'? Wouldn't that have been a fine way for me to fulfil the duty of a paraphraser? But the knotty difficulty, they say, needed to be explained. That was not what the paraphraser professed he would do; he only recounts the text in a clearer way, especially since there is no agreement among the Doctors, and those who try hardest to untie this knot give off enough sweat and heat.

But if someone says I should have avoided the error of those who want oaths to be absolutely eliminated from the entire lives of Christians, there is more danger in people's ordinary practices, since by swearing they often learn to perjure themselves and by perjuring themselves often they learn to consider perjury a slight fault. For nowadays there are plenty of swearers and perjurers everywhere. It was necessary to recall mortals, who are prone to evil, from this Charybdis.[132] That is the reason we see this practice in Scripture and the early Doctors: wherever people's minds are most prone to vice, they confront them there, drawing them in the other direction

* * * * *

132 *Adagia* III vii 41

with figures and hyperboles, so that virtue might be established in a middle position. Thus when the Lord calls people back from a lust for revenge, he cries out: 'But I say to you, do not resist evil, and if anyone strikes one of your cheeks, offer him the other.'[133] When he is preventing avarice he says: 'Give to everyone who asks.'[134] Likewise when Jerome discourages Christians from the madness of waging war, he says that war is absolutely forbidden to us;[135] when he deters clerics from the eager pursuit and accumulation of wealth, he says that clerics are not allowed to have anything except the Lord.[136] Following their example, I am accustomed from time to time to be more vehement against the direction toward which mankind by nature tends to lean and which poses the greater danger.

If God swears in any place, or Christ, or the angels, that has nothing to do with us. If the holy men of the Old Testament swear any oaths, that has nothing to do with the disciples of the gospel. The same must be said about the writings of the apostles, for they clearly proceed not from human understanding but from the breath of the Holy Spirit. Finally, when the Apostle writes to the Hebrews,[137] he does not approve of oaths, but draws an argument from a public custom – unless perhaps, when he says 'whoever struggles in an athletic contest abstains from everything,'[138] he is thought to be recommending theatrical contests to us, or when Christ told the parable about the rich man who distributes the talents to his servants so as to gain interest, he approved of usury.[139] Furthermore, apart from what I indicate in my paraphrase, as I said, I make it quite clear in my *Annotations* that I do not mean that oaths are absolutely forbidden and in no way allowable to Christians;[140] for that was permissible there but would have been inappropriate in my paraphrase. Perjury is a kind of blasphemy. The

* * * * *

133 Matt 5:39; cf Luke 6:29.
134 Luke 6:30
135 Jerome has a long and eloquent passage describing bloody and widespread warfare in *Epistola ad Heliodorum* 13–18 PL 22 599–602, but I cannot find any place where he says that warfare is absolutely forbidden to Christians (even using the search engine of the Patrologia Latina data base).
136 *Epistolae* 52.5 PL 22 531
137 Heb 6:16
138 1 Cor 9:25
139 Matt 25:14–30
140 In his annotation on Matt 5:37 Erasmus points out that Christ and the apostles swear to promote the faith and holiness; and since he says that the sermon on the mount is directed at the perfect, he implies that ordinary people are allowed to swear oaths.

danger lies on that side. There is no danger that oaths will disappear from the world, but rather that perjury will flood the earth. What about this: the language of the Lord seems to forbid not only all oaths, but also all emphatic asseverations. For he says, 'anything beyond that comes from an evil source.'[141] And, in fact, among the perfect such as the Lord hopes for here, all emphatic asseverations, such as 'believe me' or 'I am not kidding you,' would be superfluous, even though the Apostle Paul frequently asseverates and swears,[142] if he is actually swearing when he calls God to witness. For there are some who deny that Paul is swearing, but they are refuted by St Augustine, whose opinion I have long since fully embraced.[143] Thomas thinks that, when he says 'I call God to witness and by my soul,'[144] he not only swore but swore with an execration. The oath was 'I call God to witness'; the execration was 'by my soul.'[145] Some say that Christ did not forbid oaths, but only those forms which are mentioned there: 'by heaven,' 'by the earth,' 'by someone else's head,' etc, as the gentiles and the Jews then commonly swore – as if it were right to swear by God but not by creatures. But when Paul swears by his own glory,[146] he seems to swear by a creature. Again, when he writes to Philemon, 'so may I enjoy you in the Lord.'[147]

But if we accept the interpretation of the holy Fathers, oaths are totally forbidden to Christians on the grounds that whoever swears exposes himself to extremely grave danger of perjury because a human being, on account of mental weakness, or forgetfulness, or the deception of his senses, often thinks he knows what he does not, thinks he can perform what he cannot. Paul, who was safe from these dangers, rightly swore in his writings, which issued from the breath of the Holy Spirit. On the same grounds St Ambrose excuses the holy men of the Old Testament when they swear,[148] so that this precedent now has nothing to do with us, though those who approve of oaths for Christians adduce this as their most solid argument. Nevertheless, if we rely on the example of Paul, let us swear in the manner

* * * * *

141 Matt 5:37
142 See n125 above; Rom 9:1.
143 *Sermo* 180 5.5, 9.10 PL 38 974, 977–8
144 2 Cor 1:23
145 *Expositio in omnes s. Pauli epistolas, in epistolam secundam ad Corinthios* 1.5
146 Erasmus seems to refer to 2 Cor 6:11.
147 Philem 1:20
148 *In psalmum David* CXVIII *expositio* 14.14 PL 15 (1845) 1496A

of Paul. He did not swear except when promoting the gospel among the weak required him to do so. We swear for any reason whatever. And if the Waldensians stick too close to the word of the Lord and shrink from oaths excessively, for us certainly the explicit precept of the Lord ought to have had enough force to make us reluctant to accept oaths. Nowadays even those who profess to have evangelical perfection swear, and they swear more out of custom than necessity. How necessary or how very useful is it for petty masters of arts to swear?[149] The pagan Isocrates, who was not a philosopher but a rhetorician, did not want a sworn oath to be accepted unless someone was exonerating himself from a shameful crime or saving his friends from grave danger. He did not want anyone to swear for the sake of money, even if he would swear to the truth.[150] But in the lives of Christians it is more ordinary to swear than it once was among the pagans, and there are fewer scruples about oaths, as if the Lord had laid down his precept in vain.

And although it is true that the language of the Lord pertains to the perfect, nevertheless it is the duty of all Christians to strive for perfection, each according to his own strength. I would say this not because I totally condemn all oaths, but to make it apparent that I was not heedlessly cautious about approving oaths and that I stuck closer to the words of the gospel and did not stray far from the interpretation of the ancient, orthodox Fathers.

IX *His third proposition on the same subject. Luke 24*[151]
Christ forbade swearing, which had previously not been forbidden by the Law.

CENSURE
Since the moral precepts are the same in both laws and are confirmed by Christ through the gospel, it is erroneous to say that oaths are absolutely forbidden in the New Law, since they were permitted in the Old Law.

* * * * *

149 Masters of arts who were continuing their studies in theology had to swear concerning the validity of the 'credits' (*cedulae*) of the first six years of their theological studies; see Farge *Orthodoxy and Reform* 16–17.
150 *To Demonicus* 23
151 In his paraphrase of Christ's explanation of scripture Erasmus wrote 'forbidding them to swear, though the former Law had not done so' ('prohibens jurare, quod non prohibuerat Lex prior') LB VII 471C / CWE 48 240.

ERASMUS' NINTH CLARIFICATION[152]

IX If there is anything erroneous here, it is fitting to attribute it first of all to the early Doctors, who are approved by an overwhelming consensus and who teach with one voice that what was permitted to the Jews is forbidden to Christians. Now that word 'absolutely' was added by the reporters; I say only that oaths are forbidden in the same way as divorce, which was permitted to the Jews, is forbidden. I will not delay here to consider the subtle arguments of some who say that oaths were allowed in the same way as Christian laws allow brothels. It is more probable that they were allowed in such a way as not to be sinful. Otherwise the Law could seem to deceive the Jews by allowing what was illicit.

Now that distinction of Augustine, which he thought up for pedagogical reasons, separating moral, ceremonial, and judicial laws, has many difficulties if you examine it closely.[153] But, to accept it for the moment, if in moral matters the gospel adds nothing more perfect than the Law, the books of the ancient, orthodox Fathers are full of language suggesting that many things were allowed to the Jews which are forbidden to Christians and that the teaching of the gospel is much more perfect than that of Moses. If what they say is wrong, and they said it to avoid stumbling blocks for the weak, their words should be corrected rather than mine, since I followed them as authorities, and there is all the more danger in what they say in that they are read as greater authorities, even in church.

If they should say at this point that in moral matters Christ added nothing to the Law but only expressed the spiritual meaning of the Law

* * * * * .

152 Pelargus sigs c7–c7v insists that in moral matters the New Law is identical with the Old Law and does not go beyond it, citing some fairly easy examples but ignoring the one fatal to his case (the Christian command to love one's enemies, a point mentioned by Erasmus in the expanded second edition). Pelargus claims that Christ did not forbid swearing but perjury. The spiritual interpretation of the Law he thinks applies only to motivation, not to content. Relying on Thomas Aquinas *Summa posteriore partitione secundae partis* (where Aquinas relies on Deut 6:5, 13: 'Thou shalt love the Lord thy God and him alone shalt thou serve and thou shalt swear by his name'), he goes so far as to assert that the New Law not only permits but also requires swearing.

In the first edition Erasmus had written only a brief section (four sentences) contrasting the New Law with the Old (not merely murder but anger is forbidden, not merely adultery but lustful thoughts). In the second edition he expanded this greatly, concentrating on the difficult idea that the two laws are identical in moral matters and discussing the various meanings of 'law' in Scripture.

153 *Contra Faustum Manichaeum libri triginta tres* 19.2 PL 42 347–8

more clearly and more perfectly than the scribes and Pharisees, it is hardly a new feature of language to attribute to the Law what is expressed in the words of the Law and what the ordinary run of Jews thought they were bound only to observe. For Holy Scripture uses the word 'law' in various ways. When the Lord says 'the Law and the prophets up to John,'[154] he uses 'Law' to mean the types and ceremonies of the Law and 'prophets' to mean their predictions about the first coming of Christ. Likewise, when Paul says 'there is a setting aside of the former commandment because of its weakness and unprofitableness, for the Law brought nothing to perfection,'[155] he does not mean the whole Law, but the ceremonial precepts, which a little earlier he called 'the law of a carnal commandment.'[156] In this manner the early Doctors of the church say in many places that the gospel requires greater perfection than the Law does, meaning by 'Law' not that spiritual and hidden meaning but rather the words of the Law as ordinary Jews understood them. The precept which the Pharisees themselves confess is the greatest in the Law says only 'you shall love your neighbour as yourself.'[157] Did Christ add nothing to this precept when he said 'love your enemies, etc'?[158] Then too, if nothing more is required of Christians, what will we make of that text so often cited by the holy Fathers, 'more is required of him to whom more has been given'?[159] But if we interpret their words appropriately and do not judge them to be erroneous, then mine can all be received with similar candour.

x *His fourth proposition. Matthew 5*
A Christian is no less bound by his plain word than a Jew is when he swears by all that is holy.[160]

CENSURE
This proposition is erroneous and derogates from the honour of God, whose authority is invoked by an oath and for that reason a new bond of obligation is introduced.

* * * * *

154 Luke 16:16
155 Heb 7:18–19
156 Heb 7:16
157 Matt 22:39
158 Matt 5:43
159 Luke 12:48
160 Erasmus briefly defended this proposition in *Divinationes ad notata Bedae* LB IX 462B–D.

ERASMUS' CLARIFICATION

x Here the reporters' interpretation is quite different from what I meant. For I do not mean that a perjurer does not commit a graver sin than someone who does not keep his plain word but rather that a perfect Christian should be so faithful to his word that he observes what he has promised by his plain word more scrupulously than a Jew, or a Jewish person, however much he has sworn. For a Jewish person does not think he is bound by his plain promise, but for a perfect Christian his plainest word counts as an oath. And if all Christians were such, how in the long run would that derogate from the honour of God? In my judgment it would be rendered illustrious by such great integrity in his followers. The Lord wants all his followers to be perfect, and the glory of a king consists in the high moral character of his people. What room is there, then, for those frightful words 'erroneous and derogating from the honour of God'?

But if God is honoured by oaths, since it is pious to honour God, why do men of such great sanctity unanimously take a stand against oaths? And also, today, why is it that the more religious a person's outlook is the more vehemently he shrinks from oaths, so much so that many persons prefer to lose their case by refusing to swear an oath than to swear an oath, even a true one? In one of his homilies St John Chrysostom with great vehemence denies entry into church to those who swear oaths contrary to the Lord's precept – merely 'swear,' he says, not 'perjure themselves.'[161] The same Father writes concerning Matthew [5]: 'What if someone requires an oath or imposes it as necessary? Let your fear of God be stronger than any necessity. For if you always intend to bring up such qualifications, you will not observe any precepts.'[162] This is what he says. Someone who swears by the authority of God's name other than in order to honour God commits a sin, but holy persons are urged to refrain from such honour because perjury constitutes very grave contempt for God. And who does not know that a Christian who has sworn an oath is more bound than he would be by a plain promise?

For in that place the paraphrase is not comparing a Christian who has sworn an oath with one who has not, but a Christian who has not sworn with a Jew who has. And so, just as for a perfect Christian to lust after another's wife is accounted adultery and to hate one's brother is equivalent to murder, so too to fail to keep a plain promise made to one's neighbour is no less sinful for a Christian than a Jew took perjury to be. And on this point I have followed the authority of approved Doctors. Jerome says:

* * * * *

161 *Ad populum Antiochenum homiliae* 15.5 PG 49 159–60
162 *In Matthaeum homiliae* 17.5–6 PG 57 261

'The truth of the gospel does not accept oaths, but rather all the speech of a person of faith is equivalent to an oath.'[163] No one can be offended by my words if he reads the consecutive language of the paraphrase. For it is preceded by this: 'Among you, therefore, plain speech ought to be holier and stronger than any oath, however religious, among the Jews.' And after several intervening sentences, it repeats what had been said before: 'For the one is no less bound by his plain and bare word than a Jew who swears by all that is sacred; and the other is no less trusting than if an oath had intervened, etc.'[164] The earlier saying, 'ought to be holier and stronger,' is here repeated in other words, 'is no less bound.'

I beg you, reader, what do such cavils contribute to Christian piety – to pick out what you can carp at, to interpret unsuitably what was picked out and twist it to some other meaning? I am afraid that such standards, which some follow in examining the writings of the ancient Fathers, contribute more to the world than to Christ and diminish the energy of the gospel rather than strengthen it. What need is there to teach the world that oaths are very useful and necessary? Augustine places oaths among what is useful, not what is approved. For evils are also necessary. And if there is an oath that is not evil, there is certainly none that does not spring from evil; and since Matthew says 'from the evil one'[165] with the article (ἀπὸ τοῦ πονηροῦ), Chrysostom takes it to mean 'from the devil.'[166] Softening that, Augustine takes 'from evil' to apply to guilt or punishment.[167]

XI   *His fifth proposition on the same subject. Matthew 5*
There is no need in contracts to mingle in oaths, execrations, or such like, which are to bind with fear the one who promises and inspire trust in the one who demands it.

CENSURE
This proposition alleging that it is not fitting, useful, or necessary to take oaths to confirm human contracts, if it is understood to be universal, is false and comes close to the error of Wyclif.[168] For it is sometimes useful and sometimes necessary to confirm human agreements

* * * * *

163 *Commentariorum in Evangelium Matthaei libri quatuor* 1:34–7 PL 26 (1845) 39–40
164 *Paraphrasis in Evangelium Matthaei* 5.36 LB VII 33C–D / CWE 45 105
165 Matt 5:37
166 *In Matthaeum homiliae* 5–6 PG 57 261
167 *Expositio epistolae ad Galatas* 9 PL 35 2110–11; *De sermone Domini in monte secundum Matthaeum libri duo* 1.17.51 PL 34 1255–6
168 See n87 above.

with oaths, according to the magnitude of the subject which the contract concerns or the usefulness which arises from the oaths for the contracting persons or governments, as can be seen in the treaties of princes.

ERASMUS' CLARIFICATION

xi I did not set down this proposition universally; rather I am concerned only with those who are perfect in the simplicity of the gospel and have no other use for language than to signify and impart what they have in their thoughts. For the paraphrase says as follows: 'For among you who ought to have nothing on your lips that differs from your thoughts, language has no other use than for human beings to signify to each other what they think in their minds.' Immediately after this there follows: 'There is no need in contracts to mingle in oaths, etc.' If they had reported the drift of the passage, it would have given no offence. I am dealing there with the perfect. For this is what follows: 'But neither one applies to you, whom I want to be perfect in all ways, etc.'[169] Also it does not matter whether there are any such persons in the world. It is sufficient that Christ depicts and hopes for them. For rhetoricians also set forth a perfect orator, such as they say has never yet been found. Now if there were such persons as Christ depicts there, what would be the use or the appropriateness or the necessity of oaths? Are not oaths superfluous among those who never distrust, who never plan treachery? Are oaths fitting and proper where for everyone plain speech is equivalent to an oath? Is something necessary if it is not appropriate and is of no use at all?

Moreover, what need was there for that qualification 'if it is understood to be universal,' since my proposition cannot be understood universally; that is ruled out by what precedes and what follows. I do not deny that among princes, such as most of them now are, oaths are sometimes useful or necessary; nevertheless it would be more desirable if princes were so trustworthy that they entered into treaties without oaths and kept them just as if oaths had been taken. But if the example of princes swearing oaths to keep their treaties moves us to approve of oaths, the treaties which princes make and break so often ought more rightly to dissuade us from taking oaths. To say nothing, in the meantime, about businessmen and litigants, most of whom swear and forswear for trivial reasons, much to the disgrace of the name of Christian. Christ did not come into the world to concern

* * * * *

169 LB VII 33C–D / CWE 45 105

himself with the regulation of trade but to instil a heavenly philosophy in his followers. But to the same degree that oaths are praised, the energy of the gospel is depleted; it would be better if the gospel remained in its well-spring than that it should be mingled with worldly considerations.

Topic 5. Reparation for injuries

XII *The proposition of Erasmus. Luke 22[:49–51]*
If Christ had not clearly reproached the human feeling with which the apostles loved him, we would have thought that we are allowed to use weapons to defend ourselves against the violence of the wicked and to repel force with force. But as it is, since Peter was reproached for drawing his sword to protect his most innocent Lord against wicked criminals, what reason can there be after that for a Christian person to repay one injury with another?[170]

CENSURE
Although wars and conflicts among Christians are to be avoided as much as possible, nevertheless this proposition, as it stands, alleging that a war against the violence of wicked men is never licit, as if there could never be a just cause for a war to defend one's self, even if one observed the due process of law, undermines the whole government and is at odds with both natural and divine law. For otherwise the many wars waged according to God's plan would not have been mentioned in the books of Numbers, Joshua, Judges, Kings, and Maccabees. Moreover, this proposition conflicts with the writings of the Apostle and other holy men, and is in agreement with the heresy of the Poor Men of Lyon[171] and of Luther. The writer is not excused because he added 'what reason can there be after that for a Christian person to repay one injury with another?' since he made it clear in the preceding passage that it is absolutely illicit to defend ourselves with weapons or to repel force with force; from this the meaning of the author can be clearly inferred. Also Christ did not reproach Peter for that reason, as if it were never permissible to repel force with force, (provided that the moderation of a blameless defence is observed), but rather because Peter strove to defend Christ as if he were in need of

* * * * *

170 Erasmus defended this position briefly in *Supputatio* LB IX 576C–F, 616A–C, 635A–B and in *Responsio ad notulas Bedaicas* LB IX 708E–709B.
171 Another name for the Waldensians; see n72 above.

human assistance and did not voluntarily and without resistance accept the death decreed by his Father.

ERASMUS' CLARIFICATION[172]

XII Since we see that there is hardly ever any respite from wars, which normally arise from the ambition or anger of princes and thus are usually fought for the worst reasons, in my writings I frequently frighten people away from warfare, and in doing so I follow the example of the ancient Doctors of the church. Nevertheless in many places I make it clear that I do not absolutely condemn all wars, such as in my *Panegyric* to Prince Philip, the son of the emperor Maximilian, and in *The Christian Prince* addressed to the present emperor Charles, and finally in my little book *Waging War against the Turks*.[173] But, so far as this place is concerned, the first injury to me is to take what is spoken in the person of Luke in the paraphrase and is rightly spoken in those times to the heralds of the gospel, and to transfer it to my person and apply it to these times. For the censure seems to twist what the paraphrase says to us in such a way as to apply it to me and to the men of our times, whereas Luke is talking about his colleagues. Then, too, when the paraphrase says 'now,'[174] the censure applies it to the present age

* * * * *

172 Pelargus sigs D1–D1v claims that Christians have a natural right, and sometimes a duty, to ward off injury from themselves or others. He also asserts that Christ was not giving an example to us when he rebuked Peter. He says that Erasmus' paraphrase does not give the sense of Luke's words correctly but rather distorts them. He agrees with Erasmus that to use force to obtain vengeance is wrong; but he wonders why in his *Enchiridion* Erasmus is surprised that the maxim 'to repel force with force' has entered into Christian practice, since the maxim does not express a desire for vengeance but rather the aim of protecting the innocent. Hence he believes that in the paraphrase Erasmus is expressing his own view, not merely that of Luke. He acknowledges that Erasmus later in his paraphrase admits that it is allowable to repel evil directed at oneself or another; but Pelargus claims that this is merely inconsistency on Erasmus' part.

In the second edition Erasmus added lengthy sections in which he refutes Pelargus' argument from natural law and cites Ambrose in support of his own view (whereas Pelargus had cited Ambrose in his favour). He also cites canon law forbidding clerics to use offensive weapons (and makes some satirical thrusts at the higher clergy); again he insists that the paraphrase is set in Luke's period, not in modern times, when the concessions demanded by the theologians may have to be made.

173 *Panegyricus* LB IV / CWE 27; *Institutio principis christiani* LB IV / CWE 27; *De bello Turcico* LB V / CWE 64

174 The Latin has *jam*, though the paraphrase has *nunc*, but the sense is the same.

when it is written, whereas the paraphrase intends it to apply to the age when the evangelist wrote, when the preaching of the gospel was replacing the Law of Moses. For the Lord did not want the gospel to be spread by weapons or any other human assistance so that all the glory might devolve upon God. For he did not allow his apostles to do anything except to flee from one town to another[175] and to possess their souls in patience.[176] But if it was permitted to the apostles and men in apostolic times in the early years of the church to defend themselves against the pagans, whom I call wicked, I will confess that my paraphrase did not speak correctly. But Augustine, who followed after the time of the apostles by such a long interval, does not want idolaters to be suppressed by force of arms, even though at that time the power of the Christians, as he himself confesses, was such that they could have had the upper hand in a conflict; indeed he also opposes having the emperor take vengeance for the death of those slaughtered by the pagans, giving as his reason that the glory of the martyrs should not be clouded by vengeance.[177]

Someone will say that it is one thing to praise the gentleness of the ancients and quite another to deprive them of the right to defend themselves without blame. 'The right of defence,' they say, 'was not taken away from the apostles and martyrs, but in those times it was not expedient for the promotion of the gospel to use that right.' Let us grant this: as for me, when I looked back on those times when it was not expedient to repel force with force and the Lord did not want anyone to do what he himself did not do, I said nothing wicked, I think, by claiming that what was not expedient then, and what the Lord certainly forbade at that time, was not right. Moreover, if Peter was acting there as a model for bishops, St Ambrose says that the weapons of priests are prayers and tears,[178] and (if you wish) add the whole panoply in which Paul decks out the Ephesians in chapter 6[:13–17] and the Thessalonians in chapter 5[:8].

And the paraphrase is not speaking there absolutely about any sort of defence whatsoever but about that which springs from a desire for revenge. For this is how the passage begins: 'so that he might completely uproot from

* * * * *

175 Matt 10:14
176 Luke 21:19
177 *Epistola* 139 2 PL 33 536
178 The *sententia* 'arma episcopi lacrymae sunt et orationes' is attributed to Ambrose by Gratian in *Decretum* II causa 23 quaestio 8 pars 1, but it is merely a summary drawn from *Sermo contra Auxentium de basilicis tradendis* 2 PL 16 (1845) 1008A.

their souls all lust for revenge, at that time Jesus deceives them for the moment by the obscurity of his language, but he allows them to err precisely so that he might more certainly and efficaciously remove all lust for revenge.'[179] These were feelings to which the disciples were still subject at that time, when they had not yet drawn in the heavenly spirit, etc. That is sufficiently clear from the fact that when they were outraged at the Samaritan town for shutting out the Lord, they wanted him to call down heavenly fire upon it, so that the town would burn down and the people together with it.[180] And so if my statement is taken as it was spoken, that is, as concerning lust for vengeance, and is applied to men in the time of the apostles, when the gospel was to be spread by the blood of the martyrs, it in no way, shape, or form[181] condemns all wars, nor does it undermine all government, nor is it at odds with natural and divine law, but it is in agreement with the teaching of Christ and the apostles. For what right do they have to use force to repel the force of wicked men when they have been commanded to love even their enemies, to do good to those who do evil to them, to pray for their persecutors,[182] and when they have been told 'do not offer any resistance at all to evil,'[183] with which Paul chimes in by saying 'do not avenge yourselves, my dearly beloved, but leave room for wrath'?[184]

If they take natural law to mean natural instinct, it is very often quite praiseworthy not to give way to it. Nature has deeply instilled a love of propagating our species, and yet sexual continence is praised. The law of nature dictates obedience to parents and yet those who scorn their parents out of a love of holiness are praised.

What they say about the Apostle's writings I suspect refers to this place in Romans 13, 'it is not for nothing that he carries a sword.'[185] But

* * * * *

179 LB VII 453D / CWE 48 195. Perhaps the next sentence, ending in 'etc,' is in an earlier edition of the *Paraphrases* but it is not in LB.
180 Luke 9:54
181 Literally 'neither standing nor lying down nor walking' ('nec stans nec iacens nec ambulans'). The phrase 'sedens ambulans vel stans' was used literally in the rule of St Benedict. It was naturally very well known and came to be applied more generally in the sense 'in any (or no) way.' See, for example, Edmundus Martène on Benedict's rule 42 PL 66 674C and Adamarus Cibardi *Epistola de Apostolatu Martialis* PL 141 108C.
182 Matt 5:54
183 Matt 5:39
184 Rom 12:19. The wrath of God is meant, as the rest of the verse makes clear.
185 Rom 13:4

where did the Apostle teach that the disciples should take up arms against the savageness of their persecutors and kill those who wanted to kill them? What if the words 'it is allowed to repel force with force' belong to the law of the emperor,[186] not to the law of the gospel, and even so they are subject to many qualifications? How about the fact that canon law does not allow clerics offensive weapons but grants them only defensive arms?[187] By defensive arms they mean body-armour, shields, and helmets, though nowadays we interpret 'defensive' to mean arms taken up with the intention of defending, especially after popes have begun to be attended by a secular honour guard even at meals and in church, after bishops for the honour of the church have begun to journey in the company of three hundred armed horsemen, after cardinals for the sake of honour have begun to be designated deputy-commanders in the field.

For the present I will refrain from inquiring what force an example from the Old Testament has when it is transferred to the New, since many things were permitted to the Jews which were not allowed to Christians. Furthermore, what I added, 'for a Christian person to repay injury with injury,' is spoken climactically. If it was not allowed to repel force with force in that period of time when Luke wrote, it was even less permissible to repay injury with injury. Or if you take force to be that permitted by the Law, the apostles at that time were not allowed to do what was permitted to the Jews and what Christians are allowed to do today (as long as you add not only the restraint of a blameless defence but also a regard for Christian gentleness – a model which it is fitting we should emulate as well as we can). Or if you take it to mean the force of retaliating with like for like, which was granted to the moral character of the Jews, because they were excessively prone to vengeance, to keep revenge from going beyond all bounds, the second meaning is an interpretation of the first.[188] Such was the force which Peter brought to bear. The Lord was being called before a judge; Peter, a private man, was attempting murder; he was not employing legitimate power but was carried away by a burning desire for

* * * * *

186 *Digests of Justinian* ed Theodor Krueger and Paul Krueger, trans Alan Watson 4 vols (Philadelphia 1985) 43.27, IV 584. See also Hans Walther *Proverbia sententiaeque Latinitatis Medii Aevi: Lateinische Sprichwörter und Sentenzen des Mittelalters* 6 vols (Göttingen 1963) V 723 (33384b–d); and Cicero *Pro Sesto* 17.39.

187 Gratian *Decretum* II causa 23 quaestio 8 pars 1 cc 1–6 *Corpus iuris canonici* II 954.

188 Erasmus seems to mean here that this interpretation is simply a reason for the first point he has already mentioned, the force permitted to the Jews by the Law.

revenge. But for the moment I will not argue about what the Lord was reproaching in Peter. Certainly Augustine says that the Lord was displeased with everything Peter did.[189] And it is more likely that the Lord reproached Peter not only because he thought Christ had need of human assistance, but more fundamentally because the Lord wanted all defence to be eliminated from the business of the gospel. Hence, at that time the Lord acted thus to provide in himself an example to his disciples, so that, just as he himself did not want to be defended by arms against the wicked, so too they were to subject the world to the gospel armed only with the sword of the word of the Spirit[190] and depend not on human assistance but on the will of God.

For Erasmus does not say these things to the princes of these times, but rather Luke says them concerning the evangelists of his time. Hence, when they prove that all war is not absolutely condemned here, they clearly are on my side, and the censure of the theologians does not disagree with my proposition, if it is taken as a whole together with the circumstances which I add. In the paraphrase he does not allege what they suspect is there, but perhaps he indicates it in the fragment picked out and wrongly understood. But that cannot be blamed on the faculty but on the reporters or others whose efforts they employed. But how would it have been if I had made Luke speak thus to the apostles and disciples in the early years of the church: 'The fact that the Lord commanded Peter to put his sword away does not deprive you of the right to use force to repel the force of Jews and gentiles rebelling against the gospel, and to plot the death of those who murder you, or otherwise to seek vengeance against those who strip you of possessions and drive you into exile,[191] as long as there is some hope of victory'?

It seems to me that we detract a great deal from the glory of the apostles' and martyrs' victories if we say they did not resist the wicked because they could not do so. And even if they had been able to, the Lord did not wish his church to be founded and spread in this manner. Accordingly, I confess that what the theologians teach is rightly said for these times, although Christians are, alas, only too amenable to such opinions. As for me, when I wrote my paraphrase, I was regarding the origins and emergence of the church, which the Lord did not want to grow through human wealth or nobility or wisdom or human powers, so that the world might recognize

* * * * *

189 *De consensu evangelistarum* 5.17 PL 34 1167
190 Eph 6:17
191 The best known example of this is John the evangelist, who was exiled to Patmos.

that everything was being conducted by the will of God. That was the viewpoint of the early Doctors, who did not want pagans or Jews or heretics to be killed because the Lord would turn the malice of all of them to the benefit of his spouse. For that reason St Ambrose went so far as to write as follows concerning this passage in Luke:[192] 'But the Law does not forbid me to strike back and for that reason, perhaps, he says "it is sufficient" to Peter when he offered two swords, as if it was permitted up to the time of the gospel, so that justice might be learned in the Law, goodness be perfected in the gospel.'[193] This is what he says. But as for me, I not only was required to accommodate my speech to the gentleness of the gospel in my role of paraphraser but I also preferred to do so, considering how far Christian people have fallen away from the energy of the gospel. It is one thing to show how Christians can come as close to the world as possible; it is quite another to attempt to recall human conduct to its absolute archetype.

Topic 6. Matrimony

XIII *The first proposition of Erasmus. Matthew 19[:5]*
A woman who bestows her favours on another man ceases then to be a wife[194] and forfeits the rights of marriage, since she has divided the flesh which God wishes to be one and undivided.

XIV *His second proposition*
Among those committed to the gospel only one cause dissolves a marriage, the violation of marital faithfulness.[195]

XV *The third proposition. Mark 10[:12–13]*
A wife who bestows the favours of her body on another has ceased to be a wife even though she is not repudiated; and a husband who has bestowed the favours of his body on another woman has ceased to be a husband even before any divorce.[196]
The fourth proposition. Mark 10[:8]
Just as fire is not fire if it has no heat, so a marriage is not a marriage

* * * * *

192 Luke 22:38
193 *Expositio Evangelii secundum Lucam* 10.53 PL 15 (1845) 1817B
194 Erasmus briefly defended this proposition in *Divinationes ad notata Bedae* LB IX 461D–E.
195 Matt 19:9
196 In *Supputatio* LB IX 372C–375A, 652E–653C Erasmus explained at length the difficulties inherent in these three propositions and their scriptural underpinnings, arguing that what he said was not at all unorthodox.

unless two become one: one flesh cannot be made from three or four persons.

CENSURE

These four propositions, in so far as they seem to allege that the matrimonial bond is dissolved by adultery, are heretical. For the matrimonial bond is by divine law indissoluble, as is made clear by the Apostle when he wrote to the Corinthians, saying: 'I instruct those who are bound in marriage – not I but the Lord – that a wife not leave her husband, and that, if she does, she remain unmarried or be reconciled to her husband.' And again, 'a woman is bound by the law, as long as her husband is living.' And the same doctrine applies quite fully to men as well as women because the same St Paul says: 'Just as a woman does not have power over her body, but her husband, so too the husband does not have power over his body, but his wife.'[197] Moreover, the indissolubility of marriage is so thorough that it is not dissolved even by heresy (which is spiritual fornication).

ERASMUS' CLARIFICATIONS[198]

XIII, XIV, XV The words 'seem to allege' were rightly added to the censure, for, in fact, when I wrote the propositions I had nothing less in mind than the interpretation they make. I mean that a woman has ceased to be a wife when she has shown herself unworthy of being called a wife and of enjoying the benefits of marriage, just as a son who has been renounced is said not to be a son because he has lost the rights of a son, and we say that a human being who is violently inhuman has put off his humanity. And that is made clear by the words I added: 'forfeits the rights of marriage.' And the rights of marriage are leading a life together, board and lodging, a shared bed, a role in administering the household, sharing all the goods of fortune, seeking the marital debt, enjoying children, etc. If a woman has

* * * * *

197 1 Cor 7:10–11, 39, 4
198 Pelargus sig D1 briefly notes that he accepts Erasmus' (and Chrysostom's) figurative language about not being a husband or wife after committing adultery. But he is afraid that Erasmus seems to imply remarriage even if he does not mention it, since in interpreting 1 Cor 7 Erasmus takes divorce as allowing remarriage. In fact, Erasmus (and not only Erasmus) does so only in interpreting 1 Cor 7:15, the so-called Pauline privilege allowing divorce and remarriage only to a Christian spouse married to a pagan who opposes and insults Christianity. See LB VII 881A–B / CWE 43 96.
In the second edition Erasmus added nothing to this item.

lost these through her own fault, I ask you, how much of a wife is she? But if these words are so offensive, the holy Doctors did not shrink from such language. One of them, Chrysostom, on chapter 7 of the First Epistle to the Corinthians, speaks thus: 'Then again, in that passage a husband after fornication is not a husband. But in this passage even if a woman has . worshipped idols, she does not lose the right to her husband, etc.'[199] See, he says a husband is not a husband if he separates himself from a fruitful marriage. But in fact I cannot solve the puzzle of how Christ, talking to the Jews, means a divorce which separates from the act of marriage while the bond of marriage remains, since they knew of no other sort of divorce except one with the right of remarriage;[200] but I moderate my language in such a way that when I say that a marriage is broken up and a divorce occurs, my words can be understood to mean separation from bed and board, and I do not blend in any language by which I allow a right to remarry. I will not examine the testimonies cited. I have said a good deal about these in the annotation on 1 Corinthians, chapter 7.

Topic 7. Faith

xvi   *His first proposition. James 2*
   Faith which is cold in the absence of charity and does not come forward when circumstances require is not even faith; it is only an empty name of faith.
xvii   *His second proposition. James 2*
   Faith and charity are by nature very closely joined and one cannot be torn away from the other. And a little later: charity is the inseparable companion of faith.[201]
xviii   *His third proposition. In* Elenchus[202]
   It is certain that the one is the inseparable companion of the other.

CENSURE
These three propositions are heretical and contrary to the opinion of Paul and James. For Paul shows that faith can exist without charity

* * * * *

199   *Homiliae in epistolam primam ad Corinthios* 19.3 PG 61 155
200   In Matt 19:9 Jesus says a husband may send his wife away for fornication but that she is still bound to him in marriage.
201   Erasmus defended this proposition briefly in *Supputatio* LB IX 697D–F.
202   In *Divinationes ad notata Bedae* LB IX 479E–480A Erasmus very briefly defended these three propositions.

when he says: 'If I have such complete faith that I can move mountains but do not have charity, I am nothing.'[203] Also James, in the same chapter in which he says faith without works is dead,[204] uses 'faith' simply to designate that quality when it is without works, saying: 'Brothers, what good does it do for someone to say he has faith if he has no works? Can faith save him?'[205] Hence it is obvious that faith without charity or good works should be called faith.

ERASMUS'CLARIFICATIONS[206]

XVI, XVII, XVIII Everyone knows that the word 'faith' has a wide range of meanings. Even the pagans believed many things concerning God, and, according to what James says, 'the devils believe and tremble.'[207] Certainly the philosophers believe Aristotle, and the physicians believe Galen. Faith can be unformed,[208] infused and acquired, sound, weak, and dead; it can be actual and habitual. There can be faith which does not differ from opinion. There is a faith which Christ possessed and a faith which he did not. There is a faith which remains in heaven, and one which does not.[209] There is faith

* * * * *

203 1 Cor 13:2
204 James 2:20
205 James 2:14
206 Pelargus sigs D1v–D3 agrees with Erasmus that by a figure of speech faith without charity is merely a name and has no real existence. But he gives a number of rather fine-spun arguments showing that in fact unformed faith (faith without charity) has real existence and effects. He quotes from Erasmus' commentary on Psalm 1 to the effect that some are stubbornly orthodox in their belief (that is, have faith) but morally corrupt (that is, lack charity). He offers a valid argument against Erasmus' point that Paul was comparing charity with perfect faith, not with unformed faith: perfect faith in the sense in which Erasmus, and Basil and Theophylactus, use it must already have charity so that Paul would end up saying 'if someone has perfect faith (which includes charity) but does not have charity . . .'
     In the second edition Erasmus added long sections to this clarification: he insists that the meanings and questions asked by the scholastics about formed and unformed faith are not relevant to this part of the paraphrase which concerns the presence or absence of perfect faith (that is, justifying faith which has charity). The context makes it clear that in this passage in the paraphrase James' purpose is seen as pastoral, not academic.
207 James 2:19
208 Latin *informis*, that is, 'without a form or life-giving principle,' which for faith is charity
209 On these matters concerning faith (except for 'sound, weak, and dead' and 'opinion,' which are used with their normal meanings) see Thomas Aquinas *Summa theologiae* I-II q 67 a 5; II-II q 4 aa 2, 4; q 6 a 1; III q 7 a 3.

in what one has been told, and faith is sometimes used to mean trust, and
in this sense it differs very little from hope. And there may be other sorts
of faith about which the scholastics dispute with subtlety. But to discuss
these was not relevant to the paraphrase, which follows Paul and the early
interpreters and means the faith which justifies and purifies the heart. Such
faith was not had by those who boasted about their faith in opposition to
St James. This faith is by nature very closely joined to the gift of charity
and is the inseparable companion of charity. Now there is a human charity,
just as there is a human faith. For even the wicked in a certain sense love
God and their neighbour, since even the wicked love their wives, parents,
and children; and every good, whether moral or outward, can be said in a
general sense to be a gift of God. But what do these things have to do with
the evangelical gifts of the Spirit spoken of by Christ, Paul, and the other
apostles?

And so my propositions may be heretical three and four times over, if
you like, if they are given some other meaning, as long as they are Pauline
according to my meaning. Moreover, when I wrote that a dead faith which
does not work through love is not even worthy of the name 'faith,' I was
using a very common figure of speech, such as when we say that a good-
for-nothing and lazy person is no person at all or we call a flat and tasteless
wine no wine at all. Anyone who reads that whole passage in the paraphrase
will understand that that is what I meant. And the apostle James gave me
the occasion to speak in this way when he said that faith which does not
work through love is dead.[210] But the adjective 'dead' removes the substance
behind the name, though the wrongly used name still remains, just as we
say that a person is buried when in fact someone who has no soul is not
a person. Thus charity is, in some fashion, the soul of faith, giving faith
motion and action. Or better yet, charity is the handmaid of faith, and the
energy of faith is the divinely added power to purify the heart. What he
calls dead I call an empty name. And what is empty and dead I say is not
worthy to be called by the name so magnificently preached by Christ and
his apostles.

Finally, the language which immediately follows in the paraphrase
makes this very point when it says: 'For just as a body deprived of its
soul is useless and dead, so too faith, if it lacks an ever active charity, is
dead and ineffective.' Accordingly, the testimonies which they cite from
Scripture, though they are irrelevant to me, are not so solid that they admit
of no shifts in meaning. For Paul does not assert that faith is a special gift

* * * * *

210 James 2:17

of God without charity, but rather he uses a fiction to intensify the praise of charity, just as someone who says 'even if I had a thousand tongues and as many mouths, I could not tell the real story' does not at all mean that there is someone with a thousand tongues and as many mouths,[211] but by means of a fiction he emphasizes the difficulty of explaining. Using the same figure, in my opinion, Paul said 'though I speak with the tongues of men and angels.'[212] For angels do not have tongues but it is imagined that they do in order to signify some extraordinary tongues far more powerful than human ones. By a similar figure he said 'though I am unskilled in speech, but not in knowledge';[213] he was not unskilled in speech, since he spoke more than all tongues put together, but rather by a fiction he granted what was not true.

When Basil the Great cites this place in a certain letter to the people of Neocaesarea, he adds this: 'Not because any of those things mentioned can be found to be without charity but rather because St Paul wished to give testimonies to confirm what he had said, that the precept of charity is infinitely more excellent than the rest.'[214] So says Basil. And Theophylactus indicates that in this passage, in order to emphasize the pre-eminence of charity, Paul compares it with the greatest gift of all, faith, and not simply with faith but with the greatest faith, that is sound and sincere faith, by saying 'complete faith.'[215] Likewise, Chrysostom also noted that Paul did not simply mention faith but universal faith.[216] Even if we granted that some faith is found without charity, who would say that it is sound, sincere, and universal, that is, perfect in every way? Similarly, Thomas Aquinas also interprets complete faith as perfect faith.[217] If such faith is not found without charity, as Basil suggests, it is necessary that we recognize here a fiction and a hyperbole, which Quintilian also mentions among the forms of amplification.[218]

Some think that when the Apostle mentions tongues, prophecy, and knowledge in this passage, he is thinking of gifts freely given, not of gifts

* * * * *

211 Virgil *Aeneid* 6.625
212 1 Cor 13:1
213 2 Cor 11:6
214 *Epistolarum classis* II 204 (ad Neocaesarenses) 1 PG 32 745B
215 *Expositio in epistolam primam ad Corinthios* c 13 v 2 PG 124 725C
216 *Homiliae in epistolam primam ad Corinthios* 32.4 PG 61 269
217 *Expositio in omnes s. Pauli epistolas, in epistolam primam ad Corinthios* c 13 lectio 1
218 Amplification in traditional rhetoric deals not with expansion or amplification but with intensification or magnification. In this connection Quintilian deals with hyperbole in *Institutio oratoria* 8.4.29 and 8.6.68–76.

which make pleasing,[219] since the latter do not exist without charity. But then the amplification would be feeble if he were comparing charity with useless and inferior gifts, just as if a person were to intensify his praise of mankind's excellence by comparing it with a dead lion or camel. And so it is more probable that gifts which make pleasing, as they say, are being compared with gifts of the same kind, just as he does in the same chapter when he says: 'Now there remain faith, hope, and charity, these three, but the greatest of these is charity.'[220] For here he does not mean a dead faith, but a living one. Otherwise, the amplification would be weakened if he were comparing true charity with a dead faith. I know that some take refuge here in some sort of faith (I hardly know what sort) which, if it is firm, performs miracles, even without the access of charity,[221] but I do not see how such faith could be called pre-eminent, sound, and sincere. Indeed Paul extols this same justifying faith in the words 'that I can move mountains,' in order to magnify the excellence of charity. For many have justifying faith, but not a faith great enough to perform miracles. Therefore I think it is safer to follow St Basil in taking it that what is not and cannot be is here imagined to exist for the sake of emphasis.

Whether God could infuse a perfect gift of faith without the gift of charity it is not in the purview of a paraphrase to discuss. It is enough for me that what I have written is consistent with faith which justifies and, wheresoever it is present and is allowed to do so, works through love. But when James says 'if anyone says that he has faith,' he is referring to those who lack true faith and do not work through love; and a person does not have faith just because he says he does. But if a proposition is said to be heretical if it is contrary to canonical Scripture or what is clearly implied in such Scripture, and if it has been made clear that, from the passages

* * * * *

219 'Gifts freely given' (*gratiae gratis datae*) refers to gifts or charisms such as tongues, knowledge, or prophecy given to help others (mentioned by Paul in 1 Cor 12:8 and here compared with charity) whereas 'gifts which make pleasing' (*gratiae gratum facientes*) refers to gifts which unite persons with God by making them pleasing to him (now generally called 'sanctifying grace'). See Thomas Aquinas *Summa theologiae* I-II q 111 a 1; and DTC VI 1558. In his discussion Aquinas considers all the gifts except faith as gifts freely given.
220 1 Cor 13:13
221 Thomas Aquinas in his discussion of 1 Cor 13:1–2 (relying on Matt 7:22) does say that a firm faith without charity can perform miracles, but he also calls the faith to which Paul is comparing charity perfect, and he does not include it among the gifts freely given.

cited, there is no firm implication that faith can be found as a special gift of God without charity, I wonder why these propositions should be called heretical, since we find them in the writings of the most approved Doctors of the church. Now even if it were heretical to deny that faith is a special gift of God if charity is absent, what does that have to do with me, since, as I said, the drift of the language in the paraphrase makes it clear that I am speaking about justifying faith, which cannot be without charity. For what does it contribute to Christian holiness if we believe, according to the teaching of the scholastics, that among the gifts of the Spirit we must include faith without charity? Or to inquire how the gift of faith remains in the fallen angels or in Christians who have lapsed into mortal sin? Or whether what remains deserves to be called a gift of the Spirit of the gospel, since the gifts of the Spirit are fuller after the arrival of Christ than they were under the Law? Or how does it contribute to an understanding of the passage in James to call to mind how the greatest charity exists in Christ without faith, as it does in the angels – a point which is nevertheless disputed among the theologians? Certainly Durandus does not think it ungodly to say that in Christ faith is joined with charity, nor heretical to say that faith remains in heaven.[222]

James is making an effort to repress the pride of those who promise themselves salvation because of a dead faith, since they both lack charity and do not abound in good works. And the opening of this passage in the

* * * * *

222 Durandus of Saint-Pourçain, bishop of Meaux (ca 1275–1334), was a some-what bold and independent scholastic philosopher (*doctor resolutissimus*) who is known as a precursor of the nominalists. I have not been able to find that he attributes faith joined with charity to Christ in his *In Petri Lombardi sententias theologicas commentariorum libri IIII* (Venice 1571; repr Ridgewood, NJ 1964) 2 vols, or in his *Quolibeta Avenionensia tria* ed P.T. Stella (Zurich 1965). But some of his works have apparently not come down to us and some of his extant works are not easy to come by. In fact the scholastics, though they attributed the fullness of infused supernatural virtue to Christ, denied that he had faith because he had the beatific vision from the moment of his conception; see Peter Lombard *Sententiarum libri quatuor* liber 3 dist 26 a 3 PL 192 811; Thomas Aquinas *Summa theologiae* III q 7 a 3; and DTC VIII 1285. Durandus in his commentary on Lombard liber 3 dist 23 q 9 a 13 remarked in passing that Christ did not have faith. But in that commentary he did indeed point out that some have rashly insisted that to assert that souls in heaven can or do have the habit or act of faith is heretical. He denies that this assertion is heretical, arguing at length that there is no scriptural evidence against it (liber 3 dist 31 q 3 aa 1–22).

paraphrase is as follows: 'Should it be thought that the profession of faith alone is in itself sufficient for salvation? But what is faith without charity?' And a little later: 'If charity is lacking, my brothers, I ask you whether the empty name of faith will save a person. A faith which does not work through charity is fruitless; indeed it is faith in name only.' Again, somewhat later: 'Thus a profession of faith will certainly be useless if it consists merely in the name and does not do anything but is inactive, as if it were dead: it should no more be called faith than a dead human body deserves to be called human. What the soul is to the body, charity is to faith; and so if it is taken away, the mere word faith is something dead and ineffective.' And considerably further on: 'You congratulate yourself because you are persuaded that there is one God, whereas the pagans erroneously believe there are innumerable gods. You are right to do so, for in this respect you are superior. But it is vain for you to believe there is a God and only one God unless you believe in such a way as to gain salvation from him. But you will not do this unless you join charity to faith and bear witness by pious deeds both to what you believe and what you love.'[223] From these passages it is obvious that there I am concerned not with the teaching of the scholastics but with rejecting faith without good works in such a way as to get rid of the empty self-confidence of those who boast about their faith, though they do not have a true and lively faith.

I do not deny that there was some sort of faith in those who said 'in your name we have cast out demons.'[224] I do not deny that Caiphas had some sort of gift of faith when he said 'it is expedient for you that one person should die for the people.'[225] I also grant that Christians who lead very wicked lives can have some faith, though I hardly think that they truly believe everything that is necessary for salvation. But I was dealing with something else in the paraphrase. I think that those who performed miracles at that time were not completely devoid of charity. But what sort of gift of prophecy was it for Caiphas to say words which he himself did not understand? The apostles had a far different kind of prophecy. Furthermore, in Christians whose whole lives savour of the world either faith is extinguished or it is extremely weak and does not purify but rather makes their damnation more heavy. But if it is not the meaning but the words

* * * * *

223 LB VII 1127E–1128D / CWE 44 150–1
224 Luke 10:17
225 John 18:14

which give offence, why are they not offended by the words of St Gregory who interprets the banquet of the children of Job as the interaction of all gifts,[226] just as Plato said that all the moral virtues are connected with one another?[227] But I would handle these matters in such a way as to be prepared to yield to a better opinion. Indeed I do not assert what I mean but I inquire out of a desire to learn.

XIX *Erasmus' fourth proposition. John 3*
   Faith alone purifies the heart and renders it fit to believe the hidden teachings of the heavenly philosophy.[228]
XX *His fifth proposition. John 8*
   Believing is the only way to immortality.[229]
XXI *His sixth proposition. Luke 24*
   What does Christ demand from his followers except faith?[230]

CENSURE
Though faith is required to gain immortal beatitude and purify the heart, as Holy Scripture teaches, nevertheless it does not teach that faith alone is required to do this, but rather the opposite. Hence the apostle James says: 'You see that a person is justified because of works, not merely faith.'[231] And Paul says: 'For not the hearers of the Law are just in the eyes of the Lord but the doers of the Law are justified.'[232] Wherefore propositions stated with this sort of exclusion do not conform to Scripture, which everywhere preaches good works. And the same propositions are apt to be a stumbling block to little ones, as if (for example) good works were not necessary to the faithful but faith alone sufficed for salvation.

* * * * *

226 *Moralia* 1 32.44–5, 33.46 PL 75 547A–548A
227 *Republic* 4.15–17.440A–444A. Erasmus' argument seems weak here since the Paris theologians are clearly offended not merely by Erasmus' words but by his meaning; and it is the meaning and not merely the words of Gregory and Plato that the virtues cannot subsist without one another (as Erasmus insists that faith and charity must coexist).
228 Erasmus defended this proposition in *Elenchus in censuras Bedae* LB IX 501A–B and in *Supputatio* LB IX 630F–631B.
229 In *Divinationes ad notata Bedae* LB IX 482E–483A Erasmus defended this proposition very briefly.
230 Erasmus defends this proposition in *Supputatio* LB IX 620D–621E.
231 James 2:24
232 Rom 2:13

ERASMUS' CLARIFICATIONS[233]

XIX, XX, XXI In my paraphrases I treat hardly any point more often or more
carefully than that a profession of faith is not sufficient unless there is
added to it a life worthy of that profession. This is sufficiently clear in the
second chapter of James. Frequently I make the same point also in other
writings of mine so that this suspicion can by no means be made to stick
to me, as if I mean that after baptism good works are not necessary for
adults. In fact the propositions are presented in such a truncated fashion
that they might perhaps constitute a stumbling block for the weak, but
if they are read in the context of the paraphrase, I do not see how they
could offend anyone. For in the third chapter of John the whole drift of
the language makes it clear that I am speaking there about those who are
making the transition from paganism or Judaism to the grace of the gospel.
I will quote the very words of the paraphrase, which make it clear that I
am not talking about salvation as a whole but about the access to salvation:
'Nevertheless,' says the paraphrase, 'at that time, which was given over to
mercy, God did not send his Son to condemn the world for its sins but
rather by his death to confer on the world through faith the free gift of
salvation. And lest anyone perishing of his own free will should have a
pretext for his wickedness, easy access to salvation was given to everyone:
there is no demand for satisfaction for previous crimes, for the observance
of the Law, or for circumcision. Anyone who only believes in him is safe
from condemnation, since he has embraced what bestows eternal salvation
on everyone, however weighed down by the burden of sin.'[234] Here you
have the unique way to salvation. And immediately following that: 'if only
after professing the gospel he abstains from the crimes of his former life
and strives to achieve perfect piety according to the teaching of him whose
name he professes.'[235] It is treated so in the paraphrase. Do these seem
like the words of someone who scorns works after baptism? Or rather of

* * * * *

233 Pelargus (sigs D3–D3v) here sides entirely with Erasmus, noting that if the
context is taken into account Erasmus' propositions are quite unobjection-
able.
    In the second edition Erasmus adds long sections giving the context and the
basic drift of the paraphrase in the light of other scriptural texts. He also de-
votes considerable attention to showing that the word 'alone' is not totally exclusive. Here he includes an example from Thomas Aquinas' eucharistic hymn;
see n254 below. He also adds a citation from Chrysostom.
234 Erasmus quoted this passage in *Supputatio* LB IX 630B–D and briefly defended
it.
235 LB VII 522D–E / CWE 46 49

someone who invites gentile and Jew alike to the grace of the gospel in accord with a Catholic meaning? That is what Paul so often does with such ardour in his Epistles, deterring people from circumcision and trusting in the work of the Law, making both Jews and gentiles equal in the grace of faith by which the hearts of those who believe are freely purified.[236] In fact, this proposition is wrongly cited as if from John 3, when it is actually in chapter 4.[237] This error will be blamed on the copyist or printer, but it was for such censors to correct by their vigilance what was flawed by the workman's negligence.

But what is the paraphrase concerned with at that point? Excluding good works after baptism? Far from it. Rather it is showing that a person is incapable of perceiving the teaching of the gospel unless he has been purged of the vice of unbelief. Explaining the words of the Lord to the Samaritan woman, 'Woman, believe me, an hour is coming,'[238] the paraphrase speaks as follows: 'But when he is about to reveal this mystery of evangelical holiness, he speaks first of faith, without which no one is fit to hear the teaching of the gospel nor fit to worship according to the religion of the gospel. For faith alone purifies the heart and renders it fit to believe the hidden teachings of the heavenly philosophy. "Woman," he says, "have faith in me, etc."'[239] That is what the paraphrase says. Where is there any mention of the works of those baptized which is dragged in here? Is what the paraphrase says any different from what the prophet says: 'unless you believe you will not understand'?[240] Or again, from what Paul says in Hebrews 11: 'To approach God one has to believe'?[241] Furthermore, the paraphrase on John 8 says as follows: 'Unless you come to your senses, the founder of your race, Abraham, will do you no good, nor will Moses, or the priests or the Pharisees, or God the Father, though you may boast of these words. Be quite certain of this: if someone obeys my words, as I have often said, he will not see death forever. Believing alone is the way to immortality, etc.'[242] And I said 'way,' meaning the access to salvation and its threshold, as it

* * * * *

236 For example, Rom 3:29–20; 1 Cor 12:13
237 Erasmus is quite correct in pointing out this error; see LB VII 528F / CWE 46 57.
238 John 4:21
239 LB VII 528F / CWE 46 57–8
240 This seems to be a blending of Isa 6:9–10 (influenced by Matt 13:14–15) and Isa 7:9. Augustine mentiones 'nisi credideritis, non intelligebitis' as a variant of the Vulgate reading 'nisi credideritis, non permanebitis' in *De doctrina christiana* 2.12 PL 34 43.
241 Heb 11:6
242 LB VII 572F–573A

were,[243] calling the gentiles away from trusting in philosophy and the Jews
from trusting in ceremonies. In fact, faith opens up an entrance to salvation
in such a way that it also plays a principal role in leading someone onward.
Again, at Luke 24 it is clear that I am speaking about the ceremonies of
the Jews, which Christ does not demand of us when we convert to the
grace of the gospel, but rather he requires faith. These are the words of
the paraphrase: 'What does Christ demand from his followers except faith?
And therefore he calls his church, which knows nothing of the works of
the Law, a faithful city, relying totally on him alone. When you hear that
she must be redeemed in a court of law, you see that confidence in the
ceremonies of the Law is taken away.'[244] This is what the paraphrase says,
clearly excluding the ceremonies of the Jews, not works of charity.

There remain some scruples about the word 'alone,' for this exclusive
word offends some. But it is not always exclusive but frequently indicates
pre-eminence, as do 'one and only,' 'uniquely,' and 'singularly.' As, for instance, if one were to say about Plutarch, 'he is the one and only writer
who mingles the beautiful with the useful,' he does not mean that Plutarch
is the only one who does so, but that he does so in an outstanding way.
Likewise, when we say 'Peter loves John uniquely,' or 'he loves him singularly,' we do not at all mean that Peter loves no one else, but that he
loves John in an extraordinary way. Similarly, when Terence says 'he alone
is a friend to his friend,' he indicates that he is a remarkable friend. Furthermore, when Jerome writes to Heliodorus that 'this kind of piety stands
alone, to be cruel in these circumstances,'[245] he by no means excludes other
acts of piety, but he understands that it was an act of a certain extraordinary
piety to overcome one's affection for his parents for the sake of the gospel.
So too when the Apostle calls God alone wise and immortal[246] and Christ
calls God alone good,[247] they do not mean that no man is wise or that angels are mortal or that no one is good, but that these qualities apply to God
pre-eminently. Again, when the Law says 'you shall worship the Lord your
God and shall serve him alone,'[248] it does not, I think, exclude the worship
and cult of the saints but rather attributes to God the best that is in them.
Thus when David says 'one thing I asked for from the Lord, this I will seek

* * * * *

243 In *Elenchus in censuras Bedae* LB IX 501C–D and in *Supputatio* LB IX 633C–D
    Erasmus had made this point.
244 LB VII 473A / CWE 48 243
245 *Epistolae* 14.2 PL 22 348
246 Rom 16:27; 1 Tim 6:16
247 Mark 10:18; Luke 18:19
248 Matt 4:10 and Luke 4:8, citing Deut 6:13

to have, that I may dwell in the house of the Lord, etc,'[249] he does not exclude other petitions (and he himself makes many others) but he said 'one thing' because it is the chief thing. A quite similar rationale applies to 'except,' as when we say 'he thirsts after nothing except gold,' it means that he seeks for gold more than other things. But even though such an excuse should do me no good, certainly an exclusion ought to be made according to the subject at hand, as when John speaks of the Father, saying 'that they may know that you alone are the true God,'[250] he does not exclude the Son and the Holy Spirit but rather the false gods of the gentiles. Again, in chapter 9 of Luke, 'Jesus was found to be alone.'[251] How could he be alone since three of the disciples were present? But the two who spoke with him before are the ones excluded.[252] Once again, in the same chapter, 'when he was praying alone the disciples were also with him.'[253] The word 'alone' does not exclude the disciples but the rest of the crowd which was usually present. Similarly, when the church sings 'faith alone suffices' concerning the Eucharist in the sequence by St Thomas, nothing is excluded but human reason and the experience of the senses.[254] Again, when the Lord says to the ruler of the synagogue in chapter 5[:36] of Mark 'do not be afraid but only believe,' he does not exclude the other virtues but makes it known that for the performance of miracles faith is especially required. Likewise, when my paraphrase says that faith alone is required of those who approach the gospel, it does not exclude good works, which faith generates in those who have been purified, but rather philosophy or the works of the Law which preceded baptism.

And in this sentence it makes no difference whether you add or omit 'alone.' For when Paul says in Ephesians 2[:8] 'you are saved by grace,' he

* * * * *

249 Ps 26:4
250 John 17:3
251 Luke 9:36
252 That is, Moses and Elijah
253 Luke 9:18
254 The phrase *sola fides sufficit* 'faith alone suffices' comes from the sequence *Pange lingua* 'Praise, my tongue' composed by Thomas Aquinas at the request of Pope Urban IV for the feast of Corpus Christi, which he instituted in 1264. Erasmus has adapted the phrase *sensuum experientia* 'the experience of the senses' from the hymn, where the clause preceding 'faith alone suffices' is *si sensus deficit, ad firmandum cor sincerum* 'if sense perception fails, [faith alone suffices] to strengthen the well-disposed heart,' and three lines later we have the sentence: *Praestet fides supplementum sensuum defectui* 'Let faith provide help where the senses fail.' See Connelly 116–21.

excludes the works of the Law quite as much as if he had said 'by grace alone, or by faith alone, and not from works.' In the third chapter of Titus he says this more explicitly: 'not from the works of justice which we have done but according to his mercy he has saved us.'[255] And in Romans 11: 'And if from works, it is not by grace.'[256] If such words do not exclude works of charity after baptism, how shameless it is to make false accusations against my paraphrase, especially since in innumerable places it requires good works from those who profess to be Christians. And the books of orthodox writers are full of such sayings. Chrysostom's fourth sermon against the Jews: 'What is this? "I announced justice in the great church."[257] He did not say "I gave" but "I announced." Not from good deeds, not from labours, not from recompense, but from grace alone he justified our race.'[258] If such words by orthodox writers do not exclude good works after baptism, why is my paraphrase falsely accused?

And I think that no one is offended because I said 'way' to mean 'access,' since orthodox Doctors call faith the threshold of salvation. And faith is access in such a way that it continually follows the person who goes forward and plays a principal role in pious deeds. And so where is the danger of a stumbling block, and where is the disagreement with Scripture? If there is any inconvenience, blame it on the snappers-up of snippets. If they did not read either my paraphrase or my frequent responses concerning this passage, where is their theological dignity? If they read them and pretend they have not, where is their Christian sincerity? What thanks, then, do we owe to persons who foist off such shreds and patches on the most sacred faculty?

Topic 8. Certain wishes regarding the faith

XXII *Erasmus' first proposition. In the epistle prefaced to 1 Corinthians*
Would that Paul had at least revealed by whom, at what time, with what worship, what liturgy, what words that mystical bread and that sacrosanct cup of the Lord's blood were customarily consecrated.[259]

* * * * *

255 Titus 3:5
256 Erasmus paraphrases Rom 11:6.
257 Ps 39:10
258 *Adversus Iudaeos* 7.3 PG 48 919. Either Erasmus or the printer erred in giving '4' rather than '7' as the number of the sermon.
259 Erasmus defended this proposition in *Divinationes ad notata Bedae* LB IX 472C–E, in *Elenchus in censuras Bedae* LB IX 506B–C, and in *Supputatio* LB IX 676D–677C.

CENSURE

This wish is inquisitive and futile and unholy if it proceeds from the thought that many things handed down vocally from Christ through the apostles have less credibility than what is expressed in Scripture. For what it was expedient for Scripture to determine for the salvation of the faithful it has sufficiently determined. And, on the authority of Dionysius,[260] Basil, and Augustine, what has come down to us from Christ through the tradition of the apostles concerning the sacraments and many other things should not be held to have less authority than what is defined by Holy Scripture. For the Apostle teaches that what the apostles established must be retained, not only what is dug up out of the Scriptures but also what was handed down in bare words by the apostles.[261] But other matters were more conveniently and fittingly left to the disposition of the church, so that she can define and determine them as is demanded by the dignity of such great sacraments and the advancement of the church.

XXIII *His second proposition. In the epistle prefaced to 1 Corinthians*
Would that Paul had thrown somewhat more light on how souls exist separated from their bodies, whether they enjoy the glory of immortality, whether the souls of the wicked are already being tortured now, whether our prayers or other good deeds benefit them, whether they are immediately freed from suffering by the pope's indulgence, since I see that many are wavering or at least disputing about these points. That would have been superfluous if Paul had defined them clearly.[262]

CENSURE

This wish is both superfluous and dangerous. For many it could be an occasion of scandal, as if what is stated there is not supported by the adequate testimony of Scripture; but in fact it is all sufficiently defined by scriptural pronouncements, except the last clause about in-

* * * * *

260 Pseudo-Dionysius the Areopagite was thought to be the judge converted by Paul mentioned in Acts 17:34. His extensive theological writings, which have a mystical cast, date from about the fifth century and were accepted as genuine until about the time of Valla and Erasmus, who cast doubt upon their authenticity.
261 2 Thess 2:15
262 Erasmus defended this proposition in *Divinationes ad notata Bedae* LB IX 473C–D.

dulgences. For when Christ says to the good thief 'this day you will be with me in paradise,'[263] he shows that after this life the souls of the just reign in happiness with God. Paul also shows it, thinking that to die is gain, and hence desiring to be dissolved and be with Christ.[264] Moreover, since the guardian angels of mankind before the day of judgment always look upon the face of the Father, who is in heaven, by the same rationale the souls of the godly also see it, the handwriting of sin having been long since removed by the death of Christ.[265] Similarly, Scripture teaches that the souls of the wicked are assigned to the punishments of hell, since blessed Job says: 'They spend their days in wealth and in a moment they go down to hell.'[266] And concerning those who have followed perverse desires, St Judas Thaddaeus writes that they are undergoing the punishment of eternal fire.[267] Likewise St Luke writes that the rich glutton was buried in hell when he died.[268] But those who depart from this light in the friendship of God but are not fully purged of the dross of sin are helped by the prayers of the living, as Christ shows in the gospel when he urges the living to make friends with the Mammon of iniquity who will receive them into their eternal mansions when they fail.[269] Moreover, they are members of the body of Christ; hence it is right that they should be aided by the assistance of the other members of the same body. For by an ingrained natural instinct, when one member suffers, the other members suffer sympathetically. Also the royal prophet, speaking in the person of those acceptable to God, says: 'I share with all those who fear you and keep your commandments.'[270] Therefore it is clear that the prayers and other good deeds of the living help them a great deal.

But that is not a reason to assert that they are always immediately freed from punishment through indulgences. The popes do not allege this in their bulls, and it does not follow from the force of such papal bulls if they are rightly understood. For since power is given to the church not to destroy but to edify,[271] all who owe any pain whatever,

* * * * *

263 Luke 23:43
264 Phil 1:23
265 Col 2:14
266 Job 21:13
267 Jude 1:7
268 Luke 16:22
269 Luke 16:9
270 Ps 118:63
271 2 Cor 10:8

for any reason whatever, are not immediately released through such indulgences from the pain they owe, even though they are in a state of charity. Hence no mortal is certain how much satisfaction is made to God by any indulgences whatever for punishment owed by sinners. Nevertheless, even though the value of indulgences is not known to the faithful with certainty, that is no reason to hold them in contempt. They have been approved by sacred councils, popes, and the customary usage of the universal church, and for that reason it must be held with no doubt at all that they do good, since through them an abundant harvest of virtue and a large gain of satisfaction accrue to Christians.

Hence this proposition, which unfittingly sets a precedent for harmful doubts in the faith of wavering souls, constitutes a stumbling block for the unlearned and the weak, making them have doubts about points which must be held with firm faith, teachings about which it is not only pointless to doubt and to dispute about those doubts, but also not permissible. But if anyone has doubts about these points, when they come they ought not to be instructed with new texts of Scripture, but rather such downright ungodly temerity should be suppressed with legitimate punishments. Nevertheless, disputation on these points to elucidate the truth, undertaken without any hesitation and by those who have a duty to do so, is not temerarious or illicit, but pious and expedient, so that they may be ready according to Scripture, as pastors and teachers, to give an account of the faith and hope that is in them and to refute those who contradict them.[272]

ERASMUS' CLARIFICATION

XXII, XXIII Let my wish be as inquisitive and futile as you like, as long as it is godly. For in that passage I am not berating Holy Scripture as if it did not sufficiently hand down what is necessary for our salvation. Far be such impiety from me! But I want us to be more prepared against those who doubt and dissent about such matters. Since this wish springs from a godly desire, how can it be called ungodly? Sometimes charity wishes for something which cannot be done, as when Moses asks to be deleted from the book of life[273] or Paul wishes to be made anathema for the sake of his brothers.[274] Commenting in the Epistle to Philemon, Chrysostom, out of love for Paul, would long for even the smallest details about him in his

* * * * *

272 1 Pet 3:15
273 Exod 32:32
274 Rom 9:3

writings.[275] And yet what is sufficient for salvation was recorded by Paul. Chrysostom is not said for that reason to be accusing Paul; he is simply expressing a godly mental desire. But if it is ungodly, I confess that I am frequently in the grips of such a desire, though I esteem the inviolable authority of Scripture not a whit the less for that. For example, when I read in Matthew that at the death of the Lord the bodies of many holy persons rose and that after his resurrection they came into the holy city and appeared to many,[276] such a thought teases my mind. I wish it were expressly said whether they came to life before the resurrection of the Lord, and then who they were, and to whom they appeared, not because it pertains to the necessity of salvation, but because it would give pious delight to the mind.

Now there are in the mysterious writings not a few places where interpreters are marvellously tormented and do not find a way out. I think that the thought must sometimes have also come into their minds that a little more light would be desirable. For example, Augustine labours and toils and leaves no stone unturned[277] to unravel the puzzle about the blasphemy against the Spirit,[278] but even so he does not set the hearer's mind completely at rest. Such a desire does not spring from a contempt for Scripture but from a love of knowing things worth knowing. Finally I do not wish such things for my own sake, since the decision of the church is enough for me, but to use them against contentious debaters. For us a single text in Scripture is fully persuasive, but we delight in seeking out many scriptural proof texts to use against contentious persons.

Now, even though we grant that what the apostles handed down orally is to be accepted as having equal authority with what is expressed in

* * * * *

275 In his *In epistolam ad Philemonem commentarius*, argumentum PG 62 702–3 Chrysostom answers the objection that Paul's defence of one slave (and a convicted felon at that) is hardly worthy of being included among his Epistles by saying that such details are salutary and that he wishes that someone had provided us with even the smallest everyday details about the apostles because they would be morally uplifting; though Chrysostom simply refers to 'someone,' not to Paul himself, this must be the passage Erasmus has in mind. I am grateful to Professor Margaret M. Mitchell of the University of Chicago for helping me to unravel what Erasmus (and Chrysostom) meant at this point.

276 Matt 27:53

277 *Adagia* I iv 30

278 Sermo 71 *De verbis Evangelii Matthaei* cap XII 32 '... de blasphemia in Spiritum sanctum' PL 38 445–67; and *Expositio inchoata epistolae ad Romanos* 1.14–23 PL 35 2097–2105. Erasmus discussed this difficulty at length in *Divinationes ad notata Bedae* LB IX 453E–455E and briefly in *Supputatio* LB IX 549F–550A.

Holy Scripture, nevertheless the contentious will be able to indulge in evasions, denying that such points were handed down by the apostles, saying that they were either invented more recently or have crept into the church through the usage of the common people. Certainly this bolt-hole would have been blocked up for such disputers if Paul had discussed such matters more fully and explicitly. For I think that it is clear from very many of my books that I myself have no doubts about such matters. But there are many points about which not only contentious persons once had doubts but also those whose learning was matched by their piety. For example, Augustine had doubts about purgatory for a long time,[279] and he was not the only one. Even today there is no satisfactory agreement about the words our Lord used in consecration. And the words used by the apostles to consecrate cannot be perceived with sufficient clarity in Holy Scripture or the books of the ancient Doctors – so much so that we do not even know the words of consecration used by Basil, Chrysostom, or Augustine. Liturgies by the first two are extant, but they differ from one another.[280] And in a certain epistle Augustine briefly describes the substance of the mass, but among the prayers used to bless, that is consecrate, what is on the altar (for that is how he puts it) he names as the principal one the Lord's Prayer, which we do not say until after the consecration of the Lord's body and blood.[281] At this point if we say that what the apostles handed down is what is now observed in the Roman church, we certainly and willingly agree. But we barely have enough to shut the mouths of the inquisitive, as we would have if it were more clearly expressed in Holy Scripture.

Augustine, assailing some enemies on the subject of infant baptism, does not dare to assert that this practice comes down from the apostles, but he says it seems likely because it is unknown who was the originator of this precedent.[282] Moreover, churches follow different procedures. For the

* * * * *

279 In his earlier works Augustine had some hesitations and doubts about the significance of prayer for the dead and the condition of souls between death and the last judgment but he came to more definite conclusions in his later works, particularly after 413. On the development of his thought about purgatory see Joseph Ntedika L'évolution de la doctrine du purgatoire chez saint Augustin (Paris 1966); and Jacques Le Goff The Birth of Purgatory trans Arthur Goldhammer (Chicago 1984) 61–85.
280 Two forms of the liturgy of Basil may be found in PG 31 1629–46 and 1647–78. Chrysostom's liturgy may be found in PG 63 901–28.
281 Epistolae 139 2.16 PL 33 636
282 Sermo 294 17–18 PL 38 1346; Epistolae 166 8.23–4 PL 33 730–1; De Genesi ad litteram 10 22.38 PL 34 426

Roman and Greek churches differ on many points, and they once differed on matters of no small moment, such as the material elements of the Eucharist and its reception,[283] and concerning the procession of the Holy Spirit.[284] What about the fact that one and the same church differs from itself? For example, at one time the western church, and (as far as we can tell) the eastern church as well, considered it necessary to give baptized infants the body and blood of the Lord. If they drew this from Scripture, according to the interpretation of Augustine, why is it now omitted? And if it was drawn from the tradition of the apostles, it should be observed just as if it were expressed in Scripture. But in our day it has been totally eliminated, so much so that anyone who should now extend the body of the Lord to infants would be in danger of heresy.[285]

Now as for me, I have always been fully persuaded that the souls of the godly when separated from their bodies reign with Christ. This is clear from hundreds of places in my writings. But a contentious person will say that the words of Christ are wrapped in a cloud of allegory and will have doubts about what Christ there calls paradise. For the soul of Christ is believed to have descended into hell, and then forty days later he ascended into heaven. Perhaps by paradise he meant rest, which is what the gospel means by the bosom of Abraham.[286] What Paul says is clearer:

* * * * *

283 Throughout the first millennium in the churches of the West and the East there was no uniformity about whether the bread of the Eucharist was leavened or unleavened, but it began to become an issue in the charges and counter-charges that led up to the great schism of 1054, after which the Latin church tended to prefer unleavened bread, the Greek church leavened bread. See DTC I 2653–64.

284 The Nicaean-Constantinopolitan Creed (AD 325–81) states that the Holy Spirit proceeds from the Father; but in the West, beginning in Spain in the sixth century, 'and from the Son' ('filioque') was added. The change, which has very important trinitarian consequences, caused little trouble until the ninth century. When it was officially accepted by Rome in the eleventh century it became part of the strife that ended in the great schism between the Latin and Greek churches in 1054. See *Spirit of God, Spirit of Christ: Ecumenical Reflections on the Filioque Controversy* (London and Geneva 1981) 3–15; and Micael Azkoul 'Saint Photios and the Filioque' in St Photios *On the Mystagogy of the Holy Spirit* trans Holy Transfiguration Monastery (Astoria, NY 1983) 3–27.

285 From the early centuries of the church the Eucharist was immediately administered to those baptized, whether adults or infants, but from about 1200 the practice began to be discontinued until by Erasmus' time it had almost disappeared in the West (though it continued in the East). It was prohibited by the Council of Trent. See Leona Brockett *The Theology of Baptism* (Notre Dame, Ind. [1972]) 60–2.

286 Luke 16:23

'I long to be dissolved and to be with Christ.'[287] Even when he was alive
he was with Christ, but he longed for an end to his troubles and he hoped
for secure rest in return for his laborious struggle. No one doubts that the
angels contemplate the face of the Father. But it is a weak inference from
this that the same is granted to souls. They will take exception to the words
of Job, noting that formerly the souls of the godly also descended into hell
and that by 'descending into hell' Scripture means 'to die,' as in the canticle
of Ezekiel: 'I will go to the gates of hell.'[288] And in Genesis 42 the patriarch
Jacob says 'with sorrow you will lead my grey hairs to hell.'[289] They will
take exception to the words of Jude (though they are sufficiently clear) by
saying that 'undergoing' (*sustinentes*) is used to mean 'expecting,' for it is
not ἀνέχουσαι but ὑπέχουσαι. In Psalm 32, 'my soul will bear up under the
Lord' (*anima nostra sustinet Dominum*),[290] Jerome translates 'has waited for'
instead of 'will bear up.' Also in Mark 14[:34], 'bear up here and keep
watch' (*sustinete hic et vigilate*), the Greek is μείνατε, that is, 'stay' or 'wait
for.' As for the rich glutton, they will be able to evade it by saying it is a
parable, shamelessly (it is true) but with some plausibility, especially since
souls have no tongues and cannot be refreshed with water; and the soul
of Lazarus does not have a finger nor that of Abraham a bosom. Hence
fire can seem to mean remorse of conscience, cooling, the hope of freedom.
As for gaining friends from the Mammon of iniquity, it can refer to those
who are alive, who receive those who have deserved well of them into their
eternal mansions in the sense that in return for temporal goods they beg
and obtain for them eternal life by their prayers. They will take exception
to the words of the psalmist, claiming that the words of the prophet refer
to the living, and that the passage does not concern the sharing of merits
but companionship in afflictions. Certainly I do not see how what follows,
'of those keeping your commandments,' can be in any way applied to souls
stripped of their bodies. Here we have a companionship in affliction; in the
future life there will be a companionship in joy. This is the way the passage
is interpreted by the orthodox Fathers.[291]

I have not looked into what the bulls about indulgences allege, but
there is a widespread rumour that in some of them the pope gives precepts

* * * * *

287 Phil 1:23
288 Isa 13:10
289 Gen 42:38, 44:29
290 Ps 32:20
291 The scriptural text is Ps 118:63, which had been cited by the theologians. See
    Ambrose *In psalmum David* CXVIII *expositio* 8.53–4 PL 15 (1845) 1317A–D; and
    Augustine *Enarrationes in psalmos*, CXVIII 16.6 PL 37 1546–7.

to the angels of God.[292] What the pardoners usually promise is sufficiently well known.[293] No one doubts that the pope and also individual bishops can relax to some degree satisfactions imposed by men, but only for grave reasons and even then very sparingly, lest the force of ecclesiastical discipline be dissipated. But whether such power extends all the way to purgatory is doubted by not a few, who are also godly men. But whether such indulgences have been approved by sacred councils is not yet sufficiently clear. To me it seems improbable. And so I do not have an adequate understanding of what they mean when they say 'through them a large gain of satisfaction accrues to Christians,' since we see that for the most part such pardons remit legitimate satisfactions. For example, those who have grown rich by pillage and sacrilege are released from the burden of restitution, even if they despoiled churches, leaving no room for the pretext 'it is not clear to whom I should make restitution.' But if indulgences have the value of urging people to go to confession, or to reform their lives, or to do some pious work such as building a basilica or hospital, I do not see what the pope can offer except encouragement, unless he relaxes some right he holds such as excommunication, irregularity,[294] reserved cases, or such like, though in fact on these points theologians moderate their language to such a degree as to leave our minds in suspense.

Concerning the above matters, however, I have never had any doubts, nor do I think a godly person ought to have any. And I do not mention them as doubtful but as points to be fully supported. The conjunction 'whether' (*an*) in my preface indicates no more doubt than the word 'whether' (*utrum*) in the discussions of the theologians.[295] For it refers not to the matter itself

* * * * *

292 Erasmus may be referring to an indulgence originally attached to the Angelus prayer by John XXII in 1327 and allegedly (hence 'rumour') raised to a plenary indulgence by Adrian VI in 1524; see Henry Lea *A History of Auricular Confession and Indulgences in the Latin Church* 3 vols (1896; repr New York 1968) III 443–4. Or perhaps some plenary papal indulgence begged Michael as psychopomp to lead the freed souls to heaven. In iconography angels lead the souls out of purgatory into heaven; see Jacques Le Goff *The Birth of Purgatory* trans Arthur Goldhammer (Chicago 1984) 318.
293 Chaucer's pardoner gives a vivid picture of how such charlatans performed.
294 Irregularities are canonical impediments which (unless dispensed) permanently bar a man from entering the clerical state or forbid the exercise of the orders already received. They spring either from defects or from certain crimes. For ordination Erasmus himself required a dispensation from the irregularity of illegitimacy.
295 In their *summae theologiae* or commentaries on Peter Lombard's *Sentences* scholastic theologians answer questions beginning 'whether ...' but they are not expressing doubt. For example, when Thomas Aquinas asks 'whether faith

but to the minds of those considering the doubt. But if the theologians rightly dispute without giving offence, what offence do I give by wishing there were irrefutable scriptural authority against the inquisitive and the unmanageable? And that I wish for this light to use it against the contentious is clear from my words: 'because,' I say, 'I perceive that many are wavering or at least disputing about these points. That would have been superfluous if Paul had defined them clearly.' But when they say that those who have doubts about these points are not to be instructed with new texts from Scripture but should be suppressed with legitimate punishments, though that may be quite just, certainly it would be more merciful also to reclaim them from their error by sound teaching (if that can be done) and to lead them back to the right path. After all, they themselves grant that Doctors dispute in the schools so as to be prepared according to Scripture to give an account of the faith that is in them and to refute those who contradict them, and Peter added very fittingly 'with gentleness and respect.'[296] Moreover, for theologians to teach such things from Holy Scripture they consider quite fitting, but it is superfluous for me to consider points about which I have never had any doubts.

Topic 9. The Old Law

XXIV *Erasmus' first proposition. Mark 1*
Since the Law struck terror into the heart rather than love, after the Law had taught people that they were subject to sin, and that they could not refrain from it, and they likewise knew that no one could escape the judgment of God, who took strict revenge, what was there left except to tremble, shake, and despair?
'And who can love someone of whom he is in terror?'[297]

CENSURE
This proposition, alleging that the people of the Old Law could not avoid sin and were led by the knowledge of the Law more toward desperation than toward love, is an affront to the Law and to the Law-giver, God. For the Lord handed down the Law not so that it should

* * * * *

is a virtue' *Summa theologiae* II-II q 4 a 5, he has no doubt that it is; he is merely introducing a topic for analysis and discussion, together with some difficulties to be solved.
296 1 Pet 3:16
297 Erasmus defended this proposition briefly in *Supputatio* LB IX 637D–638A.

cause people to perish but rather so that they should be justified. Accordingly the Apostle says, 'indeed the Law is holy and the commandment just.' And Leviticus has the text 'keep my laws and judgments; if mankind does so it will live in them.'[298] For God did not oblige mankind by the Law of Moses to do what is impossible, since he is not able to be unjust.

ERASMUS' CLARIFICATION

XXIV To perpetrate an affront to the sacred Law and to God the Lawgiver is something wicked men do. Far be such a desire from me! Whenever Paul compares the Old Law with the gospel, he does not shrink from similar kinds of language, nor do the holy Doctors who interpret the Pauline Epistles. After I interpret them suitably, with no affront to God and the Law handed down by God, my language certainly could be accepted in the same spirit in which I said it. For when he says, 'the Law was given by Moses, but grace came from Jesus Christ,'[299] does he not seem to attribute terror to the Law without grace? And in Galatians 3, when he calls the Law a tutor preparing for Christ, does he not attribute terror to it without charity? So too when he says in the same place, 'whoever is coming from the works of the Law is under a curse.' Likewise in Galatians 3, 'Because no one is justified by the Law in the eyes of God, it is evident that the just man lives by faith, but the Law is not by faith.' Again, in the same place: 'For if the Law was given as something which could give life, righteousness would truly come from the Law, but Scripture has enclosed everything under sin, so that by faith in Jesus Christ the promise would be given to those who believe.'[300] And in Romans 3[:20]: 'Because all flesh is not justified by the works of the Law in the eyes of God, for through the Law comes knowledge of sin.' And in the next chapter he says 'the Law produces anger.'[301] Moreover, 1 Corinthians, chapter 15[:56] calls the Law the power of sin. Likewise 2 Corinthians 3[:9] calls the Law the ministration of condemnation; it calls the gospel the ministration of justice. Again, in Romans 7: 'When we were in the flesh,' he says, 'the passions of sins, which come through the Law, worked in our members to bring forth fruit for death, but now we are freed from the Law of death by which we were held.' And a little later: 'But taking occasion

* * * * *

298 Rom 7:12; Lev 18:5
299 John 1:17. Erasmus inserts this text from John in a series derived from Paul.
300 Gal 3:24–5, 10, 11–12, 21–2
301 Rom 4:15

through the commandment, sin worked all manner of concupiscence. For without the Law sin was dead, etc. But when the commandment came, sin revived.' In the same place, a little further on: 'But sin, that it may appear to be sin by that which was good, worked death in me, that by the commandment sin might become sinful beyond measure.'[302] Likewise in chapter 5[:20]: 'Law entered by stealth so that sin might abound.' Again, in Hebrews 4 he calls the Law of Moses the law of a carnal commandment. In the same place: 'The Law,' he says, 'brought nothing to perfection.' And in another place: 'in whom the Law is weakened.'[303] Likewise in Galatians 4[:22–31], comparing the two testaments, he says that the Old Testament, that is, the Mosaic law, engenders into bondage. And in Acts [15:10] Peter calls the Law a burden which neither they nor their fathers were able to bear.

Indeed, Ezekiel in chapter 20[:25] makes the Lord speak thus: 'I gave them precepts which were not good, judgments in which they shall not live.' Jerome interprets that text as applying to ceremonies: thus the sacrifices (he says), which were prescribed for a people prone to idolatry, not because they would please the Lord but to keep them from sacrificing to the demons.[304] In his work against the Jews, sermon 4, Chrysostom is even harsher, calling the Law inherently imperfect. 'For when the Apostle,' he says, 'wished to show that he rejected and invalidated the very religion itself of the Jews as completely imperfect, he chose testimony in which there is no accusation directed at those who offer the sacrifices but the bare and inherent imperfection of the religion itself is declared, etc.'[305] If it is no affront to preach such things about the Law of Moses and the author of that Law, why is my language an affront to God? Their words are pious if we understand by the word 'Law' that part of the Law which prescribes ceremonies which were abrogated by the gospel, or the letter of the Law, which kills according to Paul, or the obligation of precepts without charity, which applied to most Jews, concerning whom, on the authority of the writer of the psalms, Paul pronounces universally that all had fallen away from the

* * * * *

302 Rom 7:5–6, 8–9, 13
303 Erasmus refers not to Hebrews 4 but to Heb 7:16–19.
304 Erasmus summarizes what Jerome says at *Commentarium in Hezechielem* 6.20.23–4 PL 25 (1845) 193C–194A.
305 *Adversus Iudaeos* 7.4 PG 48 921. Here again Erasmus (or his typesetter) refers to sermon 4 where modern editions have sermon 7. Perhaps Erasmus had a manuscript in which the number was actually given as 7.

Law and that no one did good, not even one.[306] But he adds that this statement applies principally to the Jews.[307] If no one kept the Law according to Paul, if the Law was an unbearable burden according to Peter, where was the offence in saying that it is in some fashion impossible to observe the Law, which no one can observe without God's help. And so my proposition did not indicate in an unqualified way that the people under the Old Law could not refrain from sinning but that they could not do so with the help of the Law and without grace, since Paul also says 'for me to wish is at hand, but I do not find a way to carry through.'[308]

I did not say that God gave a Law by which people perished, but according to the teaching of Paul I say that the Law, which was good in itself, became for the Jews an occasion of horror and desperation. And it was this desperation which caused them to distrust themselves and take refuge in grace. I showed the outcome of the Law; I did not reproach the intention of the Lawgiver. And God is not immediately unjust if he commands something which we are not able to perform by our own powers, but rather such a plan shows his mercy by revealing us to ourselves, so that we may not trust in our own resources but take refuge in his help; in such a way a physician might prescribe for a sick man who thinks he is well that he walk a mile every day with the idea that, as soon as he recognizes the weakness of his own powers, he will turn himself over to the physician to be cured. Finally, is God doing something unjust if mankind by their own vice turn his good laws into evil?

xxv *His second proposition. Mark 1*
   The Law of Moses, by its shadows, victims, and terrors, produced hypocrites.[309]

   CENSURE
   This proposition scorns the Mosaic law once more and also God himself, who instituted such shadows, victims, and ceremonies of the Law, which was established to lead to what is good and figured forth the truth of the New Law.

   * * * * *

306 Rom 3:12; Ps 13:3
307 Rom 3:19
308 Rom 7:18
309 Erasmus defended this proposition in *Elenchus in censuras Bedae* LB IX 502C and in *Supputatio* LB IX 640B–E.

ERASMUS' CLARIFICATION[310]

xxv If someone who gives an occasion for something is never said to do it, why does Paul say 'the letter kills,'[311] though the letter of the Law is good in itself? He also says that knowledge puffs up,[312] though knowledge in its own nature is good, especially the kind he is speaking of there. For in that passage he is speaking about the Jews who boasted that they were righteous when they observed the external precepts of the Law out of a servile fear, whereas in fact they did not observe the Law, since they were riddled inwardly with vices and neglected the principal point of the whole Law. Clearly such persons are hypocrites. The theologians, I think, mean the same thing when they say 'was established to,' granting that it was the occasion for falling into hypocrisy. Since we are in substantial agreement, how am I scornful of God and the Law? Even the gospel itself was for many an occasion of evil deeds. But it is even more fitting to preach the same about the Law of Moses: since it was given to a crude and stiff-necked people, it terrified and threatened more than it soothed. Simeon speaks quite harshly in the Gospel: 'This child is set up for the fall and the resurrection of many in Israel.'[313] But Christ came into the world not to destroy, but to save, and yet he says concerning unbelievers: 'If I had not come and spoken to them, they would not have sinned.'[314] But the censure speaks just as if I had said the Law was given so that people might perish. Who could be crazy enough to say that? The paraphrase speaks of the outcome of the Law that was given, not about the intention of the Lawgiver, about the abuse of it, not the use. That is quite clear from the whole drift of the paraphrase itself, which speaks as follows, showing why Christ came into the world: 'They abused,' it says, 'the law of nature, which God had written in the hearts of

* * * * *

310 Pelargus sigs D4–D4v generally agrees with Erasmus' clarification, except that he quibbles that the Law did not give an occasion for sin but that an occasion for sin was taken from it. He supports Erasmus' position with a number of Pauline texts and a citation from Chrysostom. He calls clarification xxvi learned and elegant.
  In the second edition Erasmus' clarification is about five times as long as it is in the first. He gives the context in the paraphrase and a number of texts where the Law is not universally condemned or is not the cause but the occasion for bad effects; here he does not use any of Pelargus' examples.
311 2 Cor 3:6
312 1 Cor 8:1
313 Luke 2:34
314 John 15:22

all mortals;[315] the wisdom of the philosophers made the world more foolish than it had been. In that respect the religion of the gentiles was the worst impiety. The Law of Moses, by its shadows, victims, and terrors, produced hypocrites, etc.'[316] You hear the abuse and you see that the outcome is what is indicated.

Furthermore, how can I be seen as condemning the Law, when I praised it a little earlier because, in keeping with its time, wrapped in figures and shadows, it prepared for a knowledge of the truth, and, though it did not provide perfect righteousness by the observance of shadows and figures, it nevertheless took some steps toward it? Moreover, what is generally said about the Jews does not apply to those who understood the Law spiritually and observed it out of charity. For example, when Christ reproaches the Jews with the prophecy of Isaiah, 'this people honours me with their lips, but their hearts are far from me,'[317] he does not immediately accuse John the Baptist, Simeon, and Ann of hypocrisy. Even Paul, when he applies to the Jews the testimony of the psalmist, 'all have fallen away, they have become, all together, useless, there is no one who does good, no, not even one,'[318] does not mean that no one lived piously under the Law, but rather he uses Law to mean a precept threatening without grace and 'all' to mean the largest part of the Jews who used the rind of the Law to boast of their righteousness in the eyes of men. Such are those the psalm speaks of: 'You did not wish sacrifice and oblation; you perfected my ears; you did not demand a holocaust even for sin. Then I said, "Behold, I am coming."'[319] In this passage the Law is not condemned but rather the hypocrisy of the Jews; to dislodge their overconfidence it was necessary that Christ should come; he promised righteousness not from the works of the Law but from faith, and he purified not by outward ceremonies but by piety of mind. What he says about his ears pertains to faith, which comes through hearing;[320] what follows, 'thy law in the midst of my heart,'[321] refers to a spiritual and inward desire for holiness. And in citing Isaiah the Lord does not despise victims, fasting, the sabbaths, and the new moons of the Jews,

* * * * *

315 Jeremiah 31:33; 2 Cor 3:3
316 *Paraphrase on Mark* CWE 49 22
317 Isa 29:13, cited at Matt 15:8 and Mark 7:6
318 Rom 3:12, citing Ps 52:4
319 Ps 39:7–8
320 Rom 10:17
321 Ps 39:9

nor does he reject the Law which prescribes them, but rather he reproaches the arrogance of the Jews who think they are righteous through observing them.

But if such sayings are very frequent in both the Old and New Testaments and in the writings of the ancient and orthodox Fathers, what need was there to base an accusation of blasphemy on a few fragmentary snippets, especially since it is crystal clear from thousands of places in my works that I do not mean what the censure takes me to mean about the intention of the Lawgiver or the figures and ceremonies as established to destroy mankind? If any persons have put forth wicked teachings about such things, it is not just to aim the missiles which they deserve at the head of someone who does not do so, especially since I have long ago given a satisfactory response to such accusations.

XXVI *His third proposition. Romans 6*
The Law stimulated passions more than it repressed them.[322]

CENSURE
Here the writer did not perform the duty of the paraphraser suitably. Actually the Law in itself repressed passions more than it stimulated them. For the Law was not given by God to incite people to commit sins but rather to prevent them from doing so; otherwise it would be neither holy nor just.

ERASMUS' CLARIFICATION
XXVI Here too I indicate the outcome, not the intention, of the Lawgiver. In that sense I said 'the Law stimulated passions just as the Apostle said it causes wrath.'[323] For it was not given in order to call forth God's vengeance. 'The Law,' they say, 'in itself repressed passions more than it stimulated them.' I agree, but for many it was an occasion of stimulation – which they do not deny. Furthermore, that I am talking there about the Law without grace is made clear by the language of the paraphrase, which says: 'There is no danger that, when you do not wish to sin, it will drag you back into your former servitude, since you are now no longer subject to the Law, which stimulated passions more than it repressed them, but to the grace of God, which, just as it could free us from the tyranny of sin, so too it

* * * * *

322 Erasmus defended this proposition briefly in *Supputatio* LB IX 667A–D.
323 Rom 4:15

can prevent us from tumbling back into the tyranny of sin.'[324] So says the paraphrase.

But they say you ought to have explained more clearly what you meant. Everything cannot be repeated everywhere. For I discussed that point quite clearly in the proper places, pointing out that the conjunction *ut* does not always indicate an aim but sometimes an outcome. And when the paraphrase expounds the words of Paul in Romans 5[:20], 'the Law slipped in that sin might abound,' it did not interpret this to mean that the Law was given so that the Jews might sin more gravely but rather showed how, when they had grown worse by the occasion of the Law, it was also of some use to them in that, as their wickedness grew more and more apparent, they might acknowledge their sin.

But what did the censure mean when it said 'the Law in itself repressed passions'? If it takes 'in itself' to mean 'of itself,' that is, without grace, it is far from the truth. If 'in itself' does not exclude grace but rather the guilt of the Jews, it is clearly in my favour.[325] But, in fact, the phrase 'in itself' is not in my paraphrase. And so if there is any blasphemy in this phrase, how can it be in my paraphrase, which does not have the phrase? Rather the paraphrase simply tells about the outcome the Law had among the Jews. Then again, the paraphrase on Romans, chapter 7[:20], speaks in this fashion: 'Certainly the Law was given to suppress sin. But because of our vice the result was different. For, while the Law revealed sin but gave no strength to overcome vices, it happened that this was the occasion for a drive toward sin to be stimulated to a greater degree, since human nature is more prone to what is forbidden, etc.'[326] Thus in this entire passage I emphasize the word 'occasion' to exonerate the Law. And yet whoever foisted these fragments off on the faculty teaches the difference between a cause and an occasion as if it were a great mystery, whereas I knew it when I was hardly fifteen years old.

Although there are plenty of such passages in my paraphrase, nevertheless because of a few words[327] snipped out of context I am said to have failed completely to do the duty of a paraphraser. What about the fact that from this passage, out of which they have taken their snippet, it is quite

* * * * *

324 *Paraphrase on Romans* CWE 42 48
325 That is, if the Law together with grace removes the guilt of the Jews, then this is in Erasmus' favour because he is willing to admit that; but he is not talking about the Law in conjunction with grace.
326 CWE 42 42
327 'three words' (*tribus verbis*): *Adagia* IV iv 84

clear that I am not talking about the Law in an unqualified way but about the Law without charity? For this is what the paraphrase says: 'since you are now no longer subject to the Law, which stimulated passions more than it repressed them, but to the grace of God, etc.'[328] Since I set grace over against the Law, I make it perfectly clear that I am talking about the Law with no added help from grace.

XXVII *His fourth proposition. Matthew 5*
The principal precept in the Law is 'you shall love your neighbour and you shall hate your enemy.'[329]

CENSURE
It is false to assert that there is a precept in the Law about hating one's enemy, since there is no such precept in the Law. Wherefore, since the rule about loving one's friends and enemies pertains to morals, and what pertains to morals remains unchanged in both laws, it is clear that this writer is wrong in designating a difference between the Old and the New Law on this point.

ERASMUS' CLARIFICATION[330]
XXVII Augustine thought that what they say is not in Scripture is in fact there, explaining this text as follows: 'When the Law says "you shall hate your enemy," it is not to be taken as a command to a righteous person but as a concession to the weak.'[331] He says this in his explication of the Lord's sermon on the mount. Then again, he makes the same point against

* * * * *

328 CWE 42 38
329 In *Supputatio* LB IX 377A–378C Erasmus defended this proposition with arguments quite similar to the ones given here.
330 Pelargus sig D4v simply rejects the opinion of Augustine. He rejects Erasmus' elaborate explication of the various meanings of 'hate' as irrelevant, and claims that the meaning of 'hate' here is clear from its opposition to 'love' so that the second command is inconsistent with the first. He also claims that the refusal to enter into treaties is not equivalent to hatred. He is on weaker ground when he suggests that the second command was added by the Pharisees and was a distortion of the word of God.
In the second edition Erasmus identified the citation from Augustine (as Pelargus had), and added another from Augustine and one from Chrysostom. He added a long section casting doubt on the rule that morality in the two testaments is the same.
331 *De sermone Domini in monte* 1.21.70 PL 34 1265

Faustus. 'I ask of the Manichaeans,' he says, 'why they consider the command "you shall hate your enemy" as something specific to the Law of Moses, when it was said to the ancients in general.'[332] Chrysostom seems to mean the same thing when he says that the Lord did not require of the weak what he already taught in his own times to the more advanced.[333] First of all, then, my paraphrase followed approved authors. Furthermore, since the other points mentioned by the Lord are found in the Law, it is probable that this is also contained there, though it is not found anywhere expressed in these exact words.[334] For the Hebrews were forbidden forever to make treaties with the Amalechites, Moabites, and Ammonites.[335] This fact is brought out by those who teach that the hatred of our enemies is a precept of the Law.

And in the mystical writings[336] the word 'hate' does not always refer to the state of mind of someone who wants to hurt another person. Sometimes a person hates if he shuns, afflicts, or scorns. Someone hates his father and mother if he neglects them out of a love of holiness. Someone hates his life if he exposes it to danger for the sake of the gospel. And it is clear that God figuratively indulges in hatred and anger, but sometimes he is said to hate if he inflicts unhappiness, to love if he pours forth favours. That is the way Jerome interprets the place in Malachi concerning Esau and Idumea, where he reduced the mountains called Seir to wilderness and made the cities empty, possessed by serpents and beasts, whereas he raised up the people of Israel to wealth and honour.[337] Just as a person is said to love if he bestows favours, so too he is said to hate if he flees from someone and shuns him. Thus when the Jews were forbidden to contract

* * * * *

332 *Contra Faustum Manichaeum* 19.24 PL 42 362
333 *Commentarius in sanctum Matthaeum Evangelistam* 18.1 PG 57 265
334 Matt 5:21–43
335 Deut 23:3–6 forever forbids the Jews from making peace with the Ammonites and the Moabites, though it does not mention the Amalechites. In his commentary on Matt 5:43 Thomas Aquinas says: '"You shall hate your enemy" is nowhere found in the Law but was an addition on the part of the Jews, who thought this should perhaps be added because of what was often said in the Law. For God commanded that the Amalechites should be destroyed [1 Sam 15:18] and Exod 23:22 says "I will be an enemy to your enemies," and likewise concerning other peoples.' See Aquinas *In Matthaeum Evangelistam expositio* 5.9.
336 Meaning Scripture
337 *Commentariorum in Malachiam prophetam liber unus* 1:1 PL 25 (1845) 1545D–1546D

mixed marriages with the Ammonites and Moabites, in a sense they seemed to hate them.[338] Then, too, when the Law says 'love your neighbour,'[339] since the ordinary run of the Jews took 'neighbour' to mean a person of their nation, they interpreted the command as implying hatred of foreign nations, and for that reason they shrank from dealings with the gentiles and Samaritans, thinking they would be contaminated by fellowship with them. Hence the Lord said 'the Jews have no use for the Samaritans.'[340] And when the apostles were sent out for the first time, he commanded that they not wander off into the path of the gentiles or enter the cities of the Samaritans.[341] For this reason there is nothing to keep someone from loving and hating the same person. For example, when a strict father treats his wanton son hatefully, threatening him, beating him, tying him up, he hates him in a certain sense; on the other hand, when he wants a son who has mended his wanton ways, he loves him; so too when he provides for his external needs. Indeed, in Latin *odium* commonly means 'hardship,' as in 'you will never conquer me with your hardships,' and *odiosus* means 'troublesome.'

Although such an interpretation is not absurd and does not lack authoritative support, nevertheless I have no need to take refuge in such assistance. For I never meant that the Jews were commanded to hate their enemies with malevolence, but that they were permitted to do so; and also not that it was permitted in such a way as to be licit, but only as a concession to that nation's hardness of heart. The noun 'precept' applies only to the first clause; that this is true is clear from the adjective 'principal.' For, though there may be some precept in the Law concerning hating one's enemies, it certainly cannot be the principal one. If the interpretation of the Doctors of the church is true, namely that hatred of enemies was permitted to the Jews, whereas loving one's enemies and kindness toward them were required of Christians, I think that I was right, in accord with the ancients, to posit a difference between the Old and the New Law. Now, even though that rule of Augustine is thoroughly inviolable – that morality does not change between the two testaments, according to the hidden and spiritual sense of the Law, though there should be agreement about what is purely moral and what is not – certainly the gospel is said to add to the Law more vivid

* * * * *

338 Deut 7:3 forbids marriage with several Canaanite tribes, though it does not specifically mention the Ammonites and Moabites.
339 Lev 19:18; Matt 5:43
340 John 4:9. Actually not Christ, but the Samaritan woman says this.
341 Matt 10:5

explications, more frequent inculcations, more extraordinarily expressive examples. Moses importunes God on behalf of the people;[342] David keeps his men from Shemei;[343] but what are such incidents compared with the perpetual and wonderful mildness and kindness of the Lord? What are they compared with the indefatigable charity of the apostles, their cheerfulness in afflictions? And then if we take Law in the usual understanding of it, it is right to say that the gospel added many things to the Law.

But if we will not accept that interpretation, there are thousands of places in the books of the orthodox Fathers which would have to be condemned if they were measured by that exact standard, 'morality is the same in both testaments.' Now it does not matter that the paraphrase changes 'it was said' to 'it was commanded' since the language in both halves is imperative, 'you shall love' and 'you shall hate,' just like the phrases 'you shall not kill, you shall not steal.' It would have been clearer to use the imperative forms 'love' and 'hate,' but still the effect of the language is the same. The problem is not solved by Augustine's interpretation that the words 'you shall hate' are not a command but a concession.[344] For if you take hatred to mean a malicious desire to injure the person you hate, that was certainly not, I think, conceded to the Jews according to the spiritual sense of the Law, although the eternal law did not threaten them with any punishment.

XXVIII   *His fifth proposition. Matthew 19*

> The young man had heard Christ teaching that the precepts of the Mosaic law were not sufficient to gain the kingdom of heaven.[345]

CENSURE

This proposition is asserted temerariously; and, in that it alleges that the precepts of the Old Law (including the precepts of the decalogue) were not sufficient at that time to gain the kingdom of heaven or to merit eternal life, it conflicts with the words of Christ, who said, 'if you wish to enter into life, keep the commandments.'[346] And again, when he responded to the expert in the Law who recounted both parts

* * * * *

342 Exod 32:11–13
343 2 Sam 19:22
344 See n331 above.
345 Erasmus defends this proposition briefly in *Divinationes ad notata Bedae* LB IX 465D–E, and at greater length in *Supputatio* LB IX 590D–591B.
346 Matt 19:17

of the commandment of the Law concerning love, he said, 'do this and you will live.[347]

XXVIII I wanted to give the reason which brought the young man to Jesus and I presented one which seemed probable to me, though perhaps it would have been better not to allege something not expressed in the Gospel, especially in the person of the evangelist whose deficiency was being remedied. But in fact I have more than once warded off bad feeling from the person speaking in case something happened to be said that was less than correct. Otherwise, if you make an uproar whenever a character is introduced, then you should do so whenever Jerome arranges the language of a prophet, explaining the meaning of a passage in a paraphrase wherever the true sense of the prophet is perhaps not being grasped; so too whenever Gregory prefaces a passage with 'as if to say,' and changes the words of Scripture, putting them in the mouth of a person he introduced to speak them. Now since allegories are sometimes ambiguous, it will not be proper to explain them in the person of the evangelist. What then will we do with Ambrose when he does this, as he frequently does? And so either paraphrases ought not to have been written or some latitude should have been allowed in them. It was necessary only to avoid what the nature of the times would not allow such and such a person to say.

But if my guessing here is reprehensible, the same fault is shared by Rabanus, a man not without learning and honour, since he guesses there was another reason, namely that he had heard from the Lord that no one is worthy of the kingdom of heaven unless he has become like a little child.[349] And then he would fulfil the perfections which the Lord had taught

* * * * *

347 Luke 10:28
348 Pelargus sig D4v says that Erasmus' paraphrase is incorrect at this point because the scriptural context makes it clear that 'kingdom of heaven' here means 'eternal life.'
  In the first edition the clarification is very brief. In the second it is at least fifteen times longer. Erasmus removed the blunt statement which Pelargus found incorrect: 'In that place I call the kingdom of heaven not eternal life but the profession of the gospel.' Drawing upon Origen and Theophylactus, he explains why it is not wrong to identify the kingdom of God with eternal life in this passage. He then contrasts at length the spiritual fulfilment of the Law with a purely external compliance.
349 *Commentariorum in Matthaeum libri octo* 6.19.2 PL 107 1019D. Rabanus Maurus (c 776–856), abbot of Fulda and archbishop of Mainz, was a learned compiler of patristic and exegetic commentaries.

sitting on the mountain. And Christ, as Origen elegantly points out, was the eternal life, to whom the apostles said, 'you have the words of life.'[350] And he said concerning himself: 'Everyone who lives and believes in me will not die forever.'[351] Therefore there was nothing absurd about calling the profession of the gospel eternal life, of which Christ deprives those who do not renounce themselves. Hence, as Origen also notes, the Lord does not say 'if you wish to attain life' but 'if you wish to enter into life,'[352] as if the observance of the Law were the first rudimentary step toward the perfection of the gospel.[353] Then again, when the young man had been sent away, the Lord said to the disciples, 'how difficult it is for a rich man to enter the kingdom of heaven,'[354] indicating that the rich people of this world are hardly suitable hearers of the evangelical philosophy. What he here called 'the kingdom of heaven,' he called 'life' when he was speaking to the young man.

But if this seems forced (as coming from Origen), there is a more expeditious method if we take this text as referring to those outward commandments, 'you shall not kill, you shall not steal, etc.' What is added about loving one's neighbour is spoken according to the understanding of the general run of the Jews, who did not consider a person to be a neighbour unless he belonged to his own race or had deserved well of him. This is evident from the parable of the wounded traveller who was healed by the efforts of the Samaritan.[355] Otherwise the Lord would not have received so favourably the language in which the young man said he had observed all these things from his childhood. In fact he had observed none of them according to the spiritual understanding of the Law, which differs not at all from the gospel, according to the teaching of the theologians, to be sure. But the Lord received him very favourably, as an unpolished and straightforward Jew who was not infected with the leaven of the Pharisees and who seemed capable of being taught the evangelical philosophy.

But it is probable that from the speeches of the Lord he had gathered the opinion, more or less, that for the eternal salvation to which the Lord invited him something more was required which was not expressed in the Law. Otherwise, since the Law expressly promises life to those who observe it, what need would there have been to consult the Lord about the means

* * * * *

350 John 6:69
351 John 11:26
352 Matt 19:17
353 *Commentaria in Evangelium secundum Matthaeum* 15.12 PG 13 1285A–1287B
354 Matt 19:23
355 Luke 10:33–5

by which he could gain eternal life? But since the Lord had added to the grave precepts which had been laid down that anyone who did not fulfil them could not be his disciple or be worthy of him, he seems to block the way to salvation for all others. For no one can be saved if he is unworthy of Christ. Whoever observed the Law spiritually, though he might not have fulfilled all of it, still he would have done so if the occasion had arisen, as John the Baptist scorned his life for the sake of the truth. But that young man had not yet progressed so far, and for that reason he left Jesus and went away in sadness because he was still no more than a Jew. This is the interpretation of Theophylactus: 'Whatever good deeds you did,' he says, 'you did them in a Jewish fashion. But if you wish to be perfect, that is, to be my disciple and a Christian, go and sell all that you, etc.'[356] That is what Theophylactus says. But to make a point in passing, doesn't Theophylactus say these things in the person of Christ, paraphrasing at this juncture? But if someone should say that he understood 'perfect' wrongly in this place, as if imperfect Christians were not Christians or disciples of Christ, would it be fair to convict him of blasphemy because he brought in Christ uttering falsehoods? Or rather shall we accept the error as if he spoke it in his own person as a commentary? But this is a minor point. Hilary does not disagree with Theophylactus: 'This young man,' he says, 'is a type of the Jewish people, both arrogant under the Law and expecting from Christ nothing more than the Mosaic law, etc.'[357] The Lord cries out, 'unless your righteousness is more plentiful than that of the Scribes and Pharisees, you shall not enter the kingdom of heaven.'[358] Now the Pharisees and the Scribes observed the Law meticulously, but only according to external worship. And so if we take the Mosaic law to mean external precepts and if we take their observance according to the ordinary Jewish understanding of them, if we agree with Theophylactus in taking 'perfect' to mean 'Christian,' I think that nothing in my proposition is ungodly or contrary to Christ.

But although not all Christians are required to fulfil all the admonitions and counsels of Christ, they are nevertheless required to be disposed to fulfil them if piety should ever demand it. This was not required of the ordinary run of the Jews because the Lord had not yet expressed the full force of the Mosaic law; and if we accept Origen's interpretation, it is one thing to enter into life and another to gain eternal life. The one is elementary and belongs to simple Judaism; the other belongs to the full force of

* * * * *

356 *Enarratio in Evangelium Matthaei* 19:17–19 PG 123 356B
357 *In Evangelium Matthaei commentarius* 19.4 PL 9 1025B
358 Matt 5:20

the gospel. I never meant that before the light of the gospel came forth the Jews could not be saved by observing the precepts of the Law, provided there was no hypocrisy and faith and charity were present according to the framework of that time. For the faith that afterwards would not have been sufficient was sufficient for them. But the reply to the lawyer, 'do this and you will live,'[359] was not spoken concerning external precepts, but concerning full and perfect charity toward God and one's neighbour, a charity which includes the whole Law and also the perfection of the gospel. Furthermore, when the censure adds 'at that time,' meaning the time preceding the light of the gospel, it signifies that after the light of the gospel was brought forth the precepts of the Mosaic law were not sufficient. If they mean the external laws, I grant that is true; if they mean the moral laws, which they say are the same under both laws, those laws seem to have been sufficient. But my paraphrase refers to the time when the Lord was instructing people to prepare them for the full force of the spirit of the gospel, sowing the seeds of perfection which would sprout in the morals and minds of the disciples after they had drunk in the heavenly spirit. The censure is concerned with a different time. For this is what the paraphrase says: 'But the Lord, when he was showing the difference between the righteousness of the Jews and that of the gospel, between good according to the Jews and good according to Christians, said, "If you wish, etc." '[360] I do not think that young man was damned because he could not despise riches for the love of Christ, because the full force of the gospel had not yet shone forth, although minds were being prepared for it. From these considerations I think it is clear that the theologians and I are in agreement and that the quarrel is merely a matter of words.

xxix *His sixth proposition. 1 Tim 1*

> If genuine charity is present, what need is there for the precepts of the Law?[361]

CENSURE

This proposition, in so far as it seems to allege that for those pilgrims[362] who have charity precepts are not necessary or useful, is based on a

* * * * *

359 Luke 10:28
360 LB VII 105B–C / CWE 45 277
361 Erasmus defended this point briefly in *Supputatio* LB IX 667E–668A.
362 That is, those on earth who are on their pilgrimage toward the heavenly Jerusalem

wrong interpretation of the scriptural passage 'the Law was not laid
down for the righteous'[363] and comes close to the error of the Beguards.[364] Certainly in those words the Apostle did not exclude the
necessity of precepts, but rather he indicates the excellence of the perfect, who do good deeds not out of fear of punishment but out of the
love of virtue.

ERASMUS' CLARIFICATION[365]

XXIX Once more we mean the same thing, but my words (for heaven's sake!)
seem to come close to the error of the Beguards. For when Paul says that the
Law was not set down for the righteous, they interpret him as preaching
there about the perfection of the gospel, which acts not out of fear of punishment but out of love of virtue. The paraphrase explains that text of the
Apostle in the same sense, saying as follows: 'Whoever understands that
those who have been redeemed from the tyranny of sin by the blood of
Christ and who are driven by charity to perform willingly more than the
Law of Moses prescribes have no need for the fear or admonitions of the
Law to restrain them from vice or motivate them to do their duty; such a
person holds the Law to be good. In fact he understands that the Law has
no relevance to himself, since he has learned through the gospel not only
not to injure anyone but also to deserve well of his enemies. What need is

* * * * *

363 1 Tim 1:9
364 The Beguards were religious associations of laymen devoted to simple piety
and works of charity. They took no vows and lived in independent houses not
subject to any general rule, though their way of life (particularly in poverty)
resembled that of the Franciscan order. The parallel order for women was
that of the Beguines, which began in the Low Countries in the twelfth century about a century before the first appearance of the Beguards in Louvain.
Both groups spread widely in the Netherlands and Germany. They were condemned by several synods and popes in the thirteenth and fourteenth centuries and by the Council of Vienne in 1312, especially for their belief that
those who gain perfection in this life cannot sin and are not subject to ecclesiastical laws. Though their numbers were considerably reduced in the sixteenth
century, they were still a considerable body in Erasmus' time. See also n667
below.
365 Pelargus sig D5 agrees that Erasmus' clarification is correct and that the censors
have misunderstood what he meant.
In the second edition Erasmus confirms what Pelargus said by adding a section
as long as the original clarification; he relies especially on giving passages
which show how the context of the snippet which the theologians object to
actually denies the position of the Beguards.

there of bit or spurs if a horse is running properly and willingly?'[366] And shortly after that: 'Accordingly, the Law, which deters from vice by the fear of punishment, was in any case not founded for those who are ready and eager to perform what the Law requires, even if they do not cling to the words of the Law.'[367] Chrysostom expresses similar sentiments when he explains the text 'the end of the Law is charity,' saying that the end is fulfilment: 'The end of medicine,' he said, 'is health. And so when health is present, there is no need for precepts or warnings, etc.'[368] Theophylactus expresses the same opinion at greater length.[369] And in that text the Apostle is not speaking of just any charity but of evangelical charity which springs from a good conscience and an unfeigned faith. Such charity does not need the Law, fear, or threats to urge it to do pious deeds.

If those who brought fragments to the attention of the faculty had read my paraphrases, how could they have suspected that I agree with the Beguards, since I interpret those texts in Paul that seem to free Christians from observing precepts in such a way as to exclude the error of the Beguards. Thus, when I explain Romans 6[:14], 'you are not under the Law but under grace,' I add: 'At the same time, let no one interpret this in such a way as to think that, because I said you are free from the Law, you should sin with impunity because the Law is removed, or that the grace of God, which pardoned former sins, also granted impunity to future derelictions. Indeed we should abstain from sins all the more because we are no longer forced to act well but are motivated by merit and love. Our servitude is changed, not completely eliminated, etc.'[370] The very drift of my language here indicates that I use the word 'law' to mean the terror inspired by the Law. I explain that text in Galatians 5[:18], 'if you are led by the Spirit, you are not under the Law' thus: 'so that after you have been freed from the slavery of the Law of Moses, which is fleshly, you may lead your life according to the spiritual law of evangelical charity. This will happen if you do not measure righteousness by ceremonies and if you abstain from the desires of the flesh. You do not cease to be subject to the Law if you persevere in being subject to the desires, etc.'[371]

* * * * *

366 *Adagia* I ii 47
367 LB VII 1037B–C / CWE 44 9
368 1 Tim 1:5; Chrysostom *In epistolam primam ad Timotheum commentarius* 2.1 PG 62 509
369 Theophylactus *Commentarius in epistolam primam ad Timotheum* 1:5 PG 125 15
370 LB VII 796C / CWE 42 38–9
371 LB VII 963F / CWE 42 125

Indeed the very text from which the censure thinks the error of the Beguards arises is interpreted by the paraphrase against the Beguards, as I have made clear. Then again, explaining the text in 2 Corinthians 3[:17], 'where the Spirit is, there is liberty,' I speak as follows: 'Because the Law of Moses kept people doing their duty out of a fear of punishment, it was servile and the veil was an indication of servitude. But where there is the spirit of the Lord Jesus, which goads us secretly so that even without any command we are moved to perform the duties of piety, there liberty, etc.'[372] I say things like this in many places and I always interpret the liberty of the gospel to mean immunity from the ceremonial precepts of the Jews; from the moral precepts there is freedom only in so far as we do more when we are motivated by charity than the Jews did when they were terrorized by the Law.

I know that the Law is not useless, even for those who are furnished with faith and charity, in so far as it has the power to guide and admonish. But here the paraphrase is dealing with servile fear, which charity excludes. In other respects even those who are moved by the spirit of God do not lack fear altogether, since the church sings 'the angels also tremble';[373] but Paul is not dealing with such fear, nor is my paraphrase. Therefore I think that this is what Paul meant, as he is interpreted by approved Doctors, whom I have followed. From this it is clear how different I am from the Beguards. According to them, I think, a spiritual person is not bound by precepts and may violate them just as he pleases. As for me, I interpret the evangelical person as not free from precepts and regulations in such a way that he may violate them; rather I hold that, having his will driven by charity, he performs more than the Law commands. For the Law is a bit and a spur, so to speak. Someone who of his own free will abhors all vices and hastens toward virtue with eager joy has no need of a bit or spurs. Therefore the censure is right

* * * * *

372 LB VII 921A / CWE 43 220

373 Latin 'tremunt et angeli.' I have not found these exact words in the vast number of prayers and hymns of the mass and the divine office. The hymn *Aeterne rex altissime*, which belongs to matins from Ascension to Pentecost, contains the line 'Tremunt videntes angeli' ('The angels tremble when they see'); see Matthew Britt *The Hymns of the Breviary and Missal* (New York 1922) 156. But it may be that Erasmus is giving a shorthand reference to a clause from the ordinary preface in the mass that was frequently sung: 'Per christum Dominum nostrum. Per quem maiestatem tuam laudant angeli, adorant dominationes, tremunt potestates' ('Through our Lord Jesus Christ. Through whom the angels praise your majesty, the dominations adore it, the powers tremble before it'). The dominations and powers are, of course, two of the orders of angels. See *Missale Romanum* no 17, 1 205–6.

in softening its language: 'seems to allege.' But that doubt would have been eliminated if the paraphrase had been read instead of a fragment of it.

xxx *His seventh proposition. Galatians 4 [and 5]*
     The Law contains very many words.[374]
xxxi *His eighth proposition. In the same place*
     The Jews were for a time confined by crass religion – or rather, by superstition.

> CENSURE
>
> In these two propositions the paraphraser speaks irreverently about the Law instituted by God, calling it at one time very verbose,[375] and then a carnal religion or superstition, whereas in fact, according to Scripture, before the coming of Christ it was the wisdom of the Jews before all the nations. And the Wise Man says that the word of God and the law of the wise man is the fountain of life.[376]

ERASMUS' CLARIFICATION[377]

xxx, xxxi The harsh use[378] of the term 'wordy' gives offence, as if we did not call a letter 'wordy' if it is lengthy and abounds in words. In the Satirist[379]

* * * * *

374 Erasmus defended this proposition in *Elenchus in censuras Bedae* LB IX 508D–E and in *Supputatio* LB IX 690F–691D. The objectionable phrase comes from Erasmus' paraphrase on Galatians 5, not 4, though the paraphrase on chapter 4 mentions the simplicity of Paul's language compared to the elaborate seductions of his Judaizing enemies, who promote manifold superstitions; see CWE 42 125.

375 This is the same Latin word (*verbosissima*) which is translated 'containing many words' in Erasmus' first proposition. The theologians take the word as pejorative; Erasmus argues that it can be used in a neutral sense.

376 Prov 13:14

377 Pelargus sig D5 claims that Erasmus would have been right to tax the superstition of the Jews but that he was wrong to assert that the ceremonial law itself was superstitious.

   In the second edition Erasmus adds quotations from Cicero, Juvenal, and Jerome to show that *verbosus* need not be pejorative. He also adds a long section, which he calls grammatical but essential, on the figurative use of 'crass' as applied to the Law. He also replies to Pelargus' objection that the Lord's Prayer is not superstitious just because someone malicious recites it; certainly not, according to Erasmus, but those who promise themselves salvation by praying merely with their lips, not their minds, are superstitious.

378 Latin *abusus*: later Erasmus uses as equivalent to this the word *catachresis*, a Greek word which appears as *abusio* in Latin.

379 Juvenal 10.71–2

we read 'a verbose and grand epistle came from Capri,' where the language refers to a lengthy document such as princes usually send when dealing with some important matters. And when Cicero says 'you now have an epistle which is perhaps more verbose than you would wish,'[380] by 'more verbose' he means 'lengthier.' For this is what comes right afterwards: 'I will think that you consider it so unless you send me a reply that is even lengthier.' And in a letter to Julian the Deacon Jerome writes: 'But my present verbosity will excuse the whole blame.'[381] And I am speaking there about the infinite multitude of precepts, which are also often repeated and hammered home in the Old Law, whereas the law of the gospel gathers together such a great flock of precepts in a single phrase.[382] This has nothing to do with contempt for the Law but redounds to the glory of God's goodness, which accommodated itself to a rude, crass, and forgetful people, so that by the multitude of precepts they might be reminded of God in every possible way and so that manifold repetition might overcome their deafness and forgetfulness. Since God took on flesh for the sake of mankind, why should it be surprising that he wanted to be more verbose for the sake of mankind? But that I am speaking there not about a superfluity of words but rather about the multitude of prescriptions is testified by the words of the paraphrase, which are as follows: 'Moreover, what the Law does not bring about by its many prescriptions and threats, charity alone fulfils by a shortcut, embracing in itself the meaning and essence of the whole Law. For what the Law with its many words attempts to bring about by innumerable precepts is fulfilled completely in a single, short sentence, etc.'[383] If someone should say that the multitude of legal precepts, hammered home with so many words, repeated so often, is superfluous for those who have drawn:w in the spirit of Christ, what, I beg you, would be the crime in that?

And in many places Scripture itself provides an occasion to speak in such a way. Isaiah, chapter 10[:23]: 'For the Lord will make a consummation and an abridgement in the midst of the land.' And Paul, Romans 9[:28]: 'Consummating and shortening his word in fairness, because a shortened word will the Lord make upon the earth.' Likewise in Romans 3[384] he says that all the precepts of the Law can be embraced in one phrase, 'love your

* * * * *

380 *Epistulae familiares* 7.3.6
381 *Epistola* 6 ad Julianum Diaconum PL 22 338
382 Rom 13:9
383 LB VII 963D / CWE 42 125
384 Romans 3 is apparently a typographical error for Romans 13.

neighbour.' Likewise, soon after that, 'the fullness of the Law is love.'[385] For the fair-minded reader this harsh usage could even have a certain charm, especially since the comparison there is between the Old Testament and the New. Through Moses and the prophets God was wordy, but through the Son he was 'shortening the word upon the earth.'

Moreover, when I call the religion of the Law crass, I do not mean the whole Law, which also contains the precepts of the gospel, but the external ceremonies – circumcision, choice of foods, cattle as sacrificial victims, observing the sabbath, and such like – which do not constitute true religion but rather provided a figure of true religion. For that is the part of the Law which the Apostle was discussing. To call the Law crass or fleshly with respect to that part of it is no more contemptuous than to call the body the crass part of a human being or in the sacraments to designate that part as crass which is more obvious to the senses, as in baptism the water, salt, and anointing. Crass religion is what I call external worship, which in the Epistle to the Hebrews the Apostle puts down emphatically by comparison with the truth of the gospel.[386] Perhaps someone might suspect that the Law is said to be crass in the same way as the French call a stupid person crass. But the paraphrase itself, from which these fragments have been torn out to accuse me falsely, makes it clear that that is not what I mean. For this is what it says: 'But just as the Jews were for a time confined by carnal religion – or rather by superstition – to prevent them from completely falling away from all religion, so you at one time, etc.' And shortly thereafter: 'It is not charged against the Jews that, because of the nature of the times, they were subservient to the traditions of their forefathers, for after they were taught better things they turned away from such teachings and devoted themselves to a true zeal for piety.'[387] If it is the novelty of the figure that offends, it is very frequent in the Epistles of Paul and in orthodox interpreters, especially when the preaching of the gospel is compared to the Law of Moses. By a similar figure Paul speaks of the old man and the new man,[388] the interior person and the exterior person,[389] not meaning the whole person but only part of him. Indeed we ordinarily say the upper hand for the upper part of the hand and the middle person for the middle part of a person. These are grammatical points, I grant you, but,

* * * * *

385 Rom 13:9, 10
386 For example, Heb 10:26–8
387 LB VII 957C / CWE 42 116
388 Eph 4:22–3; Col 3:9–10
389 Rom 7:22; Eph 3:16

whatever they are, it is shameful for the most eminent theologians to be ignorant of them, and even more shameful to make false accusations based on that ignorance.

When I say such things I do not berate the faculty but rather those who foisted such bits and pieces upon the faculty in a prejudiced way. Indeed the censure does this less ingenuously because it takes Law and religion to be identical, whereas religion, properly speaking, is worship and pertains to the sacrifice of victims, which was not only crass among the Jews but also not far from the appearance of superstition and hardly different from the rites of the gentiles, except that they were offered to God. What I add, 'or rather by superstition,' is more harsh. Most of the Jews put all righteousness in those petty external observances, neglecting those which are spiritual and thus come closer to piety. In the Jews, therefore, the observance of such things was not truly religious but superstitious, that is, verging on superstition. And what prevents anyone from designating as superstitious those practices which in Isaiah the Lord rejects with disgust and contempt?[390] What do you make of the fact that approved Doctors teach that these observances were prescribed by God not because he was pleased by them but to keep a people which was prone to all sorts of evil from falling into idolatry? As I said, Jerome interprets such prescriptions not as good laws, since they were not given according to God's pleasure, but rather as temporary concessions to the hard-heartedness of the Jewish people. Certainly, by comparison with the law of the gospel, they are not without superstition. But if I had called the whole Law crass religion or rather superstition in an unqualified way, I would have spoken not only irreverently but also impiously. For according to the mystical sense the Law is spiritual and agrees with the gospel.

Therefore, just as what the theologians say is very true, that the Law was the wisdom of the Jews before all the nations, so too, once the light of the gospel was brought forth, what had previously seemed to be religion began to be superstition, especially in so far as ceremonies were concerned. And so even before then it was a kind of superstition, as compared to the light of the gospel which was to come. 'And the Law was wisdom before all the nations.' That is true, I grant you, but the Law as spiritually understood and rightly observed. Wherever there is an appearance of religion without true piety, if pretence is present, it is hypocrisy; if error and groundless confidence are present, it is superstition. St Jerome designates

* * * * *

390 Isa 29:13; Matt 15:8

as superstition the simple-mindedness of empty-headed women who carried on their persons a piece of paper with gospel texts or a fragment of the cross;[391] he does this not because to do so is in itself ungodly but because they had more confidence in these externals than in inward matters. So too when the Jews arrogantly claimed righteousness derived from victims and other external matters, neglecting the spiritual precepts of the Law, they were superstitious, not religious. Indeed, even though prayer is something which is evangelical in the highest degree; nevertheless those who pray perpetually, promising themselves salvation from speaking much[392] but feeling nothing, are praying superstitiously. And those who fast in the belief that not eating and nothing more is in itself the chief form of piety fast superstitiously. Now what could be more religious than to call upon the Lord, to extol and praise his name? And yet the Lord scornfully rejects superstitious invocation, nor does he accept superstitious praises, when he says: 'not everyone who says to me "Lord, Lord" will enter into the kingdom of heaven.'[393] Likewise: 'These people honour me with their lips, etc.'[394]

And so I will not discuss here what bearing the other texts cited have on this point. For Ecclesiasticus speaks of that sublime wisdom: 'The fountain of wisdom,' he says, 'is the word of God on high, and the entry into it is his eternal commands.'[395] And it is clear that the ceremonial prescriptions were not given except temporarily. Now, though the ceremonial prescriptions in some fashion deserve the name of wisdom, they do not deserve it except in so far as they are applied to Christ, whom they prefigure. But Solomon seems to be saying this according to the moral sense: namely, that it is very important for the salvation of a person to be correctly and wisely brought up. According to a more hidden sense, it seems to be more applicable to the gospel. For Christ is said to be the wisdom of the Father,[396] and he is that wise Son who is the glory of the Father.[397] His law is the gospel. But however these texts are explained, they are ineffective against me because I did not speak about just any part of the Law whatever, but about external ceremonies, which were abrogated by the gospel.

* * * * *

391 *Commentariorum in Evangelium Matthaei libri quatuor* 4.23.6 PL 26 (1845) 168c
392 Prov 10:19; Matt 6:7
393 Matt 7:21
394 Isa 29:13; Matt 7:21
395 Ecclus 1:5
396 1 Cor 1:24
397 Prov 10:1, 13:1, 15:20; cf Matt 16:27; Mark 8:38

Topic 10. The authors of the books of the New Testament

[XXXII] *Erasmus' first proposition. In* Elenchus[398]
A person does not have doubts about the faith simply because he has doubts about the author of a book.

CENSURE
XXXII This proposition is asserted temerariously and erroneously, by speaking as the author speaks about doubting the authors of the holy books of the New Testament, which have been accepted by the church under the names of such authors. Such are the authors of the four books of the Gospels, the seven canonical Epistles, the fourteen Epistles of Paul, the Acts of the Apostles, and the Apocalypse. For since God established those holy men as his instruments in the issuance of such books, whoever removes their names from such books or calls them into doubt detracts from their honour; and he also discourages the frequent and fruitful reading of them. Moreover, however much some have formerly had doubts about the authors of some of these books, nevertheless, once the church by its universal usage accepted them under the names of such authors and approved of them by its decision, it is now not right for a Christian to have doubts about them or to call them into doubt.

ERASMUS' CLARIFICATION[399]
XXXII The principal author of canonical Scripture is the Holy Spirit. As long as there is no doubt about him, the authority of Scripture cannot teeter at all, nor can godly persons' reading of it fall off, whatever instruments he used to extend it to us. But in fact whatever is received by the usage of the church does not immediately bind us to believe it as an article of faith.

* * * * *

398 *Elenchus in censuras Bedae* LB IX 497C–D, where Erasmus also briefly defended the proposition
399 Pelargus sigs D5–D6 points out that in his *Retractions* Augustine denied that the Book of Wisdom was written by the son of Sirach. He also gives some authorities and reasons for thinking it was not written by Philo but by Solomon, but in the end he leaves the question open. He puts off discussing the authors of the books of the New Testament to another time.
In the second edition Erasmus adds a long section discussing the naming of scriptural books at the Council of Africa (at which Augustine was present) and giving details about how Augustine, Jerome, and Cyprian varied in assigning authors to certain books of Scripture.

The church accepted the titles in that she used the commonly received titles to indicate the work that she meant – just as apocryphal books, both those of innumerable authors and those of Jeremiah, are cited not because they are by Jeremiah but because they were issued in his name. Thus the book of Job is called so not because he wrote it but because it deals with him. Similarly we speak of the book of Tobias. And so the title does not always indicate the author, just as not all the psalms which have David's name in their titles are thought to be by him.

But if the universal church accepts these titles in the sense that those who have doubts about the human author are to be reckoned ungodly, I side with her opinion as speedily as possible,[400] and I make my intellect the obedient captive of faith. But still, according to human perception, I do not believe that the Epistle to the Hebrews is by Paul or Luke, or that the second Epistle of Peter is by Peter, or that the Apocalypse is by the apostle John who wrote the Gospel. I could accumulate many arguments at this point, but it is better to avoid giving offence to the weak. For the express judgment of the church means more to me than any human arguments. But I have in my mind a trace of hesitation about whether the church accepted those titles in such a way that she not only wants the content of those books to be accepted without doubt but also requires that we accept without doubt that they issued from the authors whose names they bear in their titles. If that is the case, I condemn and reject my doubt entirely; there was no doubt at all if that is the mind of the church as inspired by the breath of the Holy Spirit. But in fact the theologians grant that the whole church can err only in those matters which are not necessarily required for the salvation of the flock; perhaps the titles are of that sort. If not, and if we are pressed so hard by titles accepted because of usage or recited in some council or other, we will be forced to believe that the book *To Paula and Eustochium on the Assumption of the Most Holy Virgin* was written by Jerome.[401]

And in the Council of Carthage, where Augustine was present, and also in the epistle of Innocent five books are attributed to Solomon:[402] Proverbs, the Song of Songs, Ecclesiastes, Ecclesiasticus, and Wisdom, even though Ecclesiasticus is not in the Hebrew canon and Wisdom did not originate among the Jews but is thought to be by Philo, who was outstanding

* * * * *

400 Literally, 'with hands and feet'; see *Adagia* I iv 15.
401 This work was frequently but falsely attributed to Jerome; see the list of such works in PL 30 (1846) 909–10.
402 Innocent I *Epistolae et decreta* Epistola 6.7 PL 20 501A–502A. Innocent mentions them without naming them, but these are the five he means.

for eloquence in Greek. Indeed, Augustine also, in his book *The Teaching of Christianity* 2.8, when he reckons up the books of the whole scriptural canon, says it is clear that Ecclesiasticus was written by Jesus the son of Sirach in imitation of Solomon. He thinks the same about Wisdom.[403] In his explanation of the Apostles' Creed, Cyprian does not even accept the Wisdom of Sirach and the Wisdom of Solomon as canonical Scripture, even though they were recited in church, as was also the *Shepherd*.[404] In the Council of Africa the books of the New Testament were listed under certain titles, but it is one thing to list them by commonly accepted titles so that you can recognize them and quite another to define them in such a way that there may be no doubt. And then the Council of Africa was not universal, even if it had issued a definite pronouncement about the titles. In a response to Jacques Lefèvre d'Etaples I once explained that even Augustine, who in a certain manner seemed to preside at that council, had doubts concerning that author.[405] But if the public usage of certain churches obliges us to believe in the

* * * * *

403 *De doctrina christiana* 2.8.18 PL 34 41
404 Erasmus included *Commentarius in symbolum apostolorum* in his editions of Cyprian (1520 and 1530) but he placed it among other tracts under the heading 'Opera quae videntur falso ascripta Cypriano' ('Works which seem to be falsely attributed to Cyprian'), and in his notes following the preface to the work he says that 'the style makes it sufficiently clear that this work is not by Cyprian, and it is said to be among the works attributed to Rufinus; and there is nothing about the phrasing which conflicts with that of Rufinus.' In his prefatory letter to Cardinal Pucci Erasmus says that the *Symbolum fidei*, which in both printed and manuscript volumes still bears Cyprian's name in the title, is current among St Jerome's works under the name of Rufinus (Allen IV Ep 1000:35–7; CWE 7 Ep 1000:37–9). But here and later in this answer to the Paris theologians Erasmus silently accepts the false ascription to Cyprian; he does the same in his *Explanatio symboli apostolorum sive catechismus* (1534) LB V prefatory letter 1133–4, 1141C–1142E / CWE 70. (For information about Erasmus' editions of Cyprian's *Opera omnia* I am grateful to Mark Crane of the Centre for Reformation and Renaissance Studies at the University of Toronto.) Perhaps Erasmus was doing what he said Augustine and others did when they cited the Epistle to the Hebrews under the usual name of Paul simply to identify it, even though they doubted that he wrote it.
    What is said here about the Wisdom of Sirach, the Wisdom of Solomon, and the *Shepherd* appears in Rufinus' *Commentarius* PL 21 374B. The *Shepherd*, composed in the first or second century after Christ by someone named Hermas, was highly revered and read in some churches; some considered it among the canonical books.
405 In *Apologia ad Jacobum Fabrum* Erasmus cited passages from Augustine showing that he clearly had doubts about whether Paul was the author of the Epistle to the Hebrews (LB IX 55C–D / CWE 83 83).

title, even in the age of Augustine and Jerome they were publicly recited under such titles.

I think the same should be said about the citations by ancient writers. Augustine cites many passages from the Epistle to the Hebrews under the name of Paul; but in some places he also cites Paul's testimony as if in doubt about the authorship.[406] St Jerome does the same thing.[407] When they cite something under the name of Paul, they are following normal usage; when they have doubts, they indicate their judgment. So, too, in many places St Cyprian cites Ecclesiasticus naming Solomon in the title, as in the Epistle to Rogatianus, also in his book *Alms* 2, likewise in his book against the Jews 2, and finally in *To Quirinus*, chapter 53.[408] He uses the same name in the title for Wisdom when he is writing to Fortunatus and in not a few other places.[409] But in the Apostles' Creed he declares that those books are not by the authors given in the titles under which they commonly circulate. What is the reason for this? When he cites texts he is not concerned about who is the author. In the Apostles' Creed he teaches what he thinks to be true. Now if it is an article of faith that the Epistle to the Hebrews was issued by the Holy Spirit through the instrumentality of the apostle Paul, my *Elenchus* stated falsely that whoever has doubts about the human author does not for that reason alone vacillate concerning the faith. I say the same about the other books of the New Testament, those, that is, about which for three hundred years and more both orthodox people and outstanding Doctors of the church have had doubts, not those about which there has never been any doubt. And if anyone who removes from these volumes their commonly received titles or calls them into doubt discourages the frequent and fruitful

* * * * *

406 When he gives the title of the Epistle Augustine rarely associates it with Paul's name and on more than one occasion he calls into doubt Paul's authorship: *De civitate Dei* 16.22 PL 41 500, *De Genesi ad litteram* 10.19.34 PL 34.423, *Quaestionum in Heptateuchum libri septem* 7.49 PL 34.812.

407 In *Apologia ad Jacobum Fabrum* LB IX 54E–55C / CWE 83 82–3 Erasmus gives the following examples from Jerome: *Commentariorum in Jeremiam prophetam libri sex* 6.31.31–2 PL 24 (1845) 883D; *Epistolae* 129 ad Dardanum 3 PL 22 1103; *Commentariorum in Evangelium Matthaei libri quatuor* 4.26.8–9 PL 26 (1845) 191C; *Commentariorum in Isaiam libri duodeviginti* 14.50.11 PL 24 (1845) 481C.

408 *Epistolae* 65.2 ad Rogatianum 2 PL 4 (1844) 395B); *Ad Quirinum, testimonia contra Iudaeos libri tres* 2.1, 3.53, PL 4 (1844) 696C–697A, 760C. But in *De opere et eleemosynis* 2 PL 4 (1844) 603B Cyprian attributes Ecclesiasticus to the Holy Spirit (and hence deems it inspired) but does not attribute it to Solomon.

409 *Epistola ad Fortunatum, de exhortatione martyrii* 1 PL 4 (1844) 655C

reading of them, that is what Cyprian did, and after him Augustine and also Jerome.

XXXIII *His third proposition, of which the first part is contained in the epistle prefaced to the* Paraphrase on Luke, *and the second is in* A Reckoning (Supputatio) *no 26*

There have always been doubts about the authorship of the Epistle to the Hebrews, and I myself (to be frank) confess that I still have doubts.[410]

CENSURE

These two propositions are arrogantly and schismatically asserted, contrary to the usage and the determination of the church in many councils: Nicaea,[411] Laodicea,[412] the third Council of Carthage (where Augustine was present),[413] the council of the seventy-two bishops presided over by Gelasius.[414] Moreover, this is clear because the author of this Epistle says that he is sending it by means of his brother Timothy, whom Paul had customarily used as a messenger for some of his other epistles.[415] St Peter also make the same point clear, since at the end of the second canonical epistle directed to the Hebrews, to whom he had sent the first one, he said that his most beloved brother Paul had written to them.[416] Likewise the great

* * * * *

410 Erasmus discussed this question in *Divinationes ad notata Bedae* LB IX 453A–B and in *Elenchus in censuras Bedae* LB IX 497B. He further defended his position in *Prologus supputationis* LB IX 443B–C and in *Supputatio* LB IX 542A–E, 594D–595F.

411 The second Council of Nicaea (AD 787) quotes Hebrews 13:5 and assigns it to the 'the divine apostle Paul'; see *The Decrees of the Ecumenical Councils* ed Norman P. Tanner 2 vols (London and Washington 1990) I 135.

412 The Council of Laodicea in Phrygia (between AD 343 and 381) in its canon 60 gave a list of canonical books which included the second Epistle of Peter and Paul's Epistle to the Hebrews; see Hefele I 323; and Mansi II 574. The council's list, however, omits the deuterocanonical books of the Old Testament and the Apocalypse in the New Testament.

413 *Concilium Carthaginense nomine tertium* capitulum 47 in Mansi III 891

414 Pope St Gelasius died at Rome AD 496. For his list of canonical books see *Conciliorum sub Gelasio habitorum relatio. Concilium Romanum I, quo a septuaginta episcopis libri sacri et authentici ab apocryphis sunt discreti sub Gelasio, anno domini 494* PL 59 157–9; and Mansi VIII 145–7.

415 Heb 13:22

416 2 Pet 3:15

Dionysius cites some things from this Epistle to the Hebrews as if he had taken it from his teacher Paul.[417] So, too, the same point is proved by Clement I,[418] Innocent I, Ambrose, Chrysostom, Gregory Nazianzen, John Damascene, Isidore,[419] and many other Catholic Doctors. It is also not true that there have always been doubts about the authorship of this Epistle to the Hebrews, since Origen writes that before his time his ancient forebears accepted it as by the apostle Paul.[420] The arrogance and stubbornness of this writer is amazing, because, whereas so many Catholic Doctors, popes, and councils have declared this epistle to be by Paul, and whereas the usage and consensus of the universal church prove the same point, this writer still has doubts, as if he were wiser than the whole world.

ERASMUS' CLARIFICATION

xxxiii The Council of Nicaea was not concerned about the authorship but about the authority of this epistle. For some persons denied the authorship of Paul to the extent that they thought it ought not to be considered as part of canonical scripture. And I think no more was undertaken in other councils. The title was added to designate the epistle, and no one denies that many cite it under the name of Paul, and I myself have frequently so cited it. If a passage in this epistle supports my case, and the person I am engaged with believes it is by Paul, why should I not call it an epistle of Paul? But those very same Doctors who, when it is convenient, assert that it is by Paul, indicate in appropriate places that they have doubts about the authorship,

* * * * *

417 See n883 below.
418 In 1 and 2 *Clement* and in his five epistles Pope St Clement I (d 101) cites the Epistle to the Hebrews but never assigns it to the apostle Paul. See J.B. Lightfoot and J.R. Harmer, *The Apostolic Fathers: Greek Texts and English Translations of Their Writings* rev Michael W. Holmes (Grand Rapids, Mich 1992) 28–127, 606; and PL 130 19–60.
419 St Ambrose (339–97), bishop of Milan, Father and Doctor of the church; St John Chrysostom (349–407), patriarch of Constantinople, Father and Doctor of the church; St Gregory Nazianzen (330–90), bishop of Constantinople, Father and Doctor of the church; St John Damascene (645–750), Father of the church; St Isidore (560–636), archbishop of Seville, Doctor of the church – all of these cited the Epistle to the Hebrews often enough, assigning it to the apostle Paul, though that in itself does not mean that they had no doubts about its authorship.
420 See n421 below.

especially Origen,[421] Jerome, and Augustine.[422] But if the Council of Nicaea, together with the others, binds everyone, why did the Doctors I mentioned dare afterwards to have doubts about the authorship – the authorship, I say, not the authority – except that they were less concerned about the title as long as the authority was established? And no one accused them of schism or of amazing arrogance and stubbornness, as if they wanted to be wiser than the whole world. Speaking of the ancients, I said that there were always doubts, not that everyone doubted. And if three or four cite it as by Paul, what is that compared to the whole scope of the ages – especially when the very same persons who cite it under the name of Paul sometimes confess that they have doubts about the authorship?

The Latin church accepted the Epistle to the Hebrews late and reluctantly, as the Greeks did the Apocalypse.[423] But I wonder what schism can arise if someone confesses that that epistle was written under the inspiration of the Holy Spirit and confesses that it is rightly received into canonical Scripture, but has doubts about whether it was written by the apostle Paul, and has those doubts in such a way that he is prepared to cast away all doubt if the church accepts the title with the intention of commanding him to believe that it is by Paul. Since I do not find this to be the case, I am not obstinate against the universal consensus of the church, and I do not waver the least bit from the faith if I profess that the epistle was brought forth by the Spirit of God but I have doubts about the human authorship. If someone reading publicly in church should omit or change the accepted titles, perhaps some priests would murmur against him, but I have not done this and would not wish others to do so. But what schism does the church have to fear if someone privately instructs the learned for pedagogical purposes?

* * * * *

421 According to Eusebius, Origen says: 'But I would say ... that the thoughts are those of the Apostle, but the phraseology and the composition are those of someone who recalled to mind the teachings of the Apostle and who, as it were, had made notes of what was said by the teacher. If any church, then, holds this Epistle to be Paul's, let it be commended for this, for not without reason have the men of old handed it down as Paul's. Who the author of the Epistle is God truly knows, but the account that has reached us from some is that Clement, who was bishop of the Romans, wrote the Epistle; from others, that Luke, who wrote the Gospel and the Acts, is the author.' See Eusebius *Ecclesiastical History* 6.25 trans Roy J. Deferrari 2 vols (New York 1933) II 50; see also PG 14 1309.
422 On the doubts of Augustine and Jerome see nn406 and 407 above.
423 Jerome *Epistolae* 129 ad Dardanum 3 PL 22 1103

What force usage has is a perplexed and disputed point, nor is it clear enough that this point is accepted by universal usage. And then, if the title is accepted, it matters in what sense it is accepted. Theologians expect more solid reasons than usage and the reputation of the church, especially when these terms are used in such various ways. And so it is due to untrammelled irritation that an insult is tacked on, 'this writer still has doubts, as if he were wiser than the whole world,' since, apart from many of the ancients, and those the chief Doctors of the church, Tommaso de Vio, Cardinal Cajetanus, who is still alive, cited this Epistle without the name of Paul, both in his book on the Eucharist against the Lutherans[424] and in other places. In one place he adds 'which the author of this Epistle handles according to the genuine meaning.'[425] If he had no doubts about the authorship, what need was there for such a periphrasis? And what angel has revealed to the theologians that the whole world thinks what they seem to have persuaded themselves to think? Certainly, as far as judgments about style are concerned, I think that I am not inferior to any theologians whatsoever.

xxxiv *His fourth proposition. In* Elenchus[426]
There have long been doubts about the second Epistle of Peter.

CENSURE
For a long time the church has also accepted this epistle under the name of Peter by usage and by definition in the council of Laodicea, in the third council of Carthage, in that of Pope Gelasius,[427] and by the decretum of Innocent the Great.[428] Moreover, from the language of the same epistle it is clear that it was written by St Peter. For in the opening the apostle Peter is mentioned as its writer and the same letter asserts that the writer was present at the transfiguration;[429] but only three of the apostles were present at it, as the evangelists testify. Hence, since

* * * * *

424 Cajetanus (1469–1534) *De missae sacrificio et ritu adversus Lutheranos in Opuscula omnia Thomae de Vio Caietani* (Lugduni: Ex officina Iuntarum 1587; repr Hildesheim 1995) III 287 tractatus 10, caput 5: 'Obiectiones ex epistola ad Hebraeos contra sacrificium Missae'
425 I have not found the place where Cajetanus adds this clause.
426 *Elenchus in censuras Bedae* LB IX 497C, where Erasmus briefly defends this doubt, relying on the authority of Jerome.
427 See nn412–14 above.
428 See n402 above.
429 1 Pet 1:17–18

it is universally accepted that neither James the Greater nor John the evangelist wrote it, it is rightly established that Peter wrote it. In the light of these facts, it is improper and fruitless to propose any doubt about its author, since no one at all can be uncertain about whether it should be attributed to St Peter.

ERASMUS' CLARIFICATION

XXXIV If it was improper to propose this to academics in passing, how was it any less improperly done by St Thomas Aquinas, who carefully informs us that there were doubts among the ancients concerning both the authorship and the authority of the Epistle to the Hebrews, some saying that it was by Luke, others by Barnabas, others by Clement, pope and martyr.[430] With what profit does Thomas mention these matters so many centuries after the Council of Nicaea? To be sure, he answered the arguments underlying such doubts, but so feebly that it would have been more satisfactory if he had not touched on them. And those were not the chief arguments supporting the doubts – namely the omission of the name and a somewhat different style.[431] There were not a few other arguments somewhat more weighty that motivated the learned. After Thomas how profitable was it for Lyra to raise the same question?[432] But they add that these doubts arose before the Council of Nicaea, even though I showed that the principal Doctors of the church had their doubts about the authorship after the council. How profitable was it for Chrysostom in his commentary on the Acts of the Apostles to remark in his preface that there were also many in his time who had doubts about the authorship of this work?[433] How profitable was it for Jerome to write about the Gospel of Mark as follows: 'But also the Gospel according to Mark, who was his pupil and interpreter, is said to be his (that is, Peter's).'[434] How profitable was it for Papias, the disciple of John the evangelist, to inform us that the story of the adulteress was not

* * * * *

430 *Expositio in omnes s. Pauli epistolas, in epistolam ad Hebraeos*, prologus
431 These are the only two arguments mentioned by Thomas Aquinas.
432 The Franciscan theologian Nicolas de Lyra (1270/5–1349) in his extraordinarily popular biblical commentary *Postilla literalis super totam bibliam* (1322–31), at the conclusion of his proemium to the Acts of the Apostles, refuted two arguments against Paul's authorship of the Epistle to the Hebrews and gave six arguments in favour of it.
433 *Commentarius in Acta apostolorum* 1.1 PG 60 13; see also *In inscriptionem altaris et in principium Actorum* 1.3 PG 57 71.
434 *De viris illustribus* 1 PL 23 (1845) 607B–609A

by John but was excerpted from the apocryphal Gospel of the Nazarenes, even though at that time the episode was read under the name of John, as it still is.[435] Why do so, except that they thought it matters for learned men not to be ignorant of such matters?

Moreover, those who had doubts about the authorship of the second Epistle of Peter were not so stupid that they did not see there the mention of the vision on the mount; but rather they suspected that that epistle was written by someone who wanted it to be read under the name of Peter and that he added the mention of the vision so as to be more persuasive. But they came by this suspicion because of the feeling and the phrasing and the force of the ideas, which seemed partly to be fashioned in imitation of the other epistle and partly not exactly congruous with the majesty of the prince of the apostles. I pass over the fact that here the mention of the titles in councils is thrown up as an objection, as if the universal church had condemned those who disagree about the titles.

xxxv *His fifth proposition, which is in* Elenchus[436]
There have long been doubts about the Apocalypse, not (I say) from heretics but from orthodox men, who nevertheless embraced it as coming from the Holy Spirit, though they were uncertain about the name of the writer.

CENSURE
The Book of the Apocalypse is manifestly recognized to have issued from St John the apostle and evangelist, both by the usage of the church and by the determination of the same in councils such as the

* * * * *

435 In his *Historia ecclesiae* 3.39 Eusebius merely reports that Papias has included a story about a woman accused before the Lord of many sins which is contained in the Gospel according to the Hebrews. In his annotation on John 8:3, discussing the problem that the story of the adulteress does not occur in most Greek manuscripts of John's Gospel, Erasmus interprets Eusebius (or Papias as reported in Eusebius) in such a way as to clarify what he says here. He thinks that Eusebius must be referring to the woman taken in adultery who was brought before the Lord in John 8:3–10, and that the Gospel according to the Hebrews cannot mean the Gospel according to Matthew (which was written in Hebrew), for then the story would have been restored to Matthew's Gospel and would not have been placed in the Gospel according to John, but rather must refer to the apocryphal Gospel of the Nazarenes LB VI 373–4.

436 *Elenchus in censuras Bedae* LB IX 497C–D

Third Council of Carthage[437] and that of St Gelasius,[438] and also in the
Synod of Toledo, in which it is said: 'The authority of many councils
and the synodical decrees of the holy bishops of Rome prescribe that
the Book of the Apocalypse is by John the evangelist and have established that it is to be accepted among the Holy Books.' At that synod
Isidore, bishop of Seville, a man outstanding for his brilliant learning, was present.[439] Furthermore, the text of the same book shows that
John was its author; for in the text the writer is said to be the John
who gave testimony to the word of God and who was for that reason
relegated to the island of Patmos.[440] Surely these statements cannot be
understood to apply to any other John but the apostle. Again, the most
holy Father Dionysius the Aeropagite (the disciple of St Paul), Innocent I,[441] Irenaeus, Justin, John Damascene, and other Catholic Doctors
and holy men bear witness to the same point. Among them Augustine,
that brilliant splendour of the church, clearly indicates this: he numbers the Alogians or Alogans among the heretics condemned by the
church precisely because they deny that John the apostle and evangelist wrote the Gospel and the Apocalypse. Hence this writer has fallen
into error in this proposition in the same manner as in the preceding
propositions by proposing the aforesaid doubt, giving offence to the
little ones, and failing to explain the determination of the church, of
sacred councils, and of saintly fathers.

ERASMUS' CLARIFICATION

xxxv In the annotation which I supply for the Apocalypse I mention which
Doctors discuss the Apocalypse and what they think about it.[442] For those
who denied it was by John the evangelist believe either that there was some
other John than the evangelist, just as they ascribed the two later epistles
not to John the evangelist but to John the priest,[443] or that whoever wrote
the book did so to make it look as if it were written by the evangelist and

* * * * *

437 See n413 above.
438 See n414 above. Neither St Gelasius nor the Council of Carthage assign the
    Apocalypse specifically to John the evangelist but only to John.
439 See chapter 17 of the fourth Council of Toledo (AD 671) in Mansi x 624. Isidore
    of Seville was present at that council.
440 Rev 1:9
441 See n402 above. Innocent mentions John, not specifically John the evangelist.
442 LB VI 1123E–1126A
443 In *Elenchus in censuras Bedae* LB IX 511D Erasmus defended his attribution of
    the later two Epistles of John to John the priest.

therefore added to it a place that was suitable for his intention.[444] If someone thinks this explanation is absurd, here I will allow it to be as absurd as he likes, as long as he knows that in that period the world was replete with apocryphal books bearing titles that did not belong to them. And also godly persons persuaded themselves that this practice was not only permissible but also dutiful. And Augustine does not deny that such persons benefited the Christian people through such fictions, though he thinks that they will receive a very great reward only if they gain pardon for the fictions.[445]

Moreover, even if we grant that that Dionysius was the Aeropagite who was a disciple of Paul – a point about which many have serious doubts – if the authority of Dionysius is so great that we are forced to believe that Epistle was written by Paul,[446] then we will be even more forcefully compelled to believe Papias, who was certainly a pupil of John the evangelist, when he writes that the story of the adulterous woman was not by John, even though it is recited as John's in church. But Augustine mentions that the Alogians were condemned not only because they had doubts about the Apocalypse, since at that time even the orthodox did not all accept the authority of the Apocalypse, but rather because they also scorned John's Gospel and considered it to be spurious, whereas the church never had any doubts about it.[447]

The Synod of Toledo alone, if indeed its words have been reported accurately, prescribes that it is by John the evangelist, whereas Innocent says only 'and the Apocalypse of John.'[448] And in the oldest Greek codex, which you would have said[449] was written a thousand years ago, the title was given as 'The Apocalypse of John the Theologian.' But Jerome argues, partly from Papias, partly from the titles, that there were two Johns, one the apostle, the other the priest.[450] But I suspect that the word 'prescribe' derives from Isidore,[451] and this is not the place to mention what I think of

* * * * *

444 That is, Patmos
445 I have not been able to find where Augustine expresses such an opinion.
446 That is, the Epistle to the Hebrews
447 *De haeresibus* 30 PL 42 31
448 See n402 above.
449 That is, if you had seen it
450 *De viris illustribus* 18 PL 23 (1845) 637A–B
451 In fact, Isidore does not use any form of *praescribere* in connection with the Apocalypse, which he simply accepts as by John the evangelist. (He does, however, mention the doubts about the authorship of the second Epistle of Peter, the Epistle of James, the second and third Epistles of John, and the Epistle to the Hebrews); see his *De origine officiorum* 1.12.11–12 PL 749B–750A.

him. The Lord judges the holiness of the man. But certainly his language displays more enthusiasm than learning or judgment. He wrote in a rude age, and he seems to have had an extensive library, which he might have been able to use more correctly if he had been more thoroughly educated. Certainly he was a compiler, as was Bede, though Bede, in my judgment, was both more learned and more eloquent.

But these objections directed at me are irrelevant, since I profess that what the universal church believes about the titles I also believe; I easily submit my perception to her authority, not in this matter only but in all others as well, as long as whatever has once crept somehow into the usage of Christians or whatever pleases some bishop or other is not immediately taken to belong to the church. But if we are to be so careful to avoid scandal, we must erase whatever Eusebius and Jerome published about these matters. Some of the judgments of learned men are silent, and it is sometimes expedient to tweak their ears to arouse them. They point a finger at me because I pass over the authority of the church. Actually, at this point I could not interrupt the flow. But I did so in an annotation which I added to the *Annotations on the Apocalypse*. We cannot drive home all points at all points. Certainly, since I gave a brief indication[452] to the learned, I never suspected that anyone would take offence at this, much less would work it up into a schism. If I had feared such a thing, I would not have said anything at all about such points. Still, if there is any quarrel here, it originates in those who make a fuss and a spectacle of such trifles. But lest anyone should attribute any less authority to the aforesaid volumes, I give them my loftiest praise.[453]

Topic 11. The Apostles' Creed. In the preface to Matthew

XXXVI *The proposition of Erasmus*

I do not know whether the Creed was issued by the apostles.[454]

* * * * *

Erasmus may feel that the use of *praescribere* in the sense 'define' or 'assert' is unacceptable. But Isidore generally uses *praescribere* in the classical sense 'appoint, prescribe.'

452 Literally, 'three words': *Adagia* III iii 83

453 He means the Epistle to the Hebrews, the second Epistle of Peter, and the Apocalypse.

454 Erasmus defended this proposition in *Divinationes ad notata Bedae* LB IX 457D–458D and also, very briefly, in *Elenchus in censuras Bedae* LB IX 497C. He treated it at some length in *Supputatio* LB IX 554B–557C but without precise evidence from the Fathers and councils.

CENSURE

Since it is to be held as part of the faith that the Creed which is said to be by the apostles was issued and promulgated by the apostles, and since the Catholic Doctors such as Clement 1 in his epistle to James the brother of the Lord, Augustine in his *Sermon* 2 on Palm Sunday and the vigil of Pentecost, and likewise Ambrose, and Leo 1,[455] and others uniformly hold that each of the apostles said what he thought when they set up the Creed, this ignorance, which serves the cause of impiety, is proposed scandalously.

ERASMUS' CLARIFICATION

xxxvi Far be it from any Christian to have any doubts about the articles which are contained in the Apostles' Creed. No less should be attributed to them than to the four Gospels. I had doubts only about whether what we have now issued from the apostles in writing. For no one doubts that they preached such doctrines. And it is probable that they conferred among themselves about the sum and substance of the preaching of the gospel and agreed on these or similar headings, as is reported in the *Ecclesiastical History*.[456] In the same place where I seem to have doubts I attribute to it an apostolic majesty and brevity, I list it as canonical Scripture, and I put in on the same level as the Gospels. And I do not doubt whether it originated with the apostles, for it could have been spoken viva voce, but whether it came down to us through them as a written document communally produced by all of them. For at that time there were perhaps many creeds circulating, and to distinguish this one it was called the Apostles' Creed as worthy of the apostles' spirit and perhaps as the oldest of all, so that, in the absence of

* * * * *

455 Clement 1 *Epistola prima Clementis ad Jacobum* PL 130 27–8. Pseudo-Augustine *Sermones* 212 and 266 PL 38 1058–60, 1225–9; neither of these sermons makes the point claimed for them here by the Paris theologians. Pseudo(?)-Ambrose *Explanatio symboli ad initiandos* PL 17 (1845) 1155D–1159B. Leo 1 *Epistolae* 31.4 PL 54 794B

456 In his *Ecclesiastical History* Eusebius does not report that the apostles did so confer and agree, but what he does report seems to make it probable that they did so: 'The Lord after his resurrection imparted knowledge to James the Just and to John and Peter, and they imparted it to the rest of the apostles, and the rest of the apostles to the seventy ... Thus, under the influence of heavenly power and with the divine cooperation, the doctrine of the Saviour, like the rays of the sun, quickly illumined the whole world; and straightaway, in accordance with the divine Scriptures, the voice of the inspired evangelists and apostles went forth through all the earth, and their words to the end of the world' (1.1 and 1.3).

any other author, it is probable that it came down to us from the apostles. Since I everywhere make such professions, why is it dangerous for anyone to doubt whether it came down to us as written by the apostles?

I have given the reasons for my doubts in this matter, of which the principal one is that the Creed is reported variously among the ancient writers, so much so that whole articles are either present or absent. For even St Cyprian testifies that this Creed existed in different forms in different churches, some of them adding elements not found in the Roman church. He thinks that such additions were made against the heretics as they sprang up. He suspects there were two reasons why such variations did not arise at Rome: one is that there were no heresies there; the other, that a catechumen who was to be baptized customarily and routinely recited the Creed publicly.[457] And Cyprian informs us that in neither the Roman nor the eastern churches did the Creed have the article 'he descended into hell,'[458] which is not lacking in our Creed today, though neither Tertullian nor Augustine mention a descent into hell when they explain the Creed.[459] We read 'the communion of saints.' Cyprian omits that article, for this reason, I think: it was added as a sort of explanation of what 'the holy church' is. Neither of them[460] touches on the last article, 'the life of the world to come,' and they do not add 'Catholic' to 'the holy church,' although Augustine adds it as an interpretation, as it were.[461] And Cyprian reads 'resurrection of this flesh,' seemingly adding the pronoun against the Origenists,[462] whereas in our Creed it is not added. How is it that in the very beginning a difference occurs? For, as the same Cyprian informs us, all the eastern churches handed it down thus: 'Credo in uno Deo Patre omnipotente.'[463] Then again, where we say 'and in Jesus Christ his only Son,' the eastern churches recite it with the addition 'that is, one God and one Lord,' which seems to be an addition directed against the Origenists or the Arians.[464] Moreover,

* * * * *

457 Rufinus (pseudo-Cyprian) *Commentarius in symbolum apostolorum* 3 PL 21 339B. See n404 above.

458 *Commentarius in symbolum apostolorum* 18 PL 21 356A.

459 Tertullian *Adversus Praxeam* 2 PL 2 (1844) 156B–157A; Augustine *De symbolo sermo ad catechumenos* PL 40 627–36

460 Cyprian and Augustine, presumably

461 *De symbolo sermo ad catechumenos* 6.14 PL 40 635

462 *Commentarius in symbolum apostolorum* 36–45 PL 21 373A–383B. See n404 above.

463 In the Latin church the Creed begins 'Credo in unum Deum Patrem omnipotentem' ('I believe in one God, the Father almighty'). The difference between the ablative and accusative cases seems merely verbal.

464 *Commentarius in symbolum apostolorum* 4 PL 21 340C. See n13 above.

in the preceding article the eastern churches not only read 'in God the Father almighty' but also add 'invisible and incapable of suffering.' Cyprian thinks that this addition was directed against Sabellius and the Patrispassianos.[465] Again, where we add 'creator of heaven and earth,' Cyprian neither recites nor explains this phrase, from which it appears that it was not present in the eastern or western churches; and it is probable that it was added against the heretics who taught that one God was the author of the Old Testament and another of the New, and that the one was just and the other good.

Here I call upon the fair-minded reader: if this Creed, which we attribute to the apostles, was issued in writing by the agreement of the apostles and for that reason is worthy of greater reverence than if it had issued from one evangelist, or certainly no less reverence, what temerity was it to add so many words to so few? Who would permit such a thing in the Gospel of Mark or Luke, who did not belong to the twelve and also wrote later only what they had heard? Nor can they get around the difficulty by saying that Cyprian, when he mentions the Creed of the eastern churches, means the Creed of Nicaea or Constantinople; for after them he could have added many others. In his whole commentary he is speaking about the same Creed. What shall we make of the fact that in the edition of the canons of the Council of Nicaea the Creed is reported differently from what is sung in church today and does not go any further than the procession of the Holy Spirit? But the Creed of the Council of Nicaea was nothing more than an explanation of the Apostles' Creed, not adding new articles but explaining the old ones. Hence we can infer that 'I believe in the Holy Spirit' was the last element of the Apostles' Creed, as it was the end of the Nicene Creed,[466] as it also was in the Creeds of Antioch, Sardica, and Carthage,[467] which seem to approve of it. But since sects made it possible to have doubts about where to find the church, the article 'in

* * * * *

465 *Commentarius in symbolum apostolorum* 5 PL 21 343C. Sabellius (c 198–220), seeking to preserve the unity of God, was perhaps the principal proponent of the trinitarian heresy that God was a single monad, the Father, successively revealed in the 'modes' of Son and Holy Spirit. Thus it was the Father who became incarnate as the Son and was crucified (thus the designation 'patripassionism,' 'father-suffering').

466 *Decrees of the Ecumenical Councils* ed Norman P. Tanner 2 vols (London and Washington 1990) 1 5

467 The Creeds of the Council of Antioch (AD 341) are given in Hefele 1 76–81; the Creed of the Council of Sardica is given in Mansi III 1225–6; the Creed of the Council of Carthage is given in Mansi III 894, 917–18.

the holy church' was added to exclude all the conventicles of the heretics. Then, because Novatius or someone like him did not receive back into the church those who had lapsed from their baptismal vows, or because someone thought that sins could be remitted apart from the sacraments of the church, it seems that 'the forgiveness of sins' was added. Afterwards, when there arose some who professed the resurrection of the soul but denied that of the body, 'the resurrection of the flesh' was added. Again, when the Origenists confessed that we will arise with bodies but not with the ones in which our minds now dwell, in the Creed which Cyprian explains (the *Aquilensian*, if I am not mistaken) the resurrection of this flesh was added. What shall we make of the fact that, as we are informed by the Faculty of Theology, some churches even today read 'I believe in the holy church,' where the ancients read 'I believe the holy church,' considering it not proper to read it out otherwise? These points are reinforced by what is said by Tertullian, a most ancient writer, in the book which he composed against Praxeas, where he listed the articles of the Apostles' Creed, which he professes came down to us together with the gospel; his recension has the same concluding element as the Nicene Creed: 'We believe in one God,' he says, 'but nevertheless under the dispensation which we call familial, so that there is also the Son of the one God, his Speech, who proceeded from him and through whom all things were made and without whom nothing was made. That he was sent by the Father into a virgin and born of her as man and God, the son of man and the Son of God, and was named Jesus Christ. That he suffered, died, and was buried according to Scripture and was revived by the Father and was taken up into heaven where he sits at the right hand of the Father, and that he will come to judge the living and the dead. Who from there, according to his promise, will send from the Father the Holy Spirit, the Paraclete, who makes holy the faith of those who believe in the Father, the Son, and the Holy Spirit. This measure, etc.'[468] Here it is clear on the face of it that in the age of Tertullian 'I believe in the Holy Spirit' was the concluding element of the Apostles' Creed, as it was of the Nicene Creed.

Finally I remember having read in some commentary or other (though the exact place escapes me) that the rest of the Creed after the procession of the Spirit was added by later councils. In passing we should note that Tertullian does not call it the Apostles' Creed but the measure of faith.

* * * * *

468 *Adversus Praxeam* 2 PL 2 156B–157A

But if the Creed which we use today had been issued by all the apostles with unanimous consent, it would deserve more reverence than any of the Gospels. What temerity, then, would it have been for the churches to add or subtract anything from such a written document since it was considered to be the utmost impiety to dare to do such a thing even in the Epistles of Paul? True, Cyprian reports that this Creed arose from a discussion of the apostles, but he reports it only as a human story: 'our ancestors,' he says, 'hand it down.' And in the middle of his explanation he speaks as follows: 'And those who have handed down the Creed also very carefully designated the time when these things were done under Pontius Pilate.'[469] He does not say 'apostles' but rather 'those who handed down the Creed,' as if he were uncertain who in fact did it. After Cyprian, Augustine in his book on the Creed never calls it the Apostles' Creed, nor does he say that it was handed down by the apostles, but rather he indicates that it was collected by the Fathers from Holy Scripture as a help to memory.[470] Antoninus says that it was issued by the universal authority of the church.[471]

Furthermore, as for sermons in which it is reported that individual apostles produced individual articles, the phraseology itself will persuade the attentive reader that they do not belong to the ones they are attributed to. Now, no matter how much Augustine or anyone else either believed such an idea or preached it to the crass multitude,[472] I do not think it is a matter of faith, especially since theologians do not agree in the division of the articles, and are more inclined to favour a division into fourteen parts rather than twelve.[473] But if the church should also order this to be believed,

* * * * *

469 *Commentarius in symbolum apostolorum* 2, 18 PL 21 337A, 356A.
470 *De symbolo sermo ad catechumenos* 1 PL 40 627; see also *Sermones* 214 In traditione symboli PL 38 1065–6.
471 St Antoninus (1389–1459), archbishop of Florence, in his *Summa theologica* part III title 31 chapter 8 assigns each article to an apostle, but concludes that, though others make different assignments, the matter is of little importance. What matters is that through the apostles the Christian people draw from Holy Scripture what strengthens the faith of all and causes those who are to be baptized to profess and believe it and those who have been baptized to hold to it firmly.
472 Pseudo-Augustine *Sermones* 140.1, 141.1 PL 39 2189–90
473 Concerning the assigning of articles to individual apostles and the division into twelve or fourteen articles see 'Divisions of the Apostles Creed' in Nicholas Ayo *The Sermon-Conferences of St. Thomas Aquinas on the Apostles' Creed* (Notre Dame, Ind 1988) 171–85.

on this point also I willingly submit my perception to her judgment. But I am surprised that this is demanded by the faculty, though Noël Béda, as strict a censor as he is, does not demand it. And the argument that some make from etymology, as if each of the apostles threw in his portion, is frivolous. For 'symbolum' signifies a sign taken over from soldiers, who recognize one another by vocal or non-vocal passwords and use them to capture deserters or enemies.[474] The idea that individual articles came from individual apostles seems to have been thought up by painters or someone who intended this to be a way to celebrate the names of the apostles and to provide a mnemonic aid to the catachumens.[475]

But it is closer to the truth to say that the Creed which we call that of the apostles was the one which, according to the Roman church and by the authority of the early Fathers, was given to the catachumens to be learned; to this some parts were added against heresies as they sprang up. Otherwise why was this Creed not added to the decrees or canons of the apostles? If these canons do not seem to be by the apostles, though they go under that title, it follows that whatever has their names in the title does not immediately proceed from them in written form.[476] Finally, though there may be authors who, without any hedging, pronounce that the Creed is by the apostles, certainly no one has pronounced that they issued it in writing. Nevertheless even that I never deny, but rather I indicate that I have doubts, and those doubts I would drop the moment that I recognize that this is what the church teaches. As it is, I hear no more than 'which is said to be by the apostles' and 'is held by the church.' Still, it is not false to say it is by the apostles, since it contains what the apostles both preached and published in the Gospels and Epistles. Hence it follows that no less authority is to be attributed to it than to canonical Scripture.

* * * * *

474 Rufinus *Commentarius in symbolum apostolorum* 2 PL 21 337B–338B gives the meaning *collatio* 'an assemblage of items' for *symbolum* as if the apostles each contributed his own article, an erroneous meaning that was frequently repeated. Rufinus also gave the meaning that Erasmus accepts (also frequently repeated): a token or password used by soldiers to distinguish friends from enemies.

475 For a full and well-documented treatment of the legend which grew up about the Apostle's Creed, and for the iconography of the apostles and the twelve articles, see Henri de Lubac *The Christian Faith: An Essay on the Structure of the Apostles' Creed* trans Richard Arnandez (San Francisco 1986) 19–53.

476 The Apostolic Canons are a collection of ecclesiastical decrees (eighty-five in the East, fifty in the West) concerning the government of the church, incorporated with the Apostolic Constitutions. Their date of origin is about AD 500.

Topic 12. The translation of Holy Scripture into a vernacular language

XXXVII *The first proposition of Erasmus. In his preface to Matthew*
I would like Holy Scripture to be translated into all languages.[477]

CENSURE

Although Sacred Scripture is by its very nature holy and good, no matter what language it may be translated into, nevertheless just how dangerous it is to permit it to be translated into the vernacular everywhere and to be read by simple, uneducated people with no explanation, so that they abuse it and do not read it piously and humbly (as is the case with most people nowadays), is sufficiently indicated by the Waldensians,[478] the Albigensians,[479] and the Turelupini,[480] who, taking

* * * * *

477 LB VII **3v. Erasmus defends this proposition very briefly in *Divinationes ad notata Bedae* LB IX 457B–C and at greater length in *Supputatio* LB IX 551E–554B, where it is combined with the following propositions in Topic 12. Two recent articles by Wim François explore the debate between the Paris theologians and Erasmus over the translation of the Bible into the vernacular: 'La condemnation par les théologiens parisiens du plaidoyer d'Érasme pour la traduction de la Bible dans la langue vulgaire (1527–1531)' *Augustiniana* 55:3–4 (2005) 357–405; and 'Petrus Sutor et son plaidoyer contre les traductions de la Bible en langue populaire (1525)' *Ephemerides Theologicae Lovanienses: Louvain Journal of Theology and Canon Law* 82:1 (2006) 139–63.

478 See n72 above.

479 A neo-Manichaean, hyperascetical sect which flourished in France in the twelfth and thirteenth centuries; it was supported by the counts of Toulouse and was finally suppressed by a lengthy and bloody crusade, supported to a large degree by popes and led unscrupulously by Simon of Montfort. Because the Albigensians believed that matter was irredeemably evil, they denied the true humanity of Christ, forbade marriage, encouraged suicide, denied purgatory and the resurrection of the body, abstained entirely from meat, and fasted rigorously.

480 This was a heretical sect which sprang up in the late fourteenth century in France, especially in the Dauphiné. It was condemned by the Inquisition in Paris in 1372 and by Pope Gregory XI in the following year. Its beliefs suggest a connection with the Beguards and the Brethren of the Free Spirit, both in an emphasis on poverty and in the notion that the 'perfect' cannot sin and are free to follow their own inclinations. In the early fourteenth century Jean Gerson noted this belief in the freedom of the 'perfect' and also reported the immorality of the Turelupini (from hearsay): 'In the manner of the Cynic philosophers they flaunt their private parts publicly and they couple in public like beasts; as naked as dogs they display and exercise their privy members'

their opportunity from such translations, spread many errors. Hence, in this age, considering the malice of mankind, such a translation is dangerous and destructive if we are speaking about all the books of Scripture with no discrimination. And if something is useful to a few, that does not mean it should rashly be permitted to all. For in a matter not necessary for salvation we should rather protect the welfare of the many by forbidding the translation than permit what is useful to a few, to the grave detriment of the many. Hence such a translation is justly condemned.

ERASMUS' CLARIFICATION

XXXVII Since Holy Scripture was formerly translated into the vernacular – for at that time weavers and sailors knew Greek and Latin – since Chrysostom piously recommends that laymen study the Divine Volumes,[481] since Jerome praises women who study Scripture[482] and since he translated the Sacred Books even into the Dalmatian language,[483] if the malice of mankind has increased to such a degree that it is necessary to deprive Christian people of one of the best things that they have, namely the reading of Holy

* * * * *

('Cynicorum philosophorum more omnia verenda publicitus gestabant et in publico velut jumenta coibant, instar canum in nuditate et exercitio membrorum pudendorum degentes'). But such accusations had been made against heretics for centuries and cannot be taken at face value. See DTC XV 1931–2.

481 Professor Brian Daley, Huisking Professor of Theology at Notre Dame University, has kindly pointed out to me several places where Chrysostom insists that the congregation listening to him – who were mainly laypeople – should study Scripture carefully, as the key to living devout Christian lives: *Homily on Matthew* 2.9–10; *Homily on John* 21.1, 23.1; *Homily on Acts* 34; *Homily on Romans* 1.1; *Homily on Hebrews* 8.9–10. He also has a pair of homilies, *On Vainglory* and *How Parents Should Bring Up Children*, which recommends teaching them a whole course of study based on Scripture. Unfortunately this was not published until 1656 (by François Combefis), so that Erasmus would not have known it (unless he saw it in manuscript).

482 *Prefatio in librum Esther* PL 28 (1845) 1434A–B

483 Professor Daley also suggests that 'the Dalmatian language' may simply refer to the kind of Latin Jerome grew up speaking in Dalmatia. He notes that there was a Dalmatian dialect which was a Romance form of Latin spoken along the Dalmatian coast and akin to Romanian, but the earliest references to it as a language come from the tenth century. A Dalmatian humanist contemporary with Erasmus, however – Marko Marulić, who is considered the 'father of Croatian humanistic studies' – called Jerome 'the brilliant crown of our Croatian language.' Perhaps Erasmus had heard such a Croatian estimate of Jerome as a proto-Dalmatian.

Scripture, certainly that is a matter for profound grief. But in times past, because the monks read Holy Scripture issued in the vernacular and uneducated people did not understand the hidden meaning, they originated the absurd heresy of the Anthropomorphites;[484] but still the use of Holy Scripture was not forbidden but rather the error was corrected.

If laypeople read canonical Scripture in the way I there advise it should be read, I think there would be much more profit in it than danger. First of all I advise that they should be prepared by their pastors with some principles and rules for understanding it. But above all let them refrain from rash judgments, and let them adore the mystery where they cannot achieve an understanding of it, and let them resort to the learned. And let them prefer to learn from a living voice rather than from reading. Let them not read at all unless they have no access to a teacher or are preparing themselves for a holy sermon explaining that passage. And let them read soberly and with the greatest reverence, as if they were reading not human language but divine oracles. Let them proceed to do so with a simple and pure mind, purged of worldly desires, and they should also say a little prayer beforehand. Since in that passage I carefully advise these and other measures, I hoped that if they were observed people could become familiar with Holy Scripture with much profit and no danger to piety and that someone who is now crude might shortly become a good student.[485]

Now if there is some danger for laypeople in reading the profound language of Scripture there is more danger in their ignorance of it. Accordingly, when the pastors are remiss, then I grant that people should resort to silent masters.[486] Moreover, whatever can be achieved by the voice of an interpreter can be achieved by the commentaries of learned men translated into the vernacular. I care nothing about the craziness put out by the Waldensians, the Albigensians, and the Turelupini, and I do not think it has anything to do with me. It is not laypeople who have caused the uproars of our times but learned men, whose authority is followed by the people, since John Huss and Wyclif[487] were expert scholastic theologians, and Balthasar, the Doctor

* * * * *

484 Because the Old Testament mentioned God's corporeal members some simple-minded people believed he had a human body; see Augustine *Epistolae* 148.4.13–14 PL 33 628. Since Erasmus mentions monks, he may well have had in mind the treatise by St Cyril of Alexandria (370–440) against some Anthropomorphite monks; see *Adversus Anthropomorphites* PL 76 1066–1132.

485 LB VII sig **2v

486 That is, books. Gellius 14.2.1

487 John Huss (1369–1415), rector and professor of theology at the University of Prague, and an enthusiastic supporter of Wyclif's teachings. He was con-

of Anabaptism,[488] was a scholastic Doctor. So also are Luther and Oecolam-padius.[489] All the heresies in the world arose almost entirely either from philosophy or from Holy Scripture wrongly understood; and no one is re-strained from reading philosophical books, but Scripture is forbidden to us.

But if some regulation from a bishop or someone else has at some time or other been issued against the temerity of the people of our time, I do not think it applies to the universal church, especially since for many centuries now Holy Scripture has been available in the vernacular translations of various nations – to which the church has turned a blind eye. In fact, what the theologians cite here is not in the preface to Matthew but in a section that was added at that time to fill up some pages accidentally left blank.[490] And all of it was cut out in later editions.[491]

XXXVIII *His second proposition. In the preface to Matthew*
They cry out against it as an intolerable offence if a woman or a tanner should speak about Holy Scripture.[492]

CENSURE
If we take proper account of the impudent boldness of many persons in our times, we should consider it an intolerable transgression that

* * * * *

demned and burnt at the stake at the Council of Constance in 1415. On Wyclif see n87 above.

488 Balthasar Hubmaier (d 1528) obtained a doctorate of theology from the University of Ingolstadt. He became a leader of the Anabaptists first in Waldshut im Breisgau (where he lent some support to the Peasants' Revolt) and later in Mikolov (Nikolsburg) in Moravia (from which he was extradited by the Austrian authorities and burnt at the stake). See CEBR.

489 Johannes Oecolampadius (1482–1531) received a doctorate of theology from the University of Basel. He was thoroughly trained in humanist studies, especially in Greek, and assisted Erasmus in editing the Greek New Testament. In the 1520s Oecolampadius tended to side with Luther and Zwingli (especially on the Eucharist and on free will) and drifted away from his former friend Erasmus. See CEBR II 24–7.

490 The section Erasmus refers to is the Preface *pio lectori* ('to the devout reader'), which concludes with the sentence: 'I added this section because the printer complained that otherwise some pages would be blank; I wanted to fill them with some matter not entirely frivolous' (LB VII **4v); Erasmus made the same point in *Supputatio* LB IX 552E. See Allen Epp 1255 intro and 1274:20–2.

491 For the editions of the *Paraphrase on Matthew* see CWE 45 xxiv–xxvii. I do not know if the Preface to the Devout Reader was omitted in any of them.

492 Erasmus defended this proposition in *Divinationes ad notata Bedae* LB IX 456C–D.

simple, uneducated people read according to their own judgment Holy
Scripture translated into their own languages, discussing it and treating arguments about difficulties in it. Still they are not forbidden to
consult among themselves about what they have heard in public sermons for the purpose of correcting their morals and arousing their
compunction and devotion, so that they may become more and more
charitable, their humility may be firmly established, and the works of
their flesh may be mortified.

ERASMUS' CLARIFICATION
xxxviii Here there is nothing which makes against me. They grant that it
is permissible for laypeople to confer among themselves about what they
have heard in sermons in order to encourage their pursuit of piety. And I
also, like them, detest ignorant persons who read Holy Scripture according
to their own judgment and argue about unnecessary difficulties. For where
the censure prudently adds 'according to their own judgment,' I also make
the same exclusion at length and with great caution in the writing from
which this proposition is excerpted.

xxxix *His third proposition. In the preface to Matthew*
If I have my way a farmer will read Holy Scripture, a carpenter will
read it, a stonecutter will read it.[493]

CENSURE
Holy Scripture bears witness that simple people are like little children, who, according to Paul, have need of milk. For they are not yet
able to tolerate and digest solid food. For solid food is for the perfect, those who have their perception habitually trained to distinguish
good and evil.[494] Hence, for such simple persons it is not an appropriate method for them to read indiscriminately whatever Holy Scripture has been translated into the vernacular. Rather the church has established for them a most fitting method, hearing the word of God
and frequenting the places where it is preached. And incidentally she
does not forbid them the use of some books of Holy Scripture, which,
when fittingly explicated, are suitable for moral edification. But still
they should read such books piously and soberly, without pride or
arrogance, so that they do not use their reading to condemn preach-

* * * * *

493 Erasmus defended this proposition in *Divinationes ad notata Bedae* LB IX 456D–F.
494 Heb 5:13–14; cf 1 Cor 3:2

ing and are not hindered from the frequent hearing of God's word. Accordingly, this proposition, posited without the prescribed moderation, shows that the one who asserted it is not in satisfactory agreement with sound doctrine.

ERASMUS' CLARIFICATION

XXXIX Here, too, we are in agreement. They permit that laypeople read the mysterious books of Scripture, but soberly and without pride, and I would not want them to be read by anyone in any other way. Nor is that proposition set down there without moderation; it is set down so only by the reporters. For as I said before, I permit the reading of the Holy Volumes with much moderation; and I command that people abstain from reading where they have access to a teacher, and in that place I do not speak indiscriminately about just any of the Sacred Volumes but rather about the New Testament and the Gospels. That is clear from what I say: 'If Christ did not deprive them of his voice, neither will I deprive them of his books.' Shortly afterwards I move on to the Old Testament: 'Among the books of the Old Testament,' I say, 'are some for which there is some reason to keep them away from uneducated people, such as Ezechiel and the Song of Songs,' signifying that reading these books is not exactly suitable for laypeople. I permit that these books should be read only so that laypeople might come to holy sermons better instructed and that they might be more willing to listen when they recognize some features and that they might understand more easily things of which they have already had a taste, as it were. For in former times preachers also explained the prophets to mixed crowds. And I do not urge laypeople to read such volumes, but I say 'I would not forbid' [introduxero], using a verb in the subjunctive mood with a potential meaning.[495] For a condition is understood: 'if I should see that they have progressed to this stage,' or some such. And shortly after that I move on from the points I touched upon about the Old Testament and call attention to the books of the New Testament: 'In fact,' I say, 'in the books of the gospel, the divine wisdom condescends marvellously to the capacity of the weak so that no one can be so uneducated that he is incapable of learning the doctrine of the gospel.'[496]

* * * * *

495 *Introduxero* could be future perfect indicative (simply an emphatic future) or perfect subjunctive (with a conditional meaning). Here Erasmus says he intended the perfect subjunctive; the conditional meaning of the subjunctive contributes to his defence.

496 LB VII sig **2v / CWE 45 10–11

And I grant that there are steps in the ages of a Christian, but it is not fitting that Christians should always remain infants. And some laypeople have marvellously powerful minds, and there is no lack of the breath of the mysterious Spirit, who often reveals to little ones what he hides from the wise.[497] And though there are some among the Christian people whom you might rightly call infants, still to consider the whole people as infantile bespeaks contempt for the flock of Christ, who have drunk in the Spirit of their Lord; it is also absurd to attribute to them a perpetual infancy. And though it is true that Scripture has milk with which it nourishes the infancy of the unlearned, still the same Scripture is milk for the weak and solid food for the more advanced.[498] And so if you take Scripture away, you provide neither milk nor solid food. Accordingly, what they say about the author of this proposition lacking sound doctrine is more of an insult than a judgment.[499]

XL *His fourth proposition. In the same preface*
And I would not forbid any person to read the prophet Ezekiel or the Song of Songs or any books of the Old Testament.[500]

CENSURE
Since by a decree of the apostolic see the reading of many such books has long since been forbidden to laypeople, and since, in the opinion of weighty authorities, those learned in the law of the Lord among the Hebrews prohibited the reading of the said books and of the first chapter of Genesis before the age of thirty,[501] the aforesaid proposition is asserted temerariously and imprudently, since the prohibition against reading such books is based on the same reason that applied when Innocent III established a decree about them, a fragment of which is reported in 'de heret. in authentica cum ex injuncto.'[502]

* * * * *

497 Matt 11:25; Luke 10:4
498 Heb 5:13–14; 1 Cor 3:2
499 The English does not catch the Latin rhyme: 'convicium est potius quam iudicium.'
500 Erasmus defended this proposition in *Divinationes ad notata Bedae* LB IX 457A.
501 In his *Commentarium in Hezechielem* CCSL 75a 3–4 Jerome says that the beginning and end of Ezekiel, together with the beginning of Genesis and the Song of Songs, were traditionally considered so difficult by the Jews that no one under the age of thirty was allowed to read them.
502 *Decretalia Gregorii IX* liber x titulus VII de hereticis, cap XII (Innocentius III)

ERASMUS' CLARIFICATION 2

XL My words are as follows: 'and I would not prohibit anyone from reading such books.'[503] I speak conditionally and concerning my own perception: if the authority were vested in me and if I should see that it is expedient for most people. Therefore I would easily put up with it if Ezekial and the Song of Songs were forbidden to laypeople, and if the malice of mankind in these times demands it, I will not offer any resistance to the regulations of bishops or of the apostolic see. Actually, in the meantime such things are today both recited and sung in church in the hearing of the people, many of whom understand Latin, though they are less expert in theology than any workman.

XLI *His fifth proposition in the same preface*

It seems inappropriate, or even ridiculous, for uneducated people and simple-minded women to mumble their psalms and the Lord's Prayer like parrots, without understanding what the sounds mean.[504]

CENSURE

This proposition, which wrongly discourages uneducated persons and simple-minded women from vocal prayer according to the rites and custom of the church, as if it were useless unless they understood it, is ungodly and erroneous, opening the way to the error of the Bohemians, who tried to celebrate church services in the vernacular.[505] Otherwise it would have been inappropriate and ridiculous under the Old Law for simple people to observe the ceremonies of the Law founded by God which they did not understand; to assert such a thing is a blasphemy against the Law and God its founder and is heretical. For the church does not allege only that we should be instructed by following the succession of the words but that by conforming ourselves to her aim, as her members (so to speak), we should pronounce the praises of God, render due thanksgiving to him, and beg for what we need. Hence, because of such an intention in the minds of those praying, their feelings are inflamed by the grace of God, their intellects

* * * * *

503 LB VII **2v / CWE 45 11. Erasmus defended this proposition in *Divinationes ad notata Bedae* LB IX 457A.
504 Erasmus defended this proposition in *Divinationes ad notata Bedae* LB IX 457D–E.
505 A general reference to the followers of John Huss (see n487 above); there were various sects among the Hussites in the fifteenth and early sixteenth centuries, but many of them used the vernacular in liturgical services.

are illuminated, their human inadequacy is relieved, and they gain
the fruit of grace and glory. It is certain that these things are gained
by those who say vocal prayers, even though they do not understand
the words. In the same way an ambassador who reports the words of
his master according to his master's command, even though he does
not understand them, furnishes an obedience pleasing to his master
and to the person to whom he is sent. Similarly, many prophecies are
sung in church which are not understood by many who sing them, but
still the enunciation and chanting of them are very useful and meritorious. Singing them displays obedience pleasing to the divine truth
which taught and revealed them. Hence it is quite clear that the fruit
of prayer does not consist only in the understanding of the words and
that it is a dangerous error to think that vocal prayer is said only to
instruct the intellect, whereas such prayer is recited chiefly to inflame
the feelings, so that by lifting ourselves up to God in the aforesaid
ways with a pious and devout heart, our minds may be restored and
our mental aim may be fulfilled by obtaining what we ask for, and so
that we may merit an illumination of our intellects, as well as other
useful and necessary benefits. Certainly such fruits are far richer than
the mere understanding of the words, which has little use if it occurs
without arousing our feelings toward God. And even if it should happen that the psalms were translated into the vernacular, it would not
follow that simple and uneducated persons would thoroughly understand their meaning.

ERASMUS'CLARIFICATION
XLI The language here is reported somewhat differently from what I proposed, for I did not simply assert that it is ridiculous for simple-minded
women to recite the psalms in Latin, but that it seems inappropriate and
even ridiculous for them to do so rather than to recite the Lord's Prayer or
the psalms in a language known to them. I confront my opponent with a
comparison so that he will either cease to condemn what he condemns or
else also condemn what seems more absurd. My words were as follows:
'Why does it seem unsuitable if someone says the Gospel in his native language, which he understands? Rather it seems to me more inappropriate
and ridiculous, etc.'[506] In every matter a pious feeling certainly ought to be
approved; thus, when the people stand up to hear the Gospel, assuming

* * * * *

506 LB VII sig **3v / CWE 45 18

a religious posture, even though they do not understand the words of the Gospel, still that pious feeling is pleasing to God. Nevertheless, it would be desirable it they understood what is being recited. The point they bring up about the ceremonies of the Jews, the mysteries of which the ordinary people did not understand, is similar. But the Jews were commanded to observe them, and the character of the times did not yet demand that the people understand the mysteries of the figures.[507] And so that blasphemous teaching does not apply to me because it has nothing to do with this subject.

But who ever recommended that simple-minded women should recite the psalms and other prayers in Latin, if they do not understand it, when they could say them in French? I grant you, the excuse for this is a pious feeling. But not everyone recites them with a pious feeling, but many women do so out of a certain feminine vanity or impropriety, sometimes drowning out even the priest with their outcries. Hence I am all the more surprised when the censure says that those who pray with words not understood do so with the mental intention of being inflamed in this way to pursue piety. It is more probable that the majority of such people fall under the reproach of the prophet: 'This people honours me with their lips, but their hearts are far from me.'[508] In that place I am not talking about the ordinary liturgy. They tell a story about a certain shepherd who was extraordinarily ignorant: since he didn't know anything else to do, he pole-vaulted over a brook three times every day and he did so in honour of the Father, Son, and Holy Spirit. God took in good part the worship of this abysmally ignorant person; but it would be inappropriate to encourage others to follow his example. And what these simple-minded women recite is not always holy. Sometimes it consists of inept trifles. If someone were to substitute a fable of Aesop for their text, their pious error would not be unpleasing to God, but still it should not receive our immediate approval. And I have never heard that it was the custom of the church for simple-minded women to pray in church in Latin, but rather this practice crept in gradually in some nations, as did many others. In Italy you would never see such a thing. And in the papal household even men are not allowed to say private prayers. For in earlier times the whole people prayed in the voice of the priest, and because they understood the words he prayed, they answered 'amen.' This vestige of the ancient practice is still preserved in the Roman church.

* * * * *

507 For example, the bronze serpent constructed by Moses, mentioned in Num 21:8, was traditionally a figure of Christ crucified; see Augustine *Sermones* 6.5.7 PL 38 62.
508 Isaiah 29:1, quoted in Matt 15:8 and Mark 7:6

I learned, however, to place little confidence in words pronounced without understanding from St Paul, who prefers five words said with their proper signification to ten thousand spoken in the spirit.[509] And he compares someone speaking in the spirit to a tuba producing a sound that is not clear; he compares it to a cymbal which sounds in vain.[510] And yet here the Apostle is dealing with those who do indeed understand what they recite, but they recite it to those who do not understand it. Therefore, if Paul acts piously when he encourages those who speak in tongues to engage in prophecy, why do I offend when I do not at all discourage simple-minded women from the pursuit of piety but rather recall them to what seems more suitable for the pursuit of piety? And I never taught what they call the dangerous doctrine that understanding alone is sufficient in the recitation of the psalms or that this was the only reason it was established that they should be recited in church. But those who do not even understand what they utter with their tongues are very far indeed from any feeling. And the very reason I want the addition of understanding is that through it the feelings may be inflamed.

But I am surprised that, whereas I am speaking of simple-minded women praying in church out of a private motive, the censure shifts over to the chant appointed by the church. If Holy Scripture, they say, were translated into the language of the people, laypeople would still not immediately understand it. I grant it, not everything, not fully; but they will understand a great deal, especially if they have been trained. And Scripture has its milk with which it nourishes those of a tender age and it also has solid food when you are more advanced;[511] in Scripture, as some pious person elegantly said, an elephant swims, a lamb walks.[512] Many persons, they

* * * * *

509 1 Cor 14:1–19
510 1 Cor 14:8, 13:1
511 Heb 5:13–14
512 The observances in use at a priory of Augustinian canons regular in Cambridgeshire, England, in 1295 closes by praising the rule of St Augustine as follows: 'On the other hand it is deep and lofty, so that the wise and the strong can find in it matter for abundant and perfect contemplation. An elephant can swim in it, and a lamb can walk in safety' ('Est eciam profunda atque alta in tantum quod sapientes atque robusti plenam atque perfectam in ipsa sorciantur contemplacionem. In ipsa enim atque elephans natat, atque agnus secure ambulat'). See *The Observances in Use at the Augustinian Priory of S. Giles and S. Andrew at Barnwell, Cambridgeshire* ed and trans John W. Clark (Cambridge 1897) 230–1. Erasmus himself was a canon regular, and, though I have not been able to find the same praise in the observances (*consuetudines*) of any other house of Augustinian canons, it would not be surprising to find it elsewhere applied to the Augustinian rule or to Scripture.

say, recite Holy Scripture, though they do not understand it. And certainly I grant that is true, but I am grieved to do so. Perhaps it is because of obedience that they recite such things in a language which ordinary people do not understand; but for them to recite reverently words not understood to the glory of God and with a general feeling of piety is a good step toward what is more perfect. For someone who loves religious practices has already made good progress. But I cannot approve of those who do not make an effort to understand when they have the intelligence, the leisure, and the opportunity to do so.

And so on this point, we agree, if I am not mistaken; and I do not see how it is dangerous to the Christian religion if simple-minded women pray in the vernacular or at least in words they understand. If they recite with pious feeling what they do not understand, they would recite all the more piously what they do understand. But why is it necessary at all for them to recite prayers in church, since it seems it would be equally meritorious if, instead of singing and reciting something, they merely heard it without understanding it but with the same feeling they have when they recite it without understanding it, or if they gazed upon ceremonies they only partly understood? But it is a strange simile about the servant who reports his Lord's commands without understanding them, as if God were pleased with the rattling off of words. Origen's comparison is more apt: he writes that, just as evil spirits are present to obey magicians who recite words they do not understand, so too angels are at hand to present to God the holy words pronounced by the godly with religious feeling, except that in that place Origen is not talking about those who recite Scripture in a language totally unintelligible to them but about passages in Scripture which are too obscure for simple people to be able to understand.[513]

To be sure, it is immensely dangerous if church services were conducted in a language known to ordinary people! (The theologians' information about the Bohemians doing this is the first I have heard of it.) In fact, it was done with no danger to piety for more than six centuries, both among the Latins and the Greeks and the Africans, and I have no doubt that

* * * * *

513 Professor Peter Martens of Saint Louis University has kindly identified the passage by Origen to which Erasmus probably refers: *Homilies on Joshua* 20, 1–2 (in Rufinus' Latin translation of the Greek in Origen's *Philocalia* 12). Professor Brian Daley of the University of Notre Dame has also pointed out other passages where Origen talks about the angels as helping ordinary people pray (in *On Prayer* 11.5) and about the magical use of language which engages the demons as helpers (in *Contra Celsum*, especially 1.24–5, 8.36–7, 8.61, 63–4).

it would still be done today among the Spanish and French if excessive and manifold corruption had not forced them to use the written language and to stick to that. For the vernacular language was never taken away from the people, but rather they withdrew from it. Then, when the Greek and Latin languages had been corrupted in different ways in different countries and there was no fixed pattern of deterioration, the absurdity of the confusion forced people to celebrate ordinary liturgies in a grammatical language. Otherwise we would have the same state of affairs in churches as if in our choirs nowadays one person would sing the chant in French, another in Spanish, another in Italian. For these three tongues arose from the corruption of the Latin language. Or it would be as if among the Greeks one person sang in the vernacular of Rhodes, another in that of Cyprus, another in that of Crete.

Hence I do not think there is any great danger in commanding simpleminded laywomen to recite their prayers in a language they know. Since the world is full of unlearned priests, clerics, and monks, we are threatened by a much greater danger that they will be put off from the pursuit of learning altogether if they learn from authoritative theologians that God is so mightily delighted by words not at all understood.

Topic 13. Those places in his paraphrases where the paraphraser departs from the ordinary usage of the church

XLIIA 'Good will among men' instead of 'men of good will'[514]
    B Before this universe of heavenly and earthly beings was founded the eternal Speech was with the eternal Father.[515] He uses the word 'Speech,' whereas we use the word 'Word,' in explaining the text 'In the beginning was the Word.'[516]

A CLARIFICATION ABOUT THESE TWO PROPOSITIONS
BLAMED HERE AS NEWFANGLED
XLIIA If I were to recite in church something different from the public usage or if I were to introduce some new reading in the codices approved

* * * * *

514 Luke 2:14. In *Divinationes ad notata Bedae* LB IX 491F Erasmus merely mentions that here he is following Greek manuscripts and there is nothing unholy or absurd about the meaning.
515 Erasmus defended this proposition briefly in *Prologus supputationis* LB IX 446E–F.
516 John 1:1

for public use, then perhaps some offence could rightly be taken. As it is, if I alter something in a work to be read privately by the learned, I see no reason to take offence. If the Greeks consistently read 'good will,'[517] if that sense of the words is pious, if that reading appears in the early Doctors of the church, why am I guilty if in my paraphrase I follow what seems to me more probable and more suitable to the energy of the gospel?[518]

B As for the use of 'Speech' for 'Word,' I responded with no lack of care in a particular book,[519] making it clear that formerly the church read indifferently 'in the beginning was the Speech' or 'in the beginning was the Word,' and that 'Speech' instead of 'Word' is frequent in older and more recent Doctors and also nowadays in the liturgy of the church, where we sing 'Your omnipotent Speech, O Lord, came down from his regal throne,'[520] so that it should not seem novel to anyone who is educated. In the words of Tertullian, which I quoted above, the Son is called the Speech instead of the Word.[521]

C *The third novelty*

There are three in heaven who furnish testimony for Christ, the Father, the Speech, and the Holy Spirit.[522] And the agreement of these three is supreme.[523] But we read: 'There are three in heaven who give testimony, the Father, the Word, and the Holy Spirit; and these three are one.'

The paraphraser gives a wrong explanation of the clause 'these three are one,' eliminating the strong testimony for belief in the unity of

* * * * *

517 That is, 'good will to men' instead of 'men of good will'
518 Erasmus defended the reading 'good will toward men' at length in his *Annotations* LB VI 231B–233F.
519 *Apologia de 'In principio erat sermo'* LB IX 111–22
520 In his defence of Erasmus' translation of λόγος as 'speech' in the first verse of John's Gospel St Thomas More cited the same liturgical verse from the introit of the mass of the Sunday within the octave of Christmas (based on Wisdom 18:15). See *Missale Romanum* no 17, I 27, and St Thomas More *Letter to a Monk in Defense of Humanism: Letter to Martin Dorp, Letter to the University of Oxford, Letter to Edward Lee, Letter to a Monk* ed Daniel Kinney, Yale Edition of the Complete Works of St. Thomas More, vol 15 (New Haven and London 1986) 240, 579–80.
521 See n468 above.
522 1 John 5:7
523 Erasmus defended this proposition very briefly in *Responsio ad notulas Bedaicas* LB IX 712B.

substance in three persons, providing a foothold to defend the heresy of Arius.[524]

CLARIFICATION

c As for the threefold testimony, I reply in my annotation on that passage.[525] I also responded in a particular book addressed to a certain Tyrologus.[526] But those who foisted off my language on the faculty acted here with little good faith, as in many other places. For the paraphrase expressly and clearly professes both points: that there is one nature in three persons and that their agreement in giving testimony is supreme. But if to deny either of these is ungodly and if I profess both, what is there to reproach me for? For the words of the paraphrase are as follows: 'Because the Spirit is also truth, as are the Father and the Son, they all have one truth as they have one nature. For there are three in heaven who furnish testimony for Christ, the Father, the Speech, and the Holy Spirit.[527] And the agreement of these three is supreme.'[528] How can I be said to favour Arius when I so clearly profess what he denies? But the ancient Greeks and Latins who fought very bitterly against the Arian sect did not use this testimony against them, either because their codices did not have this clause or because they perceived that this passage deals with bearing witness to the faith rather than having one nature. In the time of Augustine, however, some Latin writers began to hurl this weapon at the Arians.

At this point I do not know whether we are bound by a law forbidding us to offer a scriptural interpretation different from that of Ambrose,

* * * * *

524 See n13 above.
525 LB VI 1079B–1081F
526 Erasmus' *Epistola in tyrologum quendam impudentissimum calumniatorem* was printed in Basel by Froben in 1527, together with Erasmus' *De modestia profitendi linguas* and Chrysostom's *De Babyla martyre*. It is in the form of a letter to Robert Aldridge (Ep 1858). According to Allen *tyrologus* is a satirical perversion of *theologus*, meaning 'cheese-collector' (ie 'friar'). It is an answer to an unknown preacher who had fiercely (and apparently ignorantly) attacked Erasmus' translation of John 7:39 in a sermon at Paul's Cross; other opponents are also answered. Though it does not discuss the text taken up by the Paris theologians (John 5:7), the question of the Greek text as it bears upon the divinity of the Holy Spirit and the Arian heresy arises in both cases. See Allen Ep 1858 / CWE 13 Ep 1858:251–2.
527 Here Erasmus skips over about sixty-five words in his paraphrase; but he does not distort its meaning.
528 LB VII 1158C–D / CWE 44 98

Augustine, or Jerome. But it does often happen that more recent theologians reject the interpretation of the ancients. Furthermore, since it is beyond controversy that this passage deals with faith in the testimony, which consists primarily in the agreement of the witnesses, and since the agreement is confirmed by predicating the same nature,[529] and since the word 'one' does not always express the same nature (as when we read that the faithful had 'one heart and one soul'), the Arians were not put under any pressure by the testimony of this passage. If we object against the Arians that the church interprets the passage in this way, they do not accept the authority of the church and say that the church resides among them. And so here I can rightly complain of a false accusation because they present the most holy faculty with a truncated and mutilated text.

D *The fourth novelty*
From the group of disciples the Lord appointed seventy.[530] In this place we read 'seventy-two.'

CLARIFICATION
D In my annotation[531] I make it clear that the Greek codices and interpreters agree on 'seventy,' namely Cyril, Theophylactus,[532] Dorotheus,[533] and Eu-

* * * * *

529 That is, if the same nature may be predicated for all three, then all three give the same testimony.
530 Luke 10:1
531 LB VI 271F–272F, where Erasmus cites the authorities he lists here. He made the same point very briefly in *Supputatio* LB IX 613A–B.
532 Cyril *Explanatio in Lucae Evangelium* 10.1 PG 72 665; Theophylactus *Enarratio in Evangelium Lucae* 10.1–3 PG 123 833
533 Dorotheus was supposedly a bishop of Tyre martyred in the fourth century, but his very existence has been questioned in modern times; see DTC IV 1786–8. In Erasmus' time, however, and for some two centuries afterwards, a Greek work circulated under Dorotheus' name; it concerned the apostles and listed and named the seventy disciples chosen by Christ: *Synopsis de vita et morte prophetarum, apostolorum, et discipulorum Domini*; see *Propheten- und Apostellegenden nebst Jüngerkatalogen des Dorotheus und verwandte Texte* ed Theodor Schermann (Leipzig 1907) 131–60. The work was translated into English and went through at least six editions between 1577 and 1663 as an appendix to the histories of Eusebius and others; see *A Short-title Catalogue of Books Printed in England ... 1474–1640* ed A.M. Pollard, G.R. Redgrave, et al (London 1969) 10572–6; and *Short-title Catalogue of Books Printed*

sebius; and Irenaeus, Ambrose, and Jerome[534] agree with them, so that it is likely that Augustine had a faulty codex, and that others followed his lead. In following the authority of such men I do not see why I should be reproached for preferring a genuine reading to an error that had crept in. For it cannot be denied that the public readings of the church contain some errors; to correct them is not contempt for the church but dutiful service.

E *The fifth novelty*
  One of the disciples whose name was Cleophas.[535] But we read 'Cleopas.'

CLARIFICATION
E It is not clear to me whether I wrote down 'Cleophas' or 'Cleopas,' for I usually say whichever pops into my head. And I never had words with anyone about this matter. It is clear that the evangelists consistently wrote 'Cleopas.' Some German, I imagine, added the aspiration.[536] Actually, there is an error in the censure, which has got it backwards when it says I wrote down 'Cleophas,' whereas they read 'Cleopas.' This may be an error of the scribe, and it would be fine if we could attribute all the almost inexcusable faults to him.

F *The sixth novelty*
  'This is my body, which will be broken for you,' where we read 'this is my body, which will be given up for you.'[537]

* * * * *

in England ... 1650–63 ed Donald Wing, et al 3 vols 2nd ed (New York 1982) 3421–3422B.
534 Eusebius *Ecclesiastical History* 1.12 PG 21 117; Irenaeus *Contra haereses* 3.13 PG 4 912; Ambrose *Expositio Evangelii secundum Lucam libris X comprehensa* 7.44 PL 15 (1845) 1710 B; Jerome *Epistola* LXXVII *seu liber exegeticus ad Fabiolam de* XLII *mansionibus Israelitarum in deserto* 6 PL 22 704
535 Luke 24:18
536 In *De recta pronuntiatione* Erasmus mentions the German tendency to overaspiration (CWE 26 451).
537 1 Cor 11:24 (*tradetur*). Matt 26:26 and Mark 14:22 do not have the clause after *corpus* and Luke 22:19 has 'which is given for you [*datur*].' Erasmus briefly defended 'is broken' instead of 'will be given up' in *Divinationes ad notata Bedae* LB IX 474E–F, in *Elenchus in censuras Bedae* LB IX 507E, and in *Responsio ad notulas Bedaicas* LB IX 716C–D; he defended it at greater length in *Supputatio* LB IX 681C–684C.

CLARIFICATION

F In the paraphrase I mostly relied on the trustworthiness of the Greek codices, especially where they seem more correct than ours. What I set down here appears quite consistently in the Greek copies, and it is explained by orthodox interpreters. And lest we think this reading appears only among the Greeks, St Ambrose also has it. The monk Bede reports the same reading when he explains this passage.[538] But if the church reads 'is broken' or 'will be broken' up to the time of Bede, we should see whether our reading 'will be given up' arose from a scribal error or from the authoritative efforts of our ancestors. But in fact in both phrases the meaning is the same.[539] Indeed Tommaso de Vio, Cardinal Cajetanus, when he cites this text, also gives both readings, as if it did not make any difference which one you read.[540]

G *The seventh novelty*
If it should be my will that this man remain until I come, what is that to you?[541] But we read: 'Thus I wish him to remain until I come, what is that to you?'

CLARIFICATION

G In the annotation[542] I show that the particle 'thus' cannot be understood from the words of the evangelist and is even in conflict with the meaning. I show that in this text there is thorough agreement among the Greek codices and the orthodox interpreters Cyril, Chrysostom, Theophylactus. I show that Jerome has the same reading. Finally I show that in the ancient Latin codices formerly used in church to recite the Gospel, the reading is still uncorrupted. But Augustine was deceived by a faulty codex – and this is not the only place that that happened to him, as I have pointed out in some places. Where, then, is the crime if in place of a corrupt reading I restore what John wrote and what both the Greek and the Latin church formerly read? And it is probable that Gregory, Leo, and

* * * * *

538 Ambrose *Expositio Evangelii secundum Lucam libris decem comprehensa* 6.86 PL 15 (1845) 1691 A–C; Bede *In Lucae Evangelium expositio* 22:19 PL 92 596C–D. Erasmus presumably adds 'monk' to distinguish the Venerable Bede from Noël Béda.

539 In his long note on this phrase in the *Annotationes* Erasmus explains that 'given over,' 'broken up,' and 'given to' probably all refer to the breaking up of the bread in order that it be distributed to the disciples LB VI 716F–718C.

540 *Opuscula omnia . . . in tres distincta tomos* (Lyon: ex Officina Iuntarum 1587; repr 1995) III 286 Tractatus X, De missae sacrificio et ritu adversus Lutheranos cap 3

541 John 21:22

542 LB VI 419B–421B

Hugh[543] (whom they set up as examples for us to imitate) had the same reading, except that they perhaps followed the authority of Augustine too scrupulously and stumbled just as he did.

H *The eighth novelty*
I taught you how, after he returned to life, he made himself visible to many, first to Cephas, and then to the twelve.[544] He puts 'twelve' where we read 'eleven.'

CLARIFICATION
H With complete unanimity the Greeks read 'twelve' instead of 'eleven,' and they interpret it according to that reading; Chrysostom and Theophylactus[545] do so explicitly, and there should be no doubt that the other Greeks had the same reading. Among the Latins Augustine, though he grants that some Latin codices have 'eleven' instead of 'twelve,' still suspects that some persons were disturbed by the difficulty that Judas Iscariot, when he departed to meet his own fate, reduced the number of the apostles and that these people 'corrected' this text, that is, corrupted it.[546] Chrysostom unties the knot with this notion: he thinks we should believe that the Lord also appeared to Matthias, who had been chosen to fill Judas' place.[547] But what Augustine says is closer to the mark and also more acute: he suggests that this language does not refer to the number of individual apostles but rather to the number first appointed by the Lord, just as the *centumviri*[548] [hundred-men] were called by that name

* * * * *

543 Probably Hugh of St Victor (1096–1141), philosopher, theologian, mystical writer, and exegete, renowned in the universities of Erasmus' time. A canon regular of St Augustine, he taught at the monastery school of St Victor in Paris. A moderate follower of the dialectical method of Abelard and a precursor of the scholasticism of the following century, he wrote well-known works on philosophy, exegesis (especially of an allegorical sort), and mystical theology. His pupil Richard (d 1173) eschewed philosophy but wrote well-known works on dogmatic, mystical, and exegetical theology.
544 1 Cor 15:5. Erasmus briefly defended the reading 'twelve' instead of 'eleven' in *Divinationes ad notata Bedae* LB IX 475A–B, in *Elenchus in censuras Bedae* LB IX 507F, and in *Supputatio* LB IX 684B–685B.
545 Chrysostom *Homiliae in epistolam primam ad Corinthios* 38.4 PG 61 326; Theophylactus *Expositio in epistolam primam ad Corinthios* 15.5 PG 124 756
546 *De consensu evangelistarum* 25.71 PL 34 1205
547 Acts 1:21–6
548 'The hundred-men,' a body of Roman judges chosen annually for civil cases, especially inheritances. It originally consisted of 105 members, but later grew much larger.

even if it should happen by chance that they fell short of that number. St Thomas agrees with Augustine, writing as follows: 'Augustine teaches that he ought to say twelve but the text was corrupted by scribes.'[549] The point is supported by the article τοῖς ['the']: when Ambrose uses it, saying 'the eleven,' it is likely that he read 'twelve' and that the text was corrupted by scribes.[550] For 'eleven' does not signify the number consecrated by the Lord as apostles. But 'the twelve' sounds as if you were saying 'the persons who were numbered among the twelve whom the Lord first chose as apostles.' And so, since this reading appears consistently among Greek orthodox writers, since it is likely, as Augustine suspects, that the text was corrupted by some overzealous scribe, since it was written thus by the Apostle in Greek, since the ancient Latins had the same reading, since neither meaning is rejected by Augustine, though he prefers the Greek reading, I do not think any injury was done to the church if I followed the authority of great men and set down the more approved reading.

But we, they say, have another reading. If they frighten us off with such a statement, it will not be right to remove errors from public readings. We read in a psalm[551] 'my soul thirsted for God, the living fountain,' whereas in Greek and Hebrew it is 'strong living God.' Likewise in psalm 39[:9] they read 'in the midst of my heart,' where the Greek and the Hebrew agree in the reading 'in the midst of my stomach.' Some uneducated person, who thought it was absurd for the Law to be in the stomach, changed it to 'heart.' In these places would they cackle at us, 'we have a different reading'? Many such places are found in public readings. And perhaps the more correct books of the Romans have different readings from those ordinarily found among the French. Finally it is possible that Alcuin[552] and Rupert[553] had the same reading as Augustine. If they should say 'it was necessary to explain the difficulty in the paraphrase,' I could not give both readings since I speak there in the person of Paul, but I did handle the

* * * * *

549 *Expositio in omnes s. Pauli epistolas, in epistolam primam ad Corinthios* 15.1
550 Pseudo-Ambrose *Commentaria in epistolas beati Pauli, in epistolam ad Corinthios primam* 15:5 PL 17 (1845) 261C
551 Ps 41:3
552 Alcuin twice has the reading *illis undecim;* see his *Commentaria in s. Joannis Evangelium* 43.21.14 PL 100 1000B.
553 Rupert of Deutz (c 1075–1129), a Benedictine monk and abbot of the monastery at Deutz near Cologne, was a compendious liturgist, exegete, and theologian. A search of the database of the *Patrologia latina* under Rupertus Tuitiensis does not reveal any instance where he quotes or refers to 1 Cor 15:5.

difficulty as much as was permissible, speaking as follows: 'Then he was seen by all the disciples, not merely the twelve from whom the name apostle was first derived and then applied to many others.' So too when I add the article 'the.'[554] I take care of the rest in *Annotations*.[555]

1 *The ninth novelty*
We shall not all die, since that day will perhaps find some of us alive, but nevertheless we shall all be changed by the glory of immortality; by the pursuit of piety here we train ourselves, as it were, for immortality by avoiding the contagion of sin.[556] From what he sets down here in his paraphrase, it is clear that Erasmus reads 'indeed we shall not all sleep, but we shall all be changed.' But on the other hand we read 'all indeed shall rise up, but not all will be changed.'

CLARIFICATION[557]
1 Concerning this text I replied to Lee and to some other person in an individual book, and later in *Annotations*, and lastly I responded to Béda,[558] and here these things are thrown up to me as if I had not responded at all. There I show that the Greek codices consistently have my reading, and moreover that the holy Doctors of the church, Ambrose,[559] Augustine, Chry-

* * * * *

554 LB VII 906D–E
555 LB VI 734E–F
556 1 Cor 15:51. In *Divinationes ad notata Bedae* LB IX 475D Erasmus mentions that he had defended this reading at length; see n558 below.
557 Pelargus sig D6 says he would dearly like to know exactly where Tertullian supports Erasmus' reading; and he finds two places where Tertullian seems not to do so. He notes that in these places the interpretation is so obscure and involuted that it does not seem to correspond with the reading given for the text.
   Erasmus made no additions or changes in the second edition.
558 Erasmus had indeed written frequently and in detail on the text. He responded to Edward Lee in *Liber alter quo respondet reliquis annotationibus Eduardi Lei* LB IX 218D–219E. His *Apologia de loco 'Omnes quidem'* LB IX 433A–442B was directed against his superficial Carmelite critic Nicolaas Baechem of Egmond, whom he does not deign to mention here; see CEBR. He has a long note on the passage in *Annotations* LB VI 740F–743F. And he had replied to Béda twice about the text: in *Divinationes ad notata Bedae* LB IX 475D and in *Supputatio* LB IX 687A–B.
559 *Commentaria in epistolas beati Pauli, in epistolam primam ad Corinthios* 15:[51–2] PL 30 (1846) 770A–C; this work, of uncertain authorship, is now sometimes attributed to Jerome, but Erasmus attributes it unquestioningly to Ambrose when he quotes it in his note on 1 Cor 15:51 in *Annotations*.

sostom, Theophylactus, Origen,[560] Tertullian,[561] the writer of a commentary on all the Epistles of Paul whom they take to be Jerome,[562] and finally even Peter Lombard[563] agree with this opinion, so that they either follow the reading which I follow in the paraphrase and which seems genuine to me, or else they think one is free to follow either reading. Augustine openly preaches the same in his book *The Teachings of the Church*,[564] and he does so again in his answer to Dulcitius, question 3.[565] And St Thomas reports both readings, rejecting neither. Thomas also cites St Jerome,[566] who testifies in a letter to Miner[v]ius that the verb 'rise up,' which appears in our edition, never occurs in the Greek codices.[567] Hence it is probable that the text was changed by someone who did not notice that there Paul is speaking specifically about the resurrection of the godly. And I never erased any writing from the usual codices. In the paraphrase I merely interpret what is found in ancient times and what seems to be more consistent with Paul's meaning, and I do so with no harm to the usual reading among the French.

The tenth notation, containing many novelties

K 'Germana conjunx' [true wife] for 'germane compar'[568] [true companion]

L 'Solomon' for 'Salomon'

M 'Paracletus' for 'paraclitus'

* * * * *

560 See, for example, Augustine *Epistolae* 193 4.10–11 PL 33 873; Chrysostom *Homiliae in epistolam primam ad Corinthios* 42.2 PG 61 364, and *Homiliae in epistolam ad Romanos* 29.6 PG 60 591; Theophylactus *Expositio in epistolam primam ad Corinthios* 15.51 PG 124 780; Origen *Contra Celsum* 2.65 PG 11 960.

561 In his annotation on 1 Cor 15:51 Erasmus quotes Tertullian's *De resurrectione carne* 42 PL 2 (1844) 853B–854A to demonstrate that his interpretation shows he had the Greek reading that Erasmus follows, though through scribal corruption his text now has the Vulgate reading from Corinthians.

562 *Commentarius in epistolam primam ad Corinthios* 15.51 PL 30 (1846) 770

563 *Liber sententiarum* 4 dist 43 art 5

564 Erasmus seems to refer to *Liber de ecclesiasticis dogmaticis* caput 7 PL 42 1215, which does not refer to 1 Cor 15:5 but makes the point that it is permissible to hold that those living at the end of the world may put on immortality without dying. The work, though surely not by Augustine, was attributed to him in many manuscripts and even by such authorities as Peter Lombard.

565 *De octo Dulcitii questionibus* 3.3–4 PL 40 159–60

566 *Expositio in omnes s. Pauli epistolas, in epistolam primam ad Corinthios* 15.8

567 *Epistola 119 ad Minervium et Alexandrum* 12 PL 22 980; see also *Epistola 49 ad Marcellam* 3 PL 22 587–8.

568 Phil 4:3

N 'Servator' [saviour] for 'Salvator' [saviour];[569] 'Caparnaum' for 'Capharnaum'

O 'Spiritus fatidicus' [prophetic spirit] where we usually say 'Spiritus propheticus' [prophetic spirit][570]

P 'Bethesda' for 'Bethsaida'; 'Bethabara' for 'Bethania'

Q 'Melite' for 'Mitylene'

CENSURE

In these texts and not a few others like them the paraphraser, who is writing for Latin-speaking persons, temerariously departs from the common usage of the Latin church, which he ought to preserve, following in the footsteps of preceding Latin fathers such as Gregory, Leo, Prosper, Cassiodorus, Isidore, Bede, Alcuin, Haymo, Rabanus, Anselm, Bernard, Rupert, Hugh and Richard of Saint Victor,[571] and others, who adapted and submitted their judgment to the custom of the church, as their humble charity persuaded them to do, not daring to do anything that might in any way disturb the church. For in their extraordinary wisdom these most learned men knew that, after the incomparable labour expended on Holy Scripture by St Jerome, the ancient usage of the Latin church, approved for so many centuries by the overwhelming agreement of learned men and elucidated by the brilliant commentaries of Catholic Doctors, ought to be taken by Latin-speaking persons as the law and the linguistic rule[572] for Holy Scripture. Nor would anything be taken away from Greek or Hebrew writing, but each language would keep to its own usage and rules.

CLARIFICATION OF THE INDIVIDUAL ITEMS

K First, it is clear that the Greek words express the meaning which I give in the paraphrase; it is clear that Clement was of this opinion and believed that Paul had a wife, nor was there any lack of others who interpreted this text as referring to a wife. And Clement was especially able to know because

* * * * *

569 Erasmus briefly defends the use of *servator* for *salvator* in *Divinationes ad notata Bedae* LB IX 492B.

570 Erasmus defended his use of *spiritus fatidicus* in *Divinationes ad notata Bedae* LB IX 490D–E.

571 For Haymo see n9 above; for Rabanus see n349 above; for Rupert see n553 above; for Hugh and Richard of St Victor see nn9 and 543 above.

572 Arguing that 'usage' (*usus*) should be the 'linguistic rule' (*norma loquendi*), the theologians are clearly alluding to Horace's *Ars poetica* 71–2.

he lived in the time of the apostles.[573] There is nothing contrary to piety if we assign a wife to Paul, since it is believed that Peter, the prince of the whole church, had one.[574] More recent commentators, however, eager to promote chastity, have laboured to place Paul among the virgins or at least the celibate. I took the path that seemed simplest, but only in the paraphrase, which was never intended to be recited in church. Anyone who wants should think I said this in a commentary for that is how what I said in the paraphrase ought to be taken.

L The evangelists use the name 'Solomon,' but I do not deny that it is right to say 'Salomon,' and I am not annoyed with anyone who prefers to say 'Salomon' rather than 'Solomon.' I myself call him Salomon when it suits me.

M I give the same answer concerning 'paracletus.' Whoever says 'paracletus' with a circumflex accent on the second-last syllable is pronouncing a Greek word with Latin accentuation. Whoever says 'paraclitus' with an acute accent on the second syllable is pronouncing a Greek word with the Greek sound and accentuation, except that the Greek word could not have the Latin letter 'i': if you use it, the word means 'someone who turns aside from the right path'; if you write it with 'y' it means 'a person with a bad reputation.' But if you prefer a Greek accentuation in the nominative case, you must vary it according to the Greek rules in the other cases ('paraclíto, paraclítum, paráclitum'). And so it is simpler to keep the Latin accentuation which is unchanging. And still, if someone likes 'paraclitus' better, I have nothing against it.

N 'Servator' is undoubtedly a good Latin word, frequently used by approved authors to mean 'someone who bestows salvation.' I do not find 'salvator,' though I would be glad if it were found. But I never said a word against anyone who prefers 'salvator,' and I myself frequently say it. But

* * * * *

573 Here and in his long annotation on Phil 4:3 LB VI 875E–876E Erasmus defends the possibility that the Greek phrase σύζυγε γνήσιε can refer to Paul's wife. He takes as his starting point Eusebius' report that Clement says Paul had a wife (*Ecclesiastica historia* 3.30) and claims that Clement lived in the time of the apostles. He fails to note in both places that Eusebius is referring to Clement of Alexandria (d 215), not to Clement of Rome (d 101). In *Divinationes ad notata Bedae* LB IX 477D Erasmus briefly defended his translation by referring to the authority of Clement in Eusebius. He repeated the same defence in *Elenchus in censuras Bedae* LB IX 509B.

574 Peter's mother-in-law is mentioned in Mark 1:30 and Luke 4:38.

it was my intention in the paraphrase to make the language purer, so as to make the majesty and proper diction of Scripture apparent. If I were reading to a group accustomed to hearing 'salvator' I would say 'salvator.'[575] I did not write 'Caparnaum' but rather 'Capernaum,' and that is the reading in the Gospel.[576] And if the scribes err so often in the censure, what do we think they have done for so many centuries in the codices of Holy Scripture? I do not mention this to take a swipe at the theologians but so that they may be fairer to me if something similar is found in my writings because of the negligence of scribes or printers.

o 'Fatidicus' is a word that slipped from my tongue once, or at most twice, so that no one should think that I invariably say 'Spiritus fatidicus' instead of 'Spiritus propheticus.' I adapted a pagan word to religious subject matter, committing no graver offence, I think, than someone who might say 'vates' for 'prophetus' or 'vaticinia' for 'prophetiae.' 'Propheta' is spoken properly only about someone who predicts future events, but 'spiritus fatidicus' seems to have a wider meaning. Accordingly, to express that breath of the hidden Spirit I used a word appropriate to it.

p In writing Bethesda instead of the form in the Latin codices, which I showed was probably corrupt, I reinstated a form which the codices of the Greeks still preserve uncorrupted and which the approved Doctors among them retain. On our side is the etymology of the Hebrew word for 'pertaining to cattle,' which agrees with the expression 'pertaining to sheep' which is set down by the evangelist.[577] We should say the same about 'Bethania and 'Bethabara': I restored what seemed to be corrupt, using the Greek volumes and the authority of their Doctors.

q So too I changed Mitylene into Melita, and I made similar changes in many other places.

For I never thought that errors introduced by scribes or ill-educated persons had anything to do with the usage of the church. The church, if I am not mistaken, desires its codices to be as thoroughly corrected as possible.

* * * * *

575 Erasmus defended his use of *servator* and *servare* at greater length in *Divinationes ad notata Bedae* LB IX 466B–C.
576 In *Divinationes ad notata Bedae* LB IX 492D Erasmus mentions that *Capernaum* is the reading in the Greek manuscripts.
577 John 5:2

But if whatever is sung or recited in church is ascribed to the church, many things which are both said and done there are sometimes unsuitable. How is it that the church itself varies on many points, and what is read or sung in Paris does not immediately belong to the universal church? There was a time when one might fear a disturbance would break out if someone in a public congregation introduced a reading different from what the people were used to. As it is, since we are dealing with private books used by the learned, with no bearing on public reading, where, I ask you, does this disturbance of the whole church come from?

It is a fine thing, indeed, if, when we are dealing with the genuine readings which should be sought in the Hebrew and Greek sources and in the interpretations of the ancients, we should be ordered to follow the Haymos,[578] Anselms, Ruperts,[579] and Hughs.[580] But, in fact, even in their writings we sometimes find a reading different from the one from which these theologians do not want us to depart, and then too what if their extant writings frequently contain not what they wrote but what the scribes corrupted? For it is absolutely undeniable that scribes had a persistent and inauspicious obsession to change all the scriptural texts in ancient authors in accord with their acquired taste for Vulgate readings.

Now as for their prescription that after Jerome's emendations it is not permissible to depart from the usage of the church, first of all there is some debate among the learned about whether we have the Old Testament as emended by Jerome. There is even more doubt about the New Testament. But even though both were incontrovertibly his, why, after the toils of Jerome, does the church dare to sing something different from his corrections? Why is the usage not the same in all the churches? Why do those who wrote so many centuries after Jerome dare to cite Scripture in words different from his? Why do more recent writers dare to cite different readings? For it behooved them to reject whatever was different from the Vulgate. But finally, what is the use of Hebrew and Greek writings if it is not permitted to use them to correct what is corrupt in our codices? Before Jerome it was permitted to emend errors in the Sacred Volumes or to root out what was inserted, and I think it was a pious pursuit even after Jerome. The censure speaks just as if Jerome left nothing uncorrected in the Sacred Volumes or as if he never nodded or had any blind spots, or as if it were

* * * * *

578 See n9 above.
579 See n553 above.
580 See n543 above.

indubitable that this version of both testaments is Jerome's, or as if during so many centuries what he handed down had never been corrupted by scribes or uneducated and unlearned persons. If the theologians were as carefully conversant with the written remains of the ancients as they are with the questions of the scholastics, they would never have issued such censures.

Topic 14. Some propositions which seem to be set down through the inadvertence either of the paraphraser himself or of the printers

XLIII *The first proposition. Matthew 2*
Christ was circumcised at Jerusalem.[581]

CENSURE
The phrase 'at Jerusalem' should be deleted.

The second proposition. Matthew 10
In the fifth place were the names of the apostles James the son of Alphaeus and Jude the son of James.[582]

CENSURE
Instead of 'son' he should say 'brother.' For Jude was not the son of James but his brother.

The third proposition. Luke 2
When the forty-second day after the birth arrived, on which day the Law requires a male child to be presented to the Lord

CENSURE
The word 'second' should be removed. For according to the Law a male

* * * * *

581 In *Divinationes ad notata Bedae* LB IX 460C–D Erasmus argues that there is nothing improbable about this statement, but says he will delete it because Scripture does not mention exactly where Jesus was circumcised. He makes a similar argument in *Supputatio* LB IX 568F–569D.
582 In *Divinationes ad notata Bedae* LB IX 463E–464A Erasmus pointed out that he had corrected this error. In *Supputatio* LB IX 579D–580C he noted that he had made the change required by Béda but also pointed out that the correct text may have neither 'son' nor 'brother,' but may simply be 'Jude belonging to James' (*Iudas Iacobi*).

child was to be dedicated to the Lord in the temple on the fortieth day after birth, not the forty-second.[583]

The fourth proposition. Luke 2
When everything which the Law prescribed for purification had been duly carried out, they went back to Bethlehem, where the boy was born.

CENSURE
'Bethlehem' is set down instead of 'Nazareth,' nor should 'where the boy was born' be added, since Luke writes: 'And when they had completed everything according to the Law of the Lord, they went back to Galilee, to their town of Nazareth.[584]

The fifth proposition. Luke 4[:27]
Naaman the Syrian obeyed by immersing himself three times in the Jordan.

CENSURE
He said 'three times,' whereas he was ordered by Elisha to do so seven times.[585]

The sixth proposition. Matthew 27[:61]
When the others had gone away, two remained there, Mary Magdalen and another woman from the neighbourhood of the sepulchre.[586]

CENSURE
'When the others had gone away' should be deleted since Luke makes it apparent that other women besides these two visited the monument.

* * * * *

583 In *Divinationes ad notata Bedae* LB IX 492B–C Erasmus had already pointed out that this was merely a printer's error. He made the same point in *Supputatio* LB IX 603A–B.
584 Luke 2:39. In *Supputatio* LB IX 606F–607B Erasmus pointed out that this error was obviously a mere slip of the pen, which he had corrected.
585 2 Kings 5:10. In *Supputatio* LB IX 610A Erasmus noted that he had corrected this error and was grateful to the one who had pointed it out to him.
586 In *Divinationes ad notata Bedae* LB IX 466E–F Erasmus noted that his proposition is defensible but that he had nevertheless corrected it (as the Paris censors themselves noted below). He made the same point in *Supputatio* LB IX 594A–E.

The seventh proposition. John 1[:49]
Philip professed concerning Christ the same things that Peter later professed.

CENSURE
'Nathaniel' should be substituted for 'Philip.'[587] But nevertheless Nathaniel did not entirely profess the same things about Christ that the apostle Peter did.

The eighth proposition. Philippians 3[:5]
I, Paul, am a Jew, born of Jewish parents, and not from just any tribe, but from the chief tribe, that of Benjamin, from which the priests are appointed.[588]

CENSURE
Certainly something is missing here. For the tribe of Benjamin was not the chief one among the tribes of the sons of Israel, but rather the tribe of Juda, nor were the priests appointed from the tribe of Benjamin, but from the tribe of Levi. Furthermore we approve of the correction of these errors made by the writer in the following edition.

ERASMUS' CLARIFICATION
XLIII Since they approve of my effort to correct these eight places, which were corrupted by the negligence of the printers and copyists, there is no reason for me to argue about them. But from these places it could have been conjectured that I would promptly have done the same in other places if I had discovered anything that conflicted with piety. And just as they approve of my corrections here, I also have no doubt that they would have approved of the excuses I made in other places if they had known about them. But since these places have already been corrected, as the theologians were aware, why do they use language like 'should be removed,' 'should be deleted,' 'should be substituted,' as if I had not already done so? For these are not the only places that have been changed, but many others also.

* * * * *

587 In *Elenchus in censuras Bedae* LB IX 500B Erasmus had already noted that he had corrected this slip. In *Supputatio* LB IX 624F–625D Erasmus also noted that what Nathaniel said was indeed equivalent to what Peter said about Christ.
588 In *Divinationes ad notata Bedae* LB IX 477C–D Erasmus pointed out that this was merely a printer's error probably caused by the loss of a line when the type was moved from one forme to another. He gave the same explanation in *Elenchus in censuras Bedae* LB IX 509A.

In the fifth proposition a word has been omitted. For the paraphrase has 'commanded to immerse himself three times in the Jordan, he obeyed.'

Topic 15. Some propositions in which the writer did not fulfil the duty of a paraphraser

XLIV *The first proposition. Matthew 19[:9]*
Whoever puts away his wife and marries another woman commits adultery, unless the woman he puts away deserved to be put away because of her adultery.[589]

XLV *The second proposition. Matthew 24[:36]*
Not even the Son of Man knows the day and the hour of the last judgment. The Father has reserved this to himself alone.[590]

XLVI *The third proposition. Romans 8[:26]*
Even when we are silent, the Spirit of God still intercedes for us with God, and he does so not in a human fashion but with ineffable groans.

XLVII *The fourth proposition. Romans 8[:27]*
Whenever that Spirit intercedes for the saints, grieving for their afflictions, he does not intercede according to human feeling but according to the will of God.[591]

CENSURE
In these four propositions this writer did not properly fulfil the duty of a paraphraser in his paraphrase: where the paraphrase ought to make the sense clear, it does not do so, even though it is clearly explained by other Catholic Doctors. As for the first, it is certain that a man cannot take a wife even if his own wife commits adultery, since all bonds of matrimony among the faithful are indissoluble, except when a religious vow is taken after a marriage which is legitimate but not consummated. As for the second proposition, it is certain that the Son of Man, according to his humanity, knows the day and hour of the last judgment, since he knows everything that will come upon him and the Father gave all judgment to the Son in so far as he is the Son of

* * * * *

589 Erasmus defended this proposition in *Divinationes ad notata Bedae* LB IX 464D–465B.

590 Erasmus defended his explication of this proposition at some length in *Prologus supputationis* LB IX 443D–445B, in *Supputatio* LB IX 548C–549E, and in *Responsio ad notulas Bedaicas* LB IX 707B–708A, 710D–711E.

591 Erasmus defended this and the preceding proposition in *Divinationes ad notata Bedae* LB IX 471D–E. He did so at length in *Supputatio* LB IX 672E–675C.

Man; but he did not give it in such a way that before the appointed time that day and hour of judgment should be revealed to men everywhere. As for the third and fourth propositions, the Holy Spirit is said to pray and groan because his grace makes the faithful pray and groan for their wickedness and sins or for other pious and just causes, according to the uniform explanation and opinion of Catholic Doctors.

CLARIFICATIONS OF THE FOUR PROPOSITIONS ABOVE: THE FIRST[592]
XLIV I reported the contents of Christ's language, and because the passage presents manifold convolutions and many difficult questions, I was afraid to mix human commentary with the majesty of the Gospel. For what is said about separation from bed and board with the marriage bond still intact, or about a legitimate but unconsummated marriage which is dissolved by the profession of monastic vows, and other points concerning this matter can seem to be invented by human beings. But, in fact, I recast this passage as follows: 'If anyone for any reason discards his wife, just as he himself commits adultery, so too he gives his wife a reason to commit adultery.'[593] Thus I made room for the comment of St Augustine, who thinks that the exception for fornication should apply only to that clause 'he made her commit adultery.' For she was already an adulteress before she was put away.[594]

CLARIFICATION OF THE SECOND PROPOSITION
XLV I gave the reasons why I left this passage as it is. In the person of Christ I could not explain it because at that time Christ did not want it to be understood; otherwise he would have explained it. 'But you could

* * * * *

592 Pelargus sigs D6–D7v claims that Erasmus had an incorrect idea of divorce (dissolution of marriage) instead of the correct scholastic definition (separation from bed and board, with the marriage bond intact). He gives a long analysis of 1 Cor 7:11 and Rom 7:1–4 to establish the indissolubility of marriage (which Erasmus never explicitly denied).
In the second edition Erasmus made no changes or additions.
593 LB VII 103D / CWE 45 271
594 In *De conjugiis adulterinis ad Polentium liber duo* 1.10–12 PL 40 457–9 Augustine argues subtly and at length that the exception from adultery in Matt 19:9 does not allow divorce and remarriage. He refers to the parallel text in Matt 5:32, which contains the phrase 'facit eam moechari,' and seems to say that it could not apply to a wife who was already adulterous and was put away, but only to a non-adulteress wife who was put away and who then remarried and thereby became (was made) an adulteress.

have done so,' they will say, 'in the person of the evangelist.' I could have, but it was not appropriate. But this passage also presents difficulties, as is shown by the fact that the Doctors have three ways to answer the knotty question.[595] Accordingly I preferred here to leave the learned free to judge for themselves, and to indicate what I think in more appropriate places. That Christ truly did not know something would never occur to me, not in my wildest dreams.

CLARIFICATION OF THE THIRD AND FOURTH PROPOSITIONS

XLVI, XLVII Here, too, distinguished Doctors of the church have varying opinions, some interpreting the passage as applying to the Spirit of God, others to the spirit of a human being. But I did not pass over the text with no explanation at all. For I mention two spirits, the weak human spirit and that of God, which comes to the assistance of human weakness. The paraphrase is as follows: 'Nevertheless the spirit takes it in good part and struggles with the weakness of the body; but the Spirit of God breathes upon us, aiding the weakness of our flesh and lifting it up with hope so as to bear up under all afflictions, showing us what we ought to wish for or to ask for deliverance from in our prayers. For we ourselves, according to our human feelings, do not know what to wish for, etc.'[596] From this distinction it is clear that the Spirit of God requests in such a way as to help us in requesting, suggesting both what we should seek and how, breathing into us both faith and an ineffable desire for what we seek according to God. Afterwards I modulate my language in such a way as to leave the reader free to take what the Apostle says, 'that the spirit intercedes for us with ineffable groans,' as applying to the Spirit of God (in a figure of speech, of course),[597] or to the spirit of the church spiritually praying for her members,[598] or to the spirit of an individual person praying under the breath of the Divine Spirit for what contributes to salvation rather than

* * * * *

595 Thomas Aquinas *In Matthaeum Evangelium expositio* 24.3 In *Divinationes ad notata Bedae* Erasmus gave at least six attempts to solve the difficulty LB IX 455E–456B.
596 LB VII 803E–F / CWE 42 49
597 Only pseudo-Ambrose comes close to this interpretation, saying that the prayer of the Holy Spirit 'covers' our prayers and makes them efficacious; see *Commentaria in epistolas beati Pauli, in epistolam ad Romanos* 8.26–7 PL 17 (1845) 126C–127C.
598 Chrysostom *In epistolam ad Romanos* 14.7 PG 60 532–3 and Theophylactus *Expositio in epistolam ad Romanos* 8.26 PG 124 449–52 interpret the verse to mean that the Holy Spirit influences a holy person (especially the deacon) to pray for the people.

pleasure.[599] Therefore others may look to see whether there is a consensus concerning this passage among modern theologians; certainly the ancient Fathers disagreed with one another. But Paul's language is often slippery or manifold, using such a word as 'Law' or 'flesh' differently from one place to another. Likewise 'spirit' is sometimes opposed to 'flesh'; sometimes it means a mental impulse, sometimes the Spirit of God, sometimes the sound of a speaker.[600] Finally, I did not undertake there to discuss in detail all the difficulties of the New Testament, but only to indoctrinate the disdainful with a basic knowledge of the philosophy of Christ. But it we pardon commentators on Scripture whenever they skip over some passage without explaining it, all the more should we pardon a paraphraser. It is sometimes a matter of inadvertence, sometimes of weariness.

Topic 16. Merit

XLVIII   *The first proposition.* Elenchus, *annotation 192*[601]
Augustine can hardly find a place for merit.[602]

> CENSURE
> Christ finds a place for merit under the name 'work' when he says, 'call the workers and give them their reward.'[603] And the Apostle does so under the name 'labour,' saying 'everyone will receive his own reward according to his labour.'[604] And the Wise Man in Proverbs does so under the name of 'justice,' saying 'there is a reliable reward for anyone who sows justice.'[605] Again, the Apostle finds a place for merit under the name 'merit' in these words: 'Do not forget good deeds and

* * * * *

599 This is the most common interpretation. See, for example, Augustine *Epistolae* 130.15 and 194.4.17 PL 33 505, 880, and *Expositio propositionum ex epistola ad Romanos* 54 PL 35 2076; pseudo-Jerome *Commentaria in epistolas sancti Pauli, in epistolam ad Romanos* 8 PL 30 (1846) 684A–D; Bede *In Samuelem prophetam expositio allegorica* 3.7 PL 91 647A–B; and Thomas Aquinas *Expositio in omnes s. Pauli epistolas, in epistolam ad Romanos* 8.5.
600 That is, breath or words carried by breath
601 *Elenchus in censuras Bedae* LB IX 509C
602 In *Hyperaspistes* 2 Erasmus makes a similar point: 'Augustine attributes so little to free will as to grant it something in name more than in fact' CWE 77 744. See also CWE 77 717.
603 Matt 20:8
604 1 Cor 3:8
605 Prov 11:18

sharing, for God is merited by such sacrificial victims.'[606] And the Wise Man in *Ecclesiasticus* does so by choosing his words as follows: 'Mercy makes a place for everyone according to the merit of his works.'[607] And after these witnesses, in agreement with other Catholic Doctors, Augustine asserts[608] that merit is constituted from divine grace and free will which can turn in either direction so that merit is the work of both grace and free will which can turn in either direction.[609] And so this proposition, in so far as it professes that St Augustine did not clearly and certainly find a place for merit, is manifestly false and comes close to the wicked doctrine of Luther about faith and works.

ERASMUS' CLARIFICATION[610]

XLVIII I wonder why in this place they think they have to prove the existence of human merit, since I profess it in the very passage they cite. For *Elenchus* reads as follows: 'I do not totally eliminate human merit, but Augustine is hardly able to find a place for it.'[611] Moreover, if someone hardly finds a place, he still does find one. It is generally acknowledged that Augustine, especially in his old age when he was fighting against the Pelagians, is so prone to exaggerate the grace of God that you will find him leaving hardly anything to free will, which he asserts more truly than he proves.[612] Indeed,

* * * * *

606 Heb 13:16
607 Ecclus 16:15
608 The Latin does not have *asserit* but only the participle *asserens*. A word such as *dicit* may be missing.
609 Augustine makes no such assertion and does not even use the scholastic term *vertibilis* 'which can turn in either direction.' No doubt the assertion could be justified by a narrow selection of texts from his works, ignoring the broad range and intensity of his thought, especially in the late anti-Pelagian works.
610 Pelargus sigs D7v–E1 allows that Erasmus has been misrepresented by the busybody who selected this snippet, but he goes on to accuse Erasmus of misrepresenting Augustine, who he rightly insists does allow for the cooperation of free will with grace. Erasmus never denied this but he rightly pointed out that in his later anti-Pelagian works Augustine places so much emphasis on grace that he seems to allow very little room for free will. Erasmus understood the details of Augustine's position very well from his dispute with Luther over grace and free will, and makes the same accusation against Augustine at the end of *Hyperaspistes* 2 CWE 77 717 n1643.
In the second edition Erasmus made no changes or additions.
611 LB IX 509C
612 Erasmus says much the same in *Hyperaspistes* 2 CWE 77 744. But in *Hyperaspistes* 1 and 2 he had examined the whole range of Augustine's works on the questions of free will, grace, and predestination, as the index shows (CWE 77 775–6).

how tiny a share does someone assign to merit if he says that God crowns
his own gifts in us and that the very fact that we assent to impelling grace
is attributable to grace?[613] Isn't there a great difference between a gift and
merit? In the *Psalms*[614] and in other places how often does he simply deprive
mankind of merit, ascribing everything to the mercy of God? But if merit is
taken to mean what we owe to our own powers and that for which we do
not owe thanks to God, merit is a problematic word.[615] But these remarks
are beside the point, since I profess that godly men have some merit, and
I do not deny that Augustine finds a place for it, though grudgingly, since
in many places he denies that there is any human merit at all.

XLIX *The second proposition. Preface to Luke*
     Christ frees all men from all diseases of their mind, as long as they
     acknowledge the disease and trust the physician.[616]
   L *The third proposition*
     The apostles announced that everyone should do penance for their
     previous sins and that no one should trust in his own deeds but only
     in the promises of the gospel.[617]
  LI *The fourth proposition. Mark 2[:5?]*
     God does not require holocausts from sinners or votive offerings; only
     acknowledge the disease and have confidence in the physician.[618]

     CENSURE
     Although a burning faith and an honest and unsullied confidence in
     Christ and his promises contribute much toward getting from God
     what we ask, still these things are not enough unless good works are
     added to them. Therefore these three propositions, with regard to the
     second part in each of the three, which allege that trust in Christ and his

     * * * * *

613 *De gratia et libero arbitrio* 6, 9 PL 44 890, 893; *De diversis quaestionibus ad Simpli-
    cianum libri duo* 1.2 PL 40 110–27
614 *Enarrationes in psalmos,* CXVIII 7.2 PL 37 1517
615 The scholastic theologians considered merit in the context of salvation with
    great subtlety, dividing it (for starters) into *meritum de congruo* and *meritum
    de condigno.* Erasmus had entered into the question fairly thoroughly in *Hy-
    peraspistes* 1 and 2; see, for example, CWE 76 28–9 n103 and the index under
    'merit' CWE 77 798.
616 Erasmus defended this proposition in *Divinationes ad notata Bedae* LB IX 489E–
    490A and in *Supputatio* LB IX 595F–596E.
617 Erasmus defended this proposition in *Supputatio* LB IX 649A–D.
618 Erasmus defended this proposition briefly in *Supputatio* LB IX 642B–E.

promises suffice for salvation without good works, when such can be
done, lend support to the Lutheran heresy concerning faith and works.

ERASMUS' CLARIFICATION

XLIX In this fashion even honest and learned men are often deceived, that is,
when what was said by Christ, the evangelist, or the Apostle is presented as
if it were being said in these times by Erasmus. In the Preface I speak of the
grace of the gospel presented by Christ, who saved by faith in the gospel
those who could not be saved either by the wisdom of the Greeks or by the
Law of Moses. From the pagans and Jews who came to be baptized, there
was no question of the works of their former lives but only of their faith
in the Son of God himself. This language does not exclude pious works,
which after baptism are performed by faith working through love.[619] This
is what my Preface says: 'The heavenly Father, seeing that mankind was
not reformed either by human philosophy or by observing the Law, sent
his Speech, who would free everyone from all diseases of the mind, as long
as we acknowledge the disease and trust the physician.'[620] Now if we were
to twist these words to apply them to penance, the life-raft after baptism,
it is still clear that no one's sins are forgiven if he does not recognize his
guilt and hope for remission from Christ. For *tantum ut* is equivalent to
dum modo.[621] And such phrases do not always have the effect of excluding
something,[622] but often they indicate something which is particularly and
especially relevant. For example, if a father should say to his son 'as long as
you love your literary studies, there is nothing you cannot ask and obtain
from me,' his language does not give the son licence to offend in other
matters and to neglect his duties, but indicates the area to which he should
pay particular attention.

L Furthermore, what is stated in Mark[623] is obviously spoken about those
who were resorting for the first time to the grace of the gospel. And the
Apostle wanted to start out with the same opening that John the Baptist had
used: do penance and believe in the gospel. To believe in the gospel is to
have confidence in the promises of the gospel. What, then, does it promise?

* * * * *

619 Gal 5:6
620 LB VII 275–6
621 The first phrase (ie 'as long as') is used in proposition 2 above. Both phrases
    mean 'as long as, provided that.'
622 That is, good works are not excluded by such a phrase.
623 Mark 6:12

Through faith in Jesus Christ it offers everyone righteousness, that is the wiping away of all offences. I think that this opinion is both Pauline and Catholic. The clause I added, 'that no one should trust in his own deeds but only in the promises of the gospel,' pertains to the Jews, who were puffed up by the observance of the Law and thought that salvation was owed to their own righteousness, since Paul cries out, 'if from works, then not from grace.'[624] And so it is evident that this passage does not deal with the works of the baptized but with the blots of their former lives, which were once and for all freely wiped away by baptism.

LI This part of the paraphrase deals with the faith of the paralysed man,[625] who is a figure of both nations[626] while they were burdened with sin, who both obtain salvation in equal measure through faith in Christ. And I compare Christ, who healed with his omnipotent Word, with the priests of the Mosaic law, who promised the expiation of sins by various sacrifices. And just as in the paralytic Christ had no regard for anything except their faith,[627] so too in baptism he does not question either the Jews or the gentiles about the works of their former lives, but purifies the hearts of all of them alike by means of faith. Certainly it is clear that in that place I am talking about the works of the Jews and not the duties of charity because I say that Christ does not ask for holocausts or votive offerings, which provided expiation for the Jews. Hence these three propositions in no way allege in an unqualified way that faith in Christ without good works suffices for salvation; indeed the paraphrases teach the opposite in hundreds of places. And certainly they do not offer even the tiniest support to the Lutheran heresy, since my propositions speak of those who are purified by baptism whereas Luther speaks of the good works of adults after baptism. See what it comes to if you make pronouncements based on excerpted snippets! How unjust and offensive it is to cackle time and again insults and objections to which I have clearly responded. Ah, but such high and mighty men have no time to read my answers. But they ought to have had time to read either both or none at all.[628] For it is tyrannical not to wish to know them and to want to make pronouncements.

* * * * *

624 Rom 11:6
625 Mark 2:3–12
626 That is, the Jews and the gentiles
627 That is, the faith of those represented by the paralytic
628 That is, both the works to which they were objecting and the answers Erasmus had already made to their objections

LII *The fifth proposition. Luke 5*
Jesus requires no other sacrifice than a straightforward and pure trust in him.[629]

LIII *The sixth proposition. Mark 2*
Whoever reveals that he has complete confidence has offered sufficient sacrifices.

CENSURE

Since the evangelist says nothing about sacrifice in this place, if these two propositions are understood to mean that, because of what Christ did by the authority of his excellence, we are not required to do good works and to make satisfaction for the sins committed after baptism, they are heretical, since faith requires us to hold that sinners owe satisfaction for the sins they have committed after baptism, according to the decree of divine justice. Otherwise the Catholic church would not pray for the souls of the faithful departed, nor would there be any need to posit purgatory after this life.

ERASMUS' CLARIFICATION OF THE FIRST PROPOSITION

LII It is clear that the paraphrase is dealing there with the leper healed by the touch of Christ,[630] whose healing power I compare with the priests of Moses; in cases of leprosy, concerning which they did no more than judge, they prescribed certain sacrifices and demanded offerings, whereas Christ looked for no such things but was content with faith alone. The words of the paraphrase are as follows: 'For the priests of Moses neither inflicted nor eliminated leprosy, but they only judged when leprosy was present or removed. Jesus alone relieved everyone of all sorts of diseases, etc.'[631] This word 'sacrifice' does not refer to good works but to the victims of the Mosaic law and makes Christ's superiority evident.

ERASMUS' CLARIFICATION OF THE SECOND PROPOSITION

LIII Here, too, the paraphrase is dealing with the paralytic,[632] who gained health solely by the merit of faith, meaning that those who come with full confidence to the profession of the gospel have no need of Jewish sacrifi-

* * * * *

629 Erasmus defended this passage in *Divinationes ad notata Bedae* LB IX 492E–F and in *Supputatio* LB IX 611B–E.
630 Luke 5:12–15
631 LB VII 338A–B
632 Mark 2:3–12

cial victims for the expiation of sins. Hence in these propositions I do not see a single syllable which refers to those who deny that good works are required from those who have been baptized or that satisfaction must be given by those who recover from falling after baptism. Indeed they were right to add 'if,' but there was no need for such a doubt if they had either examined the passage or read what I wrote about it in my reply to Béda, especially since they here report from that reply some things against me but pass over in silence what is on my side.[633] These things are mentioned as a precaution,[634] but at the same time my reputation is undeservedly damaged.

LIV *The seventh proposition. Matthew 19*
    No work by a human being is so good as to merit the reward of eternal life.[635]

    CENSURE
    Although eternal life is by its nature such a great good that no one can merit it without divine grace, still to assert that a person cannot merit it with divine grace is heretical and contrary to Holy Scripture, which shows that one arrives at eternal life by observing God's commandments, according to Christ's words: 'If you wish to enter into eternal life, keep my commandments.'[636] Then, too, the Apostle asserts that people merit God through good deeds and sharing;[637] and the Wise Man says concerning some holy men, 'God tested them and found them worthy of him.'[638]

    * * * * *

633 In his *Divinationes ad notata Bedae* LB IX 492E–F Erasmus had remarked that Luke is not concerned with penance after baptism or with satisfaction. The reporters to the theologians turned up these points against Erasmus' but ignored the defence he gave there: that Christ, unlike the Mosaic priests, required no sacrifices but only faith for their immediate conversion.
634 Erasmus means that in his reply to Béda he excluded sins after baptism and satisfaction as a precaution against being misunderstood.
635 In *Divinationes ad notata Bedae* LB IX 465D Erasmus briefly notes that in this proposition he did not exclude human merit but only denied its equivalence to the reward of eternal life. He also remarked that he did not deny the validity of the scholastic distinction between *meritum de congruo* and *meritum de condigno*. He made a similar defence in *Supputatio* LB IX 589F–590D and in *Responsio ad notulas Bedaicas* LB IX 709E–710D.
636 Matt 19:17
637 Heb 13:16
638 Wis 3:5

ERASMUS' CLARIFICATION[639]

LIV In that passage the paraphrase is dealing with a comparison of merit and reward. Since the young man believed that Christ was nothing more than a good man, he calls him good. As a human person the Lord refused that attribute. When the young man says, 'what should I do?' he was asking about some remarkable work to which eternal life would be rightly owed. For as a Jew he admired works, but knew nothing of grace. The Lord replied that there is no such thing as a merely human work to which such a reward is absolutely owed. The words of the paraphrase are as follows: 'When he asked about a good deed, he did not mean just any good deed but some remarkable good deed which would merit life. But no mortal is absolutely good and there is no work of mortals which is so good that it merits the reward of eternal life, etc.'[640] When I speak of a 'reward' I mean in the sense of wages. When I say 'so good' I am expressing the equality of the merit and the reward. But just as no human being is perfectly and absolutely good, so too no human work, in so far as it is human, is so completely perfect that it equals the reward of eternal life.

But in this calculation, if you want to set aside for grace what is owing to grace, such a tiny portion will remain for human beings that godly people prefer to attribute everything to grace, especially since the very fact that a person assents to or cooperates with grace is attributable to grace – indeed the very fact that we are furnished with reason and a will is a gift of God. For a person does not have anything which he has not received.[641] For when Paul said 'the wages of sin are death,' he did not add, 'but the reward of those who lead godly lives is eternal life,' but rather 'but the grace of God is life eternal through Jesus Christ.'[642] I would say these things not because

* * * * *

639 Pelargus sigs E1–E1v approves of Erasmus' statement but he wishes Erasmus had added a few words about the relation between works and grace; he himself goes on to add many words about the relation, far more than Erasmus could ever have introduced into a paraphrase. But he does not really add anything Erasmus did not already imply in his clarification. He objects to Erasmus' argument that Paul did not complete his statement 'the wages of sin are death' by saying 'the reward of good living is eternal life,' since it is hardly true that whatever Paul did not say is false.
   In the second edition Erasmus added a sentence after this argument pointing out that it is not intended to deny merit but only to show how little importance it has compared to grace; but he made no other additions or changes.
640 LB VII 104F–105A / CWE 45 276
641 1 Cor 4:7
642 Rom 6:23

I exclude merit totally but in order to show how little importance it has compared to grace. I think that this opinion of mine, which it seems to me I have expressed clearly enough, agrees with that of the theologians. And so this passage has nothing in common with those who deny that holy persons have any merit or that any human work is good at all. Good works pave the way to salvation, although salvation is not owing to them in an unqualified way.

In fact Paul does not use the word 'merit,' but rather says εὐαρεστεῖται ὁ θεός, that is 'God is pleased' or 'God is reconciled' or 'God is appeased.'[643] But God tests in order to make the virtue of holy men famous; and he finds worthy of himself those whom his grace has rendered worthy. This has nothing to do with equality between reward and merit.

LV *The eighth proposition. Mark 10*
Whoever strives for a reward but would not do so unless he knew it would be given deprives himself of the reward.[644]

CENSURE
Although people ought to strive and do good works primarily out of a love of God rather than of a reward, still it is permissible for them to be moved by a reward to do good works and to struggle against temptations; and to assert the opposite of this is erroneous and contrary to Scripture. For the Apostle writes: 'whoever plows should plow in hope, and whoever thrashes should do so in the hope of obtaining fruit.'[645] Moreover, the eunuchs who castrate themselves for the kingdom of heaven are approved by Christ.[646] And the royal prophet inclined his heart 'to perform what is righteous for the sake of the recompense.'[647]

ERASMUS' CLARIFICATION
LV I think that we are also in agreement here. They confess that God should be loved for his own sake, since he is by nature the greatest power, and that he is his own primary reward, though a regard for reward and punishments stimulates the imperfect to do good works. But whoever worships God but would not worship him if he would not give some reward which is not

* * * * *

643 Heb 13:16
644 Erasmus defended this proposition in *Supputatio* LB IX 653C–F.
645 1 Cor 9:10
646 Matt 19:12
647 Ps 118:112

himself has things upside-down: he makes what is subsidiary primary and vice versa. Certainly whoever worships God in this frame of mind does not worship him as God and does not truly love God as he is commanded to do.

Topic 17. Trust in good works and merit

LVI   *The first proposition. In the conclusion of* A Discussion of Free Will Indeed Luther discusses confidence in our own merit, works, and powers in a godly and Christian way and says we must put all our confidence in God and his promises.[648]

CENSURE .

It is well known that Luther's discussion about casting away confidence in works and merit is ungodly and heretical. For he discussed them in such a way that he did not hesitate to condemn good works and merit and likewise confidence placed in them under God, which Holy Scripture approves in many places. For Scripture teaches that after this life people will be repaid for what they did while in their bodies, whether it was good or evil, and that those who did good deeds will proceed to a resurrection of life while those who did evil will go to a resurrection of judgment. This same Holy Scripture also urges Christians to perform and multiply good deeds for two reasons: first so that by sowing unsparingly in this life they may grow rich in good works and afterwards harvest a blessing, and then so that through their works they may gain certainty about their vocation and election. For St Peter exhorts the faithful as follows: 'Work hard to make your vocation and election certain through good works. If you do this you will not sin at any time.'[649] But if people are rendered certain about their vocation and election by doing good works, they will not distrust at all but will have complete confidence that their labour will not be useless in the eyes of God, who does not deceive them when he promises eternal good to those who do good works. Hence it is quite clear that the faithful rightly place their trust under God in good works as the means necessary for salvation together with the grace of God. Therefore when Erasmus approves of the opposite opinion he errs shamefully and temerariously scandalizes his readers.

* * * * *

648 *De libero arbitrio* CWE 76 88
649 2 Pet 1:10

CLARIFICATION

LVI Since in the entire *Discussion* I am fighting against the teaching of
Luther, certainly something quite absurd happened to me if at the end of
the work I underwent a sudden transformation and approved the opinion
which I had opposed with every means at my disposal. The very absurdity
of such a thing should have let them know that I did not mean what certain
people took it to mean. In fact, in these words I am so far from approving
of Luther's teaching that, by rejecting the probable objections Luther could
make, I would offer more support to the opinion of the theologians. Christ,
Paul, and the spiritual men of both testaments especially commend the love
of God, which is the fountain of all godliness and is closely connected to
the love of one's neighbour for the sake of God. They downplay their merit,
ascribing whatever good they do to God's mercy, which provides us with
eternal life not because we merit it but because he himself promised it. Because such points are read everywhere in Scripture Luther infers that they
eliminate free will. I, on the other hand, say that I have shown that they do
not completely eliminate free will. In the concluding summary of the arguments the words of *A Discussion* are as follows: 'Finally, it seems obvious
how many disagreeable, not to say absurd, consequences follow once free
will is denied; and it appears that if we accept the opinion which I have ex-
pounded, it does not invalidate Luther's assertions, which are godly (to be
sure) and Christian, that we must love God above all else, that we must remove our trust from our own merit, deeds, and powers and put it all in
God and his promises. If all this is so, I should like the reader to consider
whether he thinks it right to condemn the opinion of so many Doctors of
the church, approved by the consensus of so many ages and nations, and
to accept a number of paradoxes which are causing the present uproar in
Christendom.'[650] Thus far I have reported the words of *A Discussion*.

In Luther I approved only what raises us up from the love of worldly
things to the love of God, which calls us away from the very dangerous
reef of confidence in ourselves into the very safe port of confidence in the
grace of the gospel; but I do not approve of the reasons he gives for it and
the conclusions he draws from it, and in fact I argue against them with all
my might. No godly person denies that good works are the provisions for
the journey to eternal life, and I confess that without them a profession
of faith is not sufficient. And whoever exhorts Christians to accumulate
here in this world as many good works as they can gives holy and godly

* * * * *

650 CWE 76 88

advice. As for someone who teaches that a person should have confidence, that is, full and certain hope, in his works in so far as they are human, I do not know whether he is giving good advice. All the holiest men sing quite a different song – especially since in Latin *fiducia* ['confidence'] does not mean just any kind of hope but the principal and highest kind. Hope is accompanied by fear; confidence excludes it. In some way or other good works foster hope, just as bad deeds generate despair, though even here there is no equal balance because we commit bad deeds on our own, but it is not so much we who do our good works as the grace of God working in us. If the goodness of God attributes them to us as merit, it is still our part to ascribe all the glory to him, without whom we are nothing and can do nothing. And to the degree that a person claims anything for himself in his good works, he takes it away from the mercy of God.

Now though there may be some importance in our part in good works, still confidence in ourselves tends toward arrogance, and therefore Christ admonished his disciples that when they have carried out all the commandments they should say 'we are useless servants.'[651] Nothing is taken away from our rewards – indeed they are increased – if we consider our part in good works (if we have any) as nothing and if we say with Paul 'by the grace of God I am what I am.'[652] I would add this: in my words 'godly, to be sure,' the phrase has a diminishing force, implying that in Luther only this point is godly or somehow godly, though at fault. I am reluctant to sift through the testimony of Scripture, since I might seem to want to teach the teachers. Still, in my opinion, Peter here enjoins no more than that those who profess Christ should live up to their profession by living well and not have the grace of God in vain. If these ideas are godly, if they are in agreement with Scripture, I am amazed that Erasmus is said to err shamefully. Such notions I do not attribute to the faculty but rather to those who set forth fragments that appear to be evil because they are perversely interpreted.

LVII *The second proposition, which is in* Elenchus[653]
It is dangerous to trust in merit.

CENSURE
Since God will render unto each according to his works, the faithful ought to be sure that if they persevere in doing good and keeping

* * * * *

651 Luke 17:10
652 1 Cor 15:10
653 *Elenchus in censuras Bedae* LB IX 509C

God's commandments they will obtain eternal life. This much is included in the nature of hope. Accordingly, in this way they not only
can trust in merit but are even bound to do so; otherwise they do not
have hope. Therefore it is erroneous to assert that it is dangerous to
trust in merit in this manner. Still this trust does not exclude the grace
and mercy of God, through which people merit and are received into
eternal life. For such trust is far removed from presumption and ingratitude: it ascribes all good works to God as their principal author
and it assigns the fruit of merit principally to God's mercy, not to its
own merit or human righteousness, which is of no importance apart
from God's mercy, although, together with that mercy, human works
are required according to God's decree, works that are nevertheless
the gift of God. Still there is no human work which regularly, absolutely, and without the condition of future perseverance can assure a
person of salvation, apart from a revelation.

CLARIFICATION

LVII Since human powers play such a small part in good works, since human weakness and imperfection are such a hindrance to obeying God's
precepts, since there is such a mass of evil works compared to the good, if
the matter is to be settled by weighing one against the other, I think that
a person's trust, that is, his chief hope, can be more safely placed in the
kindness of God than in our works, that is, our own part. Whoever trusts
in his works, in the sense that I mean, is preparing to contend with the
Lord for a judgment, but woe be to us if our lives are to be measured by
the justice of God! The next-door neighbour of trust is presumption, the
greatest plague of godliness. In dangers it is safest for sailors to turn to
the shore. And in that passage I do not say merely 'it is dangerous to trust
in our merits,' but I add 'it is dangerous to trust in them, though it is safe
to preach grace.' I think that if someone were to ask Paul himself, as he
was giving up the ghost, 'are you dying with good confidence?' he would
say, 'with the very best.' But if the questioner went on to ask, 'relying on
what protection, your good deeds or the grace of God?' I think Paul would
answer: 'If I did anything right in my life, it was not I who did it but he
through me; to his mercy I attribute everything that I have gained or expect
to gain.'

But it is not immediately true that there would be no hope if someone
attributed so little to his works that he would not dare to place any hope
in them. For God's promises and his immense kindness provide a most
certain hope. Finally, it is one thing not to trust in our own works and
quite another to perform no good deeds and many evil ones. If it is modest

to attribute very little to our works, then the more perfect a person is, the less he claims for himself in his good deeds. Therefore, just as I have nothing against that modest hope which attributes everything to grace, even its own good works, although whoever has such confidence places it more truly in God than in his own works, so too I think what I wrote is true, namely that it is not safe to attribute the principal confidence about our salvation and the safeguarding of it to our works, and that it is safer to attribute the sum and substance of it to the generosity of God. Unless I am mistaken the theologians agree with me on these points, except that I explain what I mean in different language.

Topic 18. Trust in bodily ceremonies and in the statutes of the religious orders

LVIII *The first proposition. In* Elenchus[654]
The more we adhere to bodily ceremonies, the more we tend toward Judaism.

CENSURE
Although we should not have confidence in works and bodily ceremonies in such a way as to give them precedence over spiritual works, in which perfection consists, nevertheless we ought to have confidence in them under God on their own level and we ought to take them up as weapons in the fight against spiritual enemies, as Christ teaches and as the holy Fathers have handed down. Certainly ceremonies instituted by the church and the holy Fathers should not be thought to tend toward Judaism, which has already disappeared and been revoked, as the prophets predicted that it should be completely revoked. But persons who think that the church and the holy Fathers established Jewish ceremonies should not be believed to be Christians but rather ungodly heretics, Aerians, Wyclifites,[655] or Lutherans, or those corrupted by the same leaven of malice.[656] For the ceremonies of the church, by their very rationale, pertain to pre-eminent virtue, that is, to religion; and those who render them to God or perform them in matters which pertain to him do not commit any

* * * * *

654 *Elenchus in censuras Bedae* LB IX 506D–507A
655 'Aerians' refers not to the followers of Arius (see n13 above) but to the followers of Aeris (see n70 above). For the Wyclifites see n87 above.
656 1 Cor 5:8

sin but rather perform a virtuous deed and fulfil a godly duty. The church does not burden the faithful with Jewish observances by prescribing ceremonies but, quite the contrary, she uplifts them in this way and acts as a salutary leader and guide of their lives, just as someone who prescribes useful laws for a negligent and reckless people does not burden them but uplifts them, establishing guidelines and rules for living. Accordingly, the proposition written above, by speaking of confidence in bodily ceremonies, as was aforesaid, is ungodly and heretical, in agreement with the error of Aeris, Wyclif, and Luther, an error which was seized upon by a perverse understanding of that place in Scripture, 'bodily exercise is not very useful.'[657] In this text the Apostle does not intend bodily exercises to be considered worthless, as long as they are oriented toward piety and divine worship; but it is quite different if they are taken up for their own sake and by themselves, with no regard for piety and not oriented toward it.

CLARIFICATION[658]

LVIII I am so far from condemning the ceremonies and regulations of the church that I approve of them in many places and defend them in published books against those who attack them. But since the Jews attributed a great deal to bodily observances, I use Judaism to mean not the ungodliness of the Jews but prescriptions concerning external things such as clothing, food, or fasts, which have some similarity with the observances of the Jews. And in observing them (though they were established to promote piety) many Christians have a Jewish outlook, either resting content with them and neglecting the things of the spirit, or else, by a topsy-turvy judgment, attributing more to those externals than to true godliness, which consists in a state of mind. However, just as the hard-heartedness of the Jews had to be restrained by prescriptions as a sort of railing, so too the cooling of Christian charity has caused bishops to prescribe many things not dissimilar to Jewish prescriptions, though they are to be observed with a different attitude. They are a means of transport, as it were, to bring children from their infancy to

* * * * *

657 1 Tim 4:8
658 Pelargus sigs E3–E4 agrees with Erasmus but he provides a long essay justifying physical gestures and ceremonies which adds little or nothing to Erasmus' argument.
   In the second edition Erasmus made no changes and added only a short sentence unrelated to Pelargus' essay.

the spirit, just as are the visible types which inform us about spiritual matters: fasting, for example, admonishes us to restrain all fleshly desires and is also a help in doing so, weakening the flesh and lifting up the spirit.

But it is an abuse of ceremonies to place the sum and substance[659] of sanctity in them or to attribute more to them than to the things of the spirit. Sometimes they present an occasion for violating the very holiness they were established to promote. It is people who do these things that I criticize, not the ceremonies themselves. And they themselves criticize the same persons when they condemn those who take up ceremonies by themselves, as do people who rest content with them, as if perfect holiness consisted in observing them. But if we attribute to the church whatever is prescribed by the bishops or whatever is done in church, there are many episcopal regulations about which there is public protest throughout the world, and not without cause; there are many ceremonies in some churches which you could say are either superfluous or unsuitable or superstitious. For often some dean with nothing better to do or some other wretch like him thinks them up. Sometimes some old woman gets something or other to be done by giving a large sum of money. Sometimes the force of popular custom causes some things to creep in, if not to suddenly intrude. And so a person would not be speaking in an ungodly way if he said that such regulations and ceremonies place a burden on the liberty of the Christian people, especially since there are not a few of them that have nothing to do with holiness but are based on profit and ambition.

Accordingly, since our opinions coincide, my proposition offers no support to the Aerians, Wyclifites, and Lutherans, if in fact they totally condemn the regulations of the church. When they say that this saying of Paul, 'bodily exercise is not very useful, but holiness is good for everything,'[660] does not exclude bodily ceremonies established as a help to holiness, they speak the truth; but it is equally true that his statement admonishes us that much more is to be attributed to the spirit than to these external observances. Because I saw that the world was full of such people, sometimes I discourage people from admiring ceremonies and recall them to the pursuit of true holiness. And I considered that it was neither necessary nor safe to admonish them to trust in ceremonies.

Others can look to the word 'trust'; to me it means 'to rely primarily' and I find it troublesome to trust in human works and trust in ceremonies. I do not find such phrases in Holy Scripture or in the writings of holy men.

* * * * *

659 Latin 'proram et puppim' ('stem and stern'): *Adagia* 1 i 8
660 1 Tim 4:8

The passage in *Elenchus* is as follows: 'The closer we come to the spirit, the more pure is our Christianity; the more we adhere to bodily ceremonies, the more we tend toward Judaism, etc.'[661] Someone adheres to them if he rests content with them and does not make any progress toward the things for which they were established. Now so long as we take Judaism there to mean Jewish superstition, it is true that those who adhere to bodily ceremonies as the Jews do to the letter and prefer externals to inward holiness tend toward Judaism. And so, since on this point there is no disagreement between the theologians and me, farewell to the Aerians and their brotherhood! Find someone else at whom to throw insults about ungodliness and heresy; they will certainly not stick to me. Ceremonies are necessary for the weak; the perfect certainly do not disdain them to the degree of not wanting to observe them, but they attribute less to them the more progress they have made in mental holiness and mortifying the emotions.

LIX *Proposition 2. In* Elenchus[662]

It is my hope that everyone be such as not to have much need of bodily ceremonies or not to attribute that much to them.

CENSURE

In this life the faithful see God through a glass darkly[663] and are led to the invisible by the visible. To God, who is the Lord of bodies as well as spirits, we are bound to display not only interior and invisible but also external and visible service and worship, which usually are designated by the name 'ceremonies.' Therefore, so far as the state of this life is concerned, everyone has need of ceremonies or the visible worship of God. For that reason persons who disparage such ceremonies ought to be called temerarious assailants against the Christian religion, just as is the desire of this writer in this proposition, which springs from the same bilgewater of error as the preceding proposition.

CLARIFICATION

LIX What they teach here, that we owe God worship with both of our human components, since he is the Lord of bodies as well as souls, is a pious teaching and one with which I thoroughly agree. But this teaching is not the least bit inconsistent with my proposition, which hopes for nothing other

* * * * *

661 LB IX 506D–E
662 *Elenchus in censuras Bedae* LB IX 506E
663 1 Cor 13:12

than such great progress in the Christian people in those things which are of the spirit that they would have no need of external props but would freely perform the things for the observance of which those external props, as it were, were provided. For example, people are required to genuflect or bow their heads to God; they are instructed by this ceremony to submit their minds to God. The perfect person does not need this prop because he submits his mind to God whatever the condition of his body may be. And so I do not mean that the perfect do not need ceremonies in the sense that they are not bound to observe them but that they have no need of the props which are necessary for the weak. Thus a priest is commanded to say mass fasting; by this ceremony he is admonished that he should approach the sacred mysteries with a mind purified of all fleshly desires. Furthermore, someone who is very upset because he unthinkingly tasted something but is not afraid of approaching the table of the Lord with hatred and greed attributes too much to ceremonies, and it is such people I blame when I say 'or not to attribute that much to them.' 'That much,' that is, 'too much' or 'not as much as many do.' But whoever is completely devoted to approaching mass with a purified mind certainly does not neglect what is bodily, but he neither places any trust in it nor is he upset like the other priest if something untoward happens by chance; he is less concerned where there is less danger. If someone warns against the abuse of ceremonies and urges that we advance beyond them to what is more perfect, he is certainly not disparaging them. And so how does this proposition disparage ceremonies if it preserves them and encourages us to something more perfect than they are? I will add this point: they violently twist these remarks of mine by applying them to all ceremonies, whereas *Elenchus* is dealing not with divine worship but with prescriptions about food. This is quite clear from the passages singled out for criticism by Béda, to whom I am replying in *Elenchus*. Finally, just as fasting would not immediately disappear if the church provided no fixed days for it, so too worship by means of both human components would not immediately disappear if some churches or monasteries at this time had fewer ceremonies. The first Christians did not have much need for prescribed fasts because they fasted daily of their own free will. They did not need required amounts of prayer because they persevered in prayer day and night. They did not need a rule about paying tithes because on their own they laid all their resources at the feet of the apostles.[664] If someone wishes for such Christians, how, I ask you, is he

* * * * *

664 Acts 2:44–5

sinning? That being the case, the most holy faculty could have admonished without insults if they had something to say about ceremonies.

LX *The third proposition. In* Elenchus[665]
 If bishops have established any Jewish observances because of the weak, I do not condemn them.

CENSURE

This proposition, alleging that ceremonies and observances established by the church and the holy Fathers are Jewish and suitable only to the weak, is ungodly, insulting to the church, and (like the preceding propositions) drawn from an erroneous interpretation of Scripture. We have already sufficiently demonstrated before that such ceremonies and observances of the church or holy Fathers are not Jewish. But that they are fitting not only for the weak or imperfect is clearly demonstrated. For Adam was created perfect and yet a certain kind of food was prescribed for him by the Lord. The apostles were likewise perfect but they frequently devoted themselves to fasts, vigils, and prayers. They also abstained from certain kinds of food, such as blood or what had been strangled.[666] Hence it is clear how pestilent this teaching is, asserting that the perfect in this life do not need such bodily ceremonies, a teaching which certainly tends to the error of the Beguards, which was rightly condemned at the Council of Vienne.[667]

CLARIFICATION[668]

LX Someone or other reversed my sentence, which is as follows: 'But if bishops have established any Jewish observances because of the weak, I do not condemn them, but it is my hope that everyone be such as not to have much need of them or not to attribute that much to them.'[669] First of all,

* * * * *

665 *Elenchus in censuras Bedae* LB IX 506E
666 Acts 15:20
667 At this council (AD 1311) the Beguards and Beguines were condemned for holding that the perfect do not have to conform to basic ecclesiastical rules; see Mansi XXV 410. See also n364 above.
668 Pelargus sig E4v notes briefly that it would have been better not to call ceremonies Jewish, no matter who established them. But he is not particularly upset by this terminology.
 In the second edition Erasmus made no changes or additions.
669 LB IX 506E; Erasmus means that the conclusion of the sentence was treated in the preceding proposition (LIX) whereas the introductory clause is treated here.

I am talking about rules established by bishops, not the whole church; and I apply the term 'Jewish' to that feature in external prescriptions which has a certain resemblance to Jewish prescriptions; and I do not say that such things are prescribed by bishops, but I say I do not condemn them even if they should prescribe them. It is hypothetical, not declarative. And the church has revoked many such regulations, such as giving the Eucharist to infants right after baptism or forbidding a man to enter church on the day after a night during which he had to do with his wife. Accordingly, when they twist this proposition, which is speaking about the choice of food and such matters, and apply it to all the regulations of the church and the Fathers, and when they interpret them as Jewish superstition, they do so with no approval from me. And then, when they say 'not suitable,' if they mean 'not binding' I neither meant nor said that. In fact, I grant that they are more binding on the perfect than on the weak. If at that time there had been no weak persons, the church would never have established fasts or the choice of foods. As for God's intention in prescribing for Adam abstinence from the tree,[670] it has little to do with the present discussion. He is God; he can prescribe whatever he wishes for whomever he wishes; and whatever he prescribes is by that very fact to be observed because he prescribes it. But this is not true of humanity. The apostles frequently stayed awake, fasted, and prayed, but without any human prescriptions. I have already spoken about blood and strangled animals. This regulation was conceded to the invincible importunity of the Jews, and even so only temporarily. And so if my language is taken as I spoke it, there is no affront to ceremonies or to the church or to the Fathers. If Christ withdrew his body from his followers because it would hinder the strength of the Spirit,[671] why should it be surprising that Jewish prescriptions would have rendered them weak, not because they observe them but because they place their trust in them, that is, establish them as the principal constituents of righteousness or rest content with them. This opinion, if I am not mistaken, is far from the teaching of the Beguards.

LXI *The fourth proposition. Mark 2*

To my disciples (said Christ) I do not give any such rules – eat this, abstain from that, rest at this time, work at that time, dress thus, do not touch this, do not handle that – lest they remain weak forever if

* * * * *

670 Gen 2:17
671 John 16:7

they have once learned under my direction to trust bodily things of this kind.[672]

CENSURE

As far as the first part of this proposition is concerned, we say that, although Christ did not prescribe these things universally, he nevertheless left some of them to be prescribed by Peter, the other apostles, and their successors for the edification of the church, saying 'whoever hears you hears me and whoever scorns you scorns me.'[673] As for the second part, namely 'lest they remain weak forever,' in so far as it suggests that those who trust in such things as props of virtue are rendered weak and less spiritual, it is false and insulting to the church, which, under the guidance of the Holy Spirit, has established such things in order that the faithful by means of them may advance in spirit and virtue and fulfil God's precepts more suitably and easily.

CLARIFICATION[674]

LXI The theologians and I agree that Christ did not prescribe any such things. We also agree that authority was given to the apostles and their successors to establish practices that promote godliness, especially in accord with the pronouncements of Scripture. But that those who trust in external observances and rest content with them remain weak forever – if we take this as I mean it – is quite true, and yet it is not false even if taken in their sense. If external practices are performed so that by means of them people may advance toward the spirit, they are assuredly performed to strengthen human weakness. 'For the spirit is willing but the flesh is weak.'[675] And for that reason Paul said that the Law is weakened in that it cannot confer true righteousness through basins and victims.[676] The prayers and fasts prescribed by the Pharisees belong even more to weakness. For in that passage the Lord is dealing with such fasting as that.

* * * * *

672 Erasmus defended this proposition in *Supputatio* LB IX 644E–645C.
673 Luke 10:16
674 Pelargus sigs E4v–E5 denies that outward ceremonies serve only to strengthen the weak, claiming that they are also useful to those who have achieved perfect holiness.
    In the second edition Erasmus made no changes or additions.
675 Matt 26:41; Mark 14:38
676 Heb 7:16–17

Now though such regulations seem to be of some moment when taken by themselves, nevertheless, if they are compared with the deeds for which the Lord prepared his followers, they were weak, and if nothing were added to them they did not strengthen the weak. The Pharisee said: 'fast twice on the sabbath, give a tenth of your possessions to the poor, when you have taken your phylacteries out with you,[677] wash when you return from the marketplace.'[678] These were the precepts of the proud Pharisee to whom the Lord preferred the tax gatherer. But these are merely the rudiments of godliness if compared to the lofty deeds such as loving and doing good to your enemies, praying for those who torture you and cry out for your torment and death, taking up your cross, scorning your life for the sake of the gospel, rejoicing in all kinds of persecution.

Accordingly, if they allow me to use the word 'trust' to mean 'rely on' and 'stick to' to mean 'attribute too much to,' my proposition contains nothing which is opposed to the regulations of the church. Someone who trusts in external observances is misguided if he is confident that he will achieve true godliness through them without striving by means of them to advance toward the spiritual. There is no quarrel between us about meaning; the dispute is only about words. I will quote the passage from the paraphrase to make it clear that what I have said is true. This is what precedes my proposition; it is spoken in the person of Christ: 'For just as teaching a man filled with the false conviction that he possesses some skill is more troublesome than teaching a man completely ignorant of the skill, so it is extremely difficult to instruct in evangelical righteousness men who are convinced that they have attained perfect righteousness because of petty carnal observances. This indeed is the reason why I find fishermen, tax collectors, sinners, whores, and pagans more apt to learn the spiritual philosophy than scribes, Pharisees, and priests, who place religious perfection in human ceremonies. John, who stood between the Old and the New Law, tried to combine the two kinds of teaching.[679] For he did not dare to entrust this vigorous philosophy to weak minds. And whatever is human, whatever is carnal, is weak. That which is divine, spiritual, and heavenly is vigorous and strong. Hence I have chosen as my disciples raw and unformed men so as to teach them that strong and robust philosophy. I do not give them any such rules, etc.' This

* * * * *

677 Matt 23:5. On phylacteries see Deut 6:8–9 and Exod 13:9.
678 Luke 18:9–14
679 Erasmus explained this bipolarity of John the Baptist (between the Old and the New Law) at greater length in *Supputatio* LB IX 638A–639B.

makes clear what I mean by trusting in ceremonies, namely making perfect righteousness consist in them. It is also clear that I am not talking
about the regulations of the church but about the private precepts of the
Pharisees. And a little further on the Lord calls the instruction of John
and the Pharisees old wine, tasteless, as it were, and less strong; but his
instruction he calls fresh and inebriating wine, inducing contempt for all
things and even of life itself out of love for Christ.[680] That is what the
paraphrase says.

Hence what the theologians condemn they rightly condemn, but what
they condemn is not in my words, much less in my mind. But the words of
Christ, 'who hears you hears me,' suit the apostles beautifully; but if they
are applied to bishops or theologians in general, they have many exceptions.
In the apostles of Christ the Spirit undoubtedly spoke; with the bishops that
is not always the case.

LXII *Proposition 5. Luke 19*

One person displays someone of the pharisaic ilk, and says 'behold,
here is Christ.' But another points to someone else in a white cloak
and says 'lo, here is Christ.' Another, pointing out the colours and cut
of garments, cries out 'here is Christ.' Another shows someone who
eats fish and says 'here is Christ.' Another displays a eunuch and says
'here is Christ.' O Jewish and faithless tribe! Do you want to see Jesus?
Climb the tree, take for yourselves the eyes of Zachaeus.[681]

CENSURE

Although it is certain that no such confidence is to be placed in the
observance of the regulations of religious orders as in the precepts of
God, nevertheless such regulations are not to be scorned and ought to
be highly regarded: they are directed at purity of mind, a fervent love
of God, and an easier fulfilment of God's precepts, and it is certain
that through their observance many virtues are gained and many vices
suppressed. But in this proposition the writer seems to scoff at such
regulations of religious orders, the variety of habits, abstinence from
meat, and celibacy; he does so in a clever but shameless and ungodly[682]
fashion, since the Catholic church has always valued these things and

* * * * *

680 CWE 49 42–3
681 Erasmus analysed and defended this proposition in a quite similar way in
   Supputatio LB IX 613E–615F.
682 LB has the misprint *pie*.

condemned those who carp at such godly and holy institutions and disparage them in any way.

CLARIFICATION[683]

LXII First it is indisputable that the passage is not dealing with the various regulations of monks since it is spoken in the person of Luke, in whose time monks as they now are had not yet come into being. It is also clear that the passage does not condemn customary observances but rather those persons whose confidence in them led them to claim perfect holiness even though they were very far from true godliness. For the passage praises the fervour of Zachaeus, who because of his short body climbed a tree to see Jesus himself, the only one he longed to see. Delighted by his eagerness, Jesus addresses him of his own accord and offers to be his guest. This is the gentile people who attributed nothing to their own merit and did not get stuck in the letter of the Law but were lifted up toward the spirit and directed their gaze at Jesus. For they longed to see him alone, whereas the Jewish people situated righteousness in the observance of external things, opposing the spirit through trust in them.

The passage, which they cite in a mangled form, reads as follows: 'Zachaeus enjoys this happiness, being, of course, a figure of the gentiles. What is the reason? Because the Jews still remained on the ground and stuck to the flesh of the Law. For Jesus is not beheld except by those who lift themselves up from the ground of the letter of the Law to the more lofty meaning of the spirit. From this elevated platform one can see who Jesus is and where he is. Otherwise, if you remain mixed in with the crowd, that is, if you have no exceptional wisdom, you will frequently hear that deceptive phrase, "behold, Christ is here; behold, he is there."[684] The Pharisees cry out "behold, Christ is here." The Saducees cry out "behold, he is here." The Ebionites cry out "behold, he is here." One person displays someone of the pharisaic ilk, etc.' And there follows: 'The Pharisee strides erect and

* * * * *

683 Pelargus sigs E4v–E5v rightly complains that Erasmus' defence of speaking under the person of Luke (when there were no monks) is feeble and improbable, especially since he makes Luke mention the colour of garments and the white cloak, which did not apply very well to the Jews. Some, he says, will think that by attacking the rules of the religious orders Erasmus is pissing on the ashes of his father, since Erasmus belongs to a religious order. He thinks the passage could be better applied to sects and factions in general, not just to monks.

In the second edition Erasmus made no changes or additions.

684 Luke 17:21–3

lofty, pleased with himself, claiming for himself the praise of righteousness and knowledge of the Law, and while he thinks he is very great and close to Christ, he does not deign to use the tree as a help, etc.'[685] This is how the paraphrase is expressed. And so the very drift of the language makes it clear that there I am dealing with the Jews, who flattered themselves because they observed ceremonies and neglected the grace of the gospel. At that time also there were differences in sects, clothing, and regulations; nevertheless, in that passage these are not reproached in and of themselves but they are reproached because they show Christ where he is not. For the kingdom of God is within us. But perhaps the theologians suspect that I am alluding to the regulations of the monks. What if I should deny it? What if I should protest that it is unjust to indite me of the crime of ungodliness solely on the basis of suspicion?

But let us grant (what need not be granted) that there is an allusion to the monks: if such things as are there proclaimed about the Pharisees, Ebionites, and Saducees are to be found among the monks, let the energy of the gospel stand and let errors in conduct be corrected. Was there ever any Benedict or Dominic or Francis who displayed a black or white or grey cloak and said 'behold, here is Christ'?[686] In fact, they themselves intended to attribute very little indeed to their regulations by comparison with the gospel. I am convinced that the men who founded the various kinds of monks were as far as could possibly be from any such frame of mind as would place the acme of holiness in clothing or food. By eunuch I meant someone celibate. But celibacy by itself is not holiness, nor is virginity. For the foolish virgins were shut out.[687] They have inviolate bodies in vain if their minds are not pure. There was also a sect among the Jews, the Essenes, if I am not mistaken, who did not accept married men.

And so I could first of all reject the suspicion. Even though I should acknowledge it, nothing is said against the approved groups of monks but rather against the superstition of some who neglect the pursuit of true holiness and think they are pure Pauls or Anthonys because of their clothing or their abstinence from meat. If they deny that there are any monks to whom such vices apply, I will respond, with a sigh, 'would that there were fewer!' Good monks are the jewels of the church; bad ones, its cancers. But alas, good ones are all too rare. And so, just as the suspicion that in this

* * * * *

685 LB VII 427E–428A / CWE 48 133–4
686 The greyfriars were the Franciscans; the blackfriars, the Dominicans; the whitefriars, the Carmelites.
687 Matt 25:7–11

passage I am ridiculing the regulations of the monks is false, so too it is true
that I am touching on some who have a thoroughly Jewish outlook, quite
superstitious about externals, quite negligent about the things of the spirit.

LXIII *Proposition 6. Mark 2*
The colour and shape of clothing are rightly neglected whenever it is
advantageous for a person to do so.

CENSURE
This proposition, alleging that it is permissible for anyone to abandon
his habit whenever it is advantageous for him destroys the life of
the church and the monasteries and is an affront to the regulations
established by the holy Fathers and pontiffs and councils.

CLARIFICATION
LXIII How can my language allege what they take it to mean since in that
place the Lord is speaking about the external observances of the Jews, which
he says are rightly violated when either necessity urges or charity per-
suades us to do so? This is what is in the paraphrase: 'If a person who
is free from the tumult of evil passions violates the sabbath from a desire to help his neighbour, he acts piously when he violates it. Fasting is a
pious practice, but it becomes impious if what was instituted for the salvation of mankind is turned into a means of destroying mind and body.
To make vows is a religious deed but it becomes irreligious whenever a
person, through a superstitious wish to keep them, is called away from
deeds that are more closely related to true piety. Someone who offers a
gift at the altar is doing something holy, but the proffered gift is unholy if
he has not been reconciled with his neighbour. Thus the colour and shape
of clothing are rightly neglected whenever it is advantageous for a person to do so: for the person was not created for the sake of the clothing; rather it was devised for the sake of the person. In the same manner food was provided for the sake of mankind; mankind was not created
for the sake of food. Thus it is lawful to eat any kind of food when necessity requires it. Indeed all these bodily things in which you place perfect righteousness – the temple, victims, food, clothing, feast days, fasting, vows, offerings – are observed in an irreligious fashion if the salvation of your neighbour is neglected because of them, etc.'[688] This is how

* * * * *

688 *Paraphrasis in Marcum* CWE 49 45. In *Supputatio* LB IX 645C–648D Erasmus defended all of the propositions cited here.

the Lord speaks in the paraphrase. From this it is clear that Christ is saying these things about the fleshly Jews, since the temple and victims are mentioned.

But suspicion is interjected as if the paraphraser had alluded to the habit of monks. It is certain that the teaching of Jesus, though it was prompted by the Jews, also applies to us. But even if I grant that the suspected allusion is there, what is wrong about that? Isn't it right for monks to change their clothing out of necessity or for some serious reason? I know that the Carthusians, when they set out to go to their synods, are accustomed to ride in laymen's clothing for the sake of safety. What about the fact that the Roman pontiff ordered a gathering of monks who wore various cloaks to wear similar clothing so as not to scandalize the crowd?[689] Perhaps the theologians interpret 'whenever it is advantageous for a person to do so' as meaning 'whenever a person wants to.'[690] But what precedes and follows this passage makes it clear that I am talking about either necessity or some important usefulness.

But if they infer that I permit monks and priests to wear any kind of clothes according to their whim, why do they not infer by the same token that I permit everyone to violate fasts and feast days at their own whim? For the rationale by which I allow changes of clothing is no different from the one by which I allow fasting or the sabbath to be violated. In this way they pull the wool over the eyes[691] of the most holy faculty by setting forth something said by another person as if it were said by me and by plucking out bits and pieces suitable for false accusations. What follows is of the same sort.

Topic 19. Vocal prayer

LXIV *Proposition 1. In* Elenchus, *annotation* 64[692]
Christ condemns much talking in prayer.[693]

* * * * *

689 *Decretalia Gregorii* IX 3.1.12, a mandamus of Innocent III; see *Decretalium collectiones* ed Emil L. Richter and Emil Friedberg 2nd ed (Leipzig 1922) 451–2. In *Supputatio* LB IX 648B Erasmus also mentioned this papal decree and the custom of monks wearing lay clothing for the sake of safety.
690 The Latin *quoties id illi commodum fuerit* could be taken to mean either 'whenever it is convenient for him' or 'whenever it is suitable for him.'
691 *Adagia* I v 52
692 *Elenchus in censuras Bedae* LB IX 499C
693 Matt 6:7. Erasmus defended this proposition briefly in *Responsio ad notulas Bedaicas* LB IX 709B–D.

CENSURE

This proposition signifying that Christ condemned prayer that is prolix or contains many words is erroneous and foreign to a sound understanding of Scripture. For much talking is not condemned in prayer
altogether but only that which proceeds from the unbelief of someone who thinks that God does not hear or understand those who pray
unless they indulge in much talking. Explaining this, Christ says not
only 'do not talk a lot' but he adds 'as the gentiles do, for they think
that if they talk a lot they will be heard.' The saints in glory show that
much talking in prayer is not to be condemned, for after the last judgment they will not cease to praise God not only with their minds but
also with their tongues.

CLARIFICATION[694]

LXIV Concerning chapter 5 of Luke I wrote: 'Although Christ prayed frequently, still he taught his disciples that they should pray in few words
and in secret.'[695] That is clear from chapter 6 of Matthew. Now it is evident that the form of praying which the Lord prescribed for his disciples
contains few words.[696] And so it is true that Christ taught his disciples to
pray in few words. 'But,' they say, 'he does not condemn much speaking
in an unqualified way, but he adds "as the gentiles do, who, etc."' What
they proclaim is true, nor did I add 'in an unqualified way,' and my explanation is no different when I handle this passage in chapter 6 of Matthew.
The paraphrase is as follows: 'Distance yourself from the example of the
gentiles who recite prolix and verbose prayers in a set form of words, as it
were, just as if they would not get anything unless they wore God out with
the most verbose loquacity, hammering away at the same things time after
time, laying down in a wordy account what they want and when and how
they want their petitions to be granted, though often they pray for what
is harmful to them. We should ask God for the best things, not all things,

* * * * *

694 Pelargus sigs E5v–E8 claims at some length that Erasmus' clarification is un-
dermined by rather hair-splitting inconsistencies, mostly about the meaning
of *multiloquium* 'much speaking.'
In the second edition Erasmus added long passages insisting that Christ did
not condemn much speaking in an unqualified way any more than he condemned praying in public absolutely, and that Christ's recommendation of
short prayers is directed specifically to his apostles, who at that time were
still weak and were being prepared for higher perfection.

695 LB VII 342
696 Matt 6:6–13

and pray often rather than long, and with fervour rather than wordiness, and finally with our minds more than our mouths.'[697] Here I think I have faithfully rendered the meaning of the passage, which, however, does not pertain to the customary prayers of the church but rather to the arbitrary and private prayers of the Pharisees.

But elsewhere the Lord teaches that we should pray without ceasing,[698] and Paul commands us to pray without interruption.[699] 'Since these texts seem to contradict one another,' they say, 'they should have been reconciled.' It was not convenient to do so in the paraphrase. But I solved the whole difficulty quite clearly in my *Annotations*[700] and in my little book entitled *How to Pray to God.*[701] But that phrase, 'to pray without interruption,' whether you take it to apply to vocal or to silent prayer, is not spoken without a figure of speech. For someone who perseveres in the same frame of mind also prays without interruption. I do not think it is fitting to apply the phrase 'much talking,' which has bad connotations, to the lengthy prayers of Christians. And so what does my mangled proposition signify? That lengthy prayer is condemned by Christ without any qualification? By no means. But in my dispute with Béda I defend the position that what I had said is in some sense true, meaning what I had said about the words of the gospel and not dealing with their meaning. He accused me of lying; I defend myself by what I wrote. And so it is true that prayers in public are in some sense condemned if they are customarily said for the sake of ostentation or consist of much talking. The words in *Elenchus* are as follows: 'If someone commands you to go into your chamber, is he not commanding you to pray secretly? If he condemns much talking in prayer and prescribes a brief form of it, is he not commanding you to pray in few words? And yet I teach in many places that in these words I do not disapprove of the public, lengthy, and constant prayers of pious people.'[702] That is what *Elenchus* says, hardly signifying that Christ condemns the lengthy prayers of Christians. Length is one thing; much talking in the manner of the gentiles is quite another. And saying the words of a prayer with the tongue is not the same as praying. Prayer is the work of the mind rather than the body.

* * * * *

697 LB VII 36D–E / CWE 45 115
698 Luke 18:1
699 1 Thess 5:17
700 LB VI 35E–F
701 *Modus orandi Deum* LB V 1110E–1111C / CWE 70 174–5
702 *Elenchus in censuras Bedae* LB IX 499C. Erasmus also defended his position on this point in *Supputatio* LB IX 611E–613A.

And who cannot see that here the words of *Elenchus* have been mangled by someone or other in bad faith for the purpose of slander? Christ condemns much talking in prayer in much the same way as he condemns praying in public. He does not condemn either one in an unqualified way, as long as we are not offended by the use of the phrase 'much talking.' But just as he condemns those who talk a lot in prayer in the manner of the gentiles, so too he condemns those who pray in public for the sake of ostentation in the manner of the Pharisees. They will say I should have said this expressly. Indeed I have done so both carefully and clearly in the appropriate places. I have already quoted the passage about much talking. Concerning praying in secret, this is what the paraphrase says: 'You are hidden in your chamber when you speak to God with the same mental sincerity as if no one saw you. If someone prays in a large gathering and he would pray with no more lassitude and in fact perhaps with more fervour than if he were praying alone, then he is praying in a hidden chamber.'[703] This is what the paraphrase says, preventing anyone from perhaps thinking that prayers said in an assembly in church are not pleasing to God. I do the same in many other places. In *Elenchus* I merely ward off the charge of blasphemy, though even there I do not dissemble about what I mean. Thus if the words 'Christ condemns much talking in prayers' strike a false note, blame it on those who foist badly excerpted snippets upon the reader.

But in fact there can also be some excess in the prayers of Christians. And the Lord prescribed brief prayers for his disciples while they were still weak, just as he did not burden them with fasting. But the same persons, once they had drunk in the heavenly Spirit, prayed and fasted persistently by their own free choice. That the paraphrase is not speaking about our prayers but about the disciples who were still weak is made clear by my words, which are as follows: 'But one accusation comes upon the heels of another. That one originated partly with those who had been the disciples of John. For since John belonged to those on the middle ground between the Law which was soon to cease and the liberty of the gospel which was soon to emerge, he taught some things which were not completely foreign to the regulations of the Pharisees, whereas Christ, who in the opinion of many seemed inferior to John, treated his disciples with more indulgence and flexibility, at least in matters which concerned bodily observances, such as fasts and prayers. For such matters were the principal means whereby the Pharisees gained for themselves a reputation for holiness among the

* * * * *

703 LB VII 36C / CWE 45 114

people. Though Christ himself prayed frequently, nevertheless he taught his disciples to pray both in secret and with few words, and he did not require any fasting; he even closed his eyes to some matters which might seem to neglect the prescriptions of the Law, since by a different rationale he was shaping them for the strong deeds which are proper to the strength of the gospel. For it takes far more strength to pardon an injury sincerely, to deserve well even of the undeserving, to suffer the loss of your life for the welfare of your neighbour, than it does to prolong fasting till nightfall or to say some psalms with the tongue. Most of the Pharisees did what could be seen or performed hypocritically, neglecting what belongs to true and perfect virtue, etc.'[704] This makes it clear that neither the Gospel nor the paraphrase at that point is talking about the prayers of Christians, but rather[705] about the prayers prescribed by the Pharisees and by John for their disciples, which were much lengthier than what the Lord had required of his. Nevertheless we cannot assume that the disciples of Christ never prayed, but that they prayed both less frequently and more briefly. For Luke says as follows: 'Why is it that the disciples of John often fast and say prayers, and so too the followers of the Pharisees, but yours eat and drink?'[706] They did not raise the objection that they did not pray. But since fasting is there associated with prayers, when it is said that they eat and drink, it is understood that Christ's disciples prayed as well as fasted rarely.

Again, lest anyone should think that the example pertains to just any era, the paraphrase makes it clear that this leniency of our Saviour applies only to the time when the disciples were still tender nurslings in the company of the bridegroom. For the paraphrase adds in the person of Christ: 'I do not condemn prayers and fasts but in these matters for the time being I indulge my disciples so that by another rationale I may move them along little by little to stronger deeds.' And shortly thereafter: 'These deeds, which you marvel at as the pinnacle of holiness, my disciples will perform of their own free will if the situation ever requires it.' And a little later: 'They are still tender and completely dependent on the bridegroom, but a time will come, etc.'[707] For because the weakness of the human mind is not able to concentrate on the same point for a long time, Augustine also praises those little prayers which are brief but frequent outbursts of the mind.[708]

* * * * *

704 LB VII 342B–D
705 LB has & but the sense requires *sed*.
706 Luke 5:33
707 LB VII 342E–F
708 *Epistolae* 130.10.20 PL 33 501–2

We also see in those customary prayers of the church called collects how the early bishops of the church kept to a wonderful brevity.[709] Thus to praise such brevity in praying is not to condemn the lengthy prayers of Christians which are inspired by pious feeling or required by necessity or prescribed by the authority of the church. Much talking, however, in so far as it is superfluous loquacity, is to be avoided not only in prayer but in all speech.

Finally the list of heretics was extended by the Psallians or Euchites, who lived in leisure and finished off an incredible number of psalms with amazing lingual volubility. But even more shamefully misguided than they were those who said that no one ought to pray at all because God knows what everyone needs. Therefore, when the censure says that Christ condemned much talking for no other reason than that the gentiles thought that otherwise they would not be heard, it is telling the truth, although he also clearly condemns the lengthy prayers of the Pharisees, which they prolonged for the sake of ostentation or profit. The Psallians, of course, are condemned because they interpreted literally the language of the Lord when he said 'you ought to pray always and never stop.'[710] Thus there is more than one reason why much talking ought to be condemned in prayers. Perhaps the Lord is also displeased by those who think that it is a certain extraordinary piety to recite as many psalms as possible without either understanding or a pious frame of mind. I will add this. If to the theologians 'much talking' has bad connotations, as it always does in both secular and sacred writings, why are they offended when *Elenchus* says that much talking is condemned in prayer? On the other hand, if they allow the loose use of this word,[711] why in earlier censures did they reckon I was at fault when I called the Law 'verbosam' ['wordy'], since in good Latin authors 'verbosus' is found with good connotations?[712]

LXV *The second proposition. Annotations on Matthew 6*
Everywhere there are more than enough ditties, shouts, murmurs, and boomings – if those in heaven take any pleasure in such things.

* * * * *

709 'Collects' (*collectae*) are brief prayers which occur before the Epistle in the mass and again at lauds, terce, sext, none, and vespers in the divine office.
710 Luke 18:1
711 Latin *abusum*, which normally means 'wasting, misuse.' But Erasmus seems to mean *abusio*, which in rhetoric is a 'loose use, catachresis.' Or the theologians allow the misuse of *multiloquium* by allowing it to have good connotations, as in the long prayers they defend.
712 In English there seems to be no single word meaning 'wordy or verbose' that can have both bad and good connotations.

CENSURE

Wishing in every way whatsoever to conform herself to the church triumphant, in which the saints never cease to cry out continuously 'holy, holy, holy,'[713] giving glory, praise, and honour to him who lives forever and ever, the church militant instituted solemn singing in churches, by which the praise of God might be set forth and the devotion of the people aroused, so that on her own level she might imitate here on earth the behaviour of the heavenly Jerusalem toward which she constantly aspires. She was persuaded to do this by that multitude of the heavenly host which, when Christ was born, praised God, singing on high: 'Glory to God in the highest.'[714] She was persuaded by the shouts of the children praising Christ: 'Hosannah to the son of David! Blessed is he who comes in the name of the Lord.'[715] She was persuaded by Christ himself, who, before he went out to the Mount of Olives to suffer, said a hymn to demonstrate that his ministry was most pleasing to God;[716] and a hymn, according to approved authorities, is nothing other than the praise of God in song. For praise cannot be called a hymn unless it is praise of God and is sung. And so Christ used his voice to sing a hymn, passing down to the church the pattern of singing the praise of God. Nor did he sing alone but rather together with his apostles, whom he established as his vicars throughout the world so that they might teach the church what should be done. The church was persuaded by Paul and Silas, who, after they were thrown in prison, praised God in such a loud voice that they were heard by those who were posted as guards. Then after an earthquake had shaken the foundation of the prison, the gates were thrown open and the shackles of the prisoners were loosened;[717] this shows how mightily God was pleased by hymns and divine praises, especially when they are sung in a loud voice, since hymns and praises of God such as were sent forth by Paul and Silas were of such great efficacy. Finally, she was persuaded by the most ancient custom introduced by the apostles when the church began, when gatherings of Christians used to sing hymns, sometimes even before dawn.

And the Catholic church was not off the mark when she adopted the practice of singing hymns or the praises of God, since such hymns

* * * * *

713 Isa 6:3, Rev 4:8, repeated in the sanctus of the mass
714 Luke 2:14, repeated in the gloria of the mass
715 Matt 21:15; cf Luke 19:38, John 12:13, repeated in the sanctus of the mass
716 Matt 26:30; Mark 14:26
717 Acts 16:25–6

and the sung praise of God and the saints lift up the mind to what is on high,[718] inflame it with the love of God, move it to compunction, spur it on to disdain the things of the earth, and urge it to acquire virtues. Certainly with these facts in mind, the church, which is instructed by the Spirit of God, introduced music into the sacred precincts, not rejecting the harmony and sweetness of voices as a means of luring the mind toward holiness and piety, not spurning solemn singing in church, as long as it is pious and Christian, not empty, wanton, or immodest and not broken up into so many polyphonic parts that the words of the divine praise which are being sung cannot be easily understood by the audience (which is rightly to be avoided). In doing so the church has no fear of the pharisaic scandal taken by the Arians [Aerians?], Wyclifites, Lutherans, or any heretics whatsoever, who think that such praise of Christ and his saints is a disgrace which beats and tortures themselves. The church knows how to set no store by the scandal taken by heretics: they are blind and leaders of the blind.[719] Hence this proposition, alleging that solemn chant in church and the kind of highly wrought music which soothes the ears and the mind by a considerable variety of voices are not acceptable to God and the saints, is a false, temerarious, and unholy assertion and gives support to the aforementioned error of the heretics.

CLARIFICATION

LXV Indeed I thoroughly approve of what they say in this preachy discourse concerning hymns which praise God with both mind and voice in imitation of the church triumphant. But in fact those ancient bishops still breathing in the time of the recently announced gospel message were reluctant to accept in church even the simple chant which we still use today to sing the psalms, the Gospel, and the Lord's Prayer. Also Augustine, though he does not fault the practice of singing introduced by Ambrose, nevertheless wants the chant to be very similar to recitation, and he confesses that it would be a grave sin for him to be more taken by the sweetness of the voices than by the meaning of the words.[720] In the *Decretum* St Gregory also threatens priests with anathema because they were singing in church, since that function belonged to laypeople.[721]

* * * * *

718 The faculty may be thinking of the hymns in praise of God and the saints in the divine office.
719 Matt 15:14
720 *Confessions* 10.33.50 PL 32 800
721 *Corpus iuris canonici* I 317–18

But they are quite mistaken when they infer that my proposition condemns singing in church. In that passage I point out that in some religious houses prayers and chants are prescribed that are prolix and also contain much that is unworthy of divine worship, although the Council of Carthage determined that nothing should be recited in church except canonical Scripture.[722] Then I went on to mention the Euchites, who forbade monks to work with their hands so that they would not be forced to interrupt their prayers.[723] It is clear that they placed the efficacy of prayer not in a state of mind but in a mass of words. After this I add: 'Would that those who profess the philosophy of Christ would distance themselves so far from such superstition as to offer pure prayer and a victim that is spotless and pleasing to Christ. For everywhere there are more than enough ditties, shouts, murmurs, and boomings – if those in heaven take any pleasure in such things, etc.'[724] That is what I said there. By implication I point out that some people pray with an attitude similar to that of the Euchites; and I wish that all Christians would offer Christ this victim pure and spotless, that is that they would pray with a sincere frame of mind and, if the circumstances require a voice, that the mind should pray together with the voice. For precisely in this way would this victim be truly pleasing to Christ. Furthermore, where there is nothing but the noise of voices, there is a danger that the speakers hear that saying from the Gospel: 'This people honours me with their lips but their hearts are far from me.'[725] In fact, in that passage I am not talking about just any singing in church but about inappropriate singing and ditties which the feelings of empty-headed women and simple-minded men have tacked on to solemn worship. By the word 'shouts' I blame those who nowadays in many churches and even monasteries thunder and roar, both filling the church with their bellowing and obscuring everyone's voice so that no one can be understood. I apply 'murmurs' to prayers said hastily and without thought, for to say them so is more properly to murmur than to pray. I apply 'boomings' to the almost

* * * * *

722 The third Council of Carthage (397) reaffirmed the articles of the Council of Hippo (393), one of which was that 'apart from canonical Scripture nothing shall be read in church under the name of divine writings.' See Hefele II 400; and Mansi III 891, 924.
723 The Euchites (also called Messaliens or Enthusiasts) were heretics who sprang up in the fourth century and were condemned at the council of Ephesus (AD 431). Among many other unorthodox beliefs, they held that each person's inherited demon could be driven away only by ceaseless prayer uninterrupted by any labour.
724 *Annotationes in Novum Testamentum* LB VI 36B–C
725 Matt 15:8; Isa 29:13

warlike sound of organs, trumpets (straight or curved), cornets and even bombards,[726] since these have also been accepted for divine worship. Finally I conclude that because of human weakness prayers ought to be moderate and then pure, so that we sing psalms with our hearts more than our voices. The theologians themselves condemn any inappropriate kind of music in church; they confess, I think, that moderation should be applied in prayers also and in singing, either because of people's occupations or because of the squeamishness of the human temperament. Certainly I very much disagree with those who condemn fitting church music. I am now not discussing highly wrought music,[727] although Alberto Pio candidly[728] condemns it, and I disagree with him, as long as it is employed in a modest and moderate fashion.[729] And so for the censure to infer from a passage presented in a truncated form that I think that fitting church music is displeasing to God is clearly an insult, not a judgment.[730]

LXVI *The third proposition. Annotations on 1 Cor 14*
What else is heard in monasteries, in religious houses, in churches except the noise of voices?

LXVII *The fourth proposition*
The mob hears nothing but words that signify nothing.

LXVIII *The fifth proposition*
I beg you, what opinion of Christ do people have who think he is delighted by such a din of noisy voices?

CENSURE
These three propositions, in so far as they allege that no advantage arises for clerics who sing the praise of God, and likewise none for the people who listen unless they understand what the words mean, and that God is not delighted by such singing, are wicked and foreign to Catholic truth. For if the ceremonies of the Old Law were profitably

* * * * *

726 The bombard was a bass form of the double-reeded shawm, the ancestor of the modern oboe; see Don Michael Randel *Harvard Concise Dictionary of Music* (Cambridge, MA, and London 1978) 58, 346.

727 Latin *musica operosa*; Erasmus means polyphony.

728 The Latin *ingenue* implies 'in a manner befitting someone well born.' Pio was a count.

729 In *Apologia adversus rhapsodias Alberti Pii* Erasmus notes: 'Pio condemns the use of polyphonic music in church. I censure either excessive music, or music not suited to church' CWE 84 219.

730 In Latin the contrasting terms *convicium* and *judicium* rhyme.

observed by the Scribes and Pharisees and also by simple people precisely because they were ordained to promote piety or divine worship, even though their meaning was not understood, for exactly the same reason the sung praise of God and the chants turn out to be just as fruitful for the ecclesiastics who sing them as for the laypeople who are present (even though they do not understand them), since everyone has in common the intention of putting them forth, hearing them, being present at them to the glory, praise, and honour of God, in order to give thanks for the gifts they have received and to obtain from God what is useful for this life or the next – an intention which is very pleasing to God. For if the human heart is what God requires most of all, what could be more pleasing to him than for a person to exert himself with pious devotion to praise God, revere him, love him, value him, and eagerly be present at his praises? Indeed no understanding of the words can be compared with this pious intention, which is ordinarily had even by simple, rude, and uneducated people.

LXIX *The sixth proposition. Annotations on 1 Cor 14[:19]*
Why does the church hesitate to follow such a great authority? Why does it dare to differ from him? He is speaking about Paul.

CENSURE
The same thing should be said about this proposition (which alleges the same thing as the three preceding ones) as was said about them, except that this one goes beyond them by adding that the church differs from Paul by celebrating publicly in church with songs the words of which are not understood by the people – which is not true. For when Paul wrote 'but in church I would rather speak five words with my understanding than ten thousand in a tongue,'[731] he was speaking about sermons or preaching to the people, in which an abundance of words not understood is useless, not about ecclesiastical singing, which has another purpose, as was shown in the preceding censure. Accordingly the church prudently thought that the divine office should be celebrated in the Latin language. For it is not necessary for the people to understand the words that are sung, for that aforementioned pious intention of serving God, praising him, revering and loving him is more than adequate for their spiritual progress. And considering the

* * * * *

731 1 Cor 14:19

shameless temerity and arrogance of many people, it is not expedient that the divine office should be literally translated into the vernacular and the translation sung in the sacred precincts. For such a procedure would not turn out to edify the people but to destroy them, as experience has often taught. For in the church the people are like little children, who need milk, not solid food.[732] But certainly, just as when infants are fed bread and other heavy foods a deadly disease gradually infects them because they cannot tolerate or digest solid food, just so if the plain words of Holy Scripture are set before the people in the vernacular language and sung in church – which is the equivalent of solid food that is difficult to digest – they are burdened, weighed down, and often fall into heresies, scandals, and schisms, as is clearly happening today in many places.

ERASMUS' CLARIFICATION OF THE PRECEDING PROPOSITIONS
LXVI, LXVII, LXVIII, LXIX Who could make any correct pronouncement about such snippets if they are culled by malevolent persons for the sake of false accusation? Whoever reads the whole annotation will perceive that I am doing something quite different from what they seem to suspect. The same annotation contains the following words: 'Certainly let the churches have solemn singing, but let it be moderate, etc.'[733] This, I think, is not the language of someone who rejects ecclesiastical singing. But what I deplore in that passage is this: though Paul would rather say five words with understanding than ten thousand in the spirit, we on the other hand provide a great deal of singing but very little spiritual instruction, especially in convents where the women do not work with their hands but are also burdened with many hours of external prayer and singing, whereas they very rarely hear a holy sermon. I also add this: that very many think these practices constitute the highest holiness and do not progress from them to better spiritual graces. My words are as follows: 'Even this should be tolerated except that the common run of priests and monks believe that such practices constitute the highest holiness, differing a great deal from Paul, etc.'[734] I say they differ from Paul because they place the highest holiness in things to which Paul attributes the least. Up to this point I think the theologians agree with me.

* * * * *

732 1 Cor 3:2
733 LB VI 731E
734 LB VI 731D

I emphasize my deploring the rarity of preaching in churches with the point that today people do not understand what is sung or recited in church in Latin. For once, when people understood Latin and Greek, the reading of the holy volumes and the interpreters of them was just about equivalent to a sermon. But nowadays many have adopted a kind of music that makes it impossible to understand the words, even for those among the people who know Latin, because of the chattering of the voices. I say this to indicate that sermons should be provided all the more frequently. These are my words: 'Nowadays what does the mob hear but words that signify nothing? And the pronunciation is almost so bad that the words are not heard but only sounds strike the ear, etc.'[735] The thrust of this is simply that sermons should be preached more frequently to the people, especially to monks and nuns.

There remains the third proposition: 'I beg you, what opinion, etc.' But this is preceded by the following words: 'Someone who is greedier than Crassus,[736] more scurrilous than Zoilus,[737] is nevertheless thought to be holy because he dins out those little prayers in a clear voice, even though he does not understand any of them.' Right after this comes 'I beg you, what opinion of Christ do people have who think he is delighted by such a din of noisy voices, etc?'[738] It is hardly obscure that I am here dealing with those who neglect the piety of the mind and consider it the height of holiness to sound with their tongue in church things they do not understand. For by such voices Christ is not only not delighted, he is also offended. For I did not say simply 'din of noisy voices' but 'such a din of noisy voices,' referring in fact to what precedes. As for those who out of pious devotion gather in a religious fashion at solemn worship in honour of God because they believe the general notion that what is recited and done there is holy, far be it from any Christian to blame them or rank their devotion lower than those who understand but are wicked. But still a person commits no sin if he encourages them to go from these practises to what is more perfect, not so as to reject them but to perform them in a more religious fashion.

And certainly it is not necessary that analogies from the church triumphant applied to the church militant should match at all points. In heaven, where obscurity will have disappeared, there will be no need for prophecy.

* * * * *

735 LB VI 731E
736 *Adagia* I vi 74
737 *Adagia* II v 8 ·
738 LB VI 731F

Where no one is drowsy, no encouragement will be needed. Where no one mourns, there will be no need for consolation. Where no one lacks anything, there will be no need for charitable deeds. In heaven there is leisure for endless hymns. In the church militant the situation is much different. Up to this point, if I am not mistaken, we are in agreement. But this statement from the same annotation is harsher: 'Why does the church hesitate to follow such a great authority? Why does it dare to differ from him?' By 'church' I mean the external practice of the church, according to which it is now so common to sing in the spirit, whereas prophecy, which he prefers, is relatively rare. For what precedes is as follows: 'In this matter the custom of the church has changed remarkably. Paul would rather speak five words with understanding than ten thousand in the spirit. But nowadays in some regions they sing in the spirit all day long; there is no restraint or end to the singing, whereas they hardly hear once every three months a wholesome sermon exhorting them to true holiness. For that is what Paul calls speaking with understanding. I will say nothing about the sort of music introduced into divine worship which does not allow even a single word to be clearly perceived and leaves those who sing no freedom to pay attention to what they are singing. Only a jingling of words strikes the ear. Even this should be tolerated except that the common run of priests and monks believe that such practices constitute the highest holiness, differing a great deal from Paul. Why does the church hesitate to follow such a great authority? Why does it dare to differ from him, etc?'[739] From this it is crystal clear that I am not condemning ecclesiastical singing but I am only amazed that so much is made of what the Apostle values least and that what he values most is so rare. The theologians respond to my amazement, saying that in that passage Paul is not dealing with recitations or ecclesiastical psalms but rather with sermons to the people, in which an abundance of words not understood is useless. If we accept this there would be no difference between prophecy and speaking in the spirit, except that the latter is spoken in an unknown tongue. But Paul is placing them in totally different categories. And who would be so stupid as to preach to Germans in French?

But even if what they assume were an accepted fact, the public recitation of the Sacred Volumes and their interpreters to a crowded audience is a sort of sermon, and, as far as this point is concerned, it falls under the same rules as a sermon. For they are also recited to the people, and in some regions the people are commanded to be present at matins and the

*　*　*　*　*

739 LB VI 731C–D

other hours, at mass, and at evening hymns, under pain of hellfire.[740] And St Thomas writes that the readings at matins, the Epistle, and the Gospel are still in the church as if they were spoken in tongues, for they are recited and afterwards explained. Therefore someone who recites the Gospel speaks in the spirit; someone who explains it to the people prophesies. I leave it to others to say whether to hear words not understood is milk for little children in Christ. I rather think that the same Scripture understood is milk for little children and solid food for those who are stronger; but in any case it is shameful for them to remain infants forever and to hang forever on their mother's breast. And if it is a quick-acting poison to have a grammatical understanding of what the singing in church means, then the Greeks as well as the Latins were in the greatest danger, since up to the time of St Gregory and later everything was recited in the ordinary language of the people. And the Indians still conduct their prayers and liturgy in their vernacular language.[741]

But this has nothing to do with me. It is enough for me that my propositions do not preach anything like the interpretations some have put upon them. I wish that the singing in all churches were like that of Christ when he sang a hymn with his disciples,[742] and that of Paul and Silas when they prayed in prison, praising the Lord.[743] For they did not belt out words not understood, or bellow indecently, or make a great noise like chattering

* * * * *

740 In his *Apologia adversus rhapsodias Alberti Pii* CWE 84 218–19 Erasmus mentions that in England farmers were required to attend matins and the other hours under pain of damnation when they ought to have been working to provide for their families.

741 The word 'still' suggests that Erasmus is not referring to the West Indians (who had never had a Christian liturgy in their own languages) but to the East Indian Christians of Kerala or Malabar in southern India, who had had their own Syriac liturgy for centuries when the Portuguese under Vasco da Gama landed there in 1498. The imported Latin rite and the native Syriac rite lived in harmonious juxtaposition throughout most of the sixteenth century, according, for example, to the testimony of St Francis Xavier and St Ignatius Loyola not long after Erasmus' death. Even after the disastrous Synod of Diamper (1599), in which the Portuguese attempted to suppress the Syriac rite, the liturgy in the Syriac language survived. See Archibald A. King *The Rites of Eastern Christendom* 2 vols (Rome 1947) II 431–60. I do not know what access Erasmus had to information about the Syro-Malabar church in India but he must have had contact with important imperial and Spanish sources for many years.

742 Matt 26:30; Mark 14:26

743 Acts 16:25

birds. As for how they sing in heaven or how the angels sang when Christ
was born, I do not know. Certainly the account of their singing in Luke is
very brief.[744] But there can be no doubt that that heavenly harmony is sung
with the greatest gladness, whereas in churches today and even in some
monasteries the liturgy is sung with such distaste that it generates distaste
in those who hear it. And that manifold kind of singing has also crept into
monasteries; for they believe, I imagine, that the Blessed Virgin would take
it amiss unless she had her daily mass – and before her Son at that – and that
she takes delight only in a variegated harmony of voices which antiquity
seems not to have known at all, with the organ joining in now and then. At
the same time, right in the middle of the service, you hear the indecent and
uncontrolled noise made by the devotees of Dionysus: the church is burdened with unnecessary salaries and the best part of the children's lives is
wasted, brought up as they are among the devotees of Dionysus. When they
grow up they are good for nothing but singing and drinking. To warn about
these points and others like them is not Wyclifite but godly and dutiful.[745]

Topic 20. The celibacy of priests

LXX *The first proposition. 1 Tim 3*
Because in a bishop chastity is very commendable, if it happens that
someone does not spurn this pleasure altogether, it should be seen to
that he was or is the husband of only one wife.[746]

CENSURE

Since in the western church when priests receive holy orders they voluntarily and solemnly bind themselves to live continently, this counsel,
which disparages the ordinance of the Latin church concerning celibacy
as if it would have been better had that decree never been laid down,
is unholy, contrary to the splendour of ecclesiastical chastity, and derived from the condemned teaching of Wyclif and Luther. For anyone who has bound himself to chastity of his own accord can remain
chaste with the help of God.

* * * * *

744 Luke 2:13–14
745 For a collection of Erasmus' remarks on music and musicians see Clement
     A. Miller 'Erasmus on Music' *The Musical Quarterly* 52 (1966) 332–49. On the
     rowdy singers hired as substitutes for canons see *Young Choristers, 650–1700*,
     ed Susan Boynton and Eric Rice (Woodbridge, Suffolk 2008) 160–1.
746 Erasmus defended this proposition very briefly in *Supputatio* LB IX 696B–C.

LXXI *The second proposition.* Elenchus, *annotation 197*[747]
Bishops marry wives today among the Greeks, even after receiving ordination.[748]

CENSURE
This proposition is asserted temerariously.

ERASMUS' CLARIFICATIONS LXX AND LXXI[749]

It is not fair to twist what I said in the person of Paul which pertains to his times and attribute it to my person and these times, especially since I have responded to it quite clearly. At that time a man with one wife, even when she was alive, was accepted into the priesthood, that is, into the office of a bishop. But in this passage what is Paul doing? First he wants a man to be chosen who on his own offers himself as an example of perfect chastity. If such a person is not available, he wants to go to the next best, namely someone who did not remarry after the death of his first wife. The third best is to choose someone who has married one wife and does not plan to remarry if she dies. This language has nothing to do with those who nowadays marry contrary to their vows and contrary to the public and ancient custom of the Roman church. Furthermore, I do not know what counsel they condemn; 'as if it would have been better,' they say, 'if that decree about the celibacy of priests had never been laid down.' Certainly there is nothing like that in my language; I am only explaining what Paul prescribed to Timothy. Hence I think that this censure was added to this proposition through an error of the scribes.

It is of no interest to me now how willingly the western churches accept a vow of chastity. Among the French in the time of Jerome those

* * * * *

747 *Elenchus in censuras Bedae* LB IX 510B
748 This proposition is defended very briefly in *Responsio ad notulas Bedaicas* LB IX 712E.
749 Pelargus sigs E7–E8v gives the slightly varying interpretations of Chrysostom and Theophylactus but he does not find anything amiss in Erasmus' clarification.
    In the second edition Erasmus added a short section noting that sacerdotal celibacy was not always the rule and that the priesthood would be better served if the church followed the old rule that no one should be ordained under the age of thirty and only after proving himself in minor orders.
    In *Divinationes ad notata Bedae* LB IX 488A–489A Erasmus defended at some length his recommendations about relaxing the rule of clerical celibacy, and he did the same more briefly in *Elenchus in censuras Bedae* LB IX 510A–B.

who had wives were admitted to the priesthood, and the Germans argue
that that law was never accepted by general consent but was always rejected
by many. Would that the law were kept which was once rightly established
– that no one under thirty years old be ordained a priest or be ordained
to major orders unless he had shown good promise in the minor orders.
Nowadays on one and the same day a layman under twenty-five becomes
a cleric, subdeacon, deacon, and priest. What I added in *Elenchus*, that even
today among the Greeks priests marry after receiving holy orders, but only
one woman and a virgin, I learned from Greeks at Venice when I was active
there. But in fact *Elenchus* does not approve of this, but merely tells about
what is done.

Topic 21. Original sin

LXXII *The proposition of Erasmus. Rom 5[:12]*
> The evil which arose from the first parent of the human race flowed
> down to all his posterity in that there is no one who does not follow
> the example of our first parents.[750]

CENSURE
The paraphraser is here interpreting the text of the Apostle: 'in Adam
all sinned,' or 'in whom[751] all sinned.' According to a sound interpretation this cannot be understood to mean actual sin, since not all
have committed actual sins. For children who have not yet reached the
age of reason have never been susceptible to actual sin. Therefore the
paraphraser explicates the aforesaid text in an incorrect and distorted
manner. And that interpretation favours the Pelagian heresy.

CLARIFICATION[752]
LXXII It is clear that the discussion in this passage begins and ends with actual sin. They think that only the clause 'in whom all have sinned' pertains

* * * * *

750 Erasmus defended this proposition briefly in *Divinationes ad notata Bedae* LB
IX 469A–B. For more information about the difficulties surrounding Rom 5:12
and Erasmus' reaction to them see *Paraphrases on Romans and Galatians* CWE 42
34 n12.
751 LB has *in quem* here for *in quo*. The text is Rom 5:12. See CWE 42 34–5.
752 In his *Annotationes* (1535) LB VI 585B–590C Erasmus has a long note which repeats much of the defence he gave in a long passage in *Responsio ad collationes* (1529) LB IX. He gives evidence from Origen, Pseudo-Jerome, [Pseudo-]
Ambrose, Chrysostom, and Theophylactus to show that Rom 5:12 refers not

properly to original sin. But Origen,[753] or Jerome,[754] interprets this very text
as applying to personal sin, as does Ambrose also, although at this point in
his commentary he seems to touch on original sin.[755] Likewise, the scholiast
who goes under Jerome's name clearly explains this whole passage as about
personal sin, not at all disturbed by the universal word 'all,' which stands
for 'most'; for general language does not exclude the exception of a privi-
leged few.[756] Chrysostom is of the same opinion,[757] as, I have no doubt, are
many others. We also explained that the phrase ἐφ' ὅ or ἐφ' ᾧ more probably
means 'in so far as all have sinned' rather than 'in whom all have sinned.'
For it is not ἐν ᾧ. Nor is it probable that the Apostle is dealing with infants
in this passage since nowhere in the writings of the Apostle and the evangelists is there any word which expressly applies to infants, and in those
times only adults were baptized – which, though it cannot be demonstrated
with firm arguments, nevertheless seems probable and next to certain.

* * * * *

to original sin but to sins committed in imitation of Adam's sin. Pelargus sigs
E8v–F2v attempts to refute all of Erasmus' arguments. He notes Augustine's
argument that if imitation were meant, the source of sin would have been
given as Satan, not Adam. Moreover death existed before the Law, when sin
was not imputed. Children are so numerous, he notes, that they hardly constitute a minor exception. He argues that ἐφ' ᾧ can mean 'through whom' as
well as 'in so far as.' He claims that Chrysostom, Theophylactus (correctly understood), and Ambrose do not support Erasmus' position (though he ignores
Origen). He claims that the argument from the lack of the second death and
therefore of the first is invalid because original sin does cause the first death
(that of the soul) and also part of the second (the pain of loss, but not the torment of hell). Pelargus misnumbers this proposition as LXXI.
In the second edition Erasmus adds only a few short phrases and clauses, one
of which, however, seems to reply to Pelargus' opening question: how can
Erasmus prove that in the time of the apostles only adults were baptized? In
the second edition Erasmus adds: 'though it cannot be demonstrated with firm
arguments, nevertheless [it] seems probable and next to certain.'

753 Origen *Commentary on the Gospel According to John* trans Ronald E. Heine 2 vols
(Washington 1989) 20.388, I 285; and Origen *Commentary on the Epistle to the
Romans* trans Thomas P. Scheck 2 vols (Washington 2001) 5.1, 3, 14, 20, I 303–4,
310–11, 313

754 It is puzzling here that Erasmus should make Jerome an alternative (*or*) to Origen. Origen's commentary on Romans was translated by Rufinus, not Jerome;
and Jerome himself did not interpret 'in whom all have sinned' as applying
to actual, not original, sin.

755 Pseudo-Ambrose *Commentaria in epistolas beati Pauli, in epistolam ad Romanos*
5:12–13 PL 17 (1845) 92A–94A

756 *Commentaria in epistolas sancti Pauli, in epistolam ad Romanos* 5 PL 30 (1846) 668B–
D; the commentator makes the point that 'all' does allow for a few exceptions.

757 *Commentarius in epistolam ad Romanos* 10.1 PG 60 473–6

Now if you take death to mean hell, which is not inflicted except for a mortal sin, it is certain that Adam's sin, which merited eternal torment, did not flow down to all mankind but only part of the pain and the loss of grace or original righteousness. For sin was the first death of the soul; the second was hell, that is, the torment of eternal fire. Therefore, just as this death of the soul does not flow down, so too the second also does not if they die without baptism. Therefore, since it seemed strained to haul in the mention of the sin of infants in the middle of the discourse (if it is even proper to speak of such a thing), since the ancients interpret the entire passage as applying to personal sin, and the Apostle's Greek words seem to have that meaning, I followed what seemed smoother and less strained, but at the same time I moderated my language so as not to exclude original sin but rather to affirm it.[758]

But Augustine vehemently insists that this text must be taken to refer only to original sin, especially when he is battling with Pelagius and Julian.[759] But I do not think that we are always obliged to accept the interpretation of Doctors, however much they are approved of, as articles of faith, especially if we are in agreement with the teaching of the church. We also freely profess original sin. The only dispute is about whether this text can be explained without it. The oldest exegetes thought it can be and explained it in that way. And Pelagius does not immediately triumph if Paul is here speaking about adults. Then too Pelagius will not learn this from us since he saw long ago that this text of Paul does not necessarily and properly pertain to original sin.

Topic 22. The temporal punishment of children because of the sins of their parents

LXXIII *The proposition of Erasmus. John 9[:3]*[760]
As the Law teaches,[761] God does not punish children because of the

* * * * *

758 In his paraphrase on Romans 5 Erasmus once expressed the descent of Adam's sin in an ambiguous way that could be taken to refer to inherited depravity. But in three other places in the paraphrase on Romans 5 he explicitly states that sin spread to all mankind because all have sinned in imitation of Adam. See CWE 42 34–5 and 147nn.

759 See, for example, *De natura et gratia contra Pelagium* 8.9, 39.46, 41.48 PL 44 251, 269–70, 270–1; in *Contra secundam Juliani responsionem imperfectum opus* Augustine refers to Rom 5:12 no less than thirty-two times.

760 LB VII 575 / CWE 46 121

761 Deut 24:16

transgressions of their parents unless the children emulate the vices of their parents.[762]

CENSURE

This proposition, if it is understood as universal, alleging that God never punishes children even temporally because of the crimes of their parents unless they imitate their parents' crimes, as if that would conflict with divine justice or natural equity, is heretical and contrary to Sacred Scripture, which frequently points out children punished in that way. For that was the case of the children drowned in the flood with their parents.[763] It was the case of those who perished in the fire in Pentapolis.[764] It was the case of the infant son of David who perished because of the adultery and homicide committed by his father.[765] And the Law which teaches that children are not punished for the wickedness of their fathers[766] should be understood as meaning not temporal punishment but rather eternal punishment.

CLARIFICATION[767]

LXXIII In that place I followed approved Doctors of the church, Chrysostom

* * * * *

762 Erasmus defended this proposition in *Elenchus in censuras Bedae* LB IX 501D–E and in *Supputatio* LB IX 633D–634A.
763 Gen 7:17–23
764 Wis 10:6; Gen 14:12
765 2 Kings 12:19
766 Deut 24:16
767 Pelargus sigs F2v–F4v notes in passing that the second half of Erasmus' proposition is irrelevant, since if children are punished for imitating the sins of their parents, they are being punished for their own sins, not those of their parents. But on the whole he heartily endorses Erasmus' defence, disagreeing (with apologies) with the opinion of the Paris theologians that the passage in Deuteronomy 24 refers to eternal, not temporal, punishment, since the punishments in that passage are issued by a human judge who has no competence to condemn to eternal punishment. He argues that temporal punishment is not truly punishment unless it is directed against someone who is guilty. He touches briefly on the difficulty that infants who die unbaptized seem to be punished for the sin of Adam, but original sin, which is transmitted to them by propagation, is in some sense their sin. He also rejects the argument that children under the authority of their parents are in a sense part of their parents as fruit is part of a tree and that to punish them is in some sense to punish the parents.
In the second edition Erasmus avoids a difficulty brought up by Pelargus by adding the sentence 'But if that is the case ... but for their own.' He

and Theophylactus, [768] who agrees with him; they declare that it would be unjust for God to punish someone for the transgressions of others. And they are not talking about the pain of hell but about physical blindness. And there is a law in Deuteronomy 24[:16]: 'fathers shall not be killed for their children, nor children for their fathers, but everyone shall die for his own sin.' The same idea appears in Ezekiel 18[:2–5] and Jeremiah 31[:29–30]. On the other hand, in Exodus 34 it is written: 'you who punish the sons and grandsons to the third and fourth generations for the wickedness of their fathers.'[769] They solve this puzzle in this way: The punishment due to wrongdoers is not inflicted on those who do not deserve it, but rather the same punishment is waiting for their posterity if they imitate the crimes of their ancestors. But if that is the case, they cannot properly be said to be punished for the sins of their ancestors but for their own. Then again, they solve the difficulty about the infants swallowed up in the flood by saying that was not punishment but rather the mercy of the Lord who took the children away early to keep them from turning out like their ancestors. In a similar way they settle the question arising from the words of the Lord in Matthew 23[:35], 'that all the just blood may come upon you,' by saying that they were not being punished for the crimes of their ancestors but for their own crimes, in which they surpassed the wickedness of their forebears.

If this is a pious opinion which is supported by illustrious authorities, why is there any mention of heresy here? Or what sort of courtesy is it to croak the same things at me so often, not without insults, even though I have already responded to them both in *Divinationes* and in *Elenchus* and *Supputationes*?[770] Moreover, what sort of specimen of Christian sincerity is it to carefully pick out of my replies whatever is open to false accusations and to overlook so much that they approve of by not speaking of it, according to the saying in the comedy, 'their silence is sufficient praise.' They also overlook the point that every external calamity that is inflicted is not immediately to be taken as punishment. Sometimes it is material for holiness; sometimes it is evidence demonstrating the power of God. Finally

* * * * *

also adds a section in which he seems to borrow two points from Pelargus: that the external calamities are not always punishment but may be material for holiness and that the seeming punishment of children may actually be punishment of the parents in the children.

768 Chrysostom *Commentarius in sanctum Joannem apostolum et evangelistam* 56.1 PG 59 305–7; Theophylactus *Commentarius in Joannis Evangelium* 9.1–2 PG 124 40–1

769 Exod 34:7

770 *Divinationes ad notata Bedae* LB IX 483A–B; *Elenchus in censuras Bedae* LB IX 501D–E; *Supputatio* 92 LB IX 633D–634A

when children are punished for the misdeeds of their parents, the parents are punished in the children more truly than the children because of the parents. The punishment is truly in the parents; in the children the calamity redounds to the punishment of the parents. According to this way of thinking my proposition, even if it is understood as universal, is true and Christian.

But if there are any places in Scripture which seem to contradict this opinion, they are not spoken literally but employ a figure of speech. Now if I had said that God punishes the sins of ancestors in their posterity even to the fifth generation, I would have been told that this proposition is heretical and clearly contrary to scriptural texts in Jeremiah 31 and Ezekiel 18. Now, when I give a different opinion based on the language of the Gospel, which I am interpreting, I nevertheless am told that this proposition, if it is understood as universal, is heretical and a different passage is brought up against it.

Topic 23. The punishment of heretics

LXXIV *The first proposition. Matt 13[:24–30]*
The servants who want to gather the tares before it is time are those who think that pseudo-apostles and archheretics should be eliminated by being put to the sword and killed, whereas the householder does not want them to be destroyed but tolerated, to see if perhaps they may come to their senses and become wheat instead of tares. But if they do not, they should be kept in reserve for their judge, to whom they will one day render their punishment.[771]

CENSURE
Since it is held in the Catholic faith that it is not only allowable but obligatory to punish pertinacious heretics with the ultimate punishment when this can be done without harm or danger to the commonwealth, and since there is no other way to attend to and maintain their salvation and that of others, and since the contrary is the error of the Cathars, the Waldensians,[772] and Luther, which has been condemned by general councils and imperial laws, the paraphraser has not performed the duty of a pious expositor by using so many words to lead the reader into a perverse meaning and by not clearly revealing the Catholic truth contrary to it, which the paraphraser could have easily

* * * * *

771 Erasmus defended this proposition in *Divinationes ad notata Bedae* LB IX 464A–C.
772 For the Catharists see n116 above; for the Waldensians see n72 above.

done by adding a few words of explanation, showing that what he writes here should be applied to the time of the apostles and martyrs, when tyrants cruelly persecuted the church, not when Christian princes are in power and have dominion of the world or a good part of it; when they make laws suitable for extirpating heretics, they have truly fought for their prince, Christ. Certainly the paraphraser ought to have explained this, and since he did not, he made it possible for his readers to stumble as if it were now not allowable to do what it was not possible to do in the time of the apostles and martyrs. In this way he also seemed to support the aforementioned heresies. Nor is there any room for him to excuse himself by saying that he took what we said as understood. For however much he may have taken for granted what he says he did, nevertheless he does not explain this in the same place, and readers are likely to take it far differently than he says he meant it to be taken. Hence many also complain that not only from this proposition but from very many others they are being offered under honeyed words a cup full of scandal and error; and therefore they do not accept another excuse hidden, as they say, under a cloak of clever sophistry, the trick of saying that what is said here is not said in the person of Erasmus but in the person of Christ, and not in this era but in the time when the church had to be planted by martyrdoms, though actually such ideas, which are not expressed, are not perceived by even the most careful reader, and his words, which are expressed in the paraphrase, say something different from what is set forth in his subsequent explanation of it. Then again, they do not approve of his introducing under the person of Christ, the evangelists, or the apostles not a few ideas which learned and also pious men consider impious and erroneous.

ERASMUS' CLARIFICATION[773]

LXXIV If regard for persons offers me no assistance in the paraphrases, I will be treated harshly indeed. By this rule it will be possible to impute

* * * * *

773 Pelargus sigs F4v–F5 disagrees with the censors that the parable applies only to the early church. It is universal but it means that heretics should not be punished if doing so would cause more harm than good. Erasmus was wrong not to pay attention to Christ's condition – 'lest you pull up the wheat together with the darnel,' that is, if destroying the heretics would cause more harm than leaving them alone. Pelargus also points out that Paul does not say that

to me what is said there by unholy men; now I will be Christ, now Paul, now Caiphas. Either a paraphrase ought not to have been written at all or the person speaking had to be regarded. But I am amazed that there are any readers so stupified that they do not understand that in a paraphrase nothing is spoken in my person. And for a long time now I have shouted myself hoarse saying that my paraphrase is no different from a commentary and that if I do not get at the meaning of Scripture there is no more danger than if I made a mistake in a commentary. But, though I may have slipped elsewhere, here certainly it cannot be objected that my explanation differs from the language of Christ, which they confess is true, pious, and holy for those times.

But I am accused only for this reason, that I did not expressly say that Christ's language is not general but pertains only to the beginning of the church, which at that time indeed had to be strengthened by the blood of the martyrs and trained by the turmoil of the heretics; but as soon as the situation began to be safe, the language of Christ ceased to be valid. First, I did not dare to mix this human contrivance into the majesty of the gospel, especially since I did not find it in the ancient, orthodox exegetes and since the very words of Christ seemed to reject this meaning. What kind of a paraphraser would I have been if, when Christ says the darnel should be left until the harvest, that is, as he himself interprets it, until the end of the world, I should explain it, either in the person of Christ or that of the evangelist, as meaning until five hundred years had passed when the position of the church would have improved and it would be safe to kill them? The Lord himself prescribed the time, until the end of the world. Neither Paul nor Augustine, who follows him, taught that heretics were to be tolerated simply because it was not safe to kill them, but rather because the faith and holiness of the elect would be trained by their wickedness. 'It is necessary,' he says, 'that there be heresies so that those who are approved may be manifested among you.'[774] What if I apply this language not to external princes but to apostolic men?[775] But in fact the paraphrase is not

*　*　*　*　*

heresies should be tolerated but only that it is necessary that they occur to exercise the faithful.
In the second edition Erasmus seems to have been replying to Pelargus when he added the brief section: 'Now I hear that some people ... evangelist or of Christ.'

774 1 Cor 11:19
775 The external princes were the Roman persecutors. In other words, the passage has nothing to do with not killing them because it was not safe to do so.

entirely silent even about safety, since it has this to say: 'In the meantime the good mixed with the bad should be endured, since it is less dangerous to tolerate them than to eliminate them, etc.'[776]

Now I hear that some people twist the words of Christ to mean that the heretics should be spared only with the proviso that there is a danger that sound doctrine would be eradicated together with errors or that the bad should be killed together with the good, but that once this distinction has been removed, they should by no means be spared. Since this contrivance does not square sufficiently with the drift of the parable or with the interpretation of the ancient orthodox exegetes, I did not dare to set it down under the person of the evangelist or of Christ. When they object that the words of the paraphrase say something different from my subsequent explanation, perhaps they mean my responses to Béda. But that is not surprising. For in the paraphrase I follow the most approved Doctors of the church, Jerome, Augustine, Chrysostom, Theophylactus, and Rabanus,[777] to explain the words of the Lord; in *Supputationes* I dispute with Béda. Nevertheless, what I say more explicitly in *Supputationes* (and not only there) I imply in the paraphrase.[778]

Moreover, if so much danger hangs over us because in my paraphrase (which is read privately and only by a few) I do not expressly say that it is allowable to kill heretics, we have much more to fear from Jerome, Chrysostom, and Augustine, whose writings are read by everyone as authoritative, and that even in church.[779] Why does St Thomas in his *Catena* bring up these stumbling blocks once more, citing what is now condemned by the theologians?[780] But what good does it do to base suspicion on this passage, as if I meant that heretics should not be killed, since in published books I bat-

* * * * *

776 LB VII 80F; the Latin plays on *tolerantur quam tollerentur*.
777 Jerome *Commentariorum in Evangelium Matthaei libri quatuor* 2.13.37–42 PL 26 (1845) 93B–94B; Augustine *Quaestionum septemdecem in Evangelium secundum Matthaeum liber unus* 12(13).2 PL 35 1370; Chrysostom *Commentarius in sanctum Matthaeum evangelistam* 47.1–2 PG 58 475–8; Theophylactus *Enarratio in Evangelium Matthaei* 13.24–30 PG 123 284–5; Rabanus *Commentariorum in Matthaeum libri octo* 4.13.2 PL 107 947C–948B
778 *Supputatio* 32 LB IX 580C–583F
779 Erasmus is probably thinking of readings from these Fathers in the lessons of matins in the divine office.
780 *Catena aurea super Matthaei Evangelium* 13.4 gives substantial quotations from Chrysostom, Jerome, and Augustine supporting the idea that heretics should not be put to death.

tle against those who favour that teaching? In fact we can gather how much should be attributed to the learned men they cite[781] from the many times they have been caught maliciously and falsely indicting what was well said, how many times they have condemned what they did not understand, how many times they have made patently false objections. The canons of ancient councils make this provision: if someone does not prove one accusation of criminal activity, let him not go on to make another.[782] As it is, although I have clearly pointed out so many false and outrageous accusations in the books they have written against me up till now, nevertheless they put on a bold face and go right on making false accusations as if they had a perfect right to do so. Enough said about those learned men whose authority is thrown up to me.

LXXV *The second proposition. In* Supputationes[783]

I neither urge princes to slaughter heretics nor dissuade them. I show what belongs to the duty of a priest.

CENSURE

If it is permissible for ecclesiastics, according to the disposition of the law, to declare war or through temporal magistrates to cause it to be declared against the Turks and Jews, it is certainly no less permissible to do so against notorious heretics. In support of this point St Dominic was present with the bishops in that war which was waged against the Albigensians. And when princes are gravely delinquent by not exterminating heretics who conspire to destroy the Christian community and draw very many into their heresy, orthodox bishops are bound to use every means to induce them to do so; otherwise they themselves would sin. Therefore this proposition, in so far as it alleges that it never belongs to the sacerdotal or episcopal office to induce princes to exterminate heretics, gives an impious judgment which is not conducive to the advancement of Christians and which weakens the strength of true fortitude against the enemies of the faith.

* * * * *

781 Erasmus refers to the general claim of the theologians that many complain of the poison lurking under Erasmus' honeyed words.
782 *Decretum Gratiani* (par 2 causa 3 quest 10 cc 1–3) cites the seventh Council of Carthage and the third Council of Arles to support the rule which Erasmus paraphrases here; see *Corpus iuris canonici* I 534.
783 *Supputatio* LB IX 582F

ERASMUS' CLARIFICATION[784]

LXXV I had shown in *Supputationes* that Augustine interceded to keep even the most heretical persons from being killed,[785] and I add 'nevertheless I neither urge princes to slaughter heretics nor dissuade them,' meaning that I disagree with Augustine in so far as I think princes ought not to be discouraged from carrying out the duties of justice if the disease requires extreme remedies. In that passage I am talking about myself, not the bishops of these times, and I show that I am further away than Augustine was from the opinion of those who deny that heretics should be killed. He urges the imperial prefects not to eliminate heretics; I say I neither urge nor dissuade. I address what belongs to the duty of a priest. A priest's duty is to save heretics in the hope that they will come to their senses and not to lose anyone if he possibly can. I think this is their principal duty. If they take upon themselves something beyond this, I do not deprive them of it. And so my words by no means allege what the theologians take them to mean.

The Turks not only disagree with our faith but they also sometimes occupy Christians domains and exercise horrible cruelty against our people. I wish that we were able either to suppress them through arms or (what would be better) to draw them into the Christian community. The Jews we do not kill unless they break the laws of the princes, although they are the most determined enemies of both Christ and Christianity. What Dominic did against the Albigensians I do not know.[786] Perhaps they took up arms

* * * * *

784 Pelargus sigs F5–F5v treats propositions LXXV and LXXVI together, arguing that bishops have a perfect right and even duty to ask princes to execute heretics, noting that Pope Leo mustered troops against the Saracens besieging Rome and that Pope Adrian asked Charles to fight against the Longobards. He mentions examples such as Augustine, who ultimately approved of capital punishment for heretics, and Bernard, who asked the secular power for protection against them. He also mentions that many bishops have turned them over to the secular arm for punishment or execution.

In the second edition Erasmus added a short section in which he noted that the Turks (and perhaps also the Albigensians) waged war against Christians, who had a right to defend themselves, and that the Jews (clearly enemies of Christianity) are not killed unless they violate the secular law.

785 *Epistolae* 139.2 PL 33 535–6

786 Apart from the fact that Dominic was present in the area of the crusade against the Albigensians from 1208 to 1214 and that he was a friend of the leader of the crusade, Simon de Montfort, there is little evidence about his activities; what there is suggests that he mainly preached and ministered to the people spiritually. See M.-H. Vicaire *Saint Dominic and His Times* trans Kathleen Pond (New York 1964) 146–66.

against the Catholics. Now, as to whether the strength of true fortitude against the enemies of the faith lies in weapons I leave it to others to judge; to me, certainly, it is a strange thing to say.

LXXVI *The third proposition. Also in* Supputationes[787]
Who ever heard that orthodox bishops stirred up kings to slaughter heretics who were nothing more than heretics?

CENSURE
This proposition, alleging that it is not licit for orthodox bishops and priests to give advice and use general exhortation to lead to the extirpation of heretics who are nothing more than heretical, that is, erring in the faith stubbornly and contumaciously but not stirring up insurrection and uprisings, is set forth against the disposition of natural, divine, and human law. For if according to their office bishops and other priests ought to admonish princes to execute justice upon other malefactors according to God's arrangement and their own duty (for it is not without reason that they carry a sword),[788] certainly they have an even greater duty to do so against heretics who are nothing more than heretics, in so far as heresy is a graver sin and does more harm to the Christian commonwealth. Accordingly, if those who corrupt and falsify money, which supports the life of our bodies, are justly executed, there is even stronger reason to rightly deprive heretics of their lives, since they corrupt the faith which is the basis of our spiritual life, and which, according to the evils of our times, cannot be preserved intact without punishing heretics with death, even though they are nothing more than heretics. For when most people see that those who profess heresy are not treated any worse than others, certainly they would easily cast away all fear and join the heretics, and subsequently in the Christian commonwealth there would be a miserable calamity as the people who were formerly Christians of the Catholic faith would then, after a short passage of time, become nothing other than heretics – which, alas, is what we see nowadays. For many illustrious city states which had recently been truly Christian and famous for their Christian holiness have now lapsed from true Christianity and are nothing more than the filthy dregs and putrid bilge water of wicked heretics – which would certainly not have happened if, when

* * * * *

787 *Supputatio* LB IX 581A
788 Rom 13:4

the plague first emerged, they had been attended to by means of the wholesome severity of the laws against heretics, even though they are nothing more than heretics. Hence it is quite clear how prudently the church decided that such heretics, if they have been legitimately convicted, should be left to the justice of the secular arm. In the meantime it is not right for clerics to be unmindful of their duty. For by means of exhortation, counselling, teaching, reproving, abjuring, and other required ways they should strive to provide for the salvation of such wretched persons so as to recall them from their wickedness.

LXXVII *The fourth proposition of Erasmus, which is in his* Supputationes,[789] *as are the next three*

Augustine teaches that heretics are to be tolerated until they can be eliminated without a serious shock to the church; but Augustine takes 'eliminate' to mean 'to excommunicate.'

CENSURE

Although Augustine at one time thought that heretics ought to be handled with words and opposed with argumentation and that one should go no further, except perhaps by brandishing the sword of an anathema against the contumacious, nevertheless, when he learned by experience how much the law of secular princes against heretics promoted the required performance, he abandoned his former opinion and judged that heretics should be forced by fear of the laws and severity of punishment to reunite themselves to the one faith – a fact which is borne out in many of his books.

ERASMUS' CLARIFICATION OF THE TWO PRECEDING PROPOSITIONS[790]

LXXVI, LXXVII On this point we do not disagree. They grant that it is the duty of priests to strive to their uttermost to save heretics and get them

* * * * *

789 *Supputatio* LB IX 583C
790 Concerning proposition LXXVII Pelargus sig F6 replies to Erasmus that Augustine changed his mind and that Paul required nothing more than excommunication because there were only gentile princes who would not punish heretics and apostates.
In the second edition Erasmus added a long section in which he re-emphasizes the leniency recommended by the parable of the wheat and tares and exemplified by the practice of ancient bishops. He also points out that sometimes the accusation of heresy is ill-founded and quotes Jerome's advice that extreme caution is to be exercised in bringing such accusations.

to repent, but that nevertheless, in time of great danger to the church, it is the duty of bishops to inform princes of their duty if they are remiss, but in general; and I say I have not read of any bishops stirring up kings to slaughter heretics. For that is not reminding them in general but dictating the kind of punishment. In *Elenchus*,[791] however, I am speaking not about these times but about Augustine and the bishops of his era, for nowadays some abbots and bishops think they are offering a sacrifice most pleasing to God if they slay as many as possible with their own sword and their own hand.

And though I admit that what they say about Augustine is true, that at first he was of the opinion that the power of the emperors ought not to be sought in the affairs of the faith, but when he saw what happened, he changed his mind, so too what I wrote is equally true. But at that time he was dealing with the Donatists, who were very heretical indeed and sought to create a most dangerous split in the whole church; and they had among them the Circumcellions, a mad and cruel sort of people who killed the orthodox with the sword, mutilated them with scythes, and put out their eyes with lime mixed with vinegar.[792] Why should the emperor not suppress such people, who deserved every imaginable punishment, even if heretical error had not been added to their crimes. And even against such persons Augustine was so far from calling for capital punishment that he resisted a count who had proposed a very severe edict, fearing that he might kill someone, and he saw to it that a more lenient edict was proposed. For at that time suppression by the emperor was limited to monetary fines, the transfer of property from the churches of the Donatists to the churches of the orthodox, or, if bishops could not be corrected by any remedies, exile.[793] There is no mention of slaughtering them. And so there was never any movement to ask for the help of the emperors against Pelagius because he did not disturb the tranquillity of the commonwealth very much. In fact, even those who paid fines were given their money back through the intervention of the bishops; and bishops, if they changed their teachings, re-

* * * * *

791 This must be a slip of the pen for *Supputatio* 'Reckoning' for that is the work from which the quotations under discussion are taken.

792 On the ravages perpetrated by the Donatists, especially the Circumcellions, see Augustine *Epistolae* 88.8 PL 33 307; for Augustine's appeal to the authorities to use force to resist them see *Epistolae* 86 PL 33 296 and 89.1–8 PL 33 309–13.

793 In a letter to Count Boniface Augustine justifies fear of imperial laws as a means of restraining Donatists and perhaps bringing them back to the unity of the Catholic church; but he specifically excludes capital punishment, relying only on monetary fines and exile as means of coercion (*Epistolae* 185.7.25–6 PL 33 804–5). See also the preceding note.

tained their ecclesiastical standing. Such leniency did those times exercise against heretics, and such heretics! There are many ways of suppressing besides capital punishment. Certainly very far from such leniency are those who nowadays, when something is said that is strange or not understood, immediately cry out 'to the fire, to the fire.' On this point, therefore, there is no disagreement between me and the theologians, except that they consider what a religious plague it is for the church to be split into such factions, and hence they seem more prone to killing people, whereas I, on the other hand, am more hesitant to do so, taking into account the direction we are called to follow by the parable of the Lord, the interpretation of very holy men, and the leniency and gentleness with which ancient bishops and emperors treated heretics. I also considered how from time to time human feelings get mixed up in these affairs and how frequently such remedies turn out to have a different effect than was intended. Finally I considered that sometimes the truth is in doubt, and from time to time it happens that even the one who hurls the accusation of heresy is wrong; sometimes neither side understands the other, quarrelling about words, but really in agreement.

For Jerome was not off the mark in his *Dialogue against the Luciferians* when he says in the person of the orthodox character as follows (having said right before that it was not expedient for the church to eliminate heretics totally): 'No one,' he says, 'can take to himself Christ's palm of victory; no one can judge concerning people before the day of judgment. If the church has already been cleansed, what do we reserve for Christ to do? There is a path which among men seems right, but at the end of it they come to the depths of hell. In this uncertainty of judgment, what opinion can be certain, etc?'[794] What Jerome meant by these words will be clear to the learned. Certainly they have moved me to the extent of thinking we should not proceed to extreme remedies without trying everything to keep an innocent, or at least salvageable, person from perishing through a perverse judgment and to prevent what is right from being condemned as erroneous.

As for their exaggeration of the wickedness of heretics and schismatics by comparing them to counterfeiters and other criminals, I grant that they are plagues to the church, truly to be deplored, no less worthy of the severity of the laws than other criminals, except that, as I said, the Lord specifically calls upon us to be gentle, as do the ancient bishops, both by their writings and by their example. Because the Lord said to the adulter-

* * * * *

794 *Dialogus contra Luciferanos* 22 PL 23 (1845) 177A–B

ess, 'neither will I condemn you,'[795] the punishment of adultery has been mitigated among Christians. Because Paul predicted that the Jews would finally be gathered into the sheepfold of Christ,[796] we tolerate this wicked and blasphemous people. Perhaps this parable of the Lord ought also to have sufficient weight to cause us to treat heretics more leniently, especially those who err out of conviction, not malice, and who do not gather disciples or excite uprisings. For these are the ones I meant when I said 'nothing more than heretics,' that is, subject to a heretical error. For the contumacious and those who protect themselves by gathering disciples aim at creating a schism. Otherwise, if we think that just any deviation from the integrity of the faith deserves burning, such are found in almost all the books of the Doctors of the church. Nowadays those who say out of conviction, 'we wish to be instructed if we are wrong,' are sometimes thrown into the fire as if they were extraordinarily contumacious.

LXXVIII *His fifth proposition in the same work*[797]
The gospel orders us to avoid heretics,[798] not to burn them.

CENSURE
Although the gospel does not expressly and openly show that heretics should be burned, nevertheless the civil laws, in conformity with natural law, which is not revoked by the gospel, justly decree that they should be punished with death and be consumed by fire.

CLARIFICATION[799]
LXXVIII In order to prove from the gospel that any heretics whosoever should be consumed by fire, Béda brings up the text: 'Say to the church: "if he does not listen, let him be to you as a pagan or a tax-gatherer."'[800] I reply that in these words of the gospel Christians are admonished to avoid

* * * * *

795 John 8:11
796 Rom 11:26–7
797 *Supputatio* LB IX 582B
798 Matt 18:17; cf Tit 3:10.
799 Pelargus sigs F6–F6v notes that, though Erasmus claims not to deny the validity of capital punishment for heretics, the tendency of his clarification is to argue against it. He claims that Erasmus should have avoided the negative argument against burning heretics (that it is not mentioned in the gospel) because it was an argument used by the heretics themselves.
 In the second edition Erasmus made no changes or additions.
800 Matt 18:17

a person who is heretical and cannot be cured by the arguments that have been tried; they are not admonished to burn him. The theologians hardly deny that this is true. But because, they say, the gospel does not revoke the natural and civil law, it was later justly established that those who could not be cured in any other way should be punished by being put to death. I do not deny any of this provided that the princes are severe, not savage, provided that bishops determine the kind of heresy, according to Augustine's distinctions,[801] and that imperial laws also do so, and provided that they[802] should everywhere keep in mind the gentleness of the church.

LXXIX *His sixth proposition in the same place*[803]

Whether there are laws of the church providing that anyone should be handed over to the flames of vengeance.

CENSURE

The church does not object to the laws of temporal magistrates made for the eradication of heretics, but she does not want them to be put into execution by clerics, who are altogether committed to religious duties.

CLARIFICATION[804]

LXXIX When we were dealing with killing heretics, Béda brought up against me laws of the church. Therefore I ask whether there are laws of the church providing that anyone should be handed over to the flames of vengeance, since the church does not have any right to the secular sword. But such laws, they say, the church does not object to, although punishment is not carried out by those committed to religion. I grant this also, although it is the part of clerics everywhere to temper the severity of the laws with the gentleness of the gospel.

* * * * *

801 Erasmus seems to mean Augustine's distinction between heretics who, like the Pelagians, were peaceful and those who, like the Circumcellions and some of the Donatists, were savage and destructive.
802 That is, the princes and bishops
803 *Supputatio* LB IX 580F
804 Pelargus sig F6v notes that Erasmus does not ask this question to reproach the church for doing something unworthy, since Erasmus elsewhere denies that the law of the church provides the death penalty for heretics. But Pelargus notes that Paul cites Deuteronomy (though he mitigates it), which provides death for perverse backsliders. Hence it is allowable for secular law to prescribe death for someone already condemned to death by divine law.
In the second edition Erasmus made no changes or additions.

LXXX *His seventh proposition on the same point in the same place*[805]
To the bishops of old the ultimate punishment was an anathema.

CENSURE
Because of the hostility of tyrants in the primitive church heretics
could not be punished any more severely than by excommunication.
Nevertheless, after secular princes had submitted to the church, when
the contumely and wickedness of the heretics became evident, it was
necessary, not to say convenient, to attend to them with the temporal
sword. And the preceding four propositions support the error of the
aforementioned heretics who deny that it is permissible and expedient
to suppress contumacious heretics with the ultimate punishment, even
when some disturbance of the commonwealth springs from them and
the salvation of many persons may demand it.

CLARIFICATION
[LXXX] Here too we are in agreement. They themselves grant that what I
wrote is true. But they add that, when the times changed, imperial laws
necessarily threatened heretics with capital punishment, and I grant that
this is true. Hence I wonder how they can say that these propositions, in
which I agree with the theologians, offer support to some heretics or other
who deny that it is permissible and expedient to suppress heretics with the
ultimate punishment, even when some disturbance of the commonwealth
may spring from them and the salvation of many persons may demand
it. Such a thing is not expressed or meant in my propositions, which have
no quarrel with imperial laws but rather temper the fierceness of some
clerics. The church's gentleness once tempered the severity of princes. Now
the fierceness of some monks, if it were not restrained by the leniency of
princes, would turn into a more than Scythian cruelty.[806]

LXXXI *His eighth proposition*[807]
Articles are sought out, some of which are false, some distorted.

CENSURE
This proposition is possibly set forth here for the following reasons:
so that, when many propositions are set forth about the punishment
of heretics, those who have the zeal or authority to eradicate heretics

* * * * *

805 *Supputatio* LB IX 580F
806 *Adagia* IV ix 85
807 *Supputatio* LB IX 581C

may be admonished to carefully avoid having their zeal be excessively vehement or not sufficiently discrete, which might cause it to happen that the innocent are condemned; or so that it might not cool off more than is necessary, allowing heresies to spring up or tolerating notorious heretics without punishing them; also so that the judges who render decisions in cases concerning the faith may be of unblemished integrity so as to dispense justice justly and not deviate from a true judgment out of greed for money or some other untoward emotion; moreover so that they examine and conduct such cases concerning the faith with the greatest vigilance and diligence by relying on the law, lest perhaps negligence or carelessness, which oftentimes prevents a just judgment from being handed down, should creep in. However that may be, the proposition written above, if it is understood as applying to perverse judges, who have no reverence for God or man, sets forth something which sometimes happens. But if, indeed, it is said concerning honest and fair judges who are far removed not only from accusing falsely but also from any suspicion of it, it is false.

CLARIFICATION[808]

LXXXI This censure contains nothing with which I do not agree, except that there is no reason for any doubt about whether I am writing about perverse judges or fair and honest ones, since in that very passage I expressly say what kind of judges I am reprimanding. These are my words: 'But if those who are handling this business are such as N. shows himself to be in this little book, that is, if they spew out so much hatred, if they are so shameless, so uncontrollably eager to slander, if their judgment is so corrupt that it seems they would drive ten persons into heresy sooner than recall one person from it, would they not do a fine job of handling those reported to them? Unless I am mistaken, he would first pick out someone he would wish to injure, and, having secretly reported him, see to it that he is thrown in jail; there articles might be sought out such as most of those brought against me.'[809] They have changed 'might be sought out' to 'are sought out' as if I were speaking universally about all cases. This language does not allow anyone to doubt that I was dealing with corrupt judges. Nor does it matter whether the one I reprimand is such as I say; it is sufficient that he seems

* * * * *

808 Pelargus sig F6v says only: 'Here you are perhaps right to complain.'
In the second edition Erasmus adds only a brief sentence at the end, noting that if he is wrong about Béda's perverse judgment of him, that does not change the validity of the argument as a whole.
809 *Supputatio* LB IX 581B–C

to me to be so.[810] For if there is a mistake, it concerns a person and not the situation.

Topic 24. The failing effectiveness of the gospel

LXXXII *A proposition in the prefatory epistle to the* Paraphrase on John[811]
In all ages there has been no lack of persons who paid the gospel the honour due to it; but nevertheless in these last four hundred years its energy in most people has grown cold.[812]

CENSURE
This proposition, as concerns its last part, namely 'but nevertheless in these last four hundred years, etc,' signifying that in these last four hundred years there has been a lack of men who paid the gospel the honour due to it, is a temerarious assertion, since during these past four hundred years there have been not a few men conspicuous for their sanctity and learning, such as Bernard, Hugh and Richard of St Victor, Peter Lombard, Gratian, Thomas Aquinas, Bonaventure, Alexander of Hales, William of Paris,[813] Nicolas de Lyra, Gerson, Thomas Waldensis,[814] and very many others.

* * * * *

810 The first editions of *Declarationes* and *Supputatio* gave the name 'Bed(d)a,' which was replaced by 'N.' in the second edition of *Declarationes*. But in *Supputatio* Erasmus does go on to mention an unnamed unfair judge: 'Perhaps in other matters Béda is not such as he is in this book [that is, in his censures against Erasmus]. But I know a certain person who was like this, though I refrain from naming him because he has departed to his proper place, where he will be unhappy indeed if he finds God to be such a judge of him as he was of others' (LB IX 581D).

811 LB VII 493–4 / CWE 46 10

812 In *Divinationes ad notata Bedae* LB IX 481A–C Erasmus defended this proposition. In *Supputatio* LB IX 624B–E he argued that this proposition has nothing to do with Lutheranism and does not condemn scholastic theology altogether.

813 A Dominican theologian (d c 1314), he became the Inquisitor General of France in 1303 and played a leading role in the proceedings against the Knights Templar. His *Dialogue concerning the Seven Sacraments* was widely disseminated. (He is to be distinguished from another Paris theologian named William of Paris [d c 1486] whose *Postilla super epistolas et evangelia* was very popular.) See *Lexikon des Mittelalters* 9 vols to date (Munich and Zurich 1977–   ) IX 182.

814 Thomas Netter, a Carmelite theologian born in Saffron Walden, England, in 1370, died in Rouen in 1430. He was an adviser and diplomatic representative for Henry V and Henry VI of England, an opponent of Wyclif and his followers the Lollards, and the author of a long theological compendium in which he refuted Wyclif's positions in detail. His work was influential in the antiprotes-

CLARIFICATION

LXXXII I wonder who added this censure. It says that my proposition signifies that for these past four hundred years there has been a lack of men
who paid the gospel the honour due to it, though it clearly affirms the opposite, namely that in all centuries there has been no lack of persons who
paid the gospel the honour due to it; and I do not say that in these past four
hundred years the energy of the gospel has been extinguished but that it
has grown cold, and even that not in everyone but in most people. What is
the point, then, of that catalogue of names, from which some people would
perhaps remove many names, if we are dealing with the energy of the evangelical spirit which we feel in the early Doctors of the church? But let us
grant that they all had the energy of the gospel; that fact itself proves that
what my sentence said earlier is true, namely that there has been no century which did not exhibit some men breathing the spirit of the gospel.
I only complain that in these years people's piety has grown cold, their
minds inclined either to this world or to Judaism.[815] Anyone who wants
can read the passage and he will discover that I meant nothing other than
that.

I will not examine the catalogue of names they throw up to me. Certainly I think they were all good men, but it is one thing to be a good
man and another to breathe forth the energy of the gospel. Among them
Bernard, to be sure, seems to have most ardent feelings, but how cool he is
by comparison with Cyprian, with Jerome, etc. I know many who would not
read without laughter the names of Gratian, Alexander of Hales, William of
Paris, Nicolas de Lyra, Thomas Waldensis listed among those who breathe
forth the energy of the gospel.

Topic 25. The sabbath

LXXXIII *Erasmus' proposition. Mark 2*[816]
There will come a time when for the truly pious one day is as sacred
as another.[817]

* * * * *

tant polemic of the sixteenth century. See *Biographisch-Bibliographisches Kirchen-
lexikon* ed Friedrich Bautz and Traugott Bautz (Hamm, Herzberg, Hordheim
1990–2003) VI 636–8. See also *New Catholic Encyclopedia* 15 vols (New York
1967) X 363.
815 That is, to excessive emphasis on the externals of religion
816 LB VII 178F / CWE 49 44
817 Erasmus defended this proposition in *Supputatio* LB IX 646C–D.

CENSURE

This proposition, which alleges that the observance of the Lord's day and other feast days established profitably and piously by the church ought some day to be abolished in the church militant, since that would tend to great danger for the church, is an irrational assertion, and conforms to the error of the Beguards, who say that the third precept of the decalogue, namely 'Thou shalt keep holy the sabbath day,' is now abrogated in so far as the just are concerned.

CLARIFICATION[818]

LXXXIII First it is clear that at this point the paraphrase, in the person of Christ, is speaking about the sabbath and feasts of the Jews. The drift of the whole passage makes it evident that this is true. Whoever wants to can read it. Signifying that those ceremonies of the Law ought to be abrogated by the fervour of the gospel, the Lord speaks as follows: 'There was once a time when there was no observance of the sabbath, and there will come a time when for the truly pious one day is as sacred as another. But there never has been and there never will be a time when it was not or will not be holy to help your neighbour in need, etc.'[819] For the Jews the sabbath meant abstaining from all servile labour; a feast day meant the sacrificing of victims. The true sabbath means to have a mind free of the desires of the flesh; a true feast day means to be free for prayers and the contemplation of heavenly things. And so, when the ceremonies of the Law have been abrogated, for the truly pious any day is the sabbath and every day is a feast day, since, without being compelled by any prescript, they persevere in fasting, vigils, religious teaching, and the breaking of the bread.[820]

Christ predicted that this would be so, and Paul considers as weak those who distinguish one day from another in the manner of the gentiles and the Jews, just as he reproaches those who judge their brothers in matters

* * * * *

818 Pelargus sigs F6v–7 argues that the church rightly established cessation from servile labour on Sundays and feast days so that the faithful would have leisure to pray and contemplate heavenly matters. He considers Erasmus' defence, that he means only that such observances must yield to the duties of charity, to be obvious and a mere evasion in Erasmus' usual manner.
In the second edition Erasmus added only two short clauses refining the conflict between sabbatical leisure and the requirement of charity and defining what he means by 'figuratively.'
819 LB VII 178F / CWE 49 44
820 Luke 24:35

of food and drink.[821] And just as these words of Paul do not condemn the regulations of the church about abstinence from food, so too these words spoken in the name of Christ do not condemn feast days wisely and profitably established by the church. And my proposition does not allege any such thing as some interpret it to mean. It deals only with this point, that those external observances yield whenever the duties of charity must be provided for your neighbour if a case arises when one conflicts with the other, because this law is perpetual, whereas that one about the sabbath and feast days is not.

And so farewell to the Beguards, who deny that the days established by the church should be observed. Whether they will cease I do not know. Certainly that is not what I wrote and not what Christ said. Still the church could exist more easily without feast days than without charity. Indeed, even today, for the pious who have no less horror of sinning on ordinary days than on feast days and who are continually occupied in praying and meditating on life in heaven, all days are feast days, if we take this figuratively – that is according to the spiritual observance of feasts.

Topic 26. The church

LXXXIV *Erasmus' proposition. Mark 3*[822]
The church of Christ does not accept either the deaf or the mute or the blind or the disabled or the lame; but the synagogue has such persons.[823]

CENSURE

This proposition, set forth so distinctly, seems to allege that only the righteous are in the church militant (for that is what the passage is about) but it is not consonant with the teaching of the gospel, which compares the kingdom of heaven, which is the church militant, with a net thrown into the sea and gathering in fish of all sorts,[824] and with the Lord's field, in which darnel springs up with the wheat.[825]

* * * * *

821 Rom 14:3–5
822 LB VII 181A / CWE 49 48
823 Erasmus defended this proposition very briefly in *Divinationes ad notata Bedae* LB IX 648E–F.
824 Matt 13:47
825 Matt 13:24–6

CLARIFICATION[826]

LXXXIV In that passage Mark is speaking, I think, about the church as the bride of Christ whom he cleansed with his blood, so that she has neither spot nor wrinkle,[827] and outside of which are those who are mentally blind, maimed, deaf, or mutilated. Such persons were valued by the synagogue as worthy of honour because of the external appearance of sanctity even though they were devoid of holiness. The pharisaic leaders of the synagogue accepted such people and did not heal them. On the other hand, Christ, the master of spiritual teaching, did not accept such people in his church unless they had first been healed. That is all the paraphrase is dealing with, and I do not think there is anything here divergent from Catholic doctrine. The place in the paraphrase is as follows: 'Such were the Pharisees, who preferred to look askance at the Lord rather than to be restored by him. The synagogue has such weak persons. But the church of Christ does not accept either the deaf or the mute or the blind or the disabled or the lame. Let whoever is subject to evil come into the sight of Jesus and he will be healed. He will breathe his spirit upon us and revive what was maimed. Whoever entrusts himself to the Lord with sincere confidence will go home healed. Whoever trusts his own righteousness based on good deeds done to others is rendered worse etc.'[828] From this it is evident that the paraphrase is not speaking about the evil persons mixed with good and tolerated by the church because only God knows the human heart,[829] although such persons

* * * * *

826 Pelargus sigs F7–8 agrees that Mark is here speaking of the church triumphant. But he argues that Erasmus must be speaking of the church militant, not consistently of the church triumphant, partly because he emphasizes the comparison with the synagogue (there is no point in comparing the church triumphant with the synagogue). He claims Erasmus is quite wrong; citations from Augustine's *Retractions*, citing Cyprian, and a definition from the Council of Constance prove that evil persons do belong to the church. He also refutes Erasmus' argument that Christ cannot have evil members in the mystical body; he claims that, though they are dead, they are in fact not cut away and may be revived because they still have faith, though not charity.

In the second edition Erasmus adds a long section noting that he was explaining the episode allegorically according to patristic exegesis such as Jerome's, and that there was no place in the paraphrase for subtle scholastic arguments about how evil men can be incorporated into the body of Christ. Here he is clearly referring to Pelargus' point about unformed faith.

827 Eph 4:27

828 LB VII 180F–181A / CWE 49 47–8

829 3 Kings 8:39

in the eyes of God are already in a certain sense outside the church. Rather it is talking about those who came forward to profess the gospel, which is spiritual and more perfect.

And the paraphrase is there explaining the story of the man who had a withered hand and was healed in the synagogue, and what comes next, that whoever was afflicted rushed to Jesus and was healed by the Lord.[830] Since I was explaining the allegory in that passage, how could it be proper to argue there concerning points about which not even the scholastics are in sufficient agreement: how Christ is the head even of evil Christians; and how there is in them also an influx by means of faith without charity; and how the same persons can be members of Christ and members of Satan; and what is the difference between those cut off and those not cut off; and what is the difference between saying someone is not *in* the church and saying he is not *of* the church? Such points are not at all fitting for someone who is discussing figurative language according to the interpretation of the ancient Fathers, not according to the subtleties of the scholastics.

That maimed man was in the synagogue and was not healed by the Pharisees, who taught ceremonies, not the works of charity; but those whom Jesus receives he renders spiritually alive and active in the duties of charity. And who is unaware that evil persons are tolerated in the church, especially those who are secretly so? But it is one thing for evil persons to be tolerated by human beings and another for them to be accepted by Christ. A physician accepts a sick person whom he hopes he will set free by his care. But that celestial physician heals whomever he accepts. In treating the allegory St Jerome uses other words to say the same thing as I do: 'Until the coming of the Saviour,' he says, 'the withered hand was in the synagogue of the Jews and it did not perform the works of God. When he came to the earth, it was rendered dexterous in the apostles and restored to its original activity.'[831] Now if we do not accept a figurative interpretation, the synagogue also had good persons mixed with the bad. The parable of the net from Matthew 13[:47–50] and what they bring up about the Lord's field[832] I explain in the same way as the theologians take them. The story about the lame and the

* * * * *

830 Mark 3:1–10
831 *Commentariorum in Evangelium Matthaei libri quatuor* 2.12.13 PL 26 (1845) 78B
832 The Latin of the second edition (the phrase does not occur in the first) is 'de magna domo parabolam de sagena.' Since the censure has 'agro dominico' it looks as if the abbreviation for this phrase was misread as 'magna domo' and an 'et' was omitted before 'parabolam'; I have emended and translated accordingly.

blind invited to the banquet[833] is an allegory and is explained by the holy Doctors as applying more to those scorned by the world than to vices of the mind.

Topic 27. The Blessed Virgin Mary

LXXXV *The first proposition. Luke 1*[834]

What is offered springs from God's favour (says Gabriel to Mary), not from your merit.[835]

CENSURE

If by setting down the liberal beneficence of God with respect to the incarnation it is alleged that the Blessed Virgin in no way merited to be the mother of God – the opposite of which is sung by the church[836] – the proposition is false and derogates from the honour of the most holy Virgin.

CLARIFICATION

LXXXV This is not put forward, and I am not dealing here with merit that contributes to salvation but with the inestimable honour bestowed on the Virgin of giving birth to God. The more modest she was the less she considered herself worthy of this honour, and for that reason she was disturbed and hesitated somewhat at the language of the angel. In order to eliminate this hesitation the angel does not want her to weigh her merits, since no human merit is equal to such a great honour, but rather to consider the gratuitous benevolence of the Deity, who was pleased to have the redeemer of the world born of a humble little virgin. This favour of God the angel calls grace. Moreover, what I add, 'not from your merit,' in so far as it pertains

* * * * *

833 Luke 14:21
834 LB VII 289D
835 Erasmus defended this proposition in *Divinationes ad notata Bedae* LB IX 490E–491B and at some length in *Supputatio* LB IX 597D–600F.
836 The theologians refer to the following hymn: 'Regina coeli laetare, alleluia, / Quia quem meruisti portare, alleluia, / Resurrexit sicut dixit, alleluia, / Ora pro nobis Deum, alleluia' ('Queen of heaven, rejoice, alleluia. / The Son whom you merited to bear, alleluia, / has risen as he said, alleluia. / Pray to God for us, alleluia'). It was sung as an antiphon during the paschal season. It may have been derived from a Christmas antiphon: 'Maria Virgo semper laetare, quae meruisti Christum portare ...' ('O Virgin Mary, rejoice always, for you merited to bear Christ'). See Connelly 46–7.

to weighing the honour against the merit, concerns belonging not to merit but totally to grace.

And then, what is of little importance is not usually taken into account when we are dealing with the most important features. Furthermore, this turn of phrase is frequently found in Holy Scripture whereby it merely asserts something, as, for example, 'they offered sacrifices to demons, not to God.'[837] Sometimes there is a comparison rather than a rejection, as in 'I want mercy, not sacrifice,'[838] meaning 'I want mercy rather than sacrifice.' So too, that statement of Peter in Acts, 'you lied not to a human being but to God.'[839] For if there is no help from a figure of speech, Ananias lied also to a human being. I had no thought whatsoever of merit as understood by the Lutherans. Moreover, it is perfectly clear from hundreds of places in my writings that I do not deny that there is some merit on the part of the pious.

LXXXVI *The second proposition. In* Elenchus[840]

It is not clear to me whether it was fully revealed to the Blessed Virgin during the boyhood and infancy of Christ that he was God and man.

CENSURE

By speaking thus this proposition indicates crass ignorance of the gospels, since it is to be believed that it was fully revealed to the Virgin Mary that Christ was God and man. For this had been sufficiently pointed out to her by the angel, Elizabeth, the kings, the shepherds, and the prophets.[841]

CLARIFICATION

LXXXVI If the gospel manifestly expressed this, I would by no means have said 'it is not clear to me.' This was not fully revealed even to the apostles before they were breathed upon by the Holy Spirit. I also think it was not fully revealed to the Magi, although we read that they adored the Lord and offered mystical gifts.[842] The same can be said of Elizabeth and the

* * * * *

837 1 Cor 10:20
838 Hos 6:6, quoted at Matt 9:13, 12:7
839 Acts 5:4
840 *Elenchus in censuras Bedae* LB IX 499A
841 For the angel see Luke 1:28–35; for Elizabeth see Luke 1:41–5; for the kings see Matt 2:1–12; for the shepherds see Luke 2:8–20; for the prophets see, for example, Isaiah 57, 61, 63.
842 Gold for kingship, frankincense (for divinity?), myrrh (for suffering?)

shepherds. And the prophets proposed such a great mystery covered over and infolded, as it were. And the angel who spoke to Mary did not announce openly that the one that would be born would be true God and true man but that he would be a holy one and the Son of God, language that could also apply to an extraordinary prophet. The Divine Wisdom arranged the revelation of the mystery according to times and persons, in such a way as to be most conducive to the salvation of mankind. The full revelation was reserved to the Holy Spirit. I do not deny that this was also revealed to others in some fashion, and it is pious to believe that it was more fully revealed to the most holy Virgin than to anyone else; I was merely somewhat undecided about whether she had a full revelation of this mystery when Christ was an infant.

And one reason I am so is because of the highly approved Doctors Chrysostom and Augustine, the former of whom attributes to the Virgin some ordinary maternal feelings, as if she had the authority to command him and to be proud of him. Explaining the marriage at Cana in Galilee, he says that the words 'woman, what is that to you and me?'[843] are words of reproach to prevent his mother from saying anything like this in the future, because she had generated only his human body and was not the mother of his divine nature; but to perform miracles belonged to his divine nature. Augustine also, when the Lord had been crucified, attributes to her some lack of belief, though less than that of the apostles.[844] Clearly such things are not consistent with a perfect knowledge of his divinity. When they found him in the temple, it was more fitting for them to adore him and thank him for not withdrawing himself from them than it was to say 'Son, why have you done this to us?'[845] For such language seems reproachful. And at the marriage there was no need to say 'they have no wine.'[846] The mere thought would have been enough for God. Certainly we nowhere read that Christ was adored as God either by his mother or by Joseph when he was an infant. But if what is not clear to me is clear to the church, then it is also clear to me. Moreover, if they had perfect knowledge that he was God, certainly they also knew that he had a Father and by his authority had come to save the human race. Why, then, did they not understand the language of the Son when he said: 'did you not know that I must be about the business of my Father?'[847] Hence the comment of

* * * * *

843 John 2:4
844 *Quaestiones veteris et novi testamenti* 73 PL 35 2267–8
845 Luke 2:48
846 John 2:2
847 Luke 2:49–50

Theophylactus seems superficial when he writes that they were afraid that he would withdraw into heaven, abandoning, that is, his Father's mission.[848]. But if his mother was afraid that he would take offence and depart and therefore said 'Son, why have you done this to us?' then the reply was not fitting and she did not deserve the reproach, 'why is it that you looked for me?' Concerning this passage Ambrose wrote: 'For in other places he urges onward to a mystery; here he reproves his mother because she is still considering what is human.'[849] Moreover, the Greek commentator who is cited in the *Catena aurea* also says as follows: 'When the Lord reproaches Mary for seeking him, he very clearly implies the omission of the ties of blood.'[850] And on these words, 'and they did not understand his words,' Bede adds, 'because he was speaking to them about his divinity.'[851] Such notions are certainly not consistent with someone who knew his divine nature perfectly.

Now Elizabeth did not say 'why has it happened to me that the Mother of my God comes to me?' but 'of my Lord.' She recognized the dignity of the child, perhaps even the divinity, but still, I think, as if through a cloud. Neither Anna nor Simeon expressly referred to the divine nature of Christ, and the old man did not adore the infant but only professed that he was the Messiah.[852] It was said to the apostles, 'the Spirit, the Advocate, will call to your mind all that I have said to you.'[853] What they had perceived in a slumber, as it were, with imperfect understanding and imperfect faith, of these things the Spirit would give them full understanding and full faith. But if the perfect union of the divine nature with the human one is not clearly expressed in the gospels, if the holy doctors seem to have a different opinion about the mother of Jesus than these people do, then when I profess only that I have doubts, I could be instructed without insults. Many burn with a marvellous zeal for the most holy Virgin, vehement in magnifying the gifts bestowed on her; but there are very few who burn with eagerness to imitate her gifts. With what measure the Holy Spirit bestowed his gifts on the Virgin, only the Spirit himself knows completely.

* * * * *

848 *Enarratio in Evangelium Lucae* 2:41–50 PG 123 733C
849 *Expositio Evangelii secundum Lucam libris x comprehensa* 2.64 PL 15 (1845) 1575C
850 *Catena aurea in Lucae Evangelium* 1.13
851 *In Lucae Evangelio expositio* 2.50 PL 92 350B; Erasmus' quotation is accurate enough, though not quite exact.
852 Luke 2:25–38
853 John 14:26

LXXXVII *The third proposition. John 2*[854]

Whenever it is necessary to serve the glory of the Father, there is no need for your intervention.[855]

CENSURE

If this proposition is understood universally, that is, in such a way that at no time is there any need for the intervention of the Blessed Virgin with her Son in divine matters or those concerned with eternal salvation, it is impious and contrary to the liturgy of the church and heretical. For the bountiful Mother of God has been established by her Son as 'the happy gate of heaven,'[856] the loving advocate of sinners,' as the Catholic church sings in accordance with Scripture.

CLARIFICATION

LXXXVII I do not adequately understand what is meant by this censure. How can this language in the paraphrase be taken universally when it is dealing with Mary being reproached because as a mother she requires a miracle though she is not the mother of that nature which performs miracles, and it was not fitting to mingle human authority with a divine enterprise. The explanation given in the paraphrase is to be found among the most approved Doctors of the church,[857] nor is there anything impious about this meaning. If she is now the gate of heaven and the advocate of sinners, my paraphrase is no hindrance to her.

Topic 28. Angels

LXXXVIII *Erasmus' first proposition. In* Elenchus 152[858]

Whether an angel is superior to a human being in an unqualified way I do not know.[859]

* * * * *

854 LB VII 515B / CWE 46 39
855 In *Divinationes ad notata Bedae* LB IX 482C–D Erasmus briefly defended this proposition. In *Supputatio* LB IX 625D–629E he analysed and defended it at great length.
856 'Felix coeli porta' ('happy gate of heaven') is the fourth line in the hymn *Ave maris stella* ('Hail, star of the sea') by an unknown author (though it has sometimes wrongly been attributed to Venantius Fortunatus). It was sung at vespers on feasts of the Blessed Virgin. See Connelly 160–1.
857 See the references to Chrysostom and Augustine in CWE 46 38 n6.
858 *Elenchus in censuras Bedae* LB IX 505D
859 Erasmus defended this proposition very briefly in *Responsio ad notulas Bedaicas*

CENSURE

The ignorance of such a doubt is rightly to be blamed, since Scripture quite openly explains the point which is doubted. In fact, the king and prophet David testifies that the Son of Man is made less than the angels when he says: 'You have made him a little less than the angels.'[860]

CLARIFICATION[861]

LXXXVIII If Scripture clearly expresses the point about which I am in doubt, I will confess my ignorance. But Scripture says something quite different from what they adduce; for Paul does not write 'a little bit' or 'a little less,' but rather βραχύτι, which on the authority of Chrysostom I explained must be referred to time, not to the manner of subordination.[862] Otherwise, when the Lord is captured, charged, condemned, struck, spat upon, and crucified (for in that passage the Apostle is speaking about his passion), he was cast down not only below the angels but also below most human beings. But the text cited there to clarify the dejection of Christ seems to have been spoken in the psalm to clarify the dignity of human nature, which is next to the angels, inferior to them because of the mortality of our bodies and the vulnerability of our souls to pain.

* * * * *

LB IX 712C–D. He discusses the question at great length in *Apologia ad Fabrum* CWE 83 22–75.

860 Heb 2:7, quoting Ps 8:6

861 Pelargus sigs F8–G2 argues that βραχύτι cannot mean 'for a short time' as Erasmus claims but must mean 'a little less' in degree, because one assumes it must have the same meaning in Psalm 8:6 and in Heb 2:7; in the psalm it cannot mean 'for a short time' because that would mean that mankind would ultimately be superior to the angels in heaven. Even during the passion, to which Paul is referring, the human nature which Christ assumed was not inferior to the angels in so far as it became part of the divine hypostasis but only in so far as it contained a body not yet glorified and hence subject to suffering. Pelargus makes distinctions at length, but except for his argument about the Greek word he does not qualify or add much to Erasmus' rather brief clarification.

In the second edition Erasmus adds only a few brief phrases, clauses, and sentences adding the authority of Chrysostom, qualifying his meaning, and extending it slightly.

862 In his annotation on Heb 2:7 Erasmus had called up the authority of Chrysostom and Theophylactus for taking βραχύτι to mean 'for a short time' rather than 'to a small degree'; see Chrysostom *Enarratio in epistolam ad Hebraeos* 4.2 PG 63 39, and Theophylactus *Expositio in epistolam ad Hebraeos* 2:9 PG 125 208D–210A.

But even granted that Christ was made a little less than the angels for
the very reason that he assumed a human body,[863] it does not follow that
an angel is greater than a human being in an unqualified way. For God can
pour such great graces into human nature that it surpasses the angels; for
that is what we believe happened in the case of Jesus' mother, and God
honoured human nature far more than that of angels, namely by taking
on the seed of Abraham, not that of the angels. Finally, no angel sits at
the right hand of God, an honour given to our head and through the head
to all his members in some fashion. They will say that I spoke absolutely
concerning the nature of a human being and an angel. That this is not so is
clear from the words which immediately follow in *Elenchus*: 'Certainly God
vouchsafed more honour to mankind than to angels.'[864] But I understand
'without qualification' to mean 'in every way and without exception.' As
for their ontological status, there is no question that angels are superior to
mankind.

Topic 29. The apostle Peter

LXXXIX *Erasmus' proposition. Matthew 16*[865]

When Peter said to Christ 'you are the Christ, the Son of the living
God,'[866] he professed his certain and undoubted belief that he was
the Messiah promised by the prophets, the Son of God by a certain
unique sort of love.

CENSURE

This proposition explains the meaning of the Gospel wrongly, providing an occasion for falsely understanding the divinity of the Son of
God, as Nestorius did.[867] For Christ is not the Son of God by a certain
unique sort of love of God toward him, nor by adoption and grace,
but by origin and nature.

* * * * *

863 In his annotation on Heb 2:7 Erasmus noted that this was the opinion of
Thomas Aquinas LB VI 985D; see Aquinas *Expositio in epistolam ad Hebraeos* 2.2.9;
but it should be noted that Aquinas also gives the alternate interpretation of
paulo minus as meaning 'for a short time.'
864 *Elenchus in censuras Bedae* LB IX 505D
865 LB VII 92E / CWE 45 245
866 Matt 16:16, Mark 8:29
867 Nestorius was the patriarch of Constantinople (428–31). He promulgated the
heresy that the two natures in Christ (divine and human) are distinct and not
joined in a single personality.

CLARIFICATION

LXXXIX In the first edition of the year 1522, set in small print, and overseen by me, you will find printed 'the Son of God in a unique manner.'[868] I use 'unique' to mean 'applicable only to one person' and 'manner' to mean 'way' or 'mode,' meaning that Christ is said to be the Son of God not in an ordinary sense but in a special way in which no one else can be said to be the Son of God. 'Unique love' is not my error but the printers'. Since I point this out both in *Prologus supputationis* and in *Divinationes*, and in *Elenchus*, and in *Supputationes*,[869] I wonder why the reporters retained this censure, especially since they claim they read *Elenchus* and *Supputationes*. If I had meant that Christ is uniquely beloved of the Father, there would have been no impiety in that opinion, for the simple reason that he is called the 'Son of Charity' and the 'beloved Son.'[870] But nevertheless, I would not have expressed that opinion in such words. As it is, since I both meant and expressed the thoroughly Christian belief that Christ alone among men is by nature God, what is the point of mentioning the Nestorians. But here the faculty has been imposed upon by those who report my writings other than they should have, who are deaf to all replies and hunt only for what they can carp at.

Topic 30. The apostle Paul

XC *Erasmus' proposition. Phil 4[:3]*[871]
I beg you, my true and genuine consort.[872]

CENSURE

The paraphraser in a Latin paraphrase departs temerariously from the common Latin reading which is everywhere followed by the Catholic Doctors Augustine, Jerome, Ambrose, and many others.[873] And Jerome

* * * * *

868 The misprint was *singulari amore* 'unique love' for *singulari more* 'unique manner.'
869 LB IX 446A, 464D–F, 497E–F, 583F–585D
870 Mark 1:11, 9:6; Luke 3:22
871 LB VII 1001E / CWE 43 387
872 Erasmus defended this proposition in *Supputatio* LB IX 692E–693E.
873 The reading of the Vulgate is *germane compar* 'my sincere companion.' Augustine chooses the reading *sororem mulierem* 'sisterly woman,' and says that those who interpret the phrase as meaning *uxorem* 'wife' have been deceived by the ambiguity of the Greek word; see *De opere monachorum* 4.5 PL 40 0522. For Ambrose's view that Paul was unmarried see *Exhortatio virginitatis* 4.22 PL 16 (1845) 342D–343A. For Jerome see the next note. See also CWE 43 387 n3.

thinks we ought not to listen to those who imagine that Paul had a wife, because Paul wishes that all be like himself. Likewise, speaking of the unmarried and widows, he says it is a good thing for them to remain as he himself is,[874] and he would by no means have said such a thing if he himself had a wife.

CLARIFICATION

xc My paraphrase does not remove the reading of the church, but, leaving it intact, it points out that either opinion can be derived from the words of the Apostle. And I have no lack of authorities of whom, on this point at least, I have no lower opinion than I do of Augustine. For Clement, pope and martyr, uses this very passage to prove that Paul had a wife, though he did not take her around with him, following the example of Peter. Since he was nearer to the time of the apostles and more familiar with them, he could know about them all the more certainly than those who followed after him some centuries later.[875] The passage in 1 Cor 7 is not compelling, as I made sufficiently clear in *Annotations*.[876] For when he says 'I want all of you to be as I am,' it is clear that he is talking to those who are married and urging them by his example to practise free and perpetual continence, although he does not dare to demand it from the weak. Right afterwards he goes on to widowers and widows, urging them also by his example to persevere in celibacy and out of a love of holiness to disdain the pleasure they have experienced, as he himself did. I have not yet investigated whether Paul's wife was at that time dead but certainly he wants them to be similar to himself in refraining from the pleasure they have experienced. Then he comes back to those who are married but abstain from the marital act not out of a love of holiness but because of human obstacles. After this he goes on to virgins, and here he makes no mention of himself. But if Paul was a virgin or if he never had a wife, here was the place where he should most appropriately have said 'it is good for them to remain as I am.'

But at this point I am pressed by the authority of Jerome, Augustine, and Ambrose. But though I follow their interpretation in so many places, I am not supported by their authority. Those who were Paul's contemporaries say he had a wife. The place in the Epistle is not compelling, as I explained. How, then, did they establish that he was a virgin?

* * * * *

874 1 Cor 7:8; Jerome *Epistolae* 22.20 PL 22 407
→ n   875 See n573 above.
876 LB VI 687C–688C

Topic 31. Dionysius the Aeropagite

XCI *The proposition of Erasmus in the prefatory epistle to the paraphrase on 1 Corinthians*[877]

The Dionysius who describes very fully the ancient liturgies of the church in the second part of *The Hierarchies*, that is, the part concerning the church, seems to the learned to be someone more recent than that Areopagite.[878]

CENSURE

It is not to the truly learned but rather to the temerarious and the pursuers of novelty that the person who wrote *The Ecclesiastical Hierarchies* does not seem to be Dionysius the Aeropagite. In fact, it is clear that it was written by Dionysius the Aeropagite himself: first, from *The Ecclesiastical Hierarchies* itself and from other books by the same author; and then it is proved by the testimony of famous men; lastly it is made quite clear by the seventh general synod, in which the person who wrote *The Ecclesiastical Hierarchies* is called Dionysius the Great.[879]

CLARIFICATION

XCI I have long since ceased to argue about this prologue, although this point was set down by me in very few words and in the name of other persons;[880] and when Josse Clichtove assailed it with tooth and nail, I kept quiet, not because I had no arguments but because I thought that this dispute contributes nothing to the business of the faith and does not have much to do with holiness.[881] As for the argument which they consider to be

* * * * *

877 LB VII 849–50 / CWE 43 4
878 Erasmus touched very briefly on this proposition in *Divinationes ad notata Bedae* LB IX 472B–C, in *Elenchus in censuras Bedae* LB IX 506A, and in *Supputatio* LB IX 675E–676B.
879 The seventh ecumenical council (the second Council of Nicaea), canon 7, quotes from *The Ecclesiastical Hierarchies*, assigning the work to Dionysius the Great; see *Conciliorum Oecumenicorum Decreta* ed Joseph Alberigo et al (Freiburg im Breisgau 1962) 116.
880 That is, Erasmus attributed the opinion about the false identity of Dionysius to 'others' in the sense of the learned in general, not to himself in particular.
881 Josse Clichtove (1472/3–1543), a moderate theologian, a follower and defender of Lefèvre d'Etaples, and a supporter of humanism before the Lutheran revolt, attacked Erasmus by name in his *Antilutherus*, published in 1524,

irrefutable, namely that certain points are included in the books which convince them that they were written by the Areopagite, someone else could very easily discredit it. He would say that whoever wrote those books took great care to make them seem as if they were written by that great Dionysius. Such an idea does not seem absurd, since in that era there were swarms of such books everywhere falsely ascribed to famous men in order to recommend them. For at that time even pious men were persuaded that it would be pleasing to God if such a pretence would encourage the populace to become eager readers.

Furthermore, as for what they say about no one having any doubts except the temerarious and the uneducated, I do not know what they think about Lorenzo Valla. I do not care what they think of me. I will set forth at least one person to whom neither ignorance nor temerity can be attributed. That was the Englishman William Grocyn, a man who, while he was alive, lived with the greatest asceticism and chastity, observed most religiously the regulations of the church (almost to the point of superstition), was thoroughly learned in scholastic theology, naturally endowed with very penetrating judgment, and (in short) thoroughly versed in all fields of learning. Thirty years ago in London, at the church dedicated to St Paul, he began to lecture to a very large audience on *The Ecclesiastical Hierarchies*, and in his prefatory remarks he vented his anger at those who denied it was by that Areopagite, singling out, I think, Lorenzo Valla. But when he had already lectured for some weeks and in the process had examined the character of the author more closely and more intimately, he did not hesitate to retract[882] his former opinion before the same audience, professing that

* * * * *

for denying that the Dionysius converted by Paul was also the author of *The Ecclesiastical Hierarchies*; in doing so Erasmus was reaffirming a position already taken by Lorenzo Valla in his annotations on the New Testament, which Erasmus had discovered in manuscript and published in 1505. In *Antilutherus* Clichtove also attacked some other positions of Erasmus, but without giving his name; Béda triumphantly pointed out that Erasmus was the intended target (Ep 1642). Erasmus did not find Clichtove to be a kindred spirit, but he admired his restraint and honesty, especially by comparison with Béda. On Erasmus' discussion of Béda's accusations about Dionysius, see CEBR on Clichtove and J.-P. Massaut *Critique et tradition à la veille de la Réforme en France* (Paris 1974) 179–229. See also *Elenchus* 157–8 LB IX 506A, *Prologus supputationis* LB IX 449B, *Supputatio* LB IX 675F–676A, and Ep 1620. See also *Appendix de scriptis Clithovei* and *Dilutio* CWE 83 109–48.

882 *Adagia* I ix 59

it by no means seemed to him to be by Dionysius the Aeropagite.[883] The memory of Grocyn is still fresh;[884] I can easily be refuted if I am not telling the truth. Finally, he can be called 'the great' even if he is not the disciple of Paul. For Basil was also called 'the great' and many others as well.

Topic 32. Scholastic theology

XCII *The first proposition of Erasmus. In the prefatory epistle to the* Paraphrase on the Epistle to the Ephesians[885]

Theology now begins to be a skill rather than wisdom, really more theatrical than adapted to true holiness. Apart from ambition and avarice, it has been corrupted by other plagues: flattery, quarrelsomeness, and superstition. Through these vices it has finally come to the point where that pure and simple Christ has almost been overwhelmed by human subtleties,[886] the springs of the gospel, once crystal clear, have been choked off by the ditch of the Philistines, and the rule of Holy Scripture, twisted one way and then another, has served our feelings rather than the glory of Christ.[887] Certainly some pious-minded persons have tried to call the world back to that pristine academic simplicity and to bring us back from puddles which are now mostly muddy to those living and most pure wellsprings. The knowledge of languages and of good literature (as they say)[888] has seemed to be especially conducive to reaching that goal; neglecting them seems to have brought us to this falling off.[889]

CENSURE

This proposition has three parts. The first, which alleges that scholastic

* * * * *

883 In his *Annotations* on Acts 17:34 Erasmus gives his basic arguments against identifying the author of *The Ecclesiastical Hierarchies* with Paul's convert and reports the same story about Grocyn's recantation (LB VI 503C–F).
884 Grocyn died in 1519.
885 LB VII 967–70 / CWE 43 287
886 *Argutatio* in classical Latin meant only 'a creaking.' It does not appear in medieval dictionaries, but it is an easy formation from *argutus* 'subtle.'
887 Erasmus briefly defended these propositions in *Divinationes ad notata Bedae* LB IX 476E–477C.
888 Latin *bonae (vt vocant) litterae*. The phrase became almost a watchword of the humanists, indicating the literature of the new learning as distinct from the bad writing they wished to displace.
889 Erasmus briefly defended this proposition in *Supputatio* LB IX 691D–692D.

theology is an art which deals with human rather than divine matters and is more adapted to worldly spectacles than to holiness, is wrongly asserted by this writer, as are many other points, in order to heap ignominy upon it. For although it sometimes receives assistance from human disciplines, it does not do so without adapting such assistance to the investigation of theological truth. But if some persons delay too long in foreign disciplines, their fault should not immediately be attributed to theology, since there are many very illustrious doctors who have enlightened the whole world with their brilliant teachings; if this writer had been imbued with them, he could easily have avoided the various and shameful errors he has mixed into his books. Moreover, if theological disputations are ordinarily held before large audiences, that does not immediately mean that theology should be called theatrical; for it is advantageous to handle such matters in public in order to attend to the needs of many persons by clarifying and defending theological truths and eliminating the errors opposed to them.

The second part, beginning with the words 'Apart from ambition, etc' and alleging that the scholastic Doctors have corrupted Scripture in their expositions and have distorted it just as they wished, to support not the truth but human feelings, is devoid of truth and clearly indicates the shameless impudence of the one who proclaims it. For the approved scholastic Doctors follow no other understanding of Scripture than that which orthodox exegetes hold and have held up to this time, although they sometimes differ on some points which are not matters of faith or do not need to be explicitly believed.

The third part, beginning with the words 'Certainly some pious-minded persons, etc,' alleges two things. One is that scholastic theology has eliminated academic simplicity; it is clear that this is manifestly false, since theology is concerned with faith and morals, the correct knowledge of which constitutes academic simplicity most of all. The other is that such academic simplicity is restored by skill in languages and literary culture – which need not be granted at all. For, although these things make some contribution to theology, they nevertheless do not do so in so far as it is scholastic theology, which is primarily concerned with meaning, not with verbal correctness, which it presupposes[890] as coming from grammar.

* * * * *

890 Latin *praesupponit* is not a classical word. It had been used in the Middle Ages; see R.E. Latham *Revised Medieval Latin Word-List* (London 1965).

CLARIFICATION

XCII This censure rests on the foundation that I condemn theology itself in an unqualified way; if this is true, whatever is said here applies to the whole class of theologians. But if theology is the understanding of the Sacred Volumes, what madness would it be to condemn that which, after God, is the best and most blessed thing the church has? Therefore it is clear that I am not condemning the profession itself but rather certain persons who handle the best subject but not in the best way. In not a few places I bear witness to this point expressly and explicitly. And in the preface this is what I say: 'Theology now begins to be a skill.' And I add ambition, avarice, flattery, quarrelsomeness, and superstition, certainly not branches of learning but human vices by which that profession has been somewhat corrupted. Someone who says 'now' points out that the study of theology has deteriorated. Someone who says it is corrupted does not condemn its nature. But if someone were to speak in this way, 'now the mass begins to be the income and the provisions of ignorant and vile persons,' he does not condemn the mass but the morals of men; so too my language offers no more injury to theology, whether scholastic or not scholastic. Accordingly, what is spoken generally applies not to all theologians but to those whom I describe as follows: 'And gradually,' I say, 'it supplanted true theology, so much so that most theologians neglected skill in languages and literary culture and even the Divine Volumes themselves, and they grew old and grey in the pursuit of curious, superfluous, and excessive quibbles, as if lured to the reefs of the Sirens. Theology now begins to be a skill rather than wisdom, really more theatrical than adapted to true holiness, etc.'[891] Someone who says 'most theologians' denotes the ordinary run, not the whole profession. If there are not or have not been in former times any theologians who are more concerned with dignities than with Christ, who handle the word of God with little integrity because of greed for money, who distort Scripture to curry favour with bishops and other princes, who prefer to defend what is false rather than abandon their opinion, who attribute too much to externals, which do not constitute true holiness, and neglect those things which are more relevant to salvation, who grow old in the pursuit of curious questions, then Erasmus can rightly be convicted of vacuity. But if there are far too many mobs of such persons everywhere, to point this out is a duty owed to the profession of theology, not contempt for it.

* * * * *

891 LB VII 967–8 / CWE 43 286

And so when they say that if one theologian or another commits some fault, it is not to be attributed to theology itself, they clearly agree with me. For I have everywhere thought and said the same thing. Am I the first to complain about the morals of theologians or the deterioration of studies? Did not Jean Gerson in the second part of his sermon 'On the Four Houses' complain about corrupt theology in the following words: 'Concerning theology, not that which is reduced to wordy and sophistical loquacity and some sort of chimerical mathematics, but that which harvests the faith and sets morals in order'? This is what he says. But I suspect that the copyists have introduced an error in this sermon; for I think he wrote 'nourishes' rather than 'harvests.'[892] In the first part of his readings on Mark, when he condemns the ostentation of some persons who defend in public disputations propositions which are true according to the rigour of logic but false according to those who profess rhetoric or politics, he gives some examples: 'the church, continuing to be the church, can err'; 'God and a creature are nothing.' Then he adds: 'Certainly those who bring up such pure logic or philosophy or mathematics before such persons in public functions are acting imprudently, not to say impudently.' And a bit further on: 'Finally, why are the theologians of our times called sophistical, verbose, or even fantastical, except that, passing over what would be useful and intelligible according to the character of their audience, they betake themselves to pure logic, or metaphysics, or even mathematics, at an inappropriate place and time, etc.'[893] Likewise in the same part he says, concerning true and false visions: 'A spiritual adviser should be a theologian of this mettle, skilled both in theory and practice, not like those who are always learning but never arrive at the knowledge of truth, garrulous, verbose, impudent, quarrelsome, and (in short) abandoned to the most corrupt behaviour, etc.'[894] If such complaints, which are frequently found in this writer, who is weighty and pleasing to the Paris theologians, do no injury to scholastic theology, why am I said to condemn it when much more indigestible things are heard in our times, not only in scholastic discussions but even in sermons in church?[895]

* * * * *

892 *nutrit* rather than *metit*
893 Gerson 'De duplica logica' on Mark 1:5 in *Oeuvres complètes* III 60–1
894 Gerson 'De distinctione verarum revelationum a falsis' on Mark 1:4 in *Oeuvres complètes* III 38–9. I have not been able to find the sermon on the Four Houses to which Erasmus refers.
895 Erasmus gives many examples of such subtle and useless questions in *The Praise of Folly* CWE 27 126–8, 133–4.

But, they say, he reproves only pseudo-theologians. God forbid that he should do otherwise. But when he says 'the theologians of our time,' does he not seem to blame all of them, or most of them? And I do not see why they thought it necessary to mention that there are 'very illustrious Doctors who have enlightened the whole world with their brilliant teachings,' as if anyone would deny it, but I am only complaining that there are so few of them. And I do not call scholastic theology theatrical because it is presented publicly, for that would be to condemn the whole scholastic enterprise, but rather because in those discussions, especially the well-attended ones where the baccalaureate and licentiate degrees are conferred, many points are often proposed which are designed to display ingenuity and which are neither necessary nor useful. The theologians themselves will not, I think, deny that this is true. So much for the first part of the proposition.

As for the second part, we are in agreement. They say: 'For the approved scholastic Doctors follow no other understanding of Scripture than that which orthodox exegetes hold and have held up to this time.' I have always thought the same about approved theologians, but my quarrel is with those not approved, although approved theologians also frequently disagree with the orthodox exegetes; in my writings they sometimes call something impious and blasphemous which is clearly expressed in books by such exegetes. The reason is that not very many of them read the ancients.

What remains is the third part, in which they find fault with two points: one is that I seem to mean that academic simplicity is eliminated by scholastic theology; the other, that I indicate that academic simplicity could be restored by skill in languages and literary culture. I reply that, through the fault of some practitioners, we have a theology which is thorny with superfluous difficulties. Let anyone deny this after he has considered how much human philosophy Thomas and those like him have imported into theology, how much thorny matter Scotus also added on his part, to say nothing of the others. But at the same time I hardly know whether we agree about the word 'simplicity.' To me simplicity is opposed to curious subtleties; but they think simplicity consists in the correct understanding of faith and morals, identifying simplicity with soundness. On the second point we are clearly in agreement that scholastic theology would contribute more to academic simplicity if it abandoned ambitious and superfluous difficulties and concerned itself above all with the sources themselves; but to do this a knowledge of languages is almost necessary, not merely contributory. What they attribute to me is their concern. Certainly I am not, I think, totally unversed in the best authorities. And if scholastic theology is so powerful that it does not allow anyone to fall into error,

I wonder from where John Huss and Wyclif, and also Luther, Oecolampadius, and Balthasar,[896] drank up such a quantity of erroneous bilgewater, since they were all imbued with scholastic theology. As for what they say about my many shameful errors, I do not deny that my learning is not up to snuff and I am not unwilling to admit to human lapses, but even more such lapses could sometimes be found in the writings of the ancient orthodox Doctors, if someone considered them according to the standards of scholastic doctrine and with similar candour and fairness. And perhaps it is even more shameful that those who are held to be and wish to be considered consummate theologians make so many mistakes not by the by but with great authority and arrogance, making their pronouncement not without atrocious insults. But I would not wish this to be said about the faculty. Nevertheless there is no lack of those who will think that for such an illustrious group excuses such as the following are not adequate: 'the copyist erred,' 'this is how it was reported to us,' 'on the face of it the proposition seems to allege this,' 'this proposition understood in this or that fashion.' For the opinion of such a group ought to be clear and blameless.

[XCIII] *The second proposition. In the preface to his Hilary and what follows*[897]
Those who are no more than human have thought up a strange divinity in theological matters; and this divinity has certainly stirred up more questions and horrible uproars throughout the world than the recklessness of the Arians[898] once did.

CENSURE
Though scholastic theology has faithfully set down the truths of Catholicism in a brief and compendious form and trained its practitioners in such a way that they do not easily fall into errors, this writer in this proposition erroneously and recklessly disparages scholastic teaching, perversely doing as much as he can to draw people away from the study of it, which is useful and necessary, as is shown by holy councils, which have approved of the study of it in general and of the schools assigned by them for such training in theology, and they have endowed them with many privileges and immunities.

* * * * *

896 For Huss see n487; for Wyclif see n87; for Oecolampadius see n489; for Balthasar see n488.
897 CWE 9 Ep 1334:239–43
→ n   898 See n13 above.

CLARIFICATION

XCIII The proposition given here is not only foreshortened but also distorted. The passage in the preface is as follows: 'And in this matter some persons have recognized no limit, so that after leaving nothing undefined in theology, they have thought up a new divinity in those who are nothing more than human, etc.' First of all, someone who says 'some persons' does not mean the whole profession of the theologians. And I am speaking here about those who attribute too much to the Roman pontiff; and I know that the theologians do not approve of such flattery. That is made sufficiently clear by the little book in which they replied to Cardinal Cajetanus.[899] Furthermore, what I said has been unfairly twisted so as to apply to all of scholastic theology. And so those words, 'erroneous, temerarious, perversely drawing people away,' are nothing but insults aimed at me, though I never either wrote or said or meant any such thing. But how can the faculty make any correct pronouncements if the matter set before them is misrepresented?

XCIIII *His third proposition. In the same preface to his Hilary*[900]

How will we have the effrontery to ask for pardon when we raise so many curious, not to say impious, questions about matters so far removed from our nature, when we define so many points which can be either ignored or left ambiguous with no impairment of our salvation. Will a person have no fellowship with the Father and the Son and the Holy Spirit if he does not know how to disentangle according to the method of philosophy the question of what distinguishes the Father from the Son, what distinguishes the Holy Spirit from either of them, what is the difference between the birth of the Son from the Father and the procession of the Spirit?

* * * * *

899 In 1511 Cajetanus (Tommaso de Vio) wrote *De comparatione auctoritatis Papae et Concilii* in opposition to the schismatic Council of Pisa, which had been convened to assert the superiority of councils to the papacy. King Louis XII of France turned it over to the University of Paris so that it could refute it and assert the Gallican principal of conciliarism. The reply, *De auctoritate Ecclesiae, seu sacrorum Conciliorum eam repraesentatium, contra Thomam de Vio, Dominicanum* (Paris: Jean Granjon 1512), by Jacques Almain, was answered by Cajetanus in the same year in *Apologia de comparata auctoritate Papae et Concilii*. See *De comparatione auctoritatis Papae et Concilii* ed Vincent Pollet (Rome 1936) 3–4.

900 CWE 9 Ep 1334:173–82

xcv *His fourth proposition. In the same place*[901]

You will not be damned if you do not know whether the Spirit, when he arises from the Father and the Son, springs from one principle or two.

CENSURE

Although it is certain that simple people can be saved without a deep understanding of these mysteries, nevertheless the assertion of these propositions, in which (as is clear from what precedes them) the author implies that the studies and investigation of the Doctors, whereby, with the help and cooperation of God, they clarify and explain such divine mysteries, are superfluous and useless, is injurious to Augustine, Hilary, Jerome, Ambrose, Basil, [Gregory] Nazianzen, Chrysostom, and others, who, it is well known, did not labour in vain when they handled such subject matter. Moreover, the aforesaid propositions display contempt for holy general councils, which frequently rendered decisions, definitions, or rather clarifications out of Scripture concerning such matters as the Trinity and the consubstantiality of the Divine Persons because of the misrepresentations put forth by heretics, even though before such definitions and clarifications the church had no doubts about them.

CLARIFICATIONS

xcɪɪɪɪ, xcv Because it is clear that those ancient teachers, whenever they were forced to philosophize about the nature of God, most scrupulously asked for pardon, having spoken about this topic, I add 'how will we have the effrontery, etc.' This passage is no more than a complaint about those who raise curious and almost impious questions about similar subjects and define many points which can be either ignored or left ambiguous with no impairment of our salvation. That this is true of many persons the theologians themselves know; they are not unaware that such things are done and they do not approve of them. I do not disapprove of necessary and sober questions about the nature of God, especially if they are undertaken with fear and trembling and according to the pronouncements of Scripture. I blame curious and superfluous questions, and then I give two examples: one is what distinguishes the Father from the Son and the Holy Spirit from both; the other is whether the Father and the Son, when they breathe forth

* * * * *

901 CWE 9 Ep 1334:220–2

the third Person, are one principle or two. If you do not like these, there are ready at hand innumerable questions which are unqualifiedly curious and superfluous, some of them in the books of the theologians, some heard in the usual discussions, and some in sermons in church.

Since nothing of this sort is found in the writings of the ancients, who nevertheless ask for pardon very scrupulously when they are about to speak of matters which are beyond human understanding, I have done nothing injurious to either the holy Doctors or the councils. I do not blame either sober examinations or necessary definitions; I criticize only curious and irreligious investigations. And so what injury does my proposition do to holy Doctors such as Augustine, Hilary, and the rest, since they themselves confess that they cannot answer the question about the procession of the Holy Spirit, and that the manner of that procession must be believed rather than disputed about?[902] St Basil confesses the same thing in his book *On the Holy Spirit*.[903] Certainly the reason added by Augustine is brilliant: no one is born except from two persons, a father and a mother.[904] How then was Christ born of a virgin? Or why is it necessary that a divine birth should match a human one in every way?

Then again, my preface is not speaking of a pious and religious examination drawn from Holy Scripture, but about those who decide such questions with the assistance of human philosophy; 'if he does not know,' it says, 'how to disentangle according to the method of philosophy the question of what distinguishes the Father from the Son, etc.' What truly pious person can read without being scandalized the comments, opinions, doubts, disagreement, quarrels which Scotus, Gabriel,[905] and other modern theologians have introduced about the distinction of

* * * * *

902 Augustine admits that he cannot distinguish generation (as applied to the Son) from procession (as applied to the Holy Spirit) in *Contra Maximinum haereticum Arianorum episcopum* 2.14.1 PL 42 770–1; Hilary admits to the same inability in *De Trinitate* 12.55–6 PL 10 468C–471A.

903 *Liber de Spiritu Sancto* 18.44–6 PG 32 148–53

904 Erasmus seems to be paraphrasing Augustine here rather than quoting him. He may be thinking of the passage where Augustine draws the analogy between father, mother, and child in discussing how man was made in the image of the Trinity; see *De Trinitate* 12.6.8 PL 42 1002–3.

905 Gabriel Biel (c 1418–1495), a nominalist theologian and follower of Ockham, taught at the University of Tübingen and wrote a well-known commentary on the *Sentences* of Peter Lombard. His writings had a considerable influence on Luther. See Heiko A. Oberman *The Harvest of Medieval Theology: Gabriel and Late Medieval Nominalism* (Cambridge, Mass 1963).

Persons? In my preface I am complaining about such things, not about sober investigation.

xcvi *His fifth proposition. In the same preface to his Hilary*[906]

The points which we investigate and define are neither brought forth from Scripture, so that even if we cannot understand them we certainly ought to believe them, nor can they be proved by any arguments, conceived by any thought process, or represented as they actually are by providing any comparisons. Though the most brilliant minds have long striven with all their might to investigate them, in the final analysis all that they gain at last is to understand that they know nothing. And they contribute so little to pious living that that text from Paul was never more appropriate: 'Knowledge puffs up; charity builds up.'[907]

CENSURE

It is clear that what the Catholic Doctors and holy councils have investigated and defined concerning what must be believed about the most blessed Trinity and the divine Persons is contained in Holy Scripture, and that it is not out of place for them to set forth reasons, persuasions, comparisons, and guideposts[908] to make such great mysteries understood in some fashion. Such labour is not at all useless or fruitless but contributes a great deal to the piety of the Christian religion; this labour is gained not by knowledge which puffs up, as this writer temerariously asserts, but by charity which builds up.

* * * * *

906 CWE 9 Ep 1334:202–12
907 1 Cor 8:1. Erasmus devoted a large section of his *Antibarbarorum liber* to interpretation of this passage. He argues that Paul's intention was not to decry knowledge but to make a point about how to win converts to the new faith: 'The charity which makes concessions is more pleasing to heaven than proud knowledge which cannot give way. It is in this way that he says knowledge puffs up, if you deliberately offend your brother; and that charity builds up, if with no harm to yourself you concede something to your brother's weakness – not to mention that this situation was peculiar to their times. Superstition was too deeply rooted from past generations to be suddenly discarded, and for the establishment of the gospel teaching it was necessary to be considerate in every way' (CWE 23 72).
908 Latin *manuductiones*, not a classical word but an easy formation from the classical *manuductor* 'guide.' It had already been used in medieval times to mean 'the action of guiding'; see Albert Blaise *Lexicon Latinitatis medii aevi* (Turnhout 1975).

CLARIFICATION

xcvi This censure would be just if I had written against approved Doctors of the church, or about points which the authority of the church, drawing upon the mysterious writing of Scripture, has prescribed that we must believe about the Holy Trinity, and not about curious, vainglorious, and superfluous disputations concerning the mysteries of the divine essence. If they deny that there are any such, I will bring forth hundreds of examples from the books of the scholastics. Moreover, the noisesomeness of these quibbles, which are neither necessary nor comprehensible, is increased by the amazing intensity with which they quarrel with one another. Likewise, since the earlier censures rest on a false foundation, as I said, imagining that I am saying these things against theology itself and against the whole profession of the theologians, they have nothing to do with me. I confess that the study of theology is the most salutary of all studies; I love sound theologians with all my heart. I complain only about those features which I do not think would be approved by any approved theologian.

The Conclusion of This Work

xcvii And so this is what we judge should be determined about the assertions put forth by Erasmus. We have expressed these points at some length so that all may recognize more completely how absurd and foolish are the shameless, bold, and sacrilegious assertions of impious heretics in the past, Arians, Aerians, Waldensians, Beguards, Turelupini, Wyclifites,[909] and in our time Erasmus and the Lutherans, against the definitions and institutions of the church, and in order that they may completely reject them and their pestilent errors and adhere only to the Catholic church, which in matters of faith and morals cannot err. For in these matters she is always guided by the Holy Spirit. For this reason the Apostle writes that the church is the pillar and the bulwark of truth.[910] Hence it is perfectly clear that those who struggle against her diverge shamefully from the truth, as even the rude and uneducated, when they read these censures, may easily perceive.

* * * * *

909 For the Arians see n13 above; for the Aerians see n70 above; for the Waldensians see n72 above; for the Beguards see nn364 and 667 above; for the Turelupini see n480 above; for the Wyclifites see n87 above.
910 1 Tim 3:15

Reasons, then, are given and the testimony of the Divine Volumes is cited so that the determinations can be manifest and not ineffective. Wherefore the impiety of those who strive to such a degree to introduce grave new errors under the pretext of restoring the purity of Christianity and sound doctrine is confounded. Moreover, it was necessary to assist the weakness of those who think that whatever is set forth in brilliant and splendid language is also true, and that, on the other hand, whatever is written in rude and unpolished language is false, paying no attention to the fact that there is no less difference between one and the other than between jars and what they contain, which is often very great. For sometimes a golden jar, which is similar to ornate speeches, contains deadly poison, whereas it is clear that an earthenware jar, which is comparable to unadorned language, contains a wholesome liquid.

It was also necessary to attend to those who think that perfect and peerless theology consists in knowing Greek and Hebrew writings, whereas in fact those who know these languages, if they are not otherwise trained in the discipline of theology, should be considered grammarians, not theologians, just like those who have mastered Latin literature but progressed no further. And so, to take all of these facets into account and to show them the truth more clearly and effectively, it was worthwhile to handle the matter at some length. For in this way, for the most part, the true meaning of Scripture is revealed, the springs of heresies are dried up, and the tricks and falsities of heretics are uncovered. In this way also the dangers which arise from suspected books, or from those which, however elegantly and beautifully they are written, are nevertheless not lacking in the poison of the condemned teachings of Wyclif and Luther, are avoided.

Given in our meeting at the College of the Sorbonne, after long and mature discussion, on the 17th day of December, in the year of our Lord 1527[911]

Response to the Conclusion

XCVII I do not know who was the author of this conclusion, but he has intermingled my name, hatefully enough, with the name of Luther, without

* * * * *

911 This decision does not appear in Farge *Procès-verbaux*.

my deserving it, since in all the propositions there is not even one in which I agree with Luther or tear apart the definitions or institutions of the church, so that the faculty has condemned what was falsely reported or what some persons wrongly suspect rather than what I wrote. Although the words 'Erasmus and the Lutherans' are an outrageous insult, nevertheless I bear it with more equanimity because the intelligent reader will easily guess who the grandstander is who has mixed into these censures poison from his breast,[912] who with such insults disgraces his college more than my name, since it is abundantly clear from my writings that I never agree with impious heretics. May the Lord grant him and his fellow conspirators a healthier attitude. I do not now treat him as he deserves out of deference to the authority of the faculty, which I wish to see increased, not diminished.

Indeed I applaud their vigilance in admonishing everyone to reject errors and cleave to the church, which cannot err, but, it should be added, 'only in those things which are necessary for salvation.' But Erasmus has never knowingly diverged from this church by so much as a hair's breadth,[913] vigorously struggling against those in whose camp some wish to place me. They are also right to warn that what is elegantly expressed is not necessarily godly; but what is issued in uncultivated language is also not necessarily godly. Certainly they are quite right to warn that a person who has mastered the Latin or Greek language should not necessarily be considered a perfect theologian. For that requires meditating day and night on the law of the Lord and reading all the best authorities, and that is a matter of not a few years and not a little labour.

* * * * *

912 Erasmus means his archenemy, Noël Béda, syndic of the theological faculty of the University of Paris.
913 Literally, 'by a straw's breadth' *Adagia* I v 6

SOME ADDITIONAL PROPOSITIONS
OF ERASMUS SINGLED OUT
FOR CENSURE

There follow some propositions of Erasmus, singled out for censure by the same Faculty of Theology but not turned over to the printer because of the negligence of the copyist. Because they could not be inserted in the proper places, the faculty thought they should be added at the end.

To Topic 17.[914] **On confidence in good works and merit**
These two propositions should be added from Erasmus' tract *On the Mercy of God*.

I *The first proposition*
To how many evils are those susceptible who put their confidence in their own merits and deeds!

II *The second proposition*
Lord, how you have encompassed us with the shield of your good will! When you hear 'good will,' says Erasmus, you should understand that confidence in merits is excluded.[915]

CENSURE
It is well known that confidence in merits is twofold: one is perverse and to be avoided, namely that which attributes more to its own righteousness and merits than to the grace and mercy of God; it is swollen

* * * * *

914 The Latin has VII. The printer apparently omitted the x in XVII.
915 These two propositions from *Concio de immensa Dei misericordia* can be found at LB V 570B–C / CWE 70 101. In the first the theologians' citation omits after 'confidence' 'in dotibus corporis, in opibus, in curibus, in equis, in mundana prudentia' ('in bodily gifts, in wealth, in benefices, in horses, in worldly prudence').

with arrogance and scorns others as if it had its merits from itself and its own power, not from the grace and mercy of God; it is also enfeebled by ingratitude, giving no thanks to God who bestows all good things, ignoring the fact that he is the principal source of merits, good thoughts, feelings, and operations. 'For we are not,' as the Apostle writes, 'adequate to think of anything by ourselves as if by our own power, but our adequacy is from God who works the desire and the execution in us,'[916] but who works them in us in such a way that we also work together with him. To show this the Apostle asserts that the labour of the faithful is not useless and he warns them not to receive the grace of God in vain.[917] In himself he says that this grace of God is not in vain but works together with him;[918] hence it is clear that the human will has its action in good works, although the primary and principal action in good works is certainly owing to God and his grace, not to the human will or to free choice; by ascribing the principal action to itself, this empty, ungodly, ungrateful, and presumptuous confidence in merits or good works removes itself far away from the fountain of divine mercy and therefore it is to be avoided.

But the other kind of confidence in merits or good works is godly, humble, and not ungrateful, as was fully explained before concerning the second proposition under this topic.[919] And this confidence is not only useful for all Christian adults but also necessary; for the faithful who are adults are obliged to believe that good works together with God's grace are necessary and required to possess eternal life. They are also obliged to desire that same eternal life and to produce such good works in order to obtain it. Furthermore, they are required to judge that the blessed Lord will reward those good works as he himself has decreed and as is manifest from Scripture. The Apostle explains it clearly; for when he has first given a general description of his good works, saying 'I have fought the good fight, I have finished the race, I have kept the faith,' he immediately adds, 'as for the rest, a crown of righteousness is laid up for me, which the Lord, the just judge, will present to me on that day.'[920] And to keep anyone from thinking that the reward, the crown of blessed immortality, must be presented only

* * * * *

916 2 Cor 3:5
917 1 Cor 15:58; 2 Cor 6:6
918 Phil 2:16
919 See 176–7 above.
920 2 Tim 4:7–8

because of his good works, he adds that it is to be attributed not only to himself but also to those who love the coming of the Lord, that is, to the faithful who have laboured well in this life and who look forward to the coming of the Lord. Accordingly, the faithful should do good works in this life according to the determination of the Apostle and by doing good works have a firm expectation of being rewarded by the Lord. Otherwise they will lack the confidence of Catholic hope, without which adults are not saved. Wherefore, if the aforesaid propositions should reject and deny this sort of confidence in merits and good works, they would support the impiety of Luther; but not so if they are understood to apply to the first kind of confidence, which, as we said, is to be totally rejected.

CLARIFICATION

Now we come to the appended propositions which some drowsy copyist of the theologians did not hand over to Bade in time, even though he had five years to write them out.[921] And it is amazing that by chance these eight were left over when the conclusion of the work had already been printed. Who does not understand this chicanery, or rather this vesperial jesting?[922] Who does not understand that it was done deliberately to tie Erasmus and Luther inextricably together? – so that Erasmus should lead off as the chief at the front and also follow in the rear, and the unlearned might think he is the alpha and omega[923] of this enterprise.[924] Certainly a marvellous gravity on the part of such craftsmen!

ON THE FIRST AND SECOND PROPOSITIONS

There I teach nothing other than that confidence should be placed in the mercy of God rather than in our merits and deeds. And by confidence I

* * * * *

921 That is, the time between the original formulation of the censures in 1526 and their publication in 1531. Josse Bade was the Parisian printer of *Determinatio*.
922 Latin *jocos vesperiales*. The *vesperia* was the final proceeding in the conferral of a doctorate in theology by the Paris faculty; it consisted of the candidate's defence of theses against three examiners. Erasmus considers these last censures as the final, parting shots. See Charles du Fresne du Cange et al *Glossarium mediae et infimae Latinitatis* 6 vols (Paris 1840–6), sv *vesperia*.
923 *Adages* I i 8
924 In the printed censures of the Paris theologians, the strictures against Luther were sandwiched in between the initial section and this added appendix against Erasmus. Thus Erasmus is placed in the vanguard and the rearguard of the action.

mean simply the highest and most certain hope; for I think that as little as possible should be attributed to human merits, in so far as they are human. And it would be a modesty most pleasing to Christ if someone attributed nothing at all to them. I am quite willing to grant that good works are required in adults. But as for their denial that there can be any confidence from Christian hope unless we trust in our good deeds, no one hopes more firmly than someone who hopes in the promises and mercy of God and in the merits of Christ. And nevertheless I certainly do not reject that lowly confidence which they posit, although nowhere do I read that it was said to anyone, 'place your hope in your good deeds' or 'he has confidence in his works.'

To Topic 20. The celibacy of priests

III *A proposition from the book* Restrictions on Eating Meat[925]
Many reasons persuade us to change the law of clerical celibacy.[926]

CENSURE

In so far as this proposition alleges that there are valid reasons for changing such a law, it is false and exceedingly scandalous, and it foments in the holy church the schism and ungodly heresy of Luther. For there are many and efficacious reasons which impel us to retain the observance of the law of clerical celibacy and not change it in any way; and there are no reasons (or at least no just ones) for the opposite course. For if those who were assigned to divine worship in the Old Law, the sacraments of which were merely shadows of the sacraments of the New Law, had to abstain from intercourse as they took their turns, one after the other, in serving at the altar, and since they, on the other hand, were required to serve at the altar by a hereditary succession and were not free to refuse this duty because those who were born into the tribe of Levi had to undertake this office, there is even more reason for continence in the ministers of the altar. For they are not drafted by birth, as those were, but serve by the free choice of their own will, for no one is by any means compelled to take holy

* * * * *

925 *De esu carnium* LB IX 1201C. The full title of the work is *Epistola apologetica de interdicto esu carnium deque similibus hominum constitutionibus*; thus it includes not only restrictions on eating meat but also other man-made regulations.
926 The theologians give a paraphrase of the passage, but it is sufficiently accurate. In *Divinationes* LB IX 488A–489A Erasmus defends at some length the legitimacy and appropriateness of his recommendations about clerical celibacy.

orders; but rather whoever wishes to is ordained and whoever rejects it is not required to accept it. And upon those who take holy orders of their own free will the church, inspired by the Holy Spirit, has wisely imposed continence, considering especially the extraordinary degree of dignity of such great sacraments, than which nothing is holier, more spiritual, more divine. Wherefore it is proper for those assigned to them to be spiritual and far removed from carnal desires and the occasions of them and impulses toward them, so that they may deserve to offer the holy and spotless victim[927] with a chaste mind and an uncontaminated body and so that those who are not proficient in extraordinary holiness may not handle these marvellous and tremendous mysteries.

Moreover, those who lead a celibate life are not hindered by external occupations or concern for a wife and children to keep them from being free to engage in holy reading, prayer, meditation, and other such duties of the contemplative life. And if those who take holy orders took wives, they would certainly be less free to concentrate on the Lord. For, as the Apostle says, 'those who have wives are concerned with the things of this world, how they may please their wives, and they are divided.'[928] For this reason priests with wives, entangled with the burdens of matrimony, would live very restless lives. Because of these burdens they would have to be caught up in secular affairs, from which, however, the Apostle himself decrees that those fighting for God should abstain.[929] But those who are continent and remain celibate think about the business of the Lord, namely, how they can please God and preserve chastity and purity of mind and body. And they also keep careful watch, since they have the care of souls and are bound to render an account to the Lord for the sheep entrusted to them.

Moreover, allowing clerics to marry would also do great damage to the church. For the church would be thrown into almost endless confusion by the immense and growing multitude of sons and daughters who would have to be raised at the expense of the church. Parents passing down ecclesiastical benefices to their children one after another and reserving them to their own families by a continual succession from one generation to the next would seem to be restoring

* * * * *

927 That is, Christ in the Eucharist. The words are drawn from the prayer immediately following the consecration in the canon of the mass: 'offerimus ... hostiam sanctam, hostiam immaculatam'; see *Missale Romanum* no 17, I 208.
928 1 Cor 7:33
929 2 Tim 2:4

the Levitical priesthood which Christ the Lord, as a priest according to the order of Melchizedech, abrogated.[930]

Considering these points, we can easily assess how far from the right path they have diverged who have cast off their priesthood so thoroughly that after taking holy orders they take steps to enter into a new contract of marriage – which was never allowed, not even among the Greeks. For although the Greeks are not bound by a vow of continence with respect to their previous marriages, nevertheless, after they had been ordained priests, they were always forbidden to enter into the bonds of matrimony or to remarry after the death of their first wife. And if this is inviolably observed by the Greeks, how much more force does the law have that forbids priests of the Latin church, which has bound itself by a vow of continence, from thrusting themselves into the servitude of marriage after they have been ordained priests? And so the continence of the Latin church must be approved: it shines with holiness, it grants free access to divine pursuits, and it contributes greatly to the utility of ecclesiastical affairs.

CLARIFICATION OF THE THIRD PROPOSITION
They truly and piously discuss why it is fitting that those who handle the divine mysteries and dispense the words of heaven should be chaste, and certainly I applaud them mightily[931] for doing so. But they are considering what the thing itself demands; I am considering what is required by human weakness. I grant that some inconveniences would follow if priests were allowed to have wives, but either the church or the concern of princes could alleviate these difficulties by some ordinances. As it is, human morals being so corrupt, the most impure celibacy of priests causes far more serious inconveniences. Would that priests, all that there are, would direct their minds toward purity of life. I said there are many reasons; whether they are valid, let the luminaries of the church decide.

To Topic 32 (the last one) on scholastic theology should be added five propositions

IV *The first of these (which would be number six in the order under the topic) is from Erasmus' preface to the* Works *of Hilary.*
The most holy Hilary was not at all unaware how full of danger it is, how irreligious it may be, to speak of ineffable things, to examine

* * * * *

930 Gen 14:18; Heb 5:6, 6:20, 7:11
931 Latin *utroque favente pollice*: Horace *Epistolae* 1.18.66; *Adages* i viii 46

what is incomprehensible, to make pronouncements about what is far removed from our understanding.[932]

CENSURE

St Hilary knew that there is no danger in making pronouncements about divine matters in conformity with what is contained in Holy Scripture or what has been decided and defined by holy ecumenical councils. Otherwise he would not have gone into exile to defend them and he would have not issued extraordinary books to defend them.

CLARIFICATION

IV But in those very books which Hilary wrote on the Trinity, in more than one place he anxiously prays to God for forgiveness when he is about to speak about inexplicable matters, and he cries out that in the pursuit of religion he is forced to be irreligious.[933] No wonder, since in those very books he sometimes writes what no one would tolerate if I wrote it now. And Augustine is in no less trepidation when he is about to discuss the Trinity.[934] The theologians themselves now make allowances in interpreting some things Augustine put forth about the Trinity; some things they reject. Scripture does not deceive, but the danger is in interpreting it. For the Arians also had the Scriptures. Finally the wording itself demands great reverence. Accordingly the ancients hardly dared to speak about the divine Persons in any other words than those used by Scripture.

v *The seventh proposition. In the same preface to Hilary*

The sum and substance of our religion is peace and unanimity; they will hardly be able to stand unless we make very few definitions and on many points allow everyone to judge for himself.[935]

CENSURE

It is well known that peace and unanimity contribute not a little to the Christian religion, as long, however, as that peace and that unity are godly and correct. But if they are ungodly and foreign to the Catholic truth, as is usually the case with heretics, they do not contribute at all; indeed they thoroughly undermine Catholic piety. But

* * * * *

932 CWE 9 Ep 1334:162–5
933 *De Trinitate* 2.5 PL 10 53C–54C
934 *Confessions* 11.12 PL 32 849; *De Trinitate* 15.6.9–10, 15.7.13 PL 42 1063–4, 1066–7
935 CWE 9 Ep 1334:232–4

in order to destroy the consensus of such ungodly persons and in order to establish godly and correct concord in the church it is necessary that Catholic dogmas be frequently explained by those who have
authority in the Christian republic. By this means schisms and scandals are eliminated, budding heresies and perverse teachings are ex-
tirpated, the morals of the faithful are put in order, and the faith itself
is rooted in the hearts of Christians. Thus in the past, when heretics,
together with the accomplices in their execrable conspiracy, were per-
secuting the church, general councils were assembled where the ungodly were rejected and condemned and the church regained peace
and concord. But for this to happen often, in order to counter the
impieties and false accusations of the heretics, it was necessary for the
church to hand down definitions concerning not very few but many
points, and to make it clear what was to be held and what rejected,
and not to allow everyone to judge for himself concerning what re-
lates to piety; otherwise unanimity and concord about what belongs
to the faith could not be preserved among the faithful. Accordingly,
this proposition, which is temerariously and ignorantly asserted, factiously opens the way to dissolving the unity of the faithful and also
to disseminating pernicious errors.

CLARIFICATION

v My whole passage discourages curious and temerarious definitions about
matters beyond human understanding; it says nothing about sober and religious investigation or the decrees of ecumenical councils. For what is said
before the passage cited is as follows: 'Not that I think we should totally
condemn the investigation of tripartite philosophy[936] or metaphysical matters, as long as it takes place with intelligence that is felicitous and without
temerity in defining, without stubbornness or, that plague of concord, an
obstinate passion to win. The sum and substance of our religion is peace,
etc.' And a little afterwards: 'And in this matter some persons have recognized no limit, etc.'[937] And a good deal earlier than that: 'But what we
examine, what we define, is not taken from Holy Scripture, etc.'[938]

But if the theologians wanted to confess the truth, I think that not
even they would approve of quarrels about instants, quiddities, formali-
ties, and respects, or of supposititious propositions, considering them both

* * * * *

936 That is, physics, ethics, and politics
937 CWE 9 Ep 1334:225–40
938 CWE 9 Ep 1334:202–4

unnecessary and offensive to pious ears – for example, the question whether this proposition is possible, 'among the divine Persons God the Father hates God the Son,' or 'whether the Father could have generated more Sons.'[939] And some even more odious than these. I do not condemn what many councils have defined out of Holy Scripture against heretics, nor do I want the tranquillity of the church to be bought at the price of a fellowship of falsity; but I single out for blame numberless and curious questions, by comparison with which those that remain seem to be few, although in themselves they are many. Accordingly, this proposition, correctly understood, is not asserted temerariously or ignorantly nor does it factiously open the way to dissolving the unity of the faithful or to disseminating pernicious errors. For the concord of the church is not straightway dissolved if everyone is allowed to indulge in his own judgment[940] concerning many opinions of the scholastics, leaving untouched what the church hands down to be believed with certainty.

VI *The eighth proposition. In the same preface to Hilary*
The role of theological learning is to define nothing beyond what is set forth in Scripture but to dispense in good faith what is set forth there.[941]

CENSURE
It is not the role of theological learning to define nothing concerning the faith except what is formally and expressly contained in Holy Scripture or what is clearly deduced from that. Such is the role of Wyclifite and Lutheran impiety, since, on the authority of Dionysius, Basil, Augustine, and many other Catholic Doctors, we must give no less credence to what we have from Christ through the apostolic tradition concerning the sacraments and some other matters than we do to what is expressed in Holy Scripture. And the Apostle commands that we place our faith not only in written documents but also in traditions explained in speech alone.[942] Wherefore the aforesaid proposition is false, ungodly, and in conformity with the faithlessness of Wyclif and Luther.

* * * * *

939 For such definitions and questions see *The Praise of Folly* CWE 27 126–7 and the notes in *The Praise of Folly* ed and trans Clarence H. Miller 2nd edition (New Haven and London 2003) 88–9.
940 Cf Rom 14:5.
941 CWE 9 Ep 1334:244–6
942 2 Thess 2:14

CLARIFICATION

VI It is the part of a fair-minded reader to interpret language according to the matter at hand. I was not dealing there with the rites of the sacraments but with curious questions about the nature of God. In such matters I would not want theologians to diverge from the guidance of Scripture. If they grant that this is rightly said, what does this proposition have in common with such people as Wyclif and Luther? No one denies that we must reverently accept what was handed down by the apostles vocally, not in writing. But whatever has somehow crept into the usage of the church is not necessarily handed down by the apostles, whereas there can be no backing away from what is written. Now I am aware that Jerome and other godly men prescribe that we should accept what was handed down by our forebears just as if it had originated with the apostles; but it is against those who contumaciously neglect what was instituted by the early Fathers that such an argument is usefully directed. Nevertheless, I do not think that we should attribute as much to the ordinances of any bishops whomsoever as we ought to attribute to the prescriptions of the apostles. I am not talking about the decisions of general councils, especially the ancient councils, and decrees which have been approved by usage.

VII *The ninth proposition. In the same preface to Hilary*

Many problems are now referred to a council; it would be much more fitting if such questions were referred to another time, when the dark glass has been taken away and we see God face to face.[943]

CENSURE

By no means should the faithful consider as problems what the church has determined in general councils concerning what pertains to godliness; for, directed by the Holy Spirit, she decides there only about doctrines which must be unshakeably and inviolably held by all Christians. For this reason this proposition is asserted temerariously and arrogantly, as if the church did not know how to distinguish what is a problem from what is not, what should be defined from what should not.

CLARIFICATION

VII Far be it from me to be so mad as to think that what the church hands down concerning the faith in general councils properly convened and con-

* * * * *

943 1 Cor 13:12. CWE 9 Ep 1334:247–9

ducted should be completely revoked. I am talking about the curious questions and temerarious definitions of some theologians which are neither useful nor necessary to the faith. The whole drift of my language makes it clear that this is what I mean. And I do not understand what the censure means when it says: 'as if the church did not know how to distinguish what is a problem from what is not, what should be defined from what should not.' For in my words there is nothing related to this meaning. My opinion expresses a similarity. Just as many things are proposed today which are neither approved nor disapproved but are referred to an ecumenical council, so too many things are defined by some theologians concerning the mysteries of the divine nature which it would be better to refer to the future age when we see God face to face. In the name of Christ, I ask you, reader, does this meaning blaspheme in any way against the church or councils?

VIII *The tenth proposition. In the oft-mentioned preface to Hilary*
In some places the rabbis are ashamed because they have nothing to reply.[944]

CENSURE
Certainly in these times scholastic Doctors are afflicted with great grief and shame when they see wicked men brazenly disdain holy councils, even general ones, and likewise scorn holy Doctors, and also twist Holy Scripture everywhere at their pleasure, giving it a heretical meaning, though, on the other hand, scholastic Doctors, whom this writer contemptuously calls rabbis, have no lack of replies to the faithless teachings of Luther. For by means of manifest arguments, and those quite sound, they clearly show that his doctrine is quite mad. Wherefore the Lutherans hardly dare to encounter them and square off against them. For they fear that if they should happen to fight with them at close quarters, since they have no reasonable responses, they would be confounded and their ignorance and lack of learning would be obvious to the whole world. Hence they usually publish worthless and flaccid books, shot through with many heresies and blasphemies indeed, but not supported by any reasons, any evidence, any Scripture except what is twisted awry – as any readers with good judgment can easily perceive. For they will observe that they have no strength in argumentation but rather show off with impudent stubbornness and notorious obstinacy. For they imitate the behaviour of their fathers, the

* * * * *

944 CWE 9 Ep 1334:243–4

heresiarchs, and when, like the worst sort of deserters, they shamefully depart from the Catholic church, outside of which there is undoubtedly no salvation, they do not know how to rest in the truth,
but rather with the entire force of their malevolence they rage against
Catholic piety as if they had gone totally out of their minds.

CLARIFICATION

VIII The anger they vent here against heresiarchs is most justified, but it
has nothing to do with me. I apply 'rabbi' to theologians who resemble the
Scribes and Pharisees, who want to seem remarkably learned and therefore
are not content with what is handed down in Scripture or by the authority of
councils but rather show off their wit by making up some curiosities which
are not far from blasphemous. Accordingly, just as those who condemn all
theologians do them a great injury, so too they do themselves an injury
if they take what is said against any of the theologians as if it were said
against all of them. In the last analysis they burden me with the odium of
a capital offence without my having deserved it at all, and in this way they
do not live up to the name of theologian.

The End

THE DETERMINATION OF
THE FACULTY OF SACRED THEOLOGY
AT THE UNIVERSITY OF PARIS
CONCERNING THE *INFORMAL COLLOQUIES*
OF DESIDERIUS ERASMUS OF ROTTERDAM
HANDED DOWN IN THE MONTH OF MAY
IN THE YEAR OF OUR LORD 1526[945]

On 16 May in the year of our Lord 1526 the Faculty of Theology under the obligation of their oath met in the College of the Sorbonne to make final deliberations concerning what should be done about the book entitled *Patterns of Informal Conversation* by Desiderius Erasmus, etc. But now the same book, much enlarged, is entitled *A Book of Informal Colloquies, Useful in Many Ways*. Concerning this business there had already been much discussion, both among the deputies and in the full sitting of the Masters. And yesterday, after many proposals had been made after mass (as usual) in the faculty sitting at Saint-Maturin, in order that the material itself might be discussed more seasonably, it was put off till this day, the 16th, when, in the presence of all the Masters, what had formerly been adduced by the deputies on various occasions was repeated and called to mind: namely that the fasting and abstinence prescribed by the church are disparaged by the author of this book,

* * * * *

945 Pelargus G2–G2v says he is glad that he has read the *Colloquies* but that he wishes they had never been published. They were published at an inopportune time when some people were already mocking the church; and when they were successful Erasmus even enlarged them. Far from promoting piety among young people, they provided a pretext for impiety and fleshly desires and withdrew them from a religious life; they provided young people with jokes against the saints, ecclesiastical regulations, and even the sacraments. The virtue and Latinity of young people could have been provided for in a more appropriate way. Such joking should also be avoided by a serious theologian. Pelargus approves of the attacks on the superstitions, avarice, and carnality of priests, but he thinks it should have been done more sparingly and more seriously, certainly not in jokebooks intended for young people.
In the censures of the *Colloquies* Pelargus says he limits himself to those which seem to have a special bearing on theology.

whoever he might be; that the intercession of the Blessed Virgin Mary and the other saints is held up to ridicule; that no value, or very little, is placed on virginity, by comparison with marriage; that everyone is dissuaded from entering the religious life; likewise that arduous and difficult questions are proposed by mere grammarians, contrary to the statutes sworn to by the Masters of Arts, with the result that they can easily fall into error; and many other similar matters are badly handled in the said book. After these matters had been carefully noticed and considered, upon mature deliberation it was pronounced and concluded by unanimous consent that the reading of the aforesaid book should be forbidden to everyone, and especially to young persons, because such reading, under the pretext of gaining eloquence, corrupted youth instead of educating them, and that by all due means a great effort should be made to suppress this book and eliminate it throughout Christendom.[946]

And in order that it might be clear to all how just our judgment is and how much it conforms with reason and godliness, we have decided to append those things which we commanded to be noted, excerpted, and transcribed concerning this book of dialogues by some of us who were specially commissioned to do so and which, after mature consideration, also motivated our judgment. In publishing them in the following manner and format, the places designated in the individual dialogues should be referred to the pages of the volume given to us by the examiners and now current everywhere in the city of Paris.

Some Scandalous and Ungodly Errors in Erasmus' *Informal Colloquies*

Here follow some scandalous and ungodly errors which are contained in the book *Informal Colloquies* revised by its author, Desiderius

* * * * *

946 With only minor differences, this is entry 152 in Farge *Procès-verbaux* 136–7. As Professor Farge has kindly informed me, the faculty ordinarily met at the beginning and in the middle of each month at Saint-Mathurin (Trinitarian Order) refectory or church. Other meetings were usually held at one of the colleges, usually the Collège de la Sorbonne. The meeting in question here was at the Sorbonne, but it was held just one day after the ordinary mid-month meeting at Saint-Mathurin on May 15. The term *per juramentum* designated special meetings, important enough that the regent Doctors were expected to attend 'under the obligation of their oath.'

Erasmus of Rotterdam, in the year of our Lord 1526.[947] In this book
its author, just as if he were a pagan, ridicules, insults, tweaks, tears
apart the Christian religion and its holy ceremonies and observances,
and decrees that they should be changed.

CENSURE

1 In the dialogue *In Poor Health* he first shamelessly mocks the devotion
people have to the holy religious habit; and he alleges that a pimp's
cloak is as effective in curing a disease as a religious cowl. This is on
page 16, in the middle:[948] 'by donning a Dominican cowl, etc.'

CLARIFICATION

1 Just as the faculty is highly commendable for the scrupulous diligence
which causes it such anxiety and fear for young people, so too it is hardly
safe when it makes pronouncements based on the reports of others. For
here the faculty frankly declares that it has simply relied on the authority
of its commissioners. But who would have expected such a majestic college
to condescend to censure such childish colloquies, a collection designed to
teach young people to speak Latin by playing at it, and to prepare them
by the by to discover and refute rhetorical arguments, and finally to imbue
them with some elements of piety and enable them day by day to climb
to a level above the crass mob. This was my aim, and it seems that I have
not altogether failed to achieve it, unless I am perhaps being flattered by
people who thank me because they have had their minds improved by these
trifles of mine. It is surprising that, in a place where Poggio's *Facetiae and
Funny Questions*[949] are printed and read with impunity, such stones should

* * * * *

947 Only one 1526 edition of *Colloquia* corresponds to the page numbers given by
the Paris theologians (or their deputies), the one printed by Froben in Basel
in February 1526, E460 in *Bibliotheca Belgica: Bibliographie générale des Pays Bas*
ed F. van der Haeghen and Marie-Thérèse Lenger 7 vols (Brussels 1964–70) II
508–10.

948 *Familiarum colloquiorum formulae* 'Patterns of Informal Conversation': *In Poor
Health* CWE 39 14 / LB I 633 / ASD I-3 134:278–80

949 Poggio Bracciolini (1380–1459) was an Italian humanist and papal secretary
famous for discovering important classical manuscripts and writing serious
moral tracts. His *Facetiae* was a collection of funny and often indecent stories,
much like vernacular fabliaux. Erasmus tended to depreciate him, partly because of Poggio's bitter and often petty quarrel with Lorenzo Valla, a favourite
of Erasmus. See CEBR I 182–3.

be thrown at my *Colloquies*. Accordingly, just as I find it easy to believe that these complaints were often proposed by deputies, so too I find it unlikely that they were published with the consent of the whole faculty. To me it is not much of a secret who instigated them.

As for the savage preface, since I do not know who wrote it, I will make no reply for the time being, except for this only: it makes many fierce pronouncements, which are nowhere to be found when it comes to the passages themselves. I will correct only the heading, which I know did not come from the faculty.[950] In his *Colloquies* Erasmus, as a person who loves true piety and is eager for the glory of Christ, never ridicules or insults the Christian religion but only assails human superstition and preposterous judgments, and by doing so makes a special contribution to purifying and confirming the Christian religion. Furthermore, since the colloquies have various speakers, I think it is very unfair to attack whatever anyone says in them as if I believed it. Otherwise as one and the same person I would contradict myself; for oftentimes what one person proposes is refuted by another. If some proposal is false, it is unfair to attack the worse part as mine and overlook the other position which refutes what has been wrongly said. But because the whole passage is not quoted from the colloquies but only the censure is given, the faculty has nothing here to do with me, since they are condemning not what I wrote but what the commissaries or perhaps others set down – how reliably the facts will soon make clear.

CLARIFICATION OF THE FIRST PASSAGE

First of all, reader, take a look at how the very opening draws upon what is manifestly false. Gerard says: 'Some persons have recovered their health by donning a Dominican or Franciscan cowl.' Livinus replies: 'Perhaps the same thing would have happened had they had put on a pimp's cloak. But these things won't help one who has no faith in them.' To this Gerard replies: 'Then have faith that you may recover.' Here it is as clear as day that Gerard encourages his companion to make use of a sacred garment and says that, if he does not believe, he should cease disbelieving so that the garment may do him good. Is it not a case here of attacking the worse part and overlooking the later remark, which corrects the earlier statement? And still Livinus, who does not seem to attribute very much to garments, does not shamelessly ridicule those who are of that persuasion nor does he say

* * * * *

950 Erasmus refers not to the heading of the entry for the meeting but to the passage at its end, which introduces the censures: 'Here follow some scandalous and ungodly errors ... decrees that they should be changed.'

that a pimp's cloak has as much efficacy in curing diseases as a monk's cowl. But rather he indicates a coincidence. For it could be that someone who gets well by donning a cowl does not get well as a benefit of the cowl but rather by the power of nature or the assistance of a physician, so that the same thing would have happened no matter what he was covered with. I omit that nothing prevents the same cowl from belonging to a monk and a pimp. You see, reader, how far the language of the colloquy is from shameless derision. And what is the danger, I beg you, in attributing not very much to a monk's cowl since in these times there is so much superstition among simple folk in these matters, so much chicanery in those who promote them, that it makes sense to counter the error of the one group and the fraud of the other? As it is, the colloquy supports neither group but rather urges that he[951] use it with faith.

2 Again, he wants no one to make a vow to a saint to have his disease cured. This can be seen a little later on the same page, namely page 16, a little lower down, at this point:[952] 'Others have been cured of some disease by making vows to some saint.'

CLARIFICATION
2 In that place Gerard says this, not me, and if they posit that I have made him semi-Lutheran, what is that to me? And in fact he does not express what they take him to mean; he blames only those who make a bargain, as it were, with the saints: if you cure me, I will erect a marble statue for you; if not, I will not put one up. The passage is as follows: 'Others have been cured of some disease by making vows to some saint.' Livinus replies: 'But I make no bargains with saints.' Gerard: 'Then seek the blessing of health from Christ, in whom you do have faith, etc.' Many are of the opinion that the saints should not be invoked at all. For that reason the other person advises him to ask Christ if he has little faith in the saints. Does someone who says 'I make no bargains with the saints' by that very statement condemn all vows made to saints? But there is no lack of piety in someone who prefers to ask Christ himself rather than the saints.

3 In the dialogue *Visiting the Holy Places* he ridicules a vow to go to Jerusalem, declaring falsely that everything seen in Jerusalem is faked and contrived to entice naive and credulous folk. This is on page 31,

* * * * *

951 That is, Livinus
952 CWE 39 14:35–6 / LB I 633 / ASD I-3 134:282–3

a little past the middle, at this point:[953] 'Anything there you consider worth seeing? etc.'

CLARIFICATION

3 In this passage it is Arnold, not Erasmus, who tells the story, and I have frequently heard the same from learned persons who have been in Jerusalem. And it is probable that today it is not known for sure where Jerusalem once was, since I see that there is some doubt among the learned whether Rome was in the place where it is nowadays indicated that it was. St Jerome, who lived in that region, when he mentioned some things which are shown there to visitors today, spoke of them as doubtful, saying 'it is reported' and 'they say.' What should we think now, after so many invasions, so many changes in human affairs that have happened over and over for a thousand years and more? They say that things shown at Rome – the Veronica, the column of Solomon, the chair of Peter, his tomb – belong to this category. But what does this have to do with the Catholic faith? Men recognized as religious once thought it was nothing special to have been in Jerusalem, and I think that Christianity would be no worse off if no one ran off to Jerusalem but rather looked for the traces of Christ in books and transferred his effort and expense to the assistance of the poor.

4 In the dialogue which is called *The Confession of a Soldier* he speaks irreverently and shamefully about sacramental confession. This is to be seen on page 42, at the top, at this point:[954] 'What priest will you choose?' The other one replies: 'One I know to be as shameless and easygoing as possible.'

CLARIFICATION

4 In fact what is ridiculed there is an ungodly soldier, burdened with crimes, who thinks it is enough to do away with his sins if he tells them in some fashion or other to a priest, without any hatred of his sins or any thought of amending his life. When someone asks him what priest he would choose, he replies: 'One I know to be as shameless and easygoing as possible.' This is not the language of Erasmus but of a detestable soldier,

* * * * *

953 *De visendo loca sacra* CWE 39 37:16–17 (with title *De votis temere susceptis* 'Rash Vows') / LB I 639 / ASD I-3 147:714–15
954 *Confessio militis* CWE 39 58:37–9 (with title *Militaria* 'Military Affairs') / LB I 643A / ASD I-3 157:1035–6

who receives the following reply: 'To be sure of finding like for like,'[955] and
he adds 'when you're absolved you'll go off to communion?' The soldier
answers: 'Why not? After I have once dumped the dregs into his cowl, I
will be free of the burden; let him who absolves see to that.' Then the other
one says: 'How do you know he absolves you?' The soldier: 'I know.' 'By
what token?' The soldier: 'Because he places his hand on my head, mum-
bling something or other.' Then the other one says: 'What if he restores all
your sins to you when laying his hand upon you, muttering these words:
"I absolve you of all good deeds (of which I find none in you) and I restore your character to you and send you away just as I received you,"
etc.'[956] From the whole colloquy it is clear that it is the stupid soldier who
is being mocked there and being exposed to ridicule for the same reason
that the Spartans brought drunken slaves to a banquet.[957] For among others also there are people like this soldier. Are they now assigning to me
the person of the one ridiculing the stupidity of the soldier or that of the
soldier himself? This argues that neither the theologians nor the reporters
read the colloquies but that the task was given over to boys, who excerpted
according to their lights. Otherwise, if you gave an uneducated cloth-fuller
the colloquy translated into the vernacular, he would see that the stupidity of the soldier is being mocked, not that confession is being ridiculed,
unless perhaps St Jerome can be said to speak irreverently about fasting,
abstinence, the chastity of virgins, the holiness of monks, and the continence of clerics and priests whenever he wittily satirizes the dainty fasts
of some people who do not drink the juice of herbs from cups but sip it
up from seashells,[958] or when he makes fun of virgins wearing dark pur-
ple, tripping along on twinkle-toes, living with clerics under the name of
'chaste lovers,'[959] or when he depicts the haughtiness of monks who walk at
a snail's pace, who call for silence by tapping with their little finger, and utter words with such hauteur that they seem to be sobbing rather than speaking;[960] or again, when he makes us see the disgraceful servility of legacy-

* * * * *

955 Latin *similes labra lactucas*, 'like lips like lettuce' *Adagia* I x 71 (said of a donkey
     eating thistles), proverbial for two things or two creatures well matched
956 CWE 39 58:37–60:11 / LB I 643A–B / ASD I-3 157:1035–47
957 Plutarch *Lycurgus* 28.4, *Demetrius* 1.4, *Moralia* 239A(30); Clement of Alexandria
     Paedagogus 3.41.5
958 *Epistolae* 52.12 PL 22 537
959 *Epistolae* 22.13–14 PL 22 402. Latin *agapetae*; Jerome skewers such supercilious
     'virgins' who claim that they live with clerics only for spiritual reasons.
960 *Epistolae* 125.18 PL 22 1083; Jerome's monk spreads out his books, taps his finger
     for the attention of his students, and then holds forth with great pomposity.

hunters[961] attending the deathbeds of rich men, collecting with their hands the pus coming from their mouths;[962] or when he makes fun of certain churches (French ones, I think) which did not admit to holy orders those who did not have wives and did not commit the sacraments to them unless they had seen the swelling wombs of their wives.[963] Or does he speak irreverently about the resurrection of the body when he makes the Origenists ask, as they fondle the breasts and other parts of women, whether we will have the same members at the resurrection? But if it is pious to hold up vices to ridicule, especially without mentioning any names, why am I said to be speaking irreverently?

> 5 In the dialogue which is entitled *The Pious Duty of Youth* he judges first of all that it is not a grave sin to transgress against the ordinances of the church unless the offence is accompanied by a malicious contempt. This is clear on page 67, after the middle of the page, at this point:[964] 'Nor do I straightway regard as an offence a transgression against a human ordinance unless this is accompanied by contempt.'

CLARIFICATION

5 I use the word *piaculum* 'offence' to denote not just any sin but an enormous offence.[965] My language says no more than that it is not straightaway a horrendous sin if someone violates some human ordinance or other. But in order to make room for slander, the word *quaslibet* 'any and every' is omitted; for what I wrote was 'against any and every ordinance.'[966] If a copyist did this, why was it not corrected? But if it was deliberately changed by the commissaries, what kind of integrity that shows I leave it to others to decide. If every violation of any human ordinance whatsoever sends someone

* * * * *

961 Latin *haeredipetarum, haeredipeta*: not classical, probably in Jerome
962 *Epistolae* 52.6 PL 22 533
963 *Contra Vigilantium* 17 PL 23 (1845) 352C. The preface to the book says that Vigilantius was born in France (PL 23 337).
964 *Pietas puerilis* CWE 39 97:18–20 (with title *Confabulatio pia* 'The Whole Duty of Youth') / LB I 652B / ASD I-3 178:1742–4
965 In the Froben 1533 edition Erasmus added after 'offence' the phrase 'that is, an enormous offence' (*hoc est, enorme crimen*); see the variant at ASD I-3 178:1742.
966 The word *quaslibet* was not added to the colloquy until the Froben edition of 1529; the theologians did not include it because it was not present in the Froben edition of February 1526 that they used; see the variant at ASD I-3 178:1743. But Erasmus implies or assumes that they should have used the latest corrected edition that appeared before their censures of 1531.

to hell, then what the child said was not correct. But if none of the theologians dares to profess such a thing, what is there for them to find fault with?

6 Then he alleges that it would be sufficient to confess to God if the church had not ordained otherwise. This is clear on page 66, at the bottom, at this point:[967] 'But I confess to him who alone, etc.'

CLARIFICATION

6 Whether confession as it is practised in these times was instituted by Christ has not yet been satisfactorily proved by the theologians. In the meanwhile it is sufficient for a child or a lay person to observe it as instituted by the bishops of the church and approved by the usage of the whole Christian people. This is what Gaspar says: 'But I confess to him who alone remits sins and who has all power.' To which Erasmius responds: 'Who is that?' Gaspar: 'Christ.' Erasmius: 'You think that is sufficient?' Gaspar: 'It would be quite sufficient for me if it were so for the rulers of the church and accepted custom.' Erasmius: 'Whom, then, do you call the rulers of the church?' Gaspar: 'Popes, bishops, apostles.' Erasmius: 'And do you include Christ with these?' Gaspar: 'He is indisputably the head[968] of them all.' Erasmius: 'And author of the customary confession?' Gaspar: 'Assuredly he is the author of all good, but whether he himself instituted this confession, I leave to theologians to decide. For me, a simple boy, the authority of my elders is good enough.'[969] From these words what can be inferred except that confession should be scrupulously observed, just because of the authority of the church and public custom, even though it cannot be firmly proved to have originated in Scripture or to have been instituted by the Lord himself. This proposition alleges nothing other than what the words clearly say.

7 After this he finds fault with the theologians' method of disputation, not understanding that theologians do not waver in the faith because they ask questions concerning matters relating to the faith. For such questions do not cause them to have doubts about the faith, but rather they explain the faith more clearly. This error is contained on page 70,

* * * * *

967 CWE 39 96:36–42 / LB I 651F / ASD I-3 178:1729–31
968 *Adagia* II iii 45; cf III x 82 and IV vi 20.
969 CWE 39 96:36–97:8 / LB I 651F–652A / ASD I-3 178:1729–34 (and variants)

in the middle, at this point:[970] 'Many[971] shun theology out of fear of wavering in their Catholic faith, since they see there is nothing that is not called into question.'

CLARIFICATION

7 I beg you, what person of sound mind ever condemned scholastic disputations altogether? The boy gives two reasons why he is less inclined to study theology. 'Theology would please me best,' he says, 'did not the manners of some theologians and their ill-tempered quarrels among themselves disgust me, etc.' Someone who says 'some theologians' is singling out certain ones for blame, not all of them. To that Erasmius replies: 'Many shun theology out of a fear of wavering in their Catholic faith, since they see there is nothing that is not called into question, etc.' What then? Does this apply to the discussions at the Sorbonne? By no means. In fact, he is pointing out the deadly conflict of opinions which is now shaking the world to its foundations so that it is not safe for a boy to discuss doctrines. If he had meant the discussions of the scholastics, he would have said 'since nothing there is not called into question.' As it is, he says 'since they see,' pointing his finger at these times. And no one says theologians waver just because they dispute; but many are afraid that they would waver amidst so many doctors and scriptural texts twisted to support contradictory doctrines. For a lay person is more firmly grounded if he simply believes without disputing. For there follows in that passage: 'As for me, what I read in Sacred Scripture and the Creed called the Apostles' I believe with complete confidence, nor do I search further. The rest I leave to theologians to dispute about.'[972]

8 In the dialogue which is called *The Profane Feast* he carps at the abstinence from meat imposed by the church, as if it were opposed to the liberty of the gospel, whereas in fact it is not so opposed; rather it is an error of the Aerians[973] to think so. This occurs on page 107 of the said book, before the middle, at this point:[974] 'Charity bears with all things.'

9 And page 104, about in the middle, at this point:[975] 'And in my opinion the Jews of old had less of a burden imposed on them.'

* * * * *

970 CWE 39 99:8–10 / LB I 653B / ASD I-3 180:1810–12
971 After 'many' Erasmus added 'in these times' (*hisce temporibus*) in the Froben 1533 edition; see ASD I-3 180, variant at line 1810.
972 CWE 39 99:11–13 / LB I 653B / ASD I-3 180:1813–15
973 See n70 above.
974 *Convivium profanum* CWE 39 145:23 / LB I 665E / ASD I-3 229:88
975 CWE 39 143:29–30 / LB I 664F / ASD I-3 227:17

→ n

10 And on the same page, about in the middle, at this point:[976] 'I hate fish worse than I do a snake.' The other one replies: 'You're not alone in that.'

11 There follows: 'Who introduced this nuisance?' And many pronouncements are made in the same place against such abstinence from meat. He concludes that it would be well if such abstinence were eliminated, which is clear at the bottom of page 107, at this point:[977] 'If I were pope, etc.' And at the end of page 107.

12 In the dialogue which is entitled *The Godly Feast* he first claims that everything – choice of foods, prescribed dress, fasting, offering, prayers said merely out of duty, and rest on holy days – is connected with Judaism, an opinion especially approved of by Luther. This is shown on page 148, before the middle, at this point:[978] 'I think "sacrifice" means, etc.'

CLARIFICATION OF THE FOUR CENSURES ABOVE

8, 9, 10, 11 The colloquy from which the first four excerpts are taken was one of those which was published without my knowledge, much to my mortification and anger. For I had never kept any copy of these trifles in my possession. And hardly any of them was more foolish and inept than this colloquy. Hence, since I could not suppress it, I made many excisions and corrections.[979] It is a splendid way to treat me to blame me for everything the jokester Augustine says there. He praises an Epicurean lifestyle; he encourages a life of pleasure. But he is countered. When Augustine says it is a great bodily inconvenience for him to abstain from meat, he receives the response, 'charity bears with all things.' When he says, 'who introduced this nuisance?' the reply is, 'who showed the medicinal use of aloes, wormwood, and scammony?' These words make it clear that such abstinence, although burdensome to the body, is nevertheless useful in weakening the flesh. And when he says, 'and in my opinion the Jews of old had less of a burden imposed on them,' he receives the reply, 'In many matters it's not the fact but the intention that distinguishes us from the Jews. They refrained from

* * * * *

976 CWE 39 143:21 / LB I 694F; ASD I-3 227:9–10

977 CWE 39 146:1 / LB I 666A / ASD I-3 230:4–5

978 *Convivium religiosum* CWE 39 188:23–6 / LB I 679E / ASD I-3 247:488–9

979 It is true that *The Profane Feast* first appeared in the unauthorized first edition (1518) of the *Colloquies*, but what the theologians objected to appeared in the revised and expanded edition of 1522 (approved by Erasmus) so that he can hardly exonerate himself by referring to the unauthorized edition. See ASD I-3 6–8, 206:2656–2706, 227:1–230:119 and CWE 39 158–9 n76.

certain foods as if from unclean things that would defile the mind. We, though we know that to the pure all things are pure,[980] nevertheless deny nourishment to the lustful flesh as if to an unruly steed, so as to render it more obedient to the dictates of the spirit.' And in this fashion Christian responds to each of the rascal's arguments.

How fair-minded is it to blame me for what the rascal says when in the same dialogue I refute what he says. It would be no less absurd to blame St Thomas for the preliminary objections,[981] or St Jerome for what the Luciferian says in his dialogues, or Augustine for what the Manichaean says.[982] What crime is it for the trifler Augustine to say that he has a natural abhorrence of eating fish and for the other one to say he is not alone in this? Is this condemning an ordinance of the church or rather pointing out a peculiar quality of some physical constitutions? And nevertheless that trifler, who naturally abhors fish, confesses that he does abstain from meat, although not without some detriment to his health.

But I conclude, they say, that it would be good to eliminate this kind of abstinence. That is not said either by me or by the person whom I introduce as a speaker. For he speaks in this manner: 'If I were pope, I would urge everyone to perpetual sobriety of life, especially when a feast day was near. But I would decree that a person might eat anything for the sake of bodily health so long as he did it moderately and thankfully, and I would labour to have the decrease in corporal observances of this kind offset by increased zeal for true godliness.' This speech, though it is not entirely absurd, is nevertheless ridiculed by Christian, in these words: 'This is so important, in my judgment, that we should make you pope.' You see, reader, what it means to trust notes handed over by unskilled youths and to make no distinctions among the speakers in a work which consists entirely of dialogue by various persons.

CLARIFICATION OF THE FIFTH CENSURE
12 Whoever wrote this was worlds away from Christian sincerity, as many things show, but especially this: he deliberately misreports what I said in order to slander me. In the dialogue someone speaks as follows: 'I think

* * * * *

980 Titus 1:15
981 In a theological *summa* these are the objections usually given in an article immediately before the response to the question asked; after an explanation of the response the objections are answered.
982 Erasmus refers to Jerome's *Dialogus contra Luciferanos* and Augustine's *Contra Faustum Manichaeum.*

"sacrifice" means whatever pertains to corporeal rites and has some connection with Judaism, such as choice of foods, prescribed dress.' He misreports this as 'are connected with Judaism,'[983] although in fact even this language contains no impiety. 'An opinion,' he says, 'especially approved of by Luther.' Actually there is no one who does not approve of this opinion, because it is quite right. But Luther's opinion is that it is ungodly to prescribe such things and foolish to observe them. And indeed what comes next in my dialogue? 'Though not to be omitted entirely at the proper occasion, these become displeasing to God if a person relies on such observances but neglects works of mercy when a brother's need calls for charity.' Do you hear, reader, this marvellous agreement with Luther? He teaches that such things are to be rejected; the dialogue teaches that they are not to be neglected.

13 Secondly, in agreement with the Beguards,[984] he claims that ecclesiastical laws do not have to be observed by the perfect, who ought not to be compelled to observe them, because 'a person who is spiritual judges all things, yet he himself is judged by no man.'[985] This is on page 143, at this point:[986] '"king" can be understood as the perfect man.'

CLARIFICATION

13 When one person had given a moral explanation of this text of Solomon, 'the king's heart is in the hand of God,'[987] another one gives it a deeper meaning, but he does so hesitantly and without insisting on anything. For he begins thus: 'I think – if you make allowance for these gray hairs – that this saying can be accommodated to a deeper meaning. "King" can be understood as the perfect man who, with his bodily passions under control, is governed solely by the power of the Holy Spirit. Moreover, to compel such a man to conform to human laws is perhaps inappropriate. Instead he should be left to his Lord, by whose spirit he is led; he is not to be judged by those regulations by which the weakness of feeble men is drawn, in one

* * * * *

983 That is, the theologians omit 'some' (*aliquid*). The Froben edition of February 1526 used by the theologians does indeed read 'aliquid habet affine cum Iudaismo,' not 'sunt affinia Iudaismo.'

984 See nn364 and 667 above.

985 1 Cor 2:15

986 CWE 39 185:41–186:1 / LB I 678B / ASD I-3 244:392–5

987 Prov 21:1

way or another, to true godliness. But if he does anything unrighteously, we ought to say with Paul: "God has taken him to himself; to his Lord he stands or falls."[988] Likewise: "A person who is spiritual judges all things, yet he himself is judged by no man."[989] Therefore nobody may prescribe to such persons, etc.' If Paul does not wish any Christian to be judged because of food or drink, why should it be a subject of wonder if Solomon thought something similar, but still this interpretation is not insisted upon but only put forward to be examined. And if there should be someone who is clearly so perfect that he is governed only by the commands of the Spirit in all matters, who would be so ungodly as to prescribe for him laws about external matters concerning which the Lord and the apostles gave no commandments, or who would dare to bind him by such ordinances? I think no one would. For the Spirit is above all human laws, above the pope and councils, however general they may be.

But since it is not clear who is such, it is not safe to open this window for the ordinary mob, lest they seize upon this as a cover for their malice. And the dialogue does not say that he is not bound but that he should not be compelled to conform and should not be judged for such deeds, but rather it should be accepted that such a man ignores what is less important in pursuit of a greater good or for some other good reason. Thus in past times hermits attached to monasteries were forgiven if their godliness had been sufficiently observed. So also in monasteries today ordinances concerning external matters are relaxed for Doctors and others striving vigorously for heroic virtues, as it is for those who have made extraordinary progress. And Jean Gerson, though he does not approve of the teachings of the Beguards, nevertheless does not deny that spiritual aspirations are not to be scorned, as long as they are not feigned, but should be examined to see if they are from God.[990]

14 Thirdly, he once more criticizes abstinence from meat. This can be seen on page 151, past the middle, at this point:[991] 'It is permissible,[992] therefore, to eat anything one likes, etc.'

* * * * *

988 Rom 14:3–4
989 1 Cor 2:15
990 Gerson *De distinctione revelationum* and *De theologia mystica* 1.8 in *Oeuvres complètes* 52–3, 255–6.
991 CWE 39 190:20–1 / LB I 680F / ASD I-3 249:557–8
992 In the Froben 1533 edition Erasmus changed *licet* 'it is permissible' to *licebat* 'it was permissible.'

CLARIFICATION

14 Once more, reader, I beg you to see what it is to judge from fragments excerpted by others, and even those often misreported. In the dialogue someone who is explaining the words of Paul, 'all things are lawful to me but not all things are expedient,'[993] speaks in the person of Paul: 'It is permissible, therefore, to eat anything one likes, and to the pure all things are pure.[994] Yet in some cases this may be inexpedient. That all things are permissible is[995] a matter of gospel liberty; but charity everywhere regards what contributes to the salvation of our neighbour and on that account frequently abstains even from what is permitted, etc.' So says the colloquy. And what is being handled there is meat offered to idols and the Jewish choice of foods. Whoever wants to can read the passage and he will discover that in that passage nothing is being discussed except the meaning of the Apostle's words, with no mention of any later ordinances of the church. But when the passage is set forth as 'Erasmus criticizes abstinence from meat, writing "it is permissible, therefore, to eat anything one likes,"' what does the faculty pronounce concerning what is set before them except that I hold a wrong opinion. But what would someone say about such calumniators if he read the colloquy and saw quite clearly that there is not a whit in it touching upon the ordinances of the church.

15 In the fourth place, he alleges that the ordinary run of Christians think their entire salvation consists in ceremonies, baptism, exorcism, catechism, salt, water, and have the greatest confidence in anointing, confession, confirmation, the Eucharist, matrimony, holy orders, as if in fact Christians hoped to be saved only by means of the sacraments without fulfilling the precepts of God. None of the Catholic Doctors takes this position; actually simple people are taught the opposite.

16 This is shown on page 160, above the middle, at this point:[996] 'If you observe the great majority of Christians, the sum and substance[997] of their salvation, etc.'[998]

* * * * *

993 1 Cor 6:12
994 Titus 1:15
995 In the Froben 1533 edition Erasmus changed *licent ... est* 'are permissible is' to *licebat ... erat* 'were permissible was.'
996 CWE 39 196:11–13 / LB I 683F / ASD I-3 255:726–7
997 Literally, the stern and bow: *Adagia* 1 i 8
998 The Froben edition of February 1526 used by the theologians has 'sum and substance of life' (*puppim et prorim vitae*), not 'of their salvation.'

17 And at the bottom of the preceding page, namely 159, speaking against
ceremonies he says: 'No wonder those who have puzzled their heads
over ceremonies[999] all their lives should die thus.'[1000]

CLARIFICATION
15, 16 It is well established that in the sacraments of the church there is
something material and something spiritual. The material does not give life
unless it is accompanied by the spiritual. And the dialogue singles out for
blame the general run of Christians, that is, the majority and the crudest
part, who think perfect godliness consists in externals and neglect those
things which truly make them godly. For example, in baptism if someone who is dipped, anointed, and initiated with other ceremonies relies
on them and does not add what is spiritual, he is dipped and anointed in
vain. The words of the colloquy are as follows: 'If you observe the general run of Christians, isn't it true that to them ceremonies are the sum and
substance of life?' Then I add examples concerning the individual sacraments. And what is it that seems to be spoken falsely: that there are such
Christians or that the entire confidence about our salvation should not be
placed in the externals of the sacraments? For in that place I am not speaking about all Christians, but about the general run of them. But, in fact,
here too the writer, whoever he was, misreported, quoting it as if I were
speaking about all Christians generally. Therefore, if they agree with me
that the whole hope of salvation should not be placed in the external ceremonies of the sacraments, if they grant that many such crude persons
are hiding under the name of Christians, I wonder what offends them or
what they mean by these words: 'as if in fact Christians hoped to be saved
only by means of the sacraments without fulfilling the precepts of God.
None of the Catholic Doctors takes this position; actually simple people
are taught the opposite.' This is what they say. If the Doctors condemn the
same thing as my dialogue, why are they taking me to task since I stand
on their side?

CLARIFICATION OF 17
Where do I say anything against ceremonies? 'No wonder,' I say, 'that those
who have puzzled their heads over ceremonies all their lives should die
thus.' What else does this say except that the reason so many die luke-

* * * * *

999 In the Froben 1533 edition Erasmus added 'only, so much' (*tantum*) before
'over ceremonies' (*in ceremoniis*).
1000 CWE 39 196 / LB I 683E / ASD I-3 255:117–18

warm and almost without faith is that all their lives they have trusted in
external things and visible sacraments and neglected what belongs to true
godliness? For this is the beginning of a disquisition on the general run of
Christians who think the sum and substance consists in externals. Is this the
same as speaking against ceremonies? Is it not rather speaking in favour of
Christian godliness? I do not know whether they suspect that this aims at
abrogating ceremonies; not only is there nothing in my words that should
have given rise to such a suspicion, but the passage expressly excludes any
such suspicion when it says: 'Indeed I approve of doing all these things but
doing them more from custom than from conviction I do not approve of.
The notion that nothing else is needed for Christianity I reject absolutely,
etc.'[1001] Time and again, reader, see what it is to render an opinion based
on notes turned over by young students; for here it is sufficiently clear
that those who wrote these things did not read the passage in the dialogue
which they are criticizing.

18 In the fifth place, he indicates that it is a mortal sin to decorate
churches, to dedicate monasteries. This can be seen on page 165, before
the middle, at this point:[1002] 'Hence it seems to me that it is hardly possible to exempt from mortal[1003] sin those who build or adorn monasteries or churches at excessive cost, when meanwhile so many of Christ's
living temples, etc.'[1004]

CLARIFICATION
18 The passage in the dialogue is as follows: 'it is robbery to lavish upon
those who will make bad use of it that which was owed to the immediate
need of our neighbours. Hence it seems to me that it is hardly possible to
exempt from mortal sin those who build or adorn monasteries or churches
at excessive cost, when meanwhile so many of Christ's living temples are in
danger of starvation, shiver in their nakedness, and are tormented by want
of the necessities of life, etc.' I beg you, reader, what is blamed here except
excessive spending, and that not unqualified but to the neglect of the poor?
The vainglory of potentates and rich men gives itself almost free rein in

* * * * *

1001 CWE 39 196:25–7 / LB I 684A / ASD I-3 255:737–9
1002 CWE 39 198:38–199:1 / LB I 684F / ASD I-3 257:787–90
1003 Here the censure reads *mortali* rather than the *capitali* found in the edition used
by the theologians. The meaning is the same, but the theologians substitute
the more usual term.
1004 1 Cor 3:16–17; 2 Cor 6:16

such things under an honourable pretext. Where, then, is the person who indicates that it is a mortal sin to adorn churches or dedicate monasteries? What would people say if they read my dialogue and compared it with this accusation?

> In the dialogue which is entitled *The Apotheosis* he praises Capnio or Reuchlin excessively, comparing his glory with that of St Jerome, and placing him in the catalogue of the saints without the authority of the Holy See, and assigning to him a prayer called a collect[1005] – none of which should have been done even in jest. For to make fun of the saints even in jest (as he says elsewhere) is neither godly nor safe. The material for jokes must be sought elsewhere.[1006]

19 The first instance occurs on page 182, about the middle, at this point:[1007] 'Jerome accosted Reuchlin with these words: "Hail, most holy colleague."'

20 The second occurs a little past the middle of page 164,[1008] at this point:[1009] 'What remains, then, but that we inscribe the holy man's name in the calendar of the saints?'

21 The third occurs about the middle of page 186, at this point:[1010] 'O God, lover of mankind, who renewed the gift of tongues, etc.'

CLARIFICATION

[19, 20,] 21 There is good reason to hope that Reuchlin lives with Christ. He was a good man to whom intellectual pursuits owe a great deal. In that place I do indeed jest, but 'who forbids us to say the truth in jest?'[1011]

* * * * *

1005 A brief prayer in the mass; Erasmus explains its history and structure in *Modus orandi Deum* LB V 1125D–1126B / CWE 70 210–12.

1006 This seems to be a paraphrase rather than a quotation. The censure may simply refer to Erasmus' defence of his satire about invocation of the saints on the grounds that the joke is against the superstition or vice of the invokers, not against the saints themselves; see, for example, *Epistola ad Dorpium* CWE 3 Ep 125:463–5; CWE 71 18; *Modus orandi Deum* LB V 1119C–F / CWE 70 197–9; *Apologia adversus Stunicae* Blasphemiae LB IX 9 366D, 368B.

1007 *De Reuchlino in divorum numero relato* CWE 39 249:13 / LB I 691B / ASD I-3 270:115–17

1008 A misprint for 184 in *Declarationes*. The faculty's *Determinatio* has CLXXXIIII.

1009 CWE 39 250:22–3 / LB I 691F / ASD I-3 271:165–6

1010 CWE 39 251:31–2 / LB I 692B / ASD I-3 273:208–12

1011 Horace *Sermones* 1.1.24

and one can joke about the saints without insulting them. Here Jerome is praised, not injured.[1012] And if Jerome, after he had written the life of Paula, called upon her, now that she was living with Christ, to assist his extreme old age with her prayers,[1013] what crime is it for me to have a similar opinion about Reuchlin? How many saints are revered by the church who have never been numbered among the saints by the See of Rome? – though actually my jest does not claim for itself the authority of that See.

22 Before the middle of page 185[1014] he wrongly says that Pius II placed Catherine of Siena among the number of the saints to please a religious order and a city.

CLARIFICATION

22 Pius was from Siena and there is a Dominican monastery there; and so it is probable that, when he had reached the apex of ecclesiastical dignity, he was asked by his fellow citizens and the monks to place that virgin in the number of the saints. The pope does not do such things at random but in response to requests. What would be wrong with doing such a thing?

23 In the dialogue which is called *The Wooer and the Maiden* he gives many examples in an effort to persuade us that marriage is to be preferred to virginity. In this he follows in the footsteps of Jovinian,[1015] if he does not even go beyond him. This is clear at the beginning of page 196, at this point:[1016] 'But meantime my virginity is gone.'

24 And at the end of the same page[1017] he says: 'A maiden is something charming, but what is more unnatural than an old maid?'

25 Secondly, he teaches that virginity is to be acquired by carnal acts – which Epicurus himself would have been afraid to say. This occurs on page 197, before the middle, at this point: 'What's this I hear? Virginity to be violated so that it may be learned?'[1018]

* * * * *

1012 The Latin plays on the sounds: 'Hic Hieronymus laudatur, non laeditur.'
1013 *Epistolae* 108.33 PL 22 906
1014 CWE 39 250:41–251:2 / LB I 692B / ASD I-3 272:181–2
1015 See n71 above.
1016 *Proci et puellae* CWE 39 264:38 (with title 'Courtship') / LB I 695E / ASD I-3 284:264
1017 CWE 39 265:15–16 / LB I 696A / ASD I-3 285:281–2
1018 CWE 39 265:26–8 / LB I 696A–B / ASD I-3 285:291–3

CLARIFICATION OF 23, 24, AND 25

In all seriousness, indeed, the amatory altercation between a wooer and a maiden is attributed to me. But which speaker do they claim I am? For the maiden refutes what the young man says. Will the language of both be attributed to me? That virgin is not destined for a convent, and it is no wonder that the young man dissuades her from virginity and encourages her to marry, for he is making his own case. And she does not praise virginity because she has decided to become a nun; rather she uses this weapon also to dissuade her lover from hurrying up the marriage because it will destroy the beauty and flower of her virginity. But a virgin past her bloom is commonly thought (and even Paul testifies to this)[1019] to be an object of opprobrium because she has not pleased any young men. And yet when the young man makes such arguments, the maiden refutes them with different arguments. But, as for their saying that I teach that virginity is acquired by carnal acts, that is by coition, such an idea never entered my mind, not even in a dream. When she pressed her suitor by praising virginity and chastity, he promised that a time would come when they could live in marriage in such a way that matrimony would differ very little from virginity. The maiden makes fun of this argument, saying: 'What's this I hear? Virginity to be violated so that it may be learned?' Because the wooer has nothing to reply to this, he wiggles out of it with a ridiculous comparison: 'Why not? As by gradually drinking less and less wine we learn temperance.' But the suitor does not take seriously his fiction that virginity is acquired by coition. For, to say nothing of Epicurus, what man in his right mind would say such a thing? But he means that chastity can be maintained in marriage when they have begotten children and the fervour of youth has subsided. What place was there for the accusation 'he teaches virginity through carnal acts,' or the statement 'which Epicurus himself would have been afraid to say'? Would that these accusations had been published under any other name than that of the Faculty of Theology! For whoever wrote them makes witty jokes, heaven knows, but in such a dim-witted way that he makes himself the laughing stock of learned men.

26 Thirdly, he prefers conjugal chastity to the chastity of priests and religious. This is clear on the same page 197, after the middle, at this point:[1020] 'But do not those who bind themselves by a vow to renounce marriage, etc.'

* * * * *

1019 1 Cor 7:36
1020 CWE 39 265:37–8 / LB I 696B / ASD I-3 285:301–2

CLARIFICATION

26 Certainly it is surprising that the suitor, joking with his fiancée, should make use of some silly argument! It is even more surprising that the theologians should treat it as if it were a scholastic dogma being seriously discussed. To be sure, according to a certain perspective a person who lives in the midst of temptations to vice and still keeps himself steadfastly undefiled is more perfect than someone who distrusts himself and hence removes the occasions and ability to sin.

27 In the dialogue *Eubulus and Catharine* he vehemently assails the state of religious life, following Lampert[1021] and saying much about it. First, he calls it 'coals' and matrimony 'a treasure.' This appears at the beginning of page 204, at this point:[1022] 'Huh! Coals instead of treasure.'[1023]

CLARIFICATION

27 Whoever singled this out for blame completely misunderstood the passage in the dialogue. For there the young man makes use of a proverb which the Greeks used to express the disappointed hopes of someone who did not get what he was looking for. The young man, who was expecting to work his way into obtaining the girl's love, falls off from that hope when he hears her speak of the religious life. The passage is as follows: 'To join a community of holy virgins. Eubulus: To become a nun? Catharine: Yes. Eubulus: Huh! Coals instead of treasure.' He does not mean that instead of the treasure of matrimony he has found the coals of virginity but that instead of what he hoped for he has found what he did not want at all. For he said this as an aside, speaking not to the girl but to himself. If the argument is made that it doesn't matter whom he is speaking to when he

* * * * *

1021 Both editions of 1532 and LB have 'Lamperius.' The theologians must be referring to François Lambert of Avignon (c 1487–1530), a Franciscan friar who left his order and married. He was instrumental in introducing Lutheranism into Hesse. He wrote books rejecting the religious life: *Rationes propter quas minoritarum conversationem habitumque rejecit* 'Reasons why he rejected the habit and way of life of the friars minor' (written in Wittenberg 1522–3, published in 1530); and *Evangelici in minoritarum regulam commentarii* 'An evangelical commentary on the rule of the friars minor' (1523?). In *Hyperaspistes 1* (CWE 76 165 n371) Erasmus replied to the attack on *De libero arbitrio* which Lambert included in *In ... Oseam ... commentarii* (1525). On Lambert see CEBR II 284.

1022 CWE 39 287:36 (with title *Virgo μισόγαμος* 'The Girl with No Interest in Marriage') / LB I 698B / ASD I-3 291:85

1023 A proverb expressing disappointed expectations: *Adagia* I ix 30

compares the proposed virginity to coals, he reveals the same good judgment by which he prefers pleasure to virtue. For in that dialogue that is
the sort of person I imagine him to be. For heaven's sake, such criticisms!
For here I will have to defend whatever a young man in love says in jest
to the maiden. For it is clear that he uses some invalid arguments, many of
which she refutes.

28 Secondly, he says that to enter the religious life against the wishes
   of one's parents is against the natural and divine law. This appears
   a little past the middle of page 208, at this point:[1024] 'Nature teaches,
   God commands, Paul admonishes, human laws decree that children
   obey their parents.'[1025]

CLARIFICATION
28 It is a lovers' quarrel. He calls the monastic life a kind of servitude. She
replies that this kind of servitude is approved of by the most approved men,
as long as it is willingly undertaken. He uses many arguments to persuade
her that a maiden is not free to withdraw against the wishes of her parents.
She responds that in a matter of religion the laws of nature lose their force.
If I had imagined two people arguing, one of them recommending the
monastic way of life and the other opposing it, wouldn't each of them have
to have appropriate language attributed to him? But in fact the young man
does not oppose monasticism in general; rather he dissuades this particular
young lady, making use of various circumstances which can be such that it
would be pious to recall one girl or another from the obligation of monastic
life: for example, if parents needed to be looked after by their daughter,
or if the monastery were such that she could live a more holy life in her
parents' house, or if those in charge of the monastery were such that her
virginity would be safer at home. And many such circumstances apply to
the young woman I introduce.

29 Thirdly, he calls the state of religious life a new servitude. This is on
   page 209, at this point:[1026] 'But under pretence of religion a new kind
   of servitude[1027] has been devised.'

* * * * *

1024 CWE 39 290:32–3 / LB I 699E / ASD I-3 294:188–9
1025 See CWE 39 297 nn28–30.
1026 CWE 39 291:2–3 / LB I 699F / ASD I-3 295:1–2
1027 In the Froben 1533 edition after the phrase 'new kind of servitude' (*novum
     servitutis genus*) Erasmus added 'at least according to the way life is lived

CLARIFICATION

29 First of all, the young lover, as I have said, is making his own case, and as is done in battle he turns every siege-engine against the maiden, using any argument whatsoever to get her to change her plan. 'Who asks whether an enemy is deceitful or honest?'[1028] And it is not entirely false that the monastic way of life is a kind of servitude. For just as a person is free if he lives just as he wishes, so too a person who depends entirely on someone else is in a certain sense a slave. For it is precisely the renunciation of their own will that they boast about. But if you look at many monasteries, what the young man said is only too true. Where Sacred Scripture is not studied, where there is no spiritual energy, where there is no charity to sweeten all things, where those in charge neither offer good example by their lives nor feed their flock with the word of God nor give loving encouragement but do nothing but rage and command in a thoroughly tyrannical way, what is this but a miserable servitude under the pretence of religion? Certainly one can live a godly life in other places, but not there. And everywhere there are plenty of such monasteries, more than enough. But in fact even what the young man says here is refuted by the maiden, as I said before. And the worst part is attributed to me.

30 In the fourth place he calls the teaching that recommends entering the religious life pharisaical and contrary to the teaching of the Apostle. This appears after the middle of page 209, at this point:[1029] 'That is a truly pharisaical doctrine. Paul teaches the contrary, that someone who is called free, etc.'[1030]

[CLARIFICATION]

30 Wherever the discipline of true religious life is absent, there they most of all lure inexperienced young people and teach them not piety but lifeless ceremonies, to say nothing of other skills not to be mentioned here. Since there is miserable slavery in such religious houses, it is pharisaical to drive simple young people there with exhortations, blandishments, and threats in order to make them sons of hell twice over.[1031] That this happens everywhere even the theologians, I think, do not deny. But what the young man is

* * * * *

nowadays in many monasteries' (*ut nunc sane in plerisque monasteriis vivitur*).
1028 Virgil *Aeneid* 2.390
1029 CWE 39 291:19 / LB I 700A / ASD I-3 295:10–11
1030 1 Cor 7:21–3
1031 Matt 23:15

getting at here is clear from what immediately follows: 'Besides your slavery is the more unfortunate because you must serve many masters, because for the most part they are foolish and vicious,[1032] because they are constantly changing and there are new ones from time to time.' Now what differs from the teaching of Paul is not straightway condemned. He gives the right to eat any food whatsoever.[1033] An ordinance of the church takes this right away. And I hardly know whether Paul would have approved of the sort of monasticism we see in our day if he had seen it. Finally, even though none of these considerations may do me any good, I can say that the young man is not disputing in the schools about how virginity compares with matrimony, but is catering to his own desire. But if in dialogues I am blamed for whatever is said, it would not even be safe to write fables, lest what the wolf and the crocodile say should be attributed to Erasmus.

31   In the fifth place he rails hostilely at the religious life. This appears at the top of page 210, at this point:[1034] 'In a matter of religion natural laws lose their force. A matter of religion is transacted in baptism. Here the question is merely one of changing dress, of a way of life that in itself is neither good nor bad.'

CLARIFICATION

31 God forbid that anyone should rail hostilely against the religious life, since it is a spotless life, an attitude free from worldly contamination, and is professed by all Christians. This is the argument of the young man, and it is inappropriate to want me to defend everything said by the rascal I have imagined. Monks boast that they have renounced the world and that they have given themselves over to Christ and subjected themselves to him. This, he says, occurs in baptism when we renounce Satan and all his pomps and pleasures, and nothing godly is done in monasteries that cannot be done as well elsewhere, or sometimes even better. What, then, is added by profession as a monk? The superior is changed, a place is assigned, clothes, food, and other human matters are prescribed which in themselves are neither good nor bad, so that someone who observes them

* * * * *

1032 According to ASD I-3, variant at 295:12–13, and CWE 39 298 n43 'because ... vicious' was added in the Froben 1531 edition. Hence it would not have been available in 1526, when the censures were written, nor when they were published in July 1531.
1033 Rom 14:3; Col 2:16
1034 CWE 39 291:31–4 / LB I 700B / ASD I-3 295:219–21

is not straightway godly and someone is not necessarily bad if he keeps himself free of them. This is the argument not of Erasmus but of the young man, who wants the maiden to be affiliated with a hermit rather than a convent.[1035] But still he does not rail against the religious life but thinks that all Christians professed a religious life at baptism, about which many people are mistaken, attributing too little to that first and highest profession and too much to the profession of monasticism, at least that of our times.[1036]

32 In the sixth place he asserts that obedience, poverty, and chastity can be equally well observed in her parents' home as in the religious life. This appears toward the end of page 210, at this point:[1037] 'They brag about obedience. Will that praise be lacking to you if you obey your parents, whom God bids you obey, etc.'

CLARIFICATION

32 'Equally well' is not in the colloquy, but the young man says only that the praise of obedience and poverty would not be lacking to her if she obeys her parents and if she herself possesses nothing living under them. For it was once considered praiseworthy for a virgin dedicated to Christ to live with her parents.

33 In the seventh place he asserts that the ceremonies of religious life contribute nothing to godliness and do not recommend anyone in the eyes of Christ. This is occurs at the beginning of page 211, at this point:[1038] 'So what remains? The veil, linen clothing inside and out, certain rites that contribute nothing to godliness.'

CLARIFICATION

33 The young man means that clothing, food, and other externals which are prescribed for monks contribute nothing to godliness in and of themselves,[1039] and he says what he means. For when he had argued that chastity,

* * * * *

1035 Latin *anachoritidem fieri quam coenobitidem*. These coinages look like patronymics formed from *anachorita* and *coenobita*; they do not appear in the usual dictionaries of medieval Latin. The hermit is presumably the young man himself.

1036 Erasmus discusses this point in *Divinationes ad notata Bedae* LB IX 458D–459A.

1037 CWE 39 292:4–6 / LB I 700C / ASD I-3 296:232–4

1038 CWE 39 292:11–12 / LB I 700D / ASD I-3 296:238–40

1039 The phrase 'in and of themselves' (*per se*) was not added to the colloquy until the 1533 edition; see ASD I-3, variant at 296:239.

obedience, and poverty can be observed even in her parents' house, he concludes that these elements do not belong exclusively to monasticism. And
so he asks what does. He replies to himself: clothing and some ceremonies
belonging to it which, without what goes along with them, do not recommend anyone to Christ but produce hypocrites. And so it is not said in an
unqualified way that the ceremonies of the monks contribute nothing to
godliness.

34 In the eighth place he contends that to enter the religious life against
    the wishes of one's parents is illicit. This appears about the middle
    of page 211, at this point:[1040] 'Then what is this new religion that
    abrogates what the law of nature sanctioned, and the Old Law taught,
    and the law of the gospel approved.'
35 In the ninth place, on the same page a little after the aforesaid words,
    he says:[1041] 'This decree' (namely the entry into religious life against
    the wishes of one's parents) 'was not issued by God but devised in a
    council of monks.'
36 Finally, he mockingly asks the theologians to point out to him a pas-
    sage in Sacred Scripture that teaches the institution of the religious
    life, though it is sufficiently clear that many texts there do so. This oc-
    curs a little after the beginning of page 212, at this point:[1042] 'Ask these
    persons to show you any passage from Sacred Scripture that teaches
    this.'

CLARIFICATION
34 and 35 I replied to this above: the Lord commands us to leave father
and mother because of him,[1043] that is, if they call us away from the gospel,
or call upon us to do ungodly deeds, their authority is to be scorned; nevertheless, in other matters a Christian owes obedience to ungodly parents.
But what is found in Scripture about leaving the world[1044] (that is, paganism and Judaism) many apply to monasticism, whereas the world is in our
attitude, not in a place or a garment. Nowadays it is a harsh thing to leave
one's parents and to devote oneself to monks against the wishes of one's
parents, especially if the parents are godly (as I imagine them to be) and
depend on their only daughter as the main comfort of their old age. For

* * * * *

1040 CWE 39 292:25–7 / LB I 700D / ASD I-3 296:250–2
1041 CWE 39 292:27–8 / LB I 700D–E / ASD I-3 296:252–3
1042 CWE 39 293:1–2 / LB I 700F / ASD I-3 297:266–7
1043 Luke 14:26
1044 For example, 1 John 2:15

all these circumstances are present in the dialogue, and if you posit them, the argument of the young man is not absurd; and even if you do not, the subject is still open to debate.

CLARIFICATION OF 36

Whoever excerpted this passage was not sufficiently attentive. For nothing is said there about the profession of monasticism as such but only about ceremonies. For this is the argument: if you can observe everything else while living with your parents and lack nothing but the name of a nun, the clothing, and the ceremonies, the right of parents is not to be held in contempt because of such things as these, for this right does not call anyone away from godliness, not even from perfect godliness. Whether there are any texts in Scripture which teach this I do not know; I have not found any yet.

37 In the dialogue which is called *The Repentant Girl* he takes to task those who persuade people to join the religious life. This appears toward the end of page 214,[1045] at this point:[1046] 'Oh, the shamelessness of the brutes! etc.'

38 The same point occurs toward the end of page 214, at this point:[1047] 'Smart actors those! They know how to put on their plays before the simple-minded rabble.'

CLARIFICATION OF 37 AND 38

The girl had told about the wickedness and tricks used by the shameless monks to force her parents to give their consent, employing even wine as a weapon, then making threats that they were in danger of coming to a bad end if they did not allow their daughter to become a nun. Against them the young man cries out, 'Oh, the shamelessness of the brutes!' not simply against anyone who exhorts a person to the religious life, though this was not exhortation but the application of force. But when the young man afterwards cried out again, 'Smart actors those!' his exclamation does not apply to just any who exhort but to the pomp with which they publicly led the maiden, decked out like a bride, from her parents' house to the convent. The passage itself in the colloquy makes it clear that what I say is true. I have made a copious reply on the part of the young man, although it is not necessary for me to answer for whatever I make him

* * * * *

1045 In fact the quotation appears a little below the middle of page 213 in the edition used by the theologians (Froben, February 1526).

1046 *Virgo poenitens* CWE 39 303:11 / LB I 701C / ASD I-3 299:25

1047 CWE 39 304:10 / LB I 701F / ASD I-3 299:62

say – no more, by heaven, than if I were writing a comedy I would have to answer for whatever was said by any person, since the speakers there could be pimps, parasites, bawds, and whores. But in fact the young man himself at the end of the dialogue removes any little offence that might be taken by the weak. When the girl asks him whether he condemns the institution of monasticism *in toto*, 'not at all,' he says. 'But just as I would not want to argue that a girl who entered this kind of life should try to get out of it, so I would not hesitate to warn all girls, particularly the talented ones, against throwing themselves rashly into something there's no escape from afterwards, especially since in those communities virginity is often in considerable danger and you could accomplish at home whatever is accomplished there.' The other points are sophistries; his conclusion makes it clear what should seriously be thought. He does not forbid anyone to enter the monastic life, but he does not approve of doing so rashly or precipitately. I imagine the theologians think the same.

39 Moreover, he approves of her backing out of religious life as if she would be doing something good by not remaining in it. This appears toward the end of page 215, at this point:[1048] 'It is well for you that you backed out in time before committing yourself to perpetual servitude.'

CLARIFICATION

39 This too is reported differently than it is in the colloquy. For the young man does not praise the girl for backing out of the religious life, but he congratulates her because, when she felt that she could not hold out there any longer, she left at the right time before taking any vows. For it was still honourable to change her mind. The dialogue says as follows: 'It is well for you that you backed out in time before committing yourself to perpetual servitude.'

40 In the dialogue *The Soldier and the Carthusian* he makes light of the ceremonies of the religious life and eliminates all confidence in them. This can be seen at the end of page 236, at this point:[1049] 'In dress, food, little prayers, and other ceremonies you put your trust, etc.'

* * * * *

1048 CWE 39 304:25–6 / LB I 702A / ASD I-3 300:74–5. In fact it appears a bit above the middle of page 215 in the edition used by the theologians (Froben, February 1526).

1049 *Militis et Cartusiani* CWE 39 333:4–5 / LB I 709C / ASD I-3 316:90–1

41 And at the beginning of page 237, at this point:[1050] 'What others may do is not for me to judge. For my part, I by no means rely on these things and I set very little store by them.'

42 And a little later on the same page:[1051] 'A shaven head or the colour of a garment does not commend me to God.'[1052]

CLARIFICATION

40, 41, 42 Someone who makes light of the ceremonies of the monks does so rightly if he observes them but nevertheless does not place any confidence about his godliness in them but rather in the godliness of his heart and in Christ. For the soldier had objected to the Carthusian that he placed his trust in dress, food, little prayers, and other ceremonies, neglecting the pursuit of godliness. To this the Carthusian responds as follows: 'What others may do is not for me to judge. For my part, I by no means rely on these things and I set very little store by them, but I place my trust in purity of heart and in Christ.' Who sets very little store does set some store by them; whoever gives the lowest place in the economy of godliness to those things which deserve the lowest place acts correctly, as long as he observes them out of love for harmony. Will such teaching as this corrupt the minds of the young if they learn in monasteries that their primary aim should be to cleanse their feelings and that externals should indeed be observed but should not be valued so highly that they think godliness consists mainly in them? If Paul spoke piously when he said 'food does not commend us to God,'[1053] though it is pleasing to God if someone, out of a love for sobriety, either fasts in order to control his flesh or abstains from wine and gourmet food, then the Carthusian is not ungodly when he says: 'A shaven head or the colour of a garment does not commend me to God.' At least in and of themselves they do not do so.

43 In the dialogue which is entitled *The Shipwreck* he impiously thinks that the titles which the church rightly bestows on the Blessed Virgin Mary should be taken away from her. This appears at the

* * * * *

1050 CWE 39 333:6–8 / LB I 709C / ASD I-3 316:92–4
1051 CWE 39 333:15–16 / LB I 709D / ASD I-3 317:100
1052 LB I 709D adds 'certainly in and of itself' (*per se quidem*) before 'does not commend' (*non commendat*), though this reading does not appear in any authoritative edition printed during Erasmus' lifetime; see ASD I-3 317:100.
1053 1 Cor 8:8

beginning of page 218,[1054] at this point:[1055] 'The sailors were singing "Hail, holy queen,"[1056] praying to the Virgin Mother, calling her Star of the Sea,[1057] Queen of Heaven, Mistress of the World, Port of Salvation,[1058] flattering her with many other titles which the Sacred Scriptures nowhere assign to her.' This is false, since Sacred Scripture calls her the Mother of God, from which the other titles are clearly derived.

CLARIFICATION

[43] I responded on this point in such detail to the Spanish monks and to Alberto Pio that I neither wish nor need to repeat the same things so often.[1059] Since there are various persons in this dialogue, as happens in ships, and among them some rough types and also some others who are superstitious, I do not have to seriously defend what each one says, no more than if I were writing a narrative of an event such as this. If all those titles are derived from the one given to her, Mother of God (although I hardly find this title in canonical Scripture; I read only mother of Jesus), I have nothing against it; nor do I deny that all those titles and ones even more sublime[1060] are fitting for the Virgin Mother in some sense. But those crude sailors are being singled out for blame for this reason: they flatter her with such titles as if she were some empty-headed woman, whereas otherwise this class of men is vicious and debauched. And it is one thing to be in Sacred Scripture and something else to be derived from it in some way or other, not to say twisted out of it. But because of the added phrase in the colloquy, 'and flattering her with other titles,' the clause 'which the Sacred Scriptures do not assign to her' pertains more to those titles that are not expressed than to the ones given. Christian candour should interpret ambiguous language in the most favourable way. Concerning taking titles away from the Virgin nothing is said or thought; this is simply added for the sake of slander.

· * * * * *

1054 The correct page number is 248.
1055 *Naufragium* CWE 39 355:11–14 / LB I 713A / ASD I-3 327:71–4
1056 On this famous hymn of the Roman breviary (Latin *Salve regina*) see CWE 39 362 n17.
1057 See n856 above.
1058 For these titles of the Blessed Virgin see Anselm Salzer *Die Sinnbilder und Beiworte Mariens in der deutschen Literatur und lateinischen Hymnenpoesie des Mittelalters* (Darmstadt 1967) 404–8, 462:6 and 12, 463:2, 529:13 and 17, 530:3–4.
1059 *Apologia adversus monachos* LB IX 1086C–D; *Apologia adversus rhapsodias Alberti Pii* LB IX 1163E–1164B / CWE 84 243–5
1060 For example, Queen of Angels

44 And then, in the same place, he speaks irreverently of the Blessed
Virgin, comparing her to Venus and making her succeed to Venus in
taking care of sailors. Hence in the same place, after the preliminary
statement, 'What does she have to do with the sea? She never sailed,
I think. Formerly Venus was the protectress of sailors,' he says the
following: 'Since she gave up guarding them, the Virgin Mother has
succeeded this mother who was not a virgin.'[1061]

CLARIFICATION
44 Pagan superstition believed that Venus took care of sailors because she
was born out of the sea. And so the superstition of the sailors is being
laughed at because they pray to the Virgin Mother with a similar attitude.
But, in fact, this whole reply of his is obviously a joke, and to make that
clear I make the other one respond: 'Surely you're joking.'[1062] And this joke
is not aimed at the Virgin but at the sailors.[1063]

45 Moreover, he criticizes at length vows made to saints. This appears at
the end of the aforesaid page:[1064] 'Didn't you make vows to any of the
saints?' And at the beginning of the following page the other answers,
'not at all,' and adds the reason for what he said; 'because,' he says, 'I
do not make deals with the saints.'

CLARIFICATION
45 Vows are not being condemned in an unqualified way; rather the superstition of people is being mocked because they make bargains with the
saints just as if they were dealing with human affairs. For this is what follows: 'For what else is that but a bargain according to the form "I give
this so that you will do that" or "I'll do this if you'll do that"; "I'll give
a candle if I swim to safety"; "I'll go to Rome if you rescue me"?' Now
imagine that there was someone on the ship who was not unfavourable to
Lutheranism; what have I done wrong if I make up a speech fitting for
him?

* * * * *

1061 CWE 39 355:11–18 / LB I 713B / ASD I-3 327:75–7
1062 The Latin is merely *ludis*, not the *ludis tu quidem* which Erasmus gives here.
1063 Erasmus replied on this point at greater length in *Apologia adversus rhapsodias
     Alberti Pii* LB IX 1164C–D / CWE 84 246.
1064 CWE 39 356:19–22 / LB I 713E / ASD I-3 328:115–329:119. In the edition used by
     the theologians (Froben, February 1526), the page is not 'the aforesaid page'
     (248) but rather page 249.

46 He also finds fault with asking for help from saints when he needs something. This appears at the top of page 250, at this point:[1065] 'But you called on some saint for help?' The other one responded: 'Not even that,' and gives the reason: 'Because heaven's a large place, etc.'

CLARIFICATION

46 There is no fault-finding in the dialogue; it is just a joke, which nevertheless suggests that the best thing in any sort of need is to seek refuge directly in God.

47 Moreover, he mocks the invocation of a saint whose name is unknown. This appears toward the end of page 251, at this point:[1066] 'If you had invoked him by name, he would have heard.'

CLARIFICATION

47 This, too, is nothing but a joke, not condemning the invocation of an unknown saint but implying the superstition of the sailor who thinks it is better to invoke an unknown saint than Christ, who is very well known. But the Christian religion would be none the worse for it if a little less were attributed to the invocation of the saints than some people do. Furthermore, if they want they can imagine once more that the jokester is a semi-Lutheran; the language fits the speaker.

48 Moreover, he adds a joke about the Dominican religious who takes off his cowl to save himself, saying that without his cowl he cannot be recognized by St Catherine of Siena. This appears at the end of page 253, at this point:[1067] 'What became of the Dominican?' And at the beginning of page 254, at this point: 'He would have swum better if he had not thrown off his sacred cowl. With that put aside, how could Catherine of Siena recognize him?'

CLARIFICATION

48 I do not think the faith is in any danger if someone makes a joke about the cowl of some Dominican.

49 In the dialogue which is called *An Examination of the Faith*, contrary to the provisions of the law, he proposes to simple people and children

* * * * *

1065 CWE 39 356:26–9 / LB I 713E / ASD I-3 329:122–5
1066 CWE 39 357:26 / LB I 714C / ASD I-3 330:160
1067 CWE 359:5–12 / LB I 715B / ASD I-3 331:213–22

difficult and dangerous questions about the faith, including some errors. The first of these is that among the divine persons authority is
appropriate to the Father and not the Son – which is set down on page
293, at this point:[1068] 'Why, then, does Sacred Scripture call the Son
"Lord" rather than "God"?' The answer is: 'Because "God" is a name
of authority, which is appropriate to the Father.' This is false, for this
name 'God' does not denote authority in any way that would not make
it equally appropriate to all of the Persons. And in Sacred Scripture
the name 'God' is indifferently applied to the Son as well as the Father:
John, chapter 1[:1]: 'And the Word was God.' And in the last chapter
of John: 'My Lord and my God.'[1069] And in many other places.

CLARIFICATION[1070]

49 In that dialogue it is not boys who are speaking but a Lutheran theologian with an orthodox one. For not all the colloquies were written for
boys, and besides it is not right not to want boys to grow up sometime.
'Authority' is there used in the sense of 'principle' or 'source,' which cannot be unknown to the theologians since it is frequently used in this sense
by St Hilary, whose words are also reported in theological opinions. For
Hilary in some places distinguishes the Persons by calling the Father the
author, the Son the only begotten, and the Holy Spirit the lord. Likewise, in
book 9 he declares that the Father is greater than the Son for the very reason that he is the Father, that is, because of his fully perfect authority. For
this reason they call only the Father the unborn because he springs from no
one. Likewise in book 7 he calls the Father the author of the Son: 'so that
he does not differ,' he says, 'in kind but signifies the author.'[1071] Again in
book 4: 'By the very fact,' he says, 'that he is called the Father, he is shown

* * * * *

1068 *Inquisitio de fidei* CWE 39 424:27–31 / LB I 729B–C / ASD I-3 366:106–7
1069 John 20:28 (the second last chapter, not the last)
1070 Pelargus G3–G4 says that he thoroughly agrees with the meaning of *auctoritas*
    'source' or 'principle,' which Erasmus justifies from Hilary and the *Sentences*
    of Lombard. But he argues cogently and at length that *Deus* is not a name
    indicating 'authority.' He notes that Erasmus himself changed an objectionable
    phrase, 'why only the father is called God' in Scripture, to 'why does the
    Sacred Scripture quite frequently call the Son "Lord" rather than "God."' He
    denies Erasmus' argument that 'God' is a name of authority because authority
    is peculiar to the Father and because whatever is done by the Son or the
    Holy Spirit is referred to the Father as its fountainhead from which the other
    Persons also owe the fact that they exist. If this were strictly true the name
    'God' could not be applied to the Son or the Holy Spirit.
    In the second edition Erasmus made no changes or additions.
1071 *De Trinitate* 4.37 PL 10 230C

to be the author of the one he generated, a name which he has because he is understood not to have arisen from anyone else and from whom we are taught that the begotten one has his substance.'[1072] 'The church knows only one unborn God.'[1073] This is what he says. Indeed in the first book of *The Sentences*,[1074] distinction 29, throughout the discussion 'author' and 'source' are used to mean the same thing. And the theologians grant, I think, that there is in the Father a certain perfect quality of being a source which is not in the Son or the Holy Spirit.

If they should say that 'God' is the name of a nature which is common to all three Persons, I grant it; but here we are dealing with what is customary in Scripture, which frequently uses the name 'God' to designate the Father. For when we read 'God sent his Son,'[1075] 'God' is certainly the name of a Person; and when the Son is called 'God from God,'[1076] the name 'God' is applied to each Person. The same divinity is in all of them, but it is present in one manner in the Father, and in a different way in the other two. And 'God' is a name denoting source and authority, certainly so whenever it is used of the Father, making it clear that in him is the fountainhead of divinity as a whole. And he is called the first Person because the others spring from him. If these things are not said piously, I would wish them to be considered as not said at all. But in fact, to speak frankly, I suspect that there is some error in this place and that it was originally written thus: 'Because "Father" is a name denoting authority, and the most perfect quality of authority is in the Father. For he is God in such a way that he himself springs from no one, but the other Persons have from him a share in the divine nature.' I remember instructing some persons about this matter; hence I am surprised it was not changed.[1077] For it is the beginning of the question which follows: 'In the Apostles' Creed why is the Father alone expressly called God?'

Accordingly, I do not think that there is any meaning here which may offend the pious; it is only that the use of one little word, namely

* * * * *

1072 *De Trinitate* 4.9 PL 10 102B. LB has *genus* 'kind' for *genitus* 'begotten.'
1073 *De Trinitate* 4.6 PL 10 100A
1074 That is, Peter Lombard's *Sententiae*
1075 Gal 4:4; 1 John 4:9
1076 Latin, 'Deus de Deo.' This is not from Scripture but from the credo of the mass ('Deum de Deo ... Deum verum de Deo vero'); see *Missale Romanum* no 17, I 129:26–7.
1077 The Copenhagen MS does not contain this passage, and the editions give no sign of a change of this sort until the Froben edition of 1533, when the two sentences are indeed revised and expanded, but not in precisely the same way as Erasmus gives here.

'authority,' has not been sufficiently examined and has disturbed some persons. But concerning this I have replied to the Spanish monks in detail.[1078] The questioner asks why the Creed calls the Father God and the Son Lord, as frequently happens in Sacred Scripture, especially in Paul. The other answers as follows: 'Because "God" is a name denoting authority, which is appropriate to the Father; "Lord" denotes the redeemer and liberator.' At this point they bring up testimony from Scripture showing that the Son is also called God in Scripture. I wonder why they thought they should do this. For if they were afraid that from my passage someone might suspect that only the Father is to be called God, there immediately follows this: 'But in fact the Father also redeems through the Son and the Son is God from God.'[1079] Here we are dealing with names, which are ordinarily attributed more frequently in Scripture to one Person, though in fact they apply equally to all Persons, as, for example, when under the name Wisdom we understand the Son, or we attribute goodness to the Holy Spirit, whereas the same goodness and wisdom belong to all the Persons.

And the questioner does not ask why Scripture calls only the Father God, but why it does so frequently and in an unqualified way. For the word 'God,' especially in the New Testament, is frequently used to mean one Person, namely the Father. Likewise the word 'Lord' is used to refer to the Person of the Son, though either word applies equally to both. There remains only the difficulty that 'God' is a name of authority; for it means the highest source, that is, authority, and Hilary attributes authority as if it were peculiar to the Father, and for that reason in the Creeds he alone is said to be 'creator of heaven and earth.' And whatever is done by the Son or the Holy Spirit is referred to the Father as its fountainhead, from which the other Persons also owe the fact that they exist. But this literary peculiarity, or rather custom, does not exclude the other Persons from sharing in the name. 'But "God,"' they say, 'does not denote authority in any way that would not make it equally appropriate to

* * * * *

1078 *Apologia adversus monachos* LB IX 1038F–1039F
1079 In the Froben edition of 1533 Erasmus modified the passage 'Because "God" . . . God from God' to read: 'Because "God" is a name denoting authority, which is especially appropriate to the Father, who is the absolute beginning of all things and also the fountainhead of divinity itself; "Lord" is a word denoting the redeemer and liberator. But in fact the Father also redeems through the Son and the Son is God but he is from God the Father. For only the Father is from no one and holds the original status among the divine persons.' See ASD I-3 366:108–367:110 and variants.

[all][1080] the Persons.' What they say is true, and I thoroughly agree; for we are not talking about the fact but about what is customary in Scripture. For the Father is not any less equally wise because the Son is called Wisdom. I simply explained things as they are, and what I thought with my mind I expressed in language which is, in my opinion, Latin, not disagreeing about anything; and still I am blamed as erroneous. Such treatment is not to be imputed to the faculty but to those who handled such a serious matter in little tidbits and snippets plucked out by uneducated persons.

50 The second error is that confidence should not be placed in the humanity of Christ, in the Blessed Virgin and the saints, under God but at a different level; this error is set down on the aforesaid page 292,[1081] in these words: 'And do you, therefore, put your trust in Jesus? Why not?' And after a few intervening words: 'But in fact I would not tie my main hope and trust – my sheet-anchor, as they say[1082] – to him unless he were God.'

CLARIFICATION

50 As I have frequently pointed out, I use 'confidence' to mean 'principal protection.' 'Under God' is not in my dialogue. Whoever trusts a human person under God trusts God more than the person. The passage itself demonstrates that I am dealing here with the greatest confidence. 'But in fact,' it says, 'I would not tie my main hope and trust – my sheet-anchor, as they say – to him (that is, Jesus) unless he were God, etc.' Whoever speaks of a sheet-anchor wants it to be understood that he means not just any confidence, but his principal confidence. But suppose I had said merely 'I would not trust,' why should I not be allowed to say this, since the prophet says 'accursed is he who trusts in man,'[1083] speaking, namely, about the greatest confidence?[1084] If this is absolutely true and thoroughly pious, why am I blamed for making an error? If someone said something wrong about

* * * * *

1080 The Latin of the censure has *omnibus personis* 'all the persons' but in quoting it Erasmus inadvertently omitted *omnibus*.
1081 CWE 39 424:35–425:21 / LB I 729C–D / ASD I-3 367:111–17
1082 Literally, 'my sacred anchor' *Adagia* I i 24. A sheet-anchor was one used by sailors as a last resort in a storm.
1083 Jer 17:5
1084 That is, if Erasmus had said simply 'trust' (*fiderem*) instead of 'tie my sheet-anchor to,' he could still be referring to the greatest confidence, as Jeremiah does using simply *confidit*.

invoking saints, do they think it is fair to find fault when someone else said something that is right?[1085]

51 The third error is written on page 298:[1086] 'Then what is to forbid calling the Holy Spirit "Son"? Barbatius: "Because I nowhere read that he was begotten, nor do I read of his Father."' This reply is erroneous. For the Holy Spirit is not called Son because that is not read anywhere but because of the peculiar character of his emanation, by reason of which it is wrong to call him Son quite apart from Scripture altogether.

CLARIFICATION[1087]

51 This is a quibble about a word, not about meaning. For it is not written precisely because it does not exist. And St Hilary was not ashamed of this response, which they call erroneous; he did not dare to give any reason why he feared to call the Holy Spirit begotten except that he did not find it expressed in Scripture.[1088] And great theologians confess that no clear reason can be given why the Holy Spirit is not called Son except the authority of Scripture. For to give the quality of his emanation as a reason is simply verbal since the peculiar character of that emanation is ineffable and unintelligible, indeed since the word emanation is not in Holy Scripture.[1089] Besides, one who is born also emanates and the word 'proceed' is also applied to the Son. John 16[:27–8]: 'I came forth from God' and 'I came forth from

* * * * *

1085 That is, if the Lutherans say something wrong, is it fair to reprove Erasmus when he says something right?

1086 CWE 39 428:26–9 / LB I 731B / ASD I-3 371:248–9

1087 Pelargus sigs G4–G4v quotes the last sentence of Erasmus' clarification: 'It is surprising that someone who receives his essence from another is not called a son.' His only comment is: 'But should this seem surprising to anyone?'
In the second edition Erasmus added the phrase 'and to human reason' (*et humanae rationi*) at the beginning of the sentence. He also added the clause noting that Augustine applied *proceed* to the Son.

1088 *De Trinitate* 2.29, 12.55–6 PL 10 69–70, 668–71

1089 Theologians such as Thomas Aquinas take it for granted that Scripture calls only the second person Son, not the third. But Thomas distinguishes the two processions from the Father according to intellect and will. The intellectual procession can be called generation, but not the procession by way of the will (to which Scripture gives no name but which can be called 'spiration'); see *Summa theologiae* I q 27 a 4 and q 33 a 2. Erasmus knows that this is the usual distinction but denies that the second kind of procession (or emanation) can be distinguished or understood at all.

the Father,' where Augustine read 'proceeded.'[1090] And to human reason it is strange that someone who equally acquired his essence from another is not called Son.

52 The fourth error is where he says we should not believe in the holy church, on the same pages 298 and 299,[1091] in these words: 'Do you believe in the holy church? Barbatius: No.' And again, 'Why are you afraid to say "I believe in the holy church?" etc.' Since Catholic Doctors, however, give the meaning of this statement 'I believe in the holy church,' and many churches sing it so,[1092] it is temerarious to assert it is not right to say it.

CLARIFICATION[1093]

52 No one asserts there that it is not right to say 'I believe in the holy church,' but rather Cyprian is cited, whom Augustine follows. Indeed I mentioned an authority because I do not especially approve of the distinction. I rather think it is a peculiarity of the Hebrew language, just as in the gospel we read indiscriminately 'I profess him' and 'I profess in him.'[1094] If the authority of Doctors is required, the most approved Doctors of the church have demonstrated what is said in the dialogue. I have not paid any attention to what is sung in this or that church, nor do I think that whatever is sung in some churches is straightway right. They will say, 'why do

* * * * *

1090 *In Joannis Evangelium tractatus* CXXIV 42.8 PL 35 1702
1091 CWE 39 429:1–9 / LB I 731D / ASD I-3 371:253–61
1092 Like Erasmus, I have not attempted to verify what the theologians assert here. But the very authoritative tradition of the credo in the Roman missal omits 'in' before 'unam sanctam catholicam et apostolicam ecclesiam'; see *Missale Romanum* no 17, I 199.
1093 Pelargus sig G4v is in complete agreement with Erasmus. He elaborates somewhat on Thomas Aquinas' opinion (which is in agreement with Erasmus).
    In the second edition Erasmus added a brief section pointing out the inconsistency of the censors: they often accuse him of departing from the usage of the church, but here they defend those who do just that by saying 'in the holy church.'
1094 Though Pelargus agrees with Erasmus about the absence of 'in' before 'sanctam ecclesiam,' in an appended letter in *Bellaria* sigs H1v–H2 he expresses some reservations about taking the use of *in* as a Hebraism, partly because he thinks such a judgment must come from a proficient native speaker and partly because it is not taken as a Hebraism in Christ's phrases *Creditis in me* and *in me credite*. The letter is reprinted in Allen Ep 2671.

you teach what you do not approve of?' Because the meaning is pious, because it is based on great authorities. But I beg you, why am I accused of asserting something temerariously when I teach what was expressly taught by Cyprian, Augustine, Leo, Thomas Aquinas, and Jean Gerson, and, I have no doubt, countless others, and what the Catholic church constantly observes to this very day?[1095] The insult of temerity should more rightly pertain to churchlets (whatever they may be) or to the doctorlings who, with no need to do so, have dared to depart from what is customarily accepted by famous Doctors and the public usage of the church. How often am I called temerarious, arrogant, and ungodly if I indicate something which seems to be at variance with the usage of the church! Now what is charged against me as a crime is defended in other people.[1096]

53   The fifth error is where he says that evil persons do not belong to the church, which consists only of the good. This is an error contrary to the teaching of the gospel. It is set down toward the beginning of page 299, at this point:[1097] 'From the fellowship of the church anyone who commits a mortal sin is separated and cut off.' And a little later: 'The church consists of none but the good.'

CLARIFICATION[1098]

53 The word 'church' is used in various ways in Sacred Scripture; but I think that here it is called holy in the sense of applying to that hidden

* * * * *

1095 See the very detailed note on this point in CWE 39 442 n97.
1096 That is, the Paris theologians defend those who depart from ecclesiastical usage by adhering to the formulation 'I believe in the church.'
1097 CWE 39 429:8–12 / LB I 731D / ASD I-3 371:259–372:264
1098 Pelargus sigs G5–G5v says that in the colloquy Erasmus seems to be speaking not of the guiltless triumphant church but of the church spread throughout our world, and that that church certainly includes evil people. Erasmus takes church here to mean those bound together in true charity and faith, but it is not that church which is referred to in the Apostles' Creed. Moreover, even that church prays for forgiveness. Erasmus does not report the words of Barbatius correctly because the colloquy does not include the phrase *proprie dicta* 'properly so called.' (This phrase was not in the edition of the *Colloquies* used by the Sorbonne theologians but was added by Erasmus in the September 1531 edition.) If the bad are excluded from the church, then they constitute a separate church, and orthodoxy requires only one church. Dead members do remain in the mystical body of Christ (the church) with the hope that they will be revived before they are cut off or become truly not part of the body. The distinction between being 'of the church' (*de ecclesia*) and being 'in the

spouse who has no spot or wrinkle,[1099] outside of which are pagans, Jews, and Christians guilty of mortal sin, together with heretics, even though they have not been cut off by excommunication. As men they still remain in the church, but in the eyes of God they are cut off as dead members. That the dialogue means this bride of Christ who does not have any spot or wrinkle of mortal sin the context of the passage makes clear: 'who worship God the Father, who place their whole trust in his Son, who are guided by the same Spirit proceeding from him, a community from whose fellowship anyone who commits a mortal sin is cut off.' And a little afterwards: 'But the church properly so called, though it consists of none but the good, nevertheless consists of human beings who can become bad, etc.' At this point I would be glad to ask the reporter why he omitted the words 'properly so called.'[1100] Christ is alive, and it is not fitting that a living head should be joined to a body having dead members. And this is not contrary to the gospel parable of the fishing net,[1101] which does not apply to that chosen spouse known only to God but to that general church which includes everyone baptized and which tolerates good and bad persons because it does not look into

* * * * *

church' (*in ecclesia*) is a distinction without a difference which the Sorbonne rightly neglected. For example, in Acts 12:1 Herod sets out to afflict some persons 'of the church' (*de ecclesia*); among those persons were good people like the apostles James and Peter. Pelargus also notes that he has covered some of the same ground in his reflections on proposition 84 in the first section.

For a more detailed and favourable analysis of Erasmus' ecclesiological differences with the Paris theologians see J.-P. Massaut 'Erasmus, la Sorbonne et la nature de l'église' in *Colloquium Erasmianum: Actes du colloque international réuni à Mons du 26 au 29 octobre ...* (Mons 1968) 86–116.

In the second edition Erasmus added a sentence berating the deputies of the theologians for not including the phrase 'properly so called,' even though Pelargus had pointed out that it was not in the edition used by the theologians. Erasmus did so, apparently, because the phrase was in the later edition he was following when he wrote the clarification.

Erasmus also added a long section, 'But if the moderns ... belong to the church,' citing Cyprian again, reiterating his main point, making some slight concession, and pointing out that quite varied boundaries can be set for inclusion in the church.

1099 Eph 5:27

1100 'Properly so called' was not added to the text of the colloquy until September 1531, after *Determinatio* had already been published (July 1531); see CWE 39 443 n99. Though Pelargus pointed out this discrepancy to Erasmus before the appearance of the second edition of *Declarationes* in the fall of 1532, Erasmus did not correct it.

1101 Matt 13:47–8

human hearts as only God can.[1102] And so it keeps them to be judged by him.

But why they changed the proposition I do not know. For nowhere do I say that evil persons are not *of* the church but that they are not *in* the holy church which is alive and is guided by the Spirit of Christ. The theologians, I think, do not include in it those subject to mortal sin. But if the moderns have thought up something clever concerning this text,[1103] about which they nevertheless do not agree with one another, I would rather follow Cyprian, who calls the church spoken of in the Creed the bride of Christ, having no spot or wrinkle, about which the Spirit says in the Song of Songs: 'One is my dove, one is my perfect one; she is the only one of her mother, the chosen of her that bore her.'[1104] If someone says that this applies to the perfection of the faith which the church has,[1105] there are plenty of people whose faith is imperfect, even erroneous. For they place in the church schismatics and hidden heretics who have not yet been cut off or openly withdrawn from the communion of the church by word or deed. Now, since faith without charity does not sanctify a person, how can those who have nothing beyond an unformed faith[1106] be said to be in the holy church? Nor does such reasoning detract from the authority of those who preside in the church; for when they administer the sacraments, they do not do so out of anything they have but out of the treasure of the unspotted church. If they judge wrongly, they do not prejudice the sentence of God.

Still I hardly deny that Christians who lead evil lives belong in some fashion to the church, as long as they persist in the unity and peace of God's house. But the church militant properly so called consists of the predestinate, whom only God knows. And although the name 'church' became best known after the coming of Christ, nevertheless Augustine considered the church as existing from the beginning of the world.[1107] And the use of this word is extended to souls separated from their bodies, whether they reign

* * * * *

1102 2 Chron 6:30
1103 That is, 'I believe the holy church.'
1104 Rufinus (pseudo-Cyprian) *Commentarius in symbolum apostolorum* 39 PL 21 375A–B; Song 6:8
1105 That is, rather than to the members of the church; but Erasmus goes on to say that that faith must exist in the members of the church and is not always perfect.
1106 'Unformed faith' (*fides informis*) is faith without charity; see Thomas Aquinas *Summa theologiae* II-II q 4 a 4, q 6 a 2.
1107 In *De civitate Dei* 8.24.2, 13.16.1, 15.1.1 PL 42 251, 387, 437 Augustine traces the city of God, which is equivalent to the church, back to the garden of Eden.

with Christ or are still being purged in the fire of charity.[1108] Hence it is extended to the good angels, and finally to non-predestined persons because they share in the faith and the sacraments, and they think that this church is properly called Catholic because that includes the universal nature of the church. But many places in Scripture do not agree with this notion. For Christ did not cleanse the angels with his blood. I use 'church' to mean its principal part, the church militant; I do not deny that Christians who believe well but live badly belong in some fashion to the church. And I do not see how the theologians and I differ except that I think such persons do not belong to the church properly so called and they think they belong to the church.

54 The sixth error is at the top of page 300[1109] in these words: 'Outside the church there is no remission of sins.' And it is clear that if you take the church as he previously did and as he explains it, this is false, since in the church of the heretics infants receive true baptism. Some receive remission of sins also by repentance; and this happens away from the church in the said manner.

CLARIFICATION[1110]

54 Baptism performed among heretics is valid, and perhaps among the Jews also, but nevertheless the power of the baptism comes from the faith of the

* * * * *

1108 That is, whether they belong to the church triumphant in heaven or the church suffering in purgatory

1109 CWE 39 429:29 / LB I 731F / ASD I-3 372:279-80

1110 Pelargus sigs G5v–G6v agrees that outside the church there is no remission of sins. But he argues that if Erasmus takes the church to mean the congregation of only the good, the church without spot or wrinkle, then it is certainly not true that outside that church there is no remission of sin. But if one takes church in the broader sense as including also the wicked (as Pelargus does), then the argument that baptism by a heretic who is outside the church is valid, but trivial because, though the heretic is outside the church, he does not baptize outside the church if his intentions are those of the church.

Pelargus concludes by saying that these are the only points he takes up in the colloquies because elsewhere it is not certain with what intention Erasmus wrote or because he transfers the error from himself to his interlocutor. Moreover, whenever he uses the excuse of his interlocutor, he very often either justifies something silly or refutes it so weakly that he seem to be in cahoots with the interlocutor. Pelargus is very sorry that some people consider Erasmus to be a jokester and entertainer. And as Erasmus knows, there are some who think that the publication of the *Colloquies* accomplished nothing but to

church, and a heretic who baptizes having a general faith is an evil minister using the instrumentality of the church. But nevertheless, if someone is not compelled by any necessity but still is baptized by a heretic and agrees with his ungodly teachings, he does not receive remission of sins but the character [1111] only, which makes it unnecessary for him to be rebaptized. Moreover, those who come to baptism with faith are not properly outside the church, but in the vestibule of the church. And maybe in God's eyes they are in the church. The other rites are executed to confirm the community of faith in the eyes of men. Then too, no one denies that the return to the church is by means of repentance. But unless someone has departed he does not return. And anyone who is repentant in his heart is already in the church, even though according to ecclesiastical discipline he is kept away from the sacraments of the church. Finally, the grace of remission is something that belongs to that unspotted church.

55 In the dialogue *The Franciscan* he claims that it would be more fitting that the religious not differ in dress from other persons. This is clear at the top of page 335, at this point:[1112] 'What do you think? Would you consider it better for monks not to differ from others in their clothing?' The other one responds: 'Well, I think it is more straightforward and more Christian, etc.'

CLARIFICATION
55 What does it have to do with piety if we did not have in the world such an infinite variety of clothing? But in fact Conrad speaks there somewhat

* * * * *

corrupt young readers so that they scorn the saints and even the religious life itself, and that Erasmus is blasphemous because he makes fun of divine and sacred matters and seems to hurl angry curses against the saints themselves. To them it perhaps does not seem likely that some people are grateful for his colloquies because their character has been improved by reading them; rather they think that there is no one who does not become worse and loves the Christian religion less by reading his writings, especially the colloquies. But Pelargus himself would have scruples about saying these things.
In the second edition Erasmus added the phrase 'not compelled by any necessity' and the last two sentences of the clarification.
The second edition wrongly numbers the next proposition as 56 instead of 55. In this volume the correct numbering of propositions 55–70 has been restored.

1111 A technical term for a mark or quality left in the soul by those sacraments which can be received only once (baptism, confirmation, orders)
1112 *Franciscani* CWE 39 480:32–5 (with title Πτωχοπλούσιοι 'The Well-to-do Beggars') / LB I 743D / ASD I-3 399:379–82

more circumspectly than is here reported. He replies as follows: 'Well, I think it is more straightforward and more Christian not to judge anyone by his appearance, provided it is respectable and decent.' He does not condemn variety but he singles out for blame the superstition of people who judge their neighbours in this way. And yet the person who says this claims that clothing should not be changed in order not to give offence to people and to conform with accepted custom. But what is fitting for monks is to differ from others not in the shape and colour of their dress but in its simplicity and cheapness.

56 Below the middle of the same page[1113] he alleges that variety in clothing among the religious was introduced because of superstition: 'After certain additions his followers turned the matter into a superstition.'

CLARIFICATION

56 The infinite variety is not entirely without superstition; and everything is not prescribed by the church but many features have been devised by men, perhaps, indeed, in pursuit of godliness but sometimes without much knowledge. Reckon, if you can, how much variety there is in the single group of canons regular[1114] or the Crutched Friars,[1115] not to mention any others. And among these are some features so strangely affected that they are uncomfortable, even though clothing was invented for the body's comfort.

57 Moreover, he carps at the decent manner in which lawyers, judges, and doctors differ from others in dress. This can be seen at the top of page 331, at this point:[1116] 'And so to profess wisdom by dress seems to me to be the silliest folly of all.'

* * * * *

1113 CWE 39 481:9–10 / LB I 743E–F / ASD I-3 400:396–7
1114 Erasmus belonged to the Augustinian canons regular (whereas Luther was an Augustinian friar).
1115 The Crutched Friars (Fratres Cruciferi) were an order officially established in the twelfth century and finally suppressed in the seventeenth century; they took their name from a large red cross on the breast of their habit. Originally they also carried a wooden staff topped with a cross, but in the late fifteenth century this was replaced by a small silver cross; at the same time the colour of their habit was changed from brown to blue.
1116 CWE 39 478:11–13 / LB I 742C / ASD I-3 397:288–9

CLARIFICATION

57 The Innkeeper proposes this argument but it is refuted by Conrad. Hence it is hardly fair to blame me for it. No one begrudges lawyers their outfits, and I do not see what this has to do with the Catholic faith.

58 In the dialogue which is entitled *A Pilgrimage for Religion's Sake* he makes up a letter in the name of the Blessed Virgin Mary, which is funny indeed, but not far removed from blasphemy; in it the Blessed Virgin says that she is delighted that a follower of Luther has made the case that the invocation of saints is superfluous because it relieves her of much trouble from now on. She likewise threatens that if men desert the saints, she will use her weapons to avenge such wrong done to them. This occurs on page 426.[1117]

CLARIFICATION

58 This is clearly a joke, but it is directed at Zwingli, not at the Blessed Virgin. But actually the passage does not deal with the Virgin Mother but with a statue of the Virgin, highly honoured by the Swiss, which is called Mary of the Rock; the close of the letter[1118] shows that this is true: 'From our stony house, etc.'[1119] And in that passage the stone Virgin does not threaten that she will use arms to defend herself but rather she says that the other saints have weapons with which to protect themselves. This is beside the point, but from it we can deduce how faithful and careful the persons were who mutilated these fragments.[1120]

59 On page 429[1121] he rails because there are so many baptistries, so many candelabra, golden statues, organs, musical concerts – an immense expense. This appears at the beginning of page 455, at this

* * * * *

1117 *Peregrinatio religionis ergo* CWE 40 624:40–628:10 / LB I 775B–776A / ASD I-3 472:79–474:129. In the edition used by the theologians (Froben, February 1526) this passage occurs not on page 426 but on page 430.
1118 CWE 40 628:14–15 / LB I 776B / ASD I-3 474:128–9
1119 For detailed and copious information about Zwingli's iconoclasm and the statue of Mary at Mariastein in Switzerland see CWE 40 652 n14 and 653–4 nn23–5.
1120 That is, the snippets from Erasmus gathered for the Paris theologians by their deputies
1121 This page number is incorrect; the correct number is given immediately after, page 455.

point:[1122] 'What is the use of so many baptistries, etc?' But nevertheless all these things pertain to the honour and worship of God, and the poor are not abandoned because of them.

CLARIFICATION

59 In the colloquy someone criticizes only the immensely expensive adornment of churches. For he begins thus: 'I grant that the sacred vestments and vessels of the church must have a dignity appropriate to their liturgical use; I want the building also to have the grandeur due to it. But what is the use of so many baptistries, so many candelabra, so many golden statues?' When he says 'so many' he is criticizing the excessive numbers; when he says 'golden' he is criticizing the excessive expense. Whether luxury belongs to the honour of God, I do not know; whether the poor are nevertheless cared for let others judge.[1123] Certainly what is excessive there does not relieve the needs of the poor, and it often happens that what is denied to the poor a sacrilegious tyrant or ungodly soldier carries away once and for all.[1124] And nevertheless the very argument that one person makes there is resolved by another, who says: 'Every decent, sensible man favours moderation in these matters, of course. But since the fault springs from excessive devotion, it merits applause.' And a little below: 'In short, I would rather see a church abounding in sacred furnishings than bare and dirty, as some are, and more like stables than churches, etc.' Why am I not charged with this language, which could perhaps be more justly charged against me? If they say that no expense in the adornment of churches can be excessive, then they have something to condemn in the colloquy. But by the same token they will be able to say that olives have no pits.[1125]

60 He does not want the people to kiss the soles and shoes of the saints, but it is nevertheless good to do so. He indicates this at the beginning

* * * * *

1122 CWE 40 644:29–31 / LB I 784E / ASD I-3 489:708–10
1123 For Erasmus' opinions about using the riches of the church to relieve the poor see CWE 40 671–2 n163.
1124 That is, the valuables in a church or shrine are plundered by iconoclastic tyrants or marauding soldiers.
1125 *Adagia* I ix 73: 'There is nothing hard inside an olive or outside a nut,' a proverb applied to those who assert something manifestly false. See Horace *Epistolae* 2.1.30.

of page 360, at this point:[1126] 'But it is[1127] shameless to push shoes, soles, and underwear at one to be kissed.' There follows the remark, 'I won't pretend it wouldn't be better to leave those things undone, etc.'

CLARIFICATION

60 Is it also part of the faith to kiss the rotten leather and scraps of linen that belonged to the saints, especially if they present no vestiges of how they lived? And yet the colloquy does not condemn those who kiss such things out of a feeling of piety but those who thrust them at you to be kissed, especially when it could be that the shoe they thrust at you did not belong to St Thomas but to some butcher or pimp. For that passage deals with the shoe of Thomas of Acre,[1128] which was thrust out by some wretched beggar on the road, not in the church.

61 In the dialogue *The Butcher and the Fishmonger* he says the choice of food was abrogated by the judgment of God and the Apostle. This appears on page 472, a little past the middle:[1129] 'The Lord has abrogated the

* * * * *

1126 CWE 40 648:33–5 / LB I 786E / ASD I-3 492:822–3

1127 In the Froben 1533 edition Erasmus changed 'is' (*est*) to 'seems to me' (*mihi videtur*).

1128 The Order of St Thomas of Acre, named after St Thomas Becket, was established in Acre in the Holy Land in the late twelfth century to care for the sick and to ransom prisoners. Its members had been canons regular and their rule was originally that of St Augustine. In the beginning of the thirteenth century they became a military order (following the rule of the Knights Templar), but in the following century they reverted to their original status and mission. St John's Hospital for lepers in London belonged to them; apart from Acre their major house was in London, and they owned extensive properties in London and elsewhere in England and Ireland. The place where Erasmus and Colet were presented with the shoe was Harbledown, where there was a leper hospital named St Nicholas, but I have discovered no evidence that it belonged to the order. See A.J. Forey 'The Military Order of St Thomas of Acre' *The English Historical Review* 354 (July 1977) 481–503. In *Modus orandi Deum* LB V 1119F / CWE 70 198 the shoe here presented to be kissed is specifically said to be allegedly that of Thomas Becket, the former bishop of Canterbury. The old man with the shoe may have been begging for the leper hospital at Harbledown or the one in London; Erasmus' point is that he was not connected to the Canterbury shrine.

1129 CWE 40 683:30–1 (with title Ἰχθυοφαγία 'A Fish Diet') / LB I 791A / ASD I-3 502:234–5

Jewish choice of foods, not by his example, to be sure, but by his judgment, etc.'

CLARIFICATION

61 It is clear from the whole drift of this passage that it deals with the abolition of Jewish ceremonies, to which the choice of food belongs. If Christ and the apostle Paul did not abrogate the Jewish distinction of foods, Erasmus lied. But if all the orthodox admit this, why is he accused? But that the passage does not deal with the regulations of the church is clear from what precedes and what follows. For the question is put in this way: 'What passage of Scripture openly teaches that Jews converted to the gospel are freed from subjection to the Mosaic law?' The other one replies: 'That was foretold by the prophets, etc. And so the Lord abrogated the Jewish distinction of foods, not by his example, to be sure, but by his judgment, when he said: "a person is not defiled by what enters into his mouth,"[1130] even then preparing his disciples to scorn the ceremonies of the Jews. Peter was likewise admonished about it in a vision,[1131] and he was once again taught by Paul that nothing is unclean which God has made clean.'[1132] He[1133] adds that there is no doubt that what Christian people do today, scorning the precepts of the Jews and eating pork and eels, was handed down by the apostles. And right after that: 'And so the Jews were not so much emancipated as weaned from superstitious reverence of the Law, as though from milk to which they were thoroughly accustomed but which was now inappropriate. And the Law was not abrogated but that part of it which was now superfluous was bidden to yield.' Again a little later: 'Now at first the Jews were wrenched with difficulty from their accustomed ways, etc.'[1134] The whole drift of that passage is arguing about Jewish ceremonies, not Christian regulations. Since that is beyond dispute, what has Erasmus done wrong? Such it is not to read the passage and to believe the notes of young men. Nor is there much need to argue from what precedes and what follows, since the passage itself which they cite is as follows: 'The Lord abrogated the Jewish choice of food, not by his example, to be sure, but by his judgment.' Why did the person who read this omit 'Jewish'?[1135] Why but

* * * * *

1130 Matt 15:11
1131 Acts 10:10–16, 11:4–10
1132 Gal 2:12–14; Rom 14:20; cf Acts 10:15.
1133 That is, the Fishmonger, who has just been quoted
1134 CWE 683:37–684:12 / LB I 691B–C / ASD I-3 502:242–53
1135 'Jewish' (*Iudaicum*) was not added to 'the choice of foods' (*Ciborum . . . delectum*)

to make way for slander? And such things are thrust upon the theological faculty!

62 He seems also to find fault with the ceremonies of the church concerning fasting, abstinence from meat, diversity of dress, shaving of the head, and some other practices, and also with the obligation of baptism, confession, and matrimony. This appears on page 475, from beginning to end.[1136] But he excuses what he said on the aforesaid page; he does this at the top of page 476, at this point:[1137] 'You're quite mistaken, butcher.'

63 But afterwards he considers that the regulations and ceremonies of the church, which he calls carnal, should be changed. That is clear a little past the top of page 477, at this point:[1138] 'In argument you are certainly dull-minded enough. But today there are fully as many reasons, it seems to me, why these carnal observances ought to be treated as matters of choice, not of obligation.' And a little past the middle of page 477, at this point:[1139] 'Since, therefore, the harvest is so abundant, it seems most urgent for the spreading of the Christian religion that, as the apostles removed the burden of the Mosaic law to keep the gentiles from backsliding, so now, to attract the weak, the rules about some things ought to be abolished. The world was saved without these in the beginning, and it could be saved now if only it had faith and evangelical love.' The same point is made throughout almost all of page 478, especially the part beginning:[1140] 'Outside the home of the church there is no salvation.'

CENSURE
And this is wicked and pernicious advice, and it is also arrogant – advice, I say, taken from the condemned teaching of both Wyclif[1141] and Luther and tending to the weakening of the Christian religion and the whole discipline of the church. And it is not true that by

* * * * *

until the Froben edition of 1529 and hence was not present in the 1526 edition used by the deputies of the Paris theologians.

1136 CWE 40 685:3–28 / LB I 792B–C / ASD I-3 503:281–504:303
1137 CWE 40 685:29 / LB I 792C / ASD I-3 504:304
1138 CWE 40 686:14–16 / LB I 792E / ASD I-3 504:325–7
1139 CWE 40 686:28–34 / LB I 793A / ASD I-3 505:339–43
1140 CWE 40 687:9 / LB I 793B / ASD I-3 505:357
1141 For Wyclif see n87 above.

such abrogation the weak would be attracted; quite the contrary, they would be all the more impelled by this to withdraw from the Christian religion. And it is certain that these things were instituted with the inspiration of the Holy Spirit and in conformity with a sound understanding of Scripture, and many practices were instituted from the tradition of the apostles, both in order to celebrate the divine mysteries with greater reverence and holiness and to promote a more genuine observance of the Christian religion; it is also certain that many of these practices belong to divine law, which is immutable and always the same and which has either been handed down in Holy Scripture or has come down to us by continuous succession from the tradition of the apostles.

Nor is there any proper analogy between the burden of the Mosaic law, which both the prophets and the apostles, inspired by the Spirit of God, perceived should be abrogated, and those things which the Holy Spirit wanted to persist in the church for its felicitous guidance even to the consummation of the world. This is clear from the fact that the church, which is always guided by the Spirit of God, quickly condemned and rejected whoever tried to change such features, such as Aeris,[1142] Vigilantius,[1143] Lambert,[1144] Jovinian, the Waldensians, the Albigensians,[1145] the Wyclifites, and finally the Lutherans, and many others. Such perverse advice, then, is heretical and blasphemous.

CLARIFICATION

62 This is proposed by the Butcher but rejected by the Fishmonger. If the refutation is welcome, why is the language of the argument charged against me?

63 Once more, this is the argument of the Butcher, who receives the response that the regulations of bishops should be obeyed without contradiction. Certainly he labels prescriptions which concern externals as carnal; and he does not urge that they be abrogated, but that the obligation

* * * * *

1142 For Aeris see n70 above.
1143 A priest of Gaul (fl 400), refuted at length by St Jerome in *Contra Vigilantium*; according to Jerome Vigilantius denied the veneration of relics, prayers to the saints, almsgiving, the celibacy of the clergy, and monasticism.
1144 Though both editions of 1532 and LB have 'Lamperius,' François Lambert must be meant. See n1021 above.
1145 For Jovinian see n71 above; for the Waldensians see n72 above; for the Albigensians see n479 above.

be removed and exhortation substituted for it. And he does not allow just anyone at all to violate such regulations but rather recommends that they be eliminated by the church if there are grave reasons for changing them. For example, if relaxing some regulations and even some teachings would cause an extraordinary expansion of Christendom, would it not be right for human laws to yield for the time being to the divine law? The divine law is to extend with all our might the glory of Christ and to attend to the salvation of our neighbours. For it commands that everyone love God with his whole heart and his neighbour as himself,[1146] whereas to abstain from food on certain days or to eat fish are human regulations. But human laws, like the medications of physicians, are usually and rightly modified according to the times, bodily characteristics, and present usage. But if we presume that there is some great advantage to the church, why does it contravene piety if the church were to relax temporarily some regulations, especially if no one is forbidden to observe the practices which are no longer obligatory? Or what is Lutheran about my language, since he teaches that all the regulations of bishops are ungodly and ought to be strenuously resisted?

But such a thing, they say, would not attract weak persons to the church but rather would weaken the whole discipline of the church. Actually, I think the discipline of the church consists in spiritual matters rather than in such externals. And if there is such great and imminent danger, how did the church flourish so long, producing so many persons who fasted and abstained and ate only vegetables, when there were no prescriptions about fasting or foods? And no one denies that our ancestors instituted these practices profitably and for serious reasons, but they were not instituted in such a way as to be irrevocable if there was a dawning hope of a great advantage, since the church itself has abrogated so many regulations for lesser causes. If anyone has any doubts about this point, he should read the decrees of the apostles and the councils and consider how few of them are observed today. And we tremble with fear that the church will immediately collapse if there is some innovation about food!

It is quite true that the Mosaic ceremonies were bestowed precisely so that they might cease at the proper time. From that, however, it follows that it is wrong to observe them now, but it does not follow that similar human regulations cannot be abrogated by the church for serious reasons. In fact what should be discussed is whether anything the apostles established, even if it is clear that it was handed down by them, binds us forever. Paul orders

* * * * *

1146 Matt 22:37–9

that women not speak in church;[1147] nowadays they sing everywhere. He forbade men to cover their heads;[1148] nowadays they do so. He commanded wives to wear a veil over their heads;[1149] nowadays in some regions they hear mass with uncovered heads, using a silken net to keep their hair from flying loose. But what makes it clear that such regulations were made with the intention that they should last till the end of the world? The fact that the church quickly rejected whoever tried to change them. No wonder, since such persons tried schismatically to render obsolete features which cannot be revised except by the authority of the church.

Finally, the Butcher does not assert but rather speaks in the manner of those who merely present a position, saying 'it seems,' so that he cannot even be said to be rendering a decision. 'A person who decides for someone else has already made up his mind, etc.' But how could the decision of the Butcher be heretical when he means something different from what is meant by that horrendous list of names, Lambert, Jovinian, the Waldensians, the Albigensians, Wyclif, and Luther? He wants the regulations of the church to be observed unless the church itself abrogates them. They teach that it is godly to scorn them vehemently and to deprive bishops and even councils of the authority to decide about them on their own. How can his advice be blasphemous when the whole matter is left to the church, which is guided by the Holy Spirit? How can it be perverse when he hopes for great glory and benefit for the church? Finally, if the Butcher's argumentation does not please them at all, it is also rejected in the dialogue. But the worse side must be charged to me.

64 In the same dialogue, *The Butcher and the Fishmonger*, he makes many other points that conform to the same opinion, as he does before the middle of page 499, at this point:[1150] 'But meanwhile where is that spiritual freedom which the apostles promise, etc?'

CLARIFICATION
64 It is true that something like this is said there by the Butcher, however not as assertions but merely as points to be discussed. The Fishmonger, however, immediately replies to him: 'I will tell you, Butcher. Christian freedom does not consist in doing as one likes, unhampered by human regulations, but in the fervour of a spirit prepared for all things, doing

* * * * *

1147 1 Cor 14:34
1148 1 Cor 11:7
1149 1 Cor 11:5–6
1150 CWE 40 702:27–8 / LB I 800B / ASD I-3 520:929–30

willingly and eagerly what we are commanded to do.' If this reply is godly,
if it is Catholic, why is it overlooked and the language of someone inquiring,
not asserting, is charged against me?

65 He indicates the same thing after the middle of page 501, at this
point:[1151] 'The world is full of pharisaical men, etc.' Likewise toward
the top of page 498, at this point:[1152] 'Finally, since human laws, which
commonly prescribe corporal practices, are guides to godliness, they
evidently come to an end when someone has attained to spiritual
vigour.' Here again he strives to revive the error of the Beguards,[1153]
as if the regulations and ceremonies of the church should be called
a guide in the same sense in which Paul calls the Old Law and its
ceremonies a guide.[1154]

CLARIFICATION
65 I beg you, by the tutelary spirit of the Sorbonne, what is this Fishmonger
pointing out?[1155] He says that the world is full of pharisaical men. But whom
is he calling Pharisees? Not those who obey the regulations of the church
but those who can claim sanctity for themselves for no other reason than
such trivial observances. For these words are added there: 'here they are
passed over for the sake of my honour.'[1156] Again, in another passage what
does the Butcher say? He gives arguments, not pronouncements. But what
answer does he get? 'Well, you bring together many arguments, some of
which I like, others I don't, and some I don't understand.'[1157] If some things
are disliked, let them think that these are the ones they condemn. And so
farewell to the Beguards!

66 Finally, the author of this dialogue complains that minor sins are punished more than serious ones. He does not consider that it is reasonable to do this in the commonwealth for purposes of self-preservation.

* * * * *

1151 CWE 40 704:12 / LB I 801B / ASD I-3 522:988–9
1152 CWE 40 701:36–8 / LB I 799F / ASD I-3 519:901–3
1153 See nn364 and 667 above.
1154 Gal 3:24
1155 Actually the Butcher, not the Fishmonger, says both texts singled out for
censure.
1156 These words do not occur after the sentence about pharisaical men or in the
whole colloquy. But at least twice the Butcher does say that he is omitting
things he dare not mention: CWE 40 705:31–2 / LB I 802A / ASD I-3 523:1045
and CWE 40 707:16–17 / LB I 802F / ASD I-3 525:1103.
1157 CWE 40 702:6–7 / LB I 800A / ASD I-3 520:910–11

This appears toward the end of page 502, at this point:[1158] 'Similarly we see many persons trust so much in corporal ceremonies, etc.' And the same on page 503, throughout almost the whole page.

CLARIFICATION

66 In this place the Butcher and the Fishmonger are in agreement, telling in turn not a few examples of the preposterous judgments of the mob, and among others it is mentioned that some people give more serious attention to minor sins:[1159] 'If a priest lets his hair grow long or wears a layman's garb, he is thrown into jail and punished severely; if he boozes in a brothel, if he whores, if he dices, if he corrupts other men's wives, if he never touches a Bible, he is nonetheless a pillar of the church.' This is what the dialogue says. The theologians say such an attitude is reasonable. Perhaps in some cases, but in the one I posit I think not. And they themselves, I think, do not approve of those who rely on bodily ceremonies, neglecting what belongs to true godliness, and who attribute what belongs to grace to their own merits, and stand still where they ought to have stepped forward to what is more perfect, and slander a neighbour on account of things neither good nor bad in themselves. For that is what the dialogue says. But if they themselves also condemn such people, I wonder why they think this passage should be singled out for blame. For why is it wrong for the dialogue to criticize the preposterous judgments of the masses, which are numberless, since to do so contributes greatly to the pursuit of true godliness? Certainly these incidents are mentioned there with that intention.

67 He does the same thing toward the bottom of page 508, at this point:[1160] 'Now, in that very precept about fasting, there are two things, etc.' He follows up on the same idea on pages 509, 520, 521, 522, and 523.

68 He carps at trust in saints on page 524,[1161] not considering that all the veneration of the saints and the trust in them are first and foremost offered to God and to them under God and because of God.

CLARIFICATION OF 67 AND 68

What is Erasmus carping at? Trust in the saints? Let the passage itself provide a response: 'How many there are who put their trust in the Virgin Mother's protection, or Christopher's, rather than in that of Christ himself?'

* * * * *

1158 CWE 40 704:39 / LB I 801D / ASD I-3 523:1015–16
1159 CWE 40 705:8–11 / LB I 801E / ASD I-3 523:1024–7
1160 CWE 40 708:21–2 / LB I 803D / ASD I-3 526:1142–3
1161 CWE 40 719:12–13 / LB I 808F / ASD I-3 535:1458–60

And he mentions some other examples of this sort. I beg you, reader, is this carping at trust in the saints or rather is it singling out for blame the preposterous judgment of foolish people? Accordingly, this censure is irrelevant to this passage, however it came to be put there.

69 In the dialogue which is called *The Funeral* the author seems to have an incorrect view of foundations for the dead[1162] and of prayers said for the dead. For he brings in a sick man who cares nothing about such things, indeed would reject them utterly, if that could be done without scandal. That can be seen toward the end of page 546, at this point]:[1163] 'Or if you deem me worthy of one funeral mass, that will be more than enough. Or if there is anything else that because of the church's public custom can scarcely be omitted without scandal to the weak, I leave that to your judgment.' There follows: 'I have no intention of buying up someone's prayers or of depriving anyone of his merits.' He says this as if those who endowed foundations for the dead were buying the prayers of others or depriving them of their merits; to say so is erroneous and ungodly.

70 And on the next page, which is 547,[1164] he seems to reject utterly all satisfaction assigned individually to dead persons, approving only the common satisfaction of all, together with the merits of Christ, and this is at the top of the page.

Conclusion of the Determination Given Above

And so, since in these dialogues Erasmus perniciously employs his eloquence to revive and somehow instil in the minds of boys, their teachers, and readers in general the condemned errors of the Aerians, Wyclifites, Joviniasts, Lambertans, Waldensians, Beguards, Lutherans, and many other heretics, if holy and Christians principles are to be instilled not only in children but in older people as well, so that they may be vigorously called and driven away from all ungodliness and blasphemy, great effort must be applied to keep any such books out of the hands of children or any Christian readers whatsoever so that

* * * * *

1162 That is, foundations such as colleges or hospitals endowed in the will of a patron for whom they were required to pray or say masses. But the Latin is odd: *de fundatione obituum*, 'about the establishment of deaths.' Erasmus (somewhat disingenuously) says he does not know what the phrase means.

1163 *Funus* CWE 40 777:23–7 / LB I 816B / ASD I-3 549:436–40

1164 CWE 40 777:27–8 / LB I 816C / ASD I-3 549:440–1

readers will not drink in this poison and thus be completely estranged
from the Christian religion.

CLARIFICATION

[69, 70] In that place I imagine a very holy man who in his lifetime did
whatever good he could, and while he was healthy and well gave to the
poor as much as his means permitted; and this he prefers to placing hope
for his salvation in papal briefs, or in requiem masses said by priests,
or in testamentary bequests. Certainly I have heard this preference vigorously approved by those who profess holiness. I do not understand what
it means 'to found deaths,' but do not those who pay a price for an-
niversary masses and such things buy the prayers of others? And do not
those who are hired to do this transfer a part of their accidental[1165] merit
to the buyer? This man thought it was superfluous to do such things at
his death since he had provided what was better when he was alive and
well.

Clarification[1166]

Someone who has so lived and so dies does not need those ordinary defences, which offer far less help than good deeds done while alive. You see,
reader, what sort of thing was written before; let others judge how well
the conclusion matches it. To the conclusion I will respond because it was
tacked on and has nothing, I think, to do with the faculty. What it says
about my employing my eloquence to revive the errors of heretics in my
colloquies and to instil them in the minds of boys, if they want to know
my intentions, I will gladly protest that this is utterly false. I would use different language if, God forbid, I had any such intention. If, however, they
twist these things to make their point, though I grant I could have erred in
many places, since I am human (or, if that is too much, semihuman), nevertheless it is clear on the face of it that I do not agree on one single teaching
with the heretics so often listed.

* * * * *

1165 Evidently a distinction depending on the difference between the Aristotelian
    categories of substance and accident. The substance of the merit arising from
    the masses or prayers is general and unchanging; but the attribution of it to
    a particular person is an accidental quality of the merit.
1166 In this clarification Erasmus defends his colloquies against the faculty's 'Con-
    clusion of the Determination Given Above,' which attacks the colloquies as
    corrupting the faith and morals of young readers.

And then there is the danger that if readers drink in these deadly poisons, they will be completely estranged from the Christian religion. Such a magnificent pronouncement by whoever crafted this conclusion, although I have shown that so much was incorrectly cited, wrongly understood, and slanderously distorted. But in these numerous propositions what props of the Christian religion are proposed? That the people believe that a monk's cowl is effective in curing diseases; that we solicit the saints while ignoring Christ; that so many people run off to Jerusalem, abandoning their wives and children, and that they think there is some extraordinary godliness in believing that all human regulations are binding under pain of hellfire; that we situate the principal function of religion in the choice of food; that in churches no adornment seems excessive but rather luxury also belongs to the honour of God; that as much emphasis as possible is placed on ceremonies, of whatever sort; that boys and girls, with contempt for their parents, run off to monasteries for trivial reasons (soon to regret their decision); that no one speaks about Christ or Holy Scripture except a theologian;[1167] that we place as much trust as possible in the saints; that we know that evil persons are not *in* the church, to be sure, but are nevertheless *of* the church; that we believe the church is marvellously enhanced by the enormous and prodigious variety of rites and clothing; that lawyers are clothed decently; that we kiss the soles and shoes of the saints; that absolutely no papal[1168] regulations should be relaxed, even with the prospect of great advantages; that the dying establish foundations for the dead and provide for as many requiem masses as possible and place the greatest confidence in them; and many other such practices.

But Christian godliness consists in loving God with our whole heart and our neighbour as ourselves,[1169] placing our best hope in Christ, putting our conduct and way of life in conformity with his teaching and example and also with the guidelines of Scripture. If someone in any way whatsoever calls us away from acting so, he is leading us instead into the danger of paganism. I make these charges against those who plucked out maimed fragments, interpreted them perversely, and thrust them upon the theological faculty, who, it seems, were duped into condemning not what I wrote but what the reporters brought to them. For I do not think the theologians had any such intentions, but if anyone interprets these censures as fairly

* * * * *

1167 Erasmus means that theologians limit those subjects to themselves by refusing to let the people read Scripture in the vernacular.
1168 Latin *pontificiarum*, which could mean 'episcopal' as well as 'papal'
1169 Matt 22:37–9

as the reporters did my writings, he would be able to accept them in that sense.[1170] I have explained my meaning in good faith and as straightforwardly as I could; nevertheless, I am prepared to make corrections if I have said anything here contrary to sound doctrine.

The End

* * * * *

1170 That is, only by judging the censures as unfairly as the reporters judged Erasmus' writings could anyone believe that the theologians intended to condemn what Erasmus wrote.

WORKS FREQUENTLY CITED

SHORT-TITLE FORMS
FOR ERASMUS' WORKS

INDEX OF SCRIPTURAL REFERENCES

GENERAL INDEX

WORKS FREQUENTLY CITED

This list provides bibliographical information for works referred to in short-title form in this volume. For Erasmus writings see the short-title list following.

Allen   *Opus epistolarum Des. Erasmi Roterodami* ed P.S. Allen, H.M. Allen, and H.W. Garrod (Oxford 1906–58) 11 vols and index

AN   Archives nationales, Paris

Argentré *Collectio judiciorum*   Charles Duplessis d'Argentré *Collectio judiciorum de novis erroribus . . . qui in ecclesia proscripti sunt et notati* 3 vols (Paris 1725–36; repr Brussels 1963)

ASD   *Opera omnia Desiderii Erasmi Roterodami* (Amsterdam 1969–)

Béda *Annotationes*   Noël Béda *Annotationum in Jacobum Fabrum Stapulensem libri duo: et in Desiderium Erasmum Roterodamum liber unus* (Paris 28 May 1526; repr Cologne 31 August 1526)

Bense   Walter F. Bense Jr 'Noël Beda and the Humanist Reformation in Paris, 1504–1534' unpublished PhD dissertation Harvard University 1967

CCSL   *Corpus christianorum, series Latina* (Turnhout 1953–)

CEBR   *Contemporaries of Erasmus: A Biographical Register of the Renaissance and Reformation* ed Peter G. Bietenholz and Thomas B. Deutscher (Toronto 1985–7; repr 2003) 3 vols

Clerval *Procès-verbaux*   Alexandre Clerval ed *Registre des procès-verbaux de la faculté de théologie de Paris* I: *1505–1523* (Paris 1917)

Connelly   *Hymns of the Roman Liturgy* ed Joseph Connelly (Westminster, Md 1957)

Corpus iuris canonici   *Corpus iuris canonici* ed Emil Richter and Emil Friedberg (Leipzig 1879–81) 2 vols

CSEL   *Corpus scriptorum ecclesiasticorum Latinorum* (Vienna, Leipzig, and Prague 1866–)

CWE   *Collected Works of Erasmus* (Toronto 1974–)

Determinatio   *Determinatio facultatis theologiae in schola Parisiensi super quam plurimis assertionibus D. Erasmi Roterodami* (Paris: Josse Bade nd [July 1531]; 2nd ed Paris nd [c 1532])

DTC

Dictionnaire de théologie catholique ed A. Vacant et al (Paris 1899–1950) 15 vols in 30 and index

Farge 'Noël Béda'

James K. Farge 'Noël Béda and the Defense of Tradition' in *Biblical Humanism and Scholasticism in the Age of Erasmus* ed Erika Rummel (Leiden 2008) 243–64

Farge *Orthodoxy and Reform*

James K. Farge *Orthodoxy and Reform in Early Reformation France: The Faculty of Theology of Paris, 1500–1543* (Leiden 1985)

Farge *Procès-verbaux*

James K. Farge ed *Registre des procès-verbaux de la faculté de théologie de l'Université de Paris, de janvier 1524 à novembre 1533* (Paris 1990)

Gerson

Oeuvres complètes de Jean Gerson ed Palémon Glorieux (Paris and New York 1960–   )

Hefele

Karl J. Hefele *A History of the Councils of the Church* trans Henry N. Oxenham (Edinburgh 1896) 5 vols

LB

Desiderii Erasmi opera omnia ed. J. Leclerc (Leiden 1703–6; repr London 1962; Amsterdam 1969) 10 vols

Liber secundus

Liber secundus registri determinationum Bibliothèque nationale de France, Paris BnF MS lat 3381B

Mansi

Sacrorum conciliorum nova et amplissima collectio: in qua ... ea omnia ... exhibentur quae Joannes Dominicus Mansi ... evulgavit (Florence 1759–98; repr Paris 1901–27) 53 vols

Missale Romanum

Missale Romanum Mediolani 1484 with *A Collation with Other Editions Printed before 1570* ed Robert Lippe, Henry Bradshaw Society 17 and 33 (London 1899 and 1907) 2 vols

Moreau *Inventaire*

Brigitte Moreau *Inventaire chronologique des éditions parisiennes du XVIe siècle 1501–1535* (Paris 1972–   )

PG

Patrologiae cursus completus ... series Graeca ed J.-P. Migne (Paris 1857–66; repr Turnhout) 161 vols, plus indexes (Paris 1912, 1928–36) 2 vols

PL

Patrologiae cursus completus ... series Latina ed J.-P. Migne 1st ed (Paris 1844–55, 1862–5; repr Turnhout) 217 vols, plus 4 vols indexes. In references to volumes of PL in which the column numbers in later editions or reprints differ from those in the first edition the date of publication of the edition cited is given.

Renouard *Imprimeurs*   Philippe Renouard *Imprimeurs et libraires parisiens du XVIe siècle: ouvrage publié d'après les manuscrits de Philippe Renouard par le service des travaux historiques de la ville de Paris* (Paris 1964–)

Rummel *Catholic Critics*   Erika Rummel *Erasmus and His Catholic Critics* (Nieuwkoop 1989) 2 vols

Titles following colons are longer versions of the short-titles, or are alternative titles. Items entirely enclosed in square brackets are of doubtful authorship. For abbreviations see Works Frequently Cited.

Acta: Acta Academiae Lovaniensis contra Lutherum *Opuscula* / CWE 71

Adagia: Adagiorum chiliades 1508, etc (Adagiorum collectanea for the primitive form, when required) LB II / ASD II-1–8 / CWE 30–6

Admonitio adversus mendacium: Admonitio adversus mendacium et obtrectationem LB X / CWE 78

Annotationes in Novum Testamentum LB VI / ASD VI-5, 6, 8, 9 / CWE 51–60

Antibarbari LB X / ASD I-1 / CWE 23

Apologia ad annotationes Stunicae: Apologia respondens ad ea quae Iacobus Lopis Stunica taxaverat in prima duntaxat Novi Testamenti aeditione LB IX / ASD IX-2

Apologia ad Caranzam: Apologia ad Sanctium Caranzam, or Apologia de tribus locis, or Responsio ad annotationem Stunicae ... a Sanctio Caranza defensam LB IX

Apologia ad Fabrum: Apologia ad Iacobum Fabrum Stapulensem LB IX / ASD IX-3 / CWE 83

Apologia ad prodromon Stunicae LB IX

Apologia ad Stunicae conclusiones LB IX

Apologia adversus monachos: Apologia adversus monachos quosdam Hispanos LB IX

Apologia adversus Petrum Sutorem: Apologia adversus debacchationes Petri Sutoris LB IX

Apologia adversus rhapsodias Alberti Pii: Apologia ad viginti et quattuor libros A. Pii LB IX / CWE 84

Apologia adversus Stunicae Blasphemiae: Apologia adversus libellum Stunicae cui titulum fecit Blasphemiae et impietates Erasmi LB IX

Apologia contra Latomi dialogum: Apologia contra Iacobi Latomi dialogum de tribus linguis LB IX / CWE 71

Apologia de 'In principio erat sermo' LB IX

Apologia de laude matrimonii: Apologia pro declamatione de laude matrimonii LB IX / CWE 71

Apologia de loco 'Omnes quidem': Apologia de loco 'Omnes quidem resurgemus' LB IX

Apologia qua respondet invectivis Lei: Apologia qua respondet duabus invectivis Eduardi Lei *Opuscula* / ASD IX-4 / CWE 72

Apophthegmata LB IV

Appendix de scriptis Clithovei LB IX / CWE 83

Appendix respondens ad Sutorem: Appendix respondens ad quaedam Antapologiae Petri Sutoris LB IX

Argumenta: Argumenta in omnes epistolas apostolicas nova (with Paraphrases)

Axiomata pro causa Lutheri: Axiomata pro causa Martini Lutheri *Opuscula* / CWE 71

Brevissima scholia: In Elenchum Alberti Pii brevissima scholia per eundem Erasmum Roterodamum CWE 84

Carmina LB I, IV, V, VIII / ASD I-7 / CWE 85–6
Catalogus lucubrationum LB I / CWE 9 (Ep 1341A)
Ciceronianus: Dialogus Ciceronianus LB I / ASD I-2 / CWE 28
Colloquia LB I / ASD I-3 / CWE 39–40
Compendium vitae Allen I / CWE 4
Conflictus: Conflictus Thaliae et Barbariei LB I
[Consilium: Consilium cuiusdam ex animo cupientis esse consultum] Opuscula /
    CWE 71

De bello Turcico: Utilissima consultatio de bello Turcis inferendo, et obiter enarratus
    psalmus 28 LB V / ASD V-3 / CWE 64
De civilitate: De civilitate morum puerilium LB I / CWE 25
Declamatio de morte LB IV
Declamatiuncula LB IV
Declarationes ad censuras Lutetiae vulgatas: Declarationes ad censuras Lutetiae
    vulgatas sub nomine facultatis theologiae Parisiensis LB IX
De concordia: De sarcienda ecclesiae concordia, or De amabili ecclesiae concordia
    [on Psalm 83] LB V / ASD V-3 / CWE 65
De conscribendis epistolis LB I / ASD I-2 / CWE 25
De constructione: De constructione octo partium orationis, or Syntaxis LB I / ASD I-4
De contemptu mundi: Epistola de contemptu mundi LB V / ASD V-1 / CWE 66
De copia: De duplici copia verborum ac rerum LB I / ASD I-6 / CWE 24
De esu carnium: Epistola apologetica ad Christophorum episcopum Basiliensem de
    interdicto esu carnium LB IX / ASD IX-1
De immensa Dei misericordia: Concio de immensa Dei misericordia LB V /
    CWE 70
De libero arbitrio: De libero arbitrio diatribe LB IX / CWE 76
De philosophia evangelica LB VI
De praeparatione: De praeparatione ad mortem LB V / ASD V-1 / CWE 70
De pueris instituendis: De pueris statim ac liberaliter instituendis LB I / ASD I-2 /
    CWE 26
De puero Iesu: Concio de puero Iesu LB V / CWE 29
De puritate tabernaculi: Enarratio psalmi 14 qui est de puritate tabernaculi sive
    ecclesiae christianae LB V / ASD V-2 / CWE 65
De ratione studii LB I / ASD I-2 / CWE 24
De recta pronuntiatione: De recta latini graecique sermonis pronuntiatione LB I /
    ASD I-4 / CWE 26
De taedio Iesu: Disputatiuncula de taedio, pavore, tristicia Iesu LB V
    CWE 70
Detectio praestigiarum: Detectio praestigiarum cuiusdam libelli Germanice scripti
    LB X / ASD IX-1 / CWE 78
De vidua christiana LB V / CWE 66
De virtute amplectenda: Oratio de virtute amplectenda LB V / CWE 29
[Dialogus bilinguium ac trilinguium: Chonradi Nastadiensis dialogus bilinguium
    ac trilinguium] Opuscula / CWE 7
Dilutio: Dilutio eorum quae Iodocus Clithoveus scripsit adversus declamationem
    suasoriam matrimonii / Dilutio eorum quae Iodocus Clithoveus scripsit ed Émile V.
    Telle (Paris 1968) / CWE 83

Divinationes ad notata Bedae: Divinationes ad notata per Bedam de Paraphrasi Erasmi in Matthaeum, et primo de duabus praemissis epistolis LB IX

Ecclesiastes: Ecclesiastes sive de ratione concionandi LB V / ASD V-4, 5
Elenchus in censuras Bedae: In N. Bedae censuras erroneas elenchus LB IX
Enchiridion: Enchiridion militis christiani LB V / CWE 66
Encomium matrimonii (in De conscribendis epistolis)
Encomium medicinae: Declamatio in laudem artis medicae LB I / ASD I-4 / CWE 29
Epistola ad Dorpium LB IX / CWE 3 (Ep 337) / CWE 71
Epistola ad fratres Inferioris Germaniae: Responsio ad fratres Germaniae Inferioris ad epistolam apologeticam incerto autore proditam LB X / ASD IX-1 / CWE 78
Epistola ad gracculos: Epistola ad quosdam impudentissimos gracculos LB X / Ep 2275
Epistola apologetica adversus Stunicam LB IX / Ep 2172
Epistola apologetica de Termino LB X / Ep 2018
Epistola consolatoria: Epistola consolatoria virginibus sacris, or Epistola consolatoria in adversis LB V / CWE 69
Epistola contra pseudevangelicos: Epistola contra quosdam qui se falso iactant evangelicos LB X / ASD IX-1 / CWE 78
Euripidis Hecuba LB I / ASD I-1
Euripidis Iphigenia in Aulide LB I / ASD I-1
Exomologesis: Exomologesis sive modus confitendi LB V
Explanatio symboli: Explanatio symboli apostolorum sive catechismus LB V / ASD V-1 / CWE 70
Ex Plutarcho versa LB IV / ASD IV-2

Formula: Conficiendarum epistolarum formula (see De conscribendis epistolis)

Hyperaspistes LB X / CWE 76–7

In Nucem Ovidii commentarius LB I / ASD I-1 / CWE 29
In Prudentium: Commentarius in duos hymnos Prudentii LB V / CWE 29
In psalmum 1: Enarratio primi psalmi, 'Beatus vir,' iuxta tropologiam potissimum LB V / ASD V-2 / CWE 63
In psalmum 2: Commentarius in psalmum 2, 'Quare fremuerunt gentes?' LB V / ASD V-2 / CWE 63
In psalmum 3: Paraphrasis in tertium psalmum, 'Domine quid multiplicate' LB V / ASD V-2 / CWE 63
In psalmum 4: In psalmum quartum concio LB V / ASD V-2 / CWE 63
In psalmum 22: In psalmum 22 enarratio triplex LB V / ASD V-2 / CWE 64
In psalmum 33: Enarratio psalmi 33 LB V / ASD V-3 / CWE 64
In psalmum 38: Enarratio psalmi 38 LB V / ASD V-3 / CWE 65
In psalmum 85: Concionalis interpretatio, plena pietatis, in psalmum 85 LB V / ASD V-3 / CWE 64
Institutio christiani matrimonii LB V / CWE 69
Institutio principis christiani LB IV / ASD IV-1 / CWE 27

[Julius exclusus: Dialogus Julius exclusus e coelis] *Opuscula* / CWE 27

Lingua LB IV / ASD IV-1A / CWE 29
Liturgia Virginis Matris: Virginis Matris apud Lauretum cultae liturgia LB V /
    ASD V-1 / CWE 69
Luciani dialogi LB I / ASD I-1

Manifesta mendacia ASD IX-4 / CWE 71
Methodus (see Ratio)
Modus orandi Deum LB V / ASD V-1 / CWE 70
Moria: Moriae encomium LB IV / ASD IV-3 / CWE 27

Notatiunculae: Notatiunculae quaedam extemporales ad naenias Bedaicas, or
    Responsio ad notulas Bedaicas / LB IX
Novum Testamentum: Novum Testamentum 1519 and later (Novum instrumentum
    for the first edition, 1516, when required) LB VI / ASD VI-2, 3

Obsecratio ad Virginem Mariam: Obsecratio sive oratio ad Virginem Mariam in
    rebus adversis, or Obsecratio ad Virginem Matrem Mariam in rebus adversis
    LB V / CWE 69
Oratio de pace: Oratio de pace et discordia LB VIII
Oratio funebris: Oratio funebris in funere Bertae de Heyen LB VIII / CWE 29

Paean Virgini Matri: Paean Virgini Matri dicendus LB V / CWE 69
Panegyricus: Panegyricus ad Philippum Austriae ducem LB IV / ASD IV-1 /
    CWE 27
Parabolae: Parabolae sive similia LB I / ASD I-5 / CWE 23
Paraclesis LB V, VI
Paraphrasis in Elegantias Vallae: Paraphrasis in Elegantias Laurentii Vallae LB I /
    ASD I-4
Paraphrasis in Matthaeum, etc LB VII / ASD VII-6 / CWE 42–50
Peregrinatio apostolorum: Peregrinatio apostolorum Petri et Pauli LB VI, VII
Precatio ad Virginis filium Iesum LB V / CWE 69
Precatio dominica LB V / CWE 69
Precationes: Precationes aliquot novae LB V / CWE 69
Precatio pro pace ecclesiae: Precatio ad Dominum Iesum pro pace ecclesiae LB IV,
    V / CWE 69
Prologus supputationis: Prologus in supputationem calumniarum Natalis Bedae
    (1526), or Prologus supputationis errorum in censuris Bedae (1527) LB IX
Purgatio adversus epistolam Lutheri: Purgatio adversus epistolam non sobriam
    Lutheri LB X / ASD IX-1 / CWE 78

Querela pacis LB IV / ASD IV-2 / CWE 27

Ratio: Ratio seu Methodus compendio perveniendi ad veram theologiam (Methodus
    for the shorter version originally published in the Novum instrumentum of 1516)
    LB V, VI

Responsio ad annotationes Lei: Responsio ad annotationes Eduardi Lei LB IX /
  ASD IX-4 / CWE 72
Responsio ad collationes: Responsio ad collationes cuiusdam iuvenis geronto-
  didascali LB IX
Responsio ad disputationem de divortio: Responsio ad disputationem cuiusdam
  Phimostomi de divortio LB IX / ASD IX-4 / CWE 83
Responsio ad epistolam Alberti Pii: Responsio ad epistolam paraeneticam Alberti
  Pii, or Responsio ad exhortationem Pii LB IX / CWE 84
Responsio ad notulas Bedaicas (*see* Notatiunculae)
Responsio ad Petri Cursii defensionem: Epistola de apologia Cursii LB X /
  Ep 3032
Responsio adversus febricitantis cuiusdam libellum LB X

Spongia: Spongia adversus aspergines Hutteni LB X / ASD IX-1 / CWE 78
Supputatio: Supputatio errorum in censuris Bedae LB IX
Supputationes: Supputationes errorum in censuris Natalis Bedae: contains
  Supputatio and reprints of Prologus supputationis; Divinationes ad notata Bedae;
  Elenchus in censuras Bedae; Appendix respondens ad Sutorem; Appendix de
  scriptis Clithovei LB IX

Tyrannicida: Tyrannicida, declamatio Lucianicae respondens LB I / ASD I-1 / CWE 29

Virginis et martyris comparatio LB V / CWE 69
Vita Hieronymi: Vita divi Hieronymi Stridonensis *Opuscula* / CWE 61

Index of Scriptural References

General Index

The design of

THE COLLECTED WORKS

OF ERASMUS

was created

by

ALLAN FLEMING

1929–1977

for

the University

of Toronto

Press